Floating Exchange Rates and the State of World Trade Payments

Floating Exchange Rates and the State of World Trade Payments

By
David Bigman and
Teizo Taya

BeardBooks
Washington, DC

Copyright © 1984 by Ballinger Publishing Company
Reprinted 2003 by Beard Books, Washington, D. C.

Library of Congress Cataloging-in-Publication Data

Floating exchange rates and the state of world trade payments.
  Floating exchange rates and the state of world trade payments / edited by David
Bigman, Teizo Taya.
    p. cm.
  Originally published: Floating exchange rates and the state of world trade payments.
Cambridge, Mass. : Ballinger Pub., Co., 1984.
  Includes bibliographical references and indexes.
  ISBN 1-58798-129-7
  1. Foreign exchange. 2. International finance. 3. International economic relations. 4.
Balance of payments. I. Bigman, David, II. Taya, Teizo. III. Title.

HD3852 .F56 2002
332.4'562--dc21

                                                          2002027739

Printed in the United States of America

To Our Children

✳

Contents

Other Beard Books on Business

Beard Books *(vertical, on left spine)*

Dangerous Dreamers: The Financial Innovators
from Charles Merrill to Michael Milkin
Robert Sobel

Distressed Securities: Analyzing and Evaluating
Market Potential and Investment
Edward I. Altman

Getting It to the Bottom Line: Management by
Incremental Gains
Richard S. Sloma

Inside Wall Street
Robert Sobel

Merger: The Exclusive Inside Story of the
Bendix-Martin Marietta Takeover War
Peter F. Hartz

No-Nonsense Planning
Richard S. Sloma

Takeover: The New Wall Street Warriors: The Men,
the Money, the Impact
Moira Johnston

The Luckiest Guy in the World
Boone Pickens

The Rise and Fall of the Conglomerate Kings
Robert Sobel

For more information on these titles and for a complete listing of
available Beard Books titles, see www.beardbooks.com

✳

List of Figures

※

List of Tables

✻

Preface

Since the collapse of the Bretton Woods system and the advent of the float in early 1973, significant changes have taken place both in the operation and in our understanding of exchange rate economics. Initially, the transition to a system that has fewer controls and allows a more free play of market forces was expected to increase efficiency, reduce impediments on trade, and gradually eliminate the external imbalances as the exchange rates gravitated to their equilibrium level.

Over the years, two facts have become increasingly apparent. First, in practice the emerging exchange rate system has evolved in directions quite different from those of a free floating system. During most of the period, the rates were tightly managed through direct interventions in the exchange market, capital controls, and monetary and interest rate policies. Second, the collapse of the fixed exchange rate system also marked the collapse of the cooperative structure that was perhaps the most important feature of the Bretton Woods agreement. The post Bretton Woods era was characterized by a lack of any form of cooperation or coordination in exchange rate or monetary policies on a global scale. The floating system itself could not have been expected to offer an automatic mechanism to correct imbalances and instabilities resulting from independent, uncoordinated policies motivated solely by national self-interests. These factors, more than any inherent weaknesses in the system itself, are responsible for the turbulance of international financial markets over the last decade.

The articles in the volume examine various aspects of these developments in the international monetary system: their implications for world trade, their effects on the stability of national economies, and the policy options of individual countries aimed at countering their adverse effects. Obviously, not all aspects could have been covered. We have, therefore, chosen to focus on the causes and the effects of the growing instability in the world money markets.

The articles are a selection from the two volumes that we have edited: *The Functioning of Flexible Exchange Rates: Theory, Evidence, and Policy Implications* and *Exchange Rate and Trade Instability: Causes, Consequences, and Remedies.* We started the work on these volumes while both of us were working at the International Monetary Fund. At that time, the Fund was still in the process of defining its role following the collapse of the system that gave birth to its creation. However, while in the early years of the float many scholars were eulogizing the IMF, a decade later the Fund has become more important and more powerful than ever and the primary caretaker of the stability of the international monetary system. Much of our work at the Fund and our subsequent work on these volumes was related to the new roles and responsibilities that the Fund assumed over the last decade.

More than just providing a stage for yet another collection of essays on exchange rates, we saw these volumes as serving the purpose of bringing together the theoreticians and the policymakers who deal with these subjects. Ultimately, it is this dialogue that carries the seeds of any new ideas that can improve the functioning of the system. The publication of this collection of articles in a student edition will make it possible to expose a still wider audience to these issues and to a range of interpretations.

In our work over the years, we were helped by many individuals too numerous to mention. We are especially indebted to our colleagues at the IMF, particularly at the Treasurer's Department, who encouraged and assisted us in many ways. We would like to express our appreciation to the editor and the staff of Ballinger Publishing Company who made our work so much more pleasant. Our primary indebtedness goes to the contributors to all three volumes whose interest and cooperation made our own work on this project a stimulating experience.

✳

Introduction

After more than a decade of experience with floating exchange rates, recent writings on the subject take a rather somber look at the past, suggesting that in many ways exchange rate economics is back to square one. First, the empirical evidence clearly discredits the ability of the structural macroeconomic models to explain the facts about exchange rates in a satisfactory manner. Second, growing skepticism has been expressed about the merits of the system and about what were previously believed to be its main attributes. Most important, past experience indicates that flexible exchange rates do not insulate the economy from external disturbances nor do they restore balance of payments equilibrium. In fact, the single most important factor threatening the stability of the international monetary system is the growing trade imbalances worldwide and particularly the large deficits of many developing countries and their mounting foreign debts that by the mid-1980s have reached crisis proportions. In this introduction we review briefly some of the recent writings on exchange rate theory and examine the dynamics of the debt crisis and its implication for the future stability of the system.

EXCHANGE RATE THEORY AFTER TEN
YEARS OF FLOATING

The 1970s saw the revival of the monetary or the asset market approach. This approach is primarily macroeconomic rather than microeconomic in nature, and as David Laidler (1981) pointed out, "it seeks to explain the behavior either of the overall balance of payments, or of the exchange rate by focusing directly on the interaction of simple aggregate relationships, rather than attempting to build up to such an explanation by way of modelling individually the determination of the various component accounts of the balance of payments" (p. 70). This is the strength of the theory, but also its weakness. On the one hand, this specification lends itself very easily to a thoroughgoing theoretical and empirical analysis; on the other hand, it ignores such important factors as the structure of supply, changes in relative prices, the structure of the financial markets, and so on. William Branson (1983) relaxed some of these assumptions and concluded that "the short-run determination of floating exchange rates by financial market equilibrium conditions has put financial structure in the center of analyses" (p. 63). The assumptions of free capital movement and perfect substitution between financial assets that underlie the conventional monetary model is therefore too strong and unwarranted.

The various versions of the exchange rate models that take the monetary approach fare very poorly with the empirical evidence. Richard Meese and Kenneth Rogoff (1983) showed that a random walk is preferable to structural models in predicting exchange rates. Jeffrey Shaffer and Bonnie Loopesko (1983) provided in-sample evidence that models tying the exchange rates to "fundamentals" help vary little in forecasting exchange rates over short horizons.

A number of reasons have been noted to explain why in the short run prices, output, and the exchange rates are susceptible to all manner of disturbances unrelated to domestic monetary policies. Jacob Frenkel (1981) emphasized the role of "news" (new shift in exchange rate policies) and their effects on traders' expectations. Thus, changes in expectations about the future course of the fundamentals may have a larger effect on the exchange rates in the short run than actual changes in the fundamentals themselves. The role of expectations in affecting even exchange rate policies has been exemplified in what has become known as the peso problem but may also be called the Israeli shekel problem (in November 1983) and the yen problem (in June 1977). In anticipation of policy changes, speculators exert such high pressures on the currency that policy change becomes imminent. Oliver Blanchard (1979) added speculative bubbles as reasons for deviations from the fundamental. David Bigman (1984) demonstrated that in a world of costly information, even under rational expectations exchange rate movements are likely to be excessive, leading to wide fluctuations in the balance of trade. William Branson (1983) emphasized the role of policy reaction in determining the exchange rate.

Along with some disillusionment with the understanding of the behavior of exchange rate and the ability of economists to offer policy guidance, growing skepticism has also been expressed about the desirability of the floating system itself. In the transition to the new system, one of its attractive features was thought to be its ability to insulate the country from external distrubances and allow autonomy with respect to its use of monetary, fiscal, and other policy instruments. Alexander Swoboda (1983) presented, however, empirical evidence suggesting that there has been *more* interdependence under flexible than under fixed exchange rates in output changes, short-run price changes, money supply, and interest rates. He proposed that "the close interdependence in business cycles that was witnessed in the 1970s may well find its origin in a world business cycle in a closely integrated international economy rather than in the transmission of distrubances from one country, or group of countries, to the rest of the world" (p. 98). In that case, different exchange rate regimes would imply different channels for the effects of the international cycles.

Rudiger Dornbusch (1983) showed that although flexible exchange rates isolate the country from world inflation trends, strong interdependence still prevails with respect to changes in the trends or any other disturbances. He asserted that "the exercise of policy autonomy becomes nearly impossible under flexible rates, because many economies are too small and open to accept the exchange rate variations induced by policy. Alternatively, the effects of policies of countries with large economies are exported and interfere with foreign internal stability" (p. 4). The so-called interest-rate war of the early 1980s is one example of interdependence. Tight monetary policy in the United States drove up its interest rates and consequently the U.S. dollar. To prevent a vicious circle of imported inflation via depreciating exchange rates, the European countries were forced to raise their own interest rates despite the negative effects on their investments and their general economic recovery.

Floating exchange rates were even blamed for the reduced discipline of the monetary authorities as they lacked the constraints existing under the fixed exchange rate system. They were also blamed for leading to excessive real exchange rate changes and for easing the transmission of inflation or deflation that resulted from monetary or fiscal dislocation in a large country aggravated by speculation pressures.

Despite these charges, the verdict against the floating system, especially in comparison with the Bretton-Woods system, is fundamentally unfair. In the latter system, fixed exchange rates were only one component. The other component was a joint and, for most of the period, binding agreement of all member countries to cooperate in maintaining the stability of the system. This cooperation involved not only a commitment in principle to fix parities but also an agreement to coordinate monetary, fiscal, and trade policies under the supervision of the International Monetary Fund. Much of the relatively poor performance of the floating system was due to the collapse of this cooperative structure rather than to inherent deficiencies in the system itself. Willem Buiter (1983) has commented that "the merit of a floating rate regime is that when the rules of the game are not followed, fixed exchange rate regimes break down while floating rate regimes simply perform poorly but continue to operate" (p. 36).

LDC DEBT AND THE STABILITY OF THE INTERNATIONAL MONETARY SYSTEM

The use of private bank funds by the less developed countries (LDCs)—especially the more advanced ones—has been practiced ever since the end of World War II. Until the oil crisis of 1973-74, however, conditions in the international credit market were generally favorable, mainly because of the credit that was made available by official institutions at fixed concessionary terms. Real interest rates, adjusted for the increase in export prices, were often negative, and the LDCs were encouraged to increase their borrowing in order to accelerate their economic growth. Indeed, in most countries the flow of capital, both from private and from public sources, fueled industrialization, permitted the purchases of necessary inputs and machinery, and allowed a high rate of investment. During the twenty-year period of the 1960s and 1970s, real domestic investment among LDCs increased by an average of 8.1 percent annually, compared to 4.4 percent for the industrial countries (World Bank Annual Report, 1982). This process was the source of and the impetus for the rapid economic growth and the unparalleled rise in the standard of living that these countries enjoyed during these years. Foreign credit also enabled countries to overcome temporary slumps that may have otherwise slowed down their growth.

In the aftermath of the oil crisis and the collapse of the Bretton-Woods system in 1973-74, the quadrupling energy prices, the sharp hike in wheat prices, and the mounting inflation worldwide have rapidly deteriorated the current account position of the non-oil-developing countries (NODCs). The main reasons are:

- Substantial worsening in their terms of trade—mainly as a result of the rise in the price of oil, which was only partly offset by the rise in the price of other primary products. In 1974 and 1975, the terms of trade of the NODCs fell by 15.6 percent (IMF, World Economic Outlook, 1982).

- Slow structural adjustments to the change in oil prices that maintained their dependence on this expensive resource.

- Continued investment process, private but mostly governmental, aimed at sustaining the rapid economic growth, allowing a further increase in the standard of living and building production capacity deemed adequate at that time for the booming world economy of the late 1970s.

- Mounting inflationary pressures, precipitated by large government deficits, continued high rates of investment (much higher than those permitted by domestic savings), and often unrealistic exchange rate policies that eroded their competitiveness in the world markets. In 1973–81 the NODCs experienced inflation at an annual rate of 29 percent compared to 12 percent for 1963–72. Nevertheless, the growth of their exports slowed down only marginally from an average rate of 6.7 percent in the 1963–72 period to 5.9 percent in 1973–81, and most of the imbalance was revealed on the import side.

Based on a cross section time-series study of a group of thirty-two NODCs for the 1973–80 period, Khan and Knight (1983) suggest that "the most important single influence on current account diseqilibrium in the NODCs was, indeed, the deterioration in their terms of trade. Next in importance were fiscal deficits and movements in the real effective exchange rate, which were of roughly equal significance. Finally, smaller, though still significant influences were exerted by movements in real foreign interest rates, trend factors, and growth in industrial countries" (p. 5).

For a number of years, however, these deficits were assumed to be short lived, eventually self-reversing, and perhaps even imminent in view of the rise in oil prices and the turmoil following the transition to flexible exchange rates. Financing the deficits without enforcing any structural adjustment was therefore considered sound and safe. The resort to private banks was also considered sound both because international institutions like the IMF or the World Bank did not command enough resources to meet such high demands and because the large private banks in Europe and in the United States were flooded with large reserves from oil-exporting countries. Indeed, the catchword of those years was "recycling the petrodollars," and the commercial banks proved to be very efficient in meeting this challenge.

Only in the late 1970s was it increasingly realized that the crisis was not temporary and the deficits in the current account of the NODCs were likely to persist for a much longer period than previously anticipated. A number of factors have prolonged these imbalances. The industrial countries entered into a recession—the deepest since the depression of the 1930s—that considerably slowed down the growth of exports and the export-led economic growth in the NODCs, especially among the semi-industrial countries (Table I-1). On top of this, the industrial countries made concerted efforts to correct their own imbalances and curb imports.[1] This effort to stabilize their exchange rates and to protect their own production and employment further reduced the flow of exports from the NODCs.

Moreover, the terms of trade of the NODCs further deteriorated and their inflation continued to rise. Finally, interest rates in the international financial markets rose quite dramatically in the early 1980s, aggravating the debt burden of the NODCs and raising their annual payments on account of the debt services (Table I-1). Thus, for instance, real annual interest rate[2] rose from an average negative rate of –1.1 percent during the 1975-80 period to a positive real rate of 17.4 percent in 1981.

Despite these alarming signs, private banks continued their practice of "have money, will travel" early in the 1980s. Motivated, of course, by the high yields, they also saw calming signs in the adjustment efforts that the borrowing countries started to make as well as the greater involvement of the IMF both in providing financial assistance and in monitoring the adjustments on which the Fund's assistance were conditioned. Net IMF financing has increased from $1.2 billion

Table I-1.   Selected Economic Indicators for Non-Oil-Developing Countries, 1979-82.

	1979	1980	1981	1982
	As Percent of Total Exports of Goods and Services			
Current account balance	–17.7	–20.4	–22.4	–19.3
External debt	119.2	112.9	124.9	143.3
Debt service	19.0	17.6	20.4	23.9
	Percentage Change			
Economic growth	5.0	4.8	2.5	1.4
Inflation	24.6	31.0	32.8	34.0
Terms of trade	0.8	–6.4	–8.1	na

Source: IMF, *World Economic Outlook*, 1982 and 1983.

in 1980 to $6.3 billion in 1982 and to more than $13 billion in 1983.

Bankers, however, have become more alert to "country risk." Some even expressed the thought that in the foreseeable future the principal of some countries' debt will have to be rolled over from year to year, thus becoming, for all practical purposes, a type of consol. By mid-1983 this pessimistic notion gave way to even more doom and gloom prophecies about the future of the international monetary system. Some borrowing countries had increasing difficulties making even the interest payments, and the rolling over of the debt that included the overdue interest payments essentially amounted to internal paper reshuffling inside the banks without any real transfer of resources. The foreign loans that were the solution to the problems of the NODCs in the mid-1970s have accumulated to such levels that they have currently become the main problem of these countries. Financial markets' outstanding credit to LDCs has risen from $36.7 billion in 1972 to $273.4 billion in 1981 and was in the range of $350 billion by the beginning of 1984.

Several factors contributed to making the foreign debt the most difficult problem facing the NODCs in the mid-1980s. For one, high interest rates still persist and by all estimates are likely to remain high for a few more years. These high rates make the repayments of interest and principal exceedingly difficult. Interest payments alone reached almost 24 percent of the total export proceeds of the NODCs. In Argentina, principal and interest payments due in 1984 on its $40 billion foreign debt will total $9 billion, but its trade surplus is expected to be only $4 billion. By the end of 1983, Argentina still owed $2 billion in overdue interest and commercial credit payments, and the new government of Raul Alfonsin formally requested that its creditor banks accept a delay in payments at least for several months.

Another factor is the large difficulties of the NODCs to carry out the necessary structural adjustments. In South Korea, for example, which saw perhaps the boldest adjustment effort, measures included a currency appreciation in 1980 by 30 percent on a trade-weighted basis, substantial real cuts in the fiscal budget, deferred investment projects, tightened credit policy, tripled interest rates, wage curbs, and the reduction of non-oil imports by 16 percent. As a result of these and other measures, real GNP declined by 6.2 percent—the first decline in over twenty years—and inflation soared to its highest level in over a decade (see Kincaid 1983). These sweeping measures are bound to cause severe political and social problems, and in some countries it is doubtful whether the existing political system can enforce—and survive—such hardships.

A third factor is the slow pace of recovery in the industrial countries. Ironically, the adjustments made by the NODCs and their efforts to lower their imports are among the reasons for the slow recovery, since 25 to 40 percent of total exports of the industrial countries is to the NODCs, and for some industries they are the main market.

Facing all these problems, many NODCs had encountered increasing difficulties in meeting their debt repayments—principal and interest—on schedule. Payments were rising while the expected income on which the maturity schedules were based had not been realized. The word "default" was hanging in the air. While the direct losses individual banks were likely to suffer in the event of default did not represent a significant proportion of their exposures, there was still the danger that a chain reaction of debts could have been triggered throughout the entire international monetary system.

To meet the debt problem, the major borrowing countries concluded arrangements in which the commercial banks themselves advanced new funds and extended all or part of the loan maturities falling in the 1982–84 period. "Rescheduling" is now becoming the bankers' catchword of the times. The number of rescheduling agreements between commercial banks and debtor countries has doubled over the last three years and the total amount involved now exceeds $37 billion. Private banks have subsequently become captives of their borrowers since many debtor countries face severe liquidity problems that made the servicing of their external debts impossible. The fundamental question surrounding all these arrangements is whether the time borrowed by stretching out maturities will allow policy changes to take their course, improve the cash flow, and eventually enable the borrowing countries to meet their obligations to their creditor.

In 1983 the commercial banks appeared to maintain practices that must be considered shortsighted if not outright greedy. They enforced stringent terms on rolling over the loans, which not only aggravated the problems of the borrowing countries but also exposed them to a higher risk of default. Mexico, for instance, was charged by its main commercial creditors' stiff rescheduling fees and premium interest rates of 2 3/8 percent above the standard international lending rate worth together more than $800 million in rolling over its $20 billion debt. In the borrowing countries, the sheer magnitude of their debt and their annual interest payments have reached proportions that make an orderly solution even more difficult. Moreover, given both economic and social constraints, the governments in these countries have difficulties adjusting their fiscal and trade policies to the extent necessary to improve domestic savings and capital formation. Even under very optimistic assumptions about increasing domestic savings, Bolin and Del Canto (1983) estimate that the fifteen principal borrowers would produce only an additional $11 billion—an amount equal to less than 50 percent of their annual debt servicing.

The combination of unfavorable conditions and inappropriate policies that have created the debt crisis in the NODCs is not likely to change in the coming years. Time itself has the effect of aggravating the problem, both by increasing the volume of the debt and by further eroding the confidence in the international banking system. The need for a reform is clear and urgent.

The crux of the problem is that presently most of the burden is being shouldered by the borrowing countries. Their governments, seeking IMF financial assistance, are required to agree to conditions that may make economic sense but also involve social and political hardships. The adjustment measures are designed to enable the countries to meet future payments of interest and principal and are tailored largely to the existing schedule of the countries' payments. Not enough consideration is given to the countries' limited abilities to implement the measures. Not enough consideration is given to the necessity that commercial banks make equal adjustments in order to make ends meet.

One direction the reform can take is a reversal of the process. First, a set of measures should be implemented—under IMF guidance and supervision—that would allow the government to make the necessary adjustments in the country but at the same time take into account its constraints. The expected adjustments would determine, in turn, the country's ability to repay its loans. The banks should agree to reschedule the payments accordingly and to ease the roll-over terms.

The debt crisis delegates a new responsibility to the IMF to negotiate an orderly solution in a way that may involve, for the first time, some form of "conditionality" on the part of the commercial banks. Given the ominous developments toward which an absence of an orderly solution may lead, this role will be well in line with the broad responsibility of the IMF to supervise the stability of the international monetary system.

NOTES

1. Thus, for instance, the industrial countries adjusted more smoothly to high oil prices, and the response of domestic demand (and supply) was more substantial than what estimates of demand elasticities—obtained through elaborate

regression analysis of past experiences—have led experts to believe. This response, coupled with the slowdown in economic activity, is responsible for the oil glut of 1982–83.

2. Eurodollar deposit rate adjusted for changes in an index of export prices of NODCs. See Khan and Knight (1983).

REFERENCES

Bigman, D. 1984. "Semi-Rational Expectations and Exchange Rate Dynamics." *Journal of International Money and Finance* (forthcoming).

Blanchard, O.J. 1979. "Speculative Bubbles, Crashes and Rational Expectations." *Economic Letters* 3: 387–89.

Bolin, W.H., and J. Del Canto. 1983. "LDC Debt: Beyond Crisis Management." *Foreign Affairs* 61: 1099–1113.

Branson, W.H. 1983a. "Economic Structure and Policy for External Balance." *IMF Staff Papers* 30: 39–66.

_____. 1983b. "A Model of Exchange-Rate Determination with Policy Reaction: Evidence from Monthly Data." Working Paper No. 1178. National Bureau of Economic Research.

Buitar, W. 1983. "Comment." *IMF Staff Papers* 30: 35–38.

Dornbusch, R. 1983. "Flexible Exchange Rates and Interdependence." *IMF Staff Papers* 30: 3–30.

Frenkel, J.A. 1981. "Flexible Exchange Rates, Prices, and the Role of "News": Lessons from the 1970s." *Journal of Political Economy* 89: 665–705.

Khan, M.S., and M. Knight. 1983. "Sources of Payments Problems in LDCs." *Finance and Development* 20: 2–5.

Kincaid, R. 1983. "Korea's Major Adjustment Effort." *Finance and Development* 20: 20–33.

Laidler, D. 1981. "Some Policy Implications of the Monetary Approach to Balance of Payments and Exchange Rate Analysis." *Oxford Economic Papers* 33: 70–84.

Meese, R.A., and K. Rogoff. 1983. "Empirical Exchange Rate Models of the Seventies: Do They Fit Out-of-Sample." *Journal of Political Economy* 91: 3–24.

Shaffer, R.J., and B.E. Loopesko. 1983. "Floating Exchange Rates After Ten Years." *Brookings Paper on Economic Activity* 1: 1–70.

Swoboda, A.K. 1983. "Exchange Rate Regimes and U.S.-European Policy Interdependence." *IMF Staff Papers* 30: 75–102.

FLOATING EXCHANGE RATES
AND THE STATE OF
WORLD TRADE PAYMENTS

✳ *Chapter 1*

Monetary Policy Under Exchange Rate Flexibility*

Rudiger Dornbusch
Massachusetts Institute of Technology

INTRODUCTION

The continuing depreciation of the dollar stands out as one of the big policy issues. It has started to impinge on U.S. monetary policy, it influences the chances for international commercial diplomacy, and it is enhanced to move toward European monetary integration. Above all, it leaves most observers with a puzzle as to the causes of the ongoing depreciation.

This chapter will, of course, not resolve the puzzle. It rather attempts to lay out the basic analytical framework that has been developed for the analysis of exchange rate questions and to relate it to the question of monetary policy. The main points to be made here are: (1) exchange rates are primarily determined in asset markets with expectations playing a dominant role: (2) the sharpest formulation of exchange rate theory is the "monetary approach," Chicago's quantity theory of the open economy; (3) purchasing power parity is a precarious reed on which to hang short-term exchange rate theory; and (4) the current account has just made it back as a determinant of exchange rates.

Subsequently, we pull together these elements to form some conjectures about the working of monetary policy under flexible rates and about the dollar depreciation. In particular we draw attention to

*Abridged version of "Monetary Policy Under Exchange Rate Flexibility," Federal Reserve Bank of Boston, Conference Series No. 20, 1979. Helpful discussions with Jeffrey Frankel, Jacob Frenkel, Stanley Fischer, and Michael Rothschild and financial support from the NSF are gratefully acknowledged.

3

the trade-off between increased net exports and the inflationary impact induced by a depreciation.

The topic covered in this chapter has received an extraordinary amount of professional attention in the last few years, and much fruitful research has been accomplished. The fine surveys by Isard (1978), Kohlhagen (1978), and Schadler (1977) will place our sketchy review in the perspective of the literature, and the books by Black (1977) and Willett (1978) help relate our topic to the ongoing policy discussions.

In this chapter we review the main strands of exchange rate theory. We start off with two rock bottom models that, in an oversimplified manner perhaps, represent exchange rate theory as viewed by the "person in the street." These models—purchasing power parity and a balance of payments theory of the exchange rate—each contain, of course, more than a germ of truth and thus serve as a useful introduction to our review.

We proceed from there to more structured models that emphasize macroeconomic interaction or the details of asset markets. These theories can be described as asset market theories of the exchange rate. Extensions of these models are then considered in an effort to add realism. These extensions deal with expectations, questions of dynamics and of indexing, and policy reaction.

PURCHASING POWER PARITY AND THE QUANTITY THEORY

Purchasing power parity theory of the exchange rate is one of those empirical regularities that are sufficiently true over long periods of time to deserve our attention but deviations from which are pronounced enough to make all the difference in the short run. Clearly, purchasing power parity (PPP) is much like the quantity theory of money and indeed can be viewed as the open economy extension of quantity theory thinking.[1]

PPP Theory

PPP theory argues that exchange rates move over time so as to offset divergent movements in national price levels. A country that experiences a hyperinflation, for example, will experience at the same time a corresponding external depreciation of its currency.

The theory leaves open two important operational questions. The first deals with the channels through which this relation between inflation differentials and depreciation will come about. The second question concerns the extent to which PPP is complete—does it hold in the short run, and is there no possibility for trend deviations over time?

The extent to which PPP holds exactly, at every point in time, and without trend deviation has been an important issue in trade theory. There is no question that theory has shown the possibility of systematic deviation that arises from the existence of nontraded goods. Specifically Balassa and Samuelson have argued that because services tend to be nontraded and labor intensive, and show low technical progress as opposed to traded manufactures, we would expect fast-growing and innovating countries to experience an increase in their real price level over time. With prices of tradeables equalized, the productivity growth in the traded sector would raise wages and the relative price of nontraded goods and thus the real price level in the fast growing countries.

A second source of systematic deviation has been pointed out by the earlier literature, including Viner, that dealt with the effect of capital flows or current account imbalance. Here it was argued that a borrowing country has a relatively high (real) price level. The argument relies on the fact that an increase in aggregate demand, financed by borrowing and a current account deficit, would raise the relative price of nontraded goods and thus the real price level. There are thus two reasons for trend deviations or systematic deviations from PPP that serve as important reservations to the generality of the theory.

Setting these reservations aside, we are still left with the issue of how rapidly and completely we expect PPP to hold and through what channels it comes about. Here the literature is considerably more diffuse. A hard core theory, associated with what Marina Whitman (1975) has aptly called "global monetarism," asserts the "law of one price." Goods produced by us and by our competitors behave as if they were perfect substitutes. Simple arbitrage by market participants will establish uniformity of price in closely integrated markets.

This hard core view is no longer very fashionable except, of course, for raw materials, commodities, and food. A more differentiated view would argue that in the short run, and perhaps even in the long run, there is substantial scope for product differentiation. Under these conditions, price adjustment is no longer a matter of arbitrage but rather becomes a question of substitution. When our prices get out of line with those of our competitors so that we become more competitive, then we would expect demand to shift toward our goods and, in a fully employed economy, to start putting upward pressure on costs and, ultimately, prices. The price adjustment here is certainly time consuming; it depends not only on substitutability between supply sources—Okun's distinction between customer and auction markets is important here—but also on the state of slack in the economy and on the expected persistence of real price changes. The description of this mechanism suggests that deviations from PPP are not only possible, but may persist for some time.

The empirical content of PPP theory can be summarized as in equation (1.1):

$$k = (1-a_1)\bar{k} + a_1 k_{-1} + a_2 z \;\; ; \;\; 0 < a_1 < 1, a_2 > 0, \quad (1.1)$$

where k and k_{-1} measure the current and lagged deviation from PPP, $\bar{k}$ is the equilibrium real price level that has perhaps a time trend, and z measures the systematic effect of borrowing or current account imbalance on the deviation from PPP. We would expect a_1 to be positive, thus showing some serial correlation or persistence in deviations from PPP.

Money, Prices, and the Exchange Rate

We turn now to a development of the "monetary approach" of exchange rate theory. This model or approach combines the quantity theory of money—fully flexible prices determined by real money demand and nominal money supply—with strict PPP to arrive at a theory of the exchange rate.

The approach can be simply formulated in terms of a combined theory of monetary equilibrium and exchange rate determination. Let M, P, V, and Y be the nominal quantity of money, the price level, velocity, and real income. Then the condition of monetary equilibrium can be written as:

$$\frac{M}{P} V(r, Y) = Y, \quad (1.2)$$

where our notation indicates that velocity may be a function of other variables, such as interest rates, r, or income.

We can rewrite equation (1.2), solving for the price level, as:

$$P = V \frac{M}{Y}, \quad (1.2')$$

which states that for a given velocity, an increase in money leads to an equiproportionate rise in the price level. A rise in velocity likewise raises the price level, while an increase in real income, by raising real money demand, would lower the equilibrium level of prices.

To go from here to a theory of the exchange rate, we draw on a strict version of PPP that states that our price level is equal to foreign prices, $P*$, converted at the exchange rate, E:

$$P = P*E, \qquad (1.3)$$

where E is the domestic currency price of foreign exchange. Substituting equation (1.3) in equation (1.2') yields an expression for the equilibrium exchange rate:

$$E = (1/P*) \, V \, \frac{M}{Y}. \qquad (1.4)$$

The equilibrium exchange rate depends on nominal money, real output, and velocity. An increase in nominal money or in velocity will depreciate the exchange rate in the same proportion. A rise in real income will lead to appreciation. What is the mechanism?

The theory argues that domestic prices are fully flexible, but are linked to world prices by PPP. Given the nominal quantity of money, any variations in the demand for money must be offset by compensating changes in the level of prices and thus in the exchange rate. An increase in real money demand, because say of an increase in real income, will be accommodated by a decline in the level of prices so as to raise the real value of the existing nominal money stock. With a decline in our prices, though, we are out of line with world prices and thus require appreciation of the exchange rate.

To complete the theory we note two extensions. First, there is symmetry in that the foreign price level, $P*$, is determined by foreign money demand and supply so that we can write equation (1.3) as

$$E = \left(\frac{M}{M*} \right) \left(\frac{V}{V*} \right) \left(\frac{Y*}{Y} \right). \qquad (1.4')$$

Clearly, then, what matters for exchange rate determination in this view is relative money supplies, velocities, and real incomes in the two countries. Our exchange rate will depreciate if, other things equal, our nominal money stock rises relative to that abroad.

The second extension is a specification of a velocity function.

Here the tradition has been to assume that velocity depends on real income and the alternative cost of holding money:

$$V = Y^{\lambda-1} \, exp(\theta r), \tag{1.5}$$

where r is the nominal rate of interest. The functional form is a matter of expositional convenience and monetary tradition.

Substituting equation (1.5) in equation (1.4') and taking logs, we obtain the standard equation of the "monetary approach":[2]

$$e = m-m^* - \lambda(y-y^*) + \theta(r-r^*), \tag{1.6}$$

where e, m, m^*, y, and y^* are logarithms of the corresponding capital letter variables.

In the final form, equation (1.6) shows that an increase in our relative money stock or a decline in our relative income will lead to depreciation, as would a rise in our relative interest rate. The last conclusion is particularly interesting since it certainly is the opposite of the conventional wisdom that a rise in interest rates will lead to appreciation. We return to the question below when we compare the relation between interest rates and the exchange rate in alternative theories. We note here the explanation: an increase in interest rates reduces the demand for real money balances. Given the nominal quantity of money, the price level has to rise to reduce the real money stock to its lower equilibrium level. With our prices thus getting out of line internationally, a depreciation is required to restore PPP.

BALANCE OF PAYMENTS THEORY OF EXCHANGE RATES

A textbook view of exchange rates will argue that the exchange rate adjusts to balance receipts and payments arising from international trade in goods, services, and assets. The current account is affected by the exchange rate because it changes relative prices and thus competitiveness; the capital account is affected to the extent that expectational considerations are important. The theory can be formulated with the help of equation (1.7):

$$BoP = 0 = C(EP^*/P, \ Y, \ Y^*) + K(r, \ r^*, \ s), \tag{1.7}$$

where BoP denotes the balance of payments, EP^*/P measures the relative price of foreign goods and thus serves as a measure of our competitiveness, C denotes the current account, K the rate of capital inflow, and s a speculative variable that we disregard for the present.

Figure 1-1 shows the schedule BB along which our balance of payments is in equilibrium, given prices, foreign income, and interest rates. A rise in E or a depreciation of the exchange makes us more competitive and thus improves the current account. To restore overall balance of payments equilibrium, lower interest rates are required so as to generate an offsetting rate of capital outflow. We can readily show that in this framework the exchange rate depends on interest rates, activity levels, relative price levels, and the exogenous determinants of the composition of world demand:

$$E = E(Y, Y^*, r, r^*, P^*/P). \qquad (1.8)$$

Specifically, an increase in our income because of, say, an autonomous increase in spending, will worsen the current account and thus

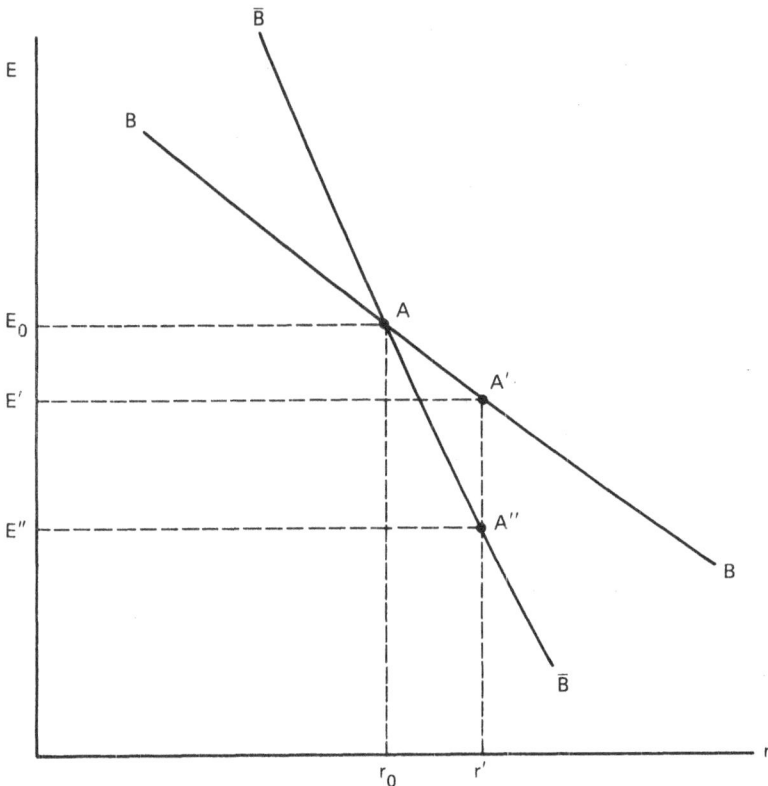

Figure 1-1.

requires an offsetting depreciation. An increase in foreign prices leads to a precisely offsetting appreciation, and an increase in our interest rate leads to an appreciation. The mechanism through which higher interest rates at home lead to an appreciation can be illustrated with the help of Figure 1-1. In the first place, the increase in interest rates will lead to a net capital inflow or a reduced rate of outflow and thus causes the overall balance of payments to move into surplus. The exchange rate will accordingly appreciate—assuming the right elasticities—until we have an offsetting worsening of the current account. This is shown by the move from *A* to *A'* on *BB*.

We may not want to stop at this point but rather recognize that the higher interest rates and the exchange appreciation will exert subsidiary domestic effects. With higher interest rates, aggregate demand declines, and thus output will fall. The same effect arises from the appreciation and the resulting deterioration of the current account. Thus we have a second round of adjustments to the decline in income that shifts the *BB* schedule inward over time. The long-run balance of payments schedule that incorporates the equilibrium level of income implied by the real exchange rate and interest rate is the steeper schedule $\overline{BB}$. In the long run we have further appreciation until point *A"* is reached.

Two points deserve emphasis here. First, the approach views changes in exchange rates as changing (almost one for one) relative prices and competitiveness. It in this respect represents a view opposite to that embodied in the monetary model. Second, it contradicts the monetary model in predicting that an increase in interest rates will lead to an appreciation. I will not pursue this model further, but rather will take a specialized version and embody it in a macroeconomic setting.

THE MUNDELL-FLEMING MODEL

The balance of payments model has drawn attention to the role of capital flows in the determination of exchange rates. This is also the perspective adopted by the modern macroeconomic approach to exchange rate determination that originated with the pathbreaking work of Mundell (1968) and Fleming (1962). Their theory argues that the exchange rate enters the macroeconomic framework of interest and output determination because changes in exchange rates affect competitiveness. Depreciation acts much in the same way as fiscal policy by affecting the level of demand for domestic goods associated with each level of output and interest rate. A depreciation shifts world demand toward our goods and thus acts in an expansionary manner.

The Mundell-Fleming model is illustrated in Figure 1-2 for the case of perfect capital mobility. Perfect capital mobility means that there is only one rate of interest at which the balance of payments can be in equilibrium. If the rate were lower, there would be outflows that would swamp any current account surplus, and the converse would be true if it were higher. This is illustrated by the horizontal *BB* schedule. The *LM* schedule is the conventional representation of monetary equilibrium. Higher income levels raise the demand for money. Given the money stock, interest rates will have to rise to contain money demand to the existing level of supply. Finally the *IS* schedule resembles that of a closed economy except that it includes as a component of demand net exports as determined by income and competitiveness. That is why a depreciation will shift the *IS* schedule out and to the right.

Consider now a monetary expansion indicated by a rightward

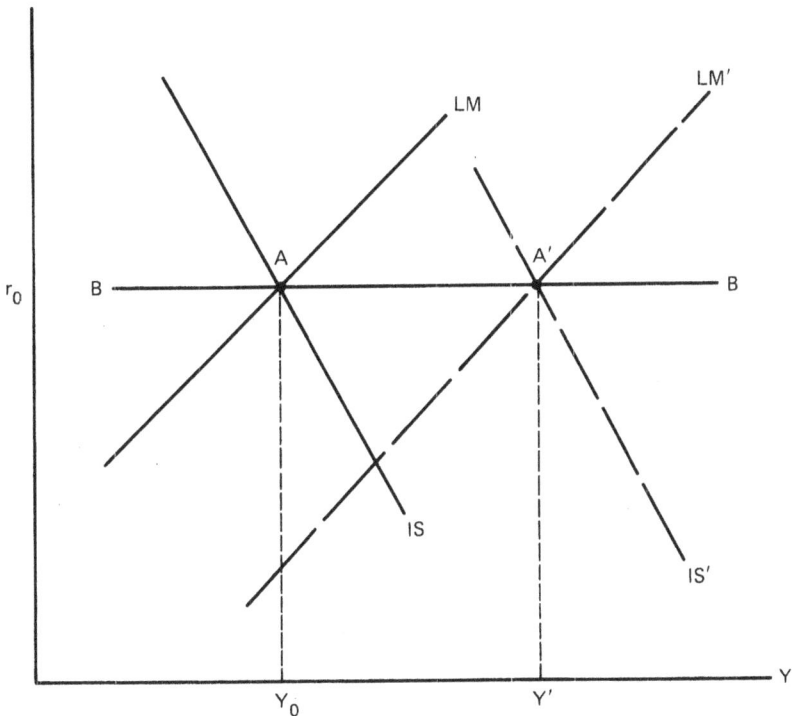

Figure 1-2.

shift of the *LM* schedule. The impact effect is of course to lower interest rates and thus to exert an expansionary effect on demand. The decline in interest rates, however, leads to exchange depreciation because of incipient capital outflows. The depreciation in turn enhances our competitiveness, raising demand and shifting the *IS* curve to the right until we reach point *A'*. Here output and income have risen sufficiently for the increased money stock to be held at the initial rate of interest.

The framework has an important lesson for exchange rate theory and monetary policy. First, under conditions of perfect capital mobility and given the world rate of interest, monetary policy works not by raising the interest-sensitive components of spending, but rather by generating a depreciation and thereby a current account surplus. Monetary policy works not through the construction sector but rather through the net export component of demand. This is, of course, a striking result, due in part to the small country assumption. It draws attention to the central role of net exports in aggregate demand and to the link between interest rates and exchange rates. It is the latter link that has become central to recent exchange rate models.

The theory implies an equilibrium exchange rate that we can obtain either from the condition of goods market equilibrium,[3]

$$E = E(r, Y, Y^*, P^*/P, \ldots), \tag{1.9}$$

or as a reduced form equation of the full system,

$$E = E(M, Y^*, \ldots), \tag{1.10}$$

where the dots denote fiscal policy variables and other exogenous determinants of goods and money demand. It is interesting to note that in equation (1.9), an increase in the (world) interest rate, because it reduces aggregate demand and thus creates an excess supply of goods, requires an offsetting depreciation that increases competitiveness and gives rise to a trade surplus.

In its present form the model has three limitations. First, there is no role whatsoever for exchange rate expectations. This point is important because it implies that strict interest equality must obtain internationally. Second, the model allows for no effect from the depreciation on domestic prices. The depreciation is not allowed to affect either the general price level, and therefore the real value of the money stock, or the price of our output, and therefore our competitiveness. It is quite apparent that in fact we should expect at least some spillover into domestic prices and that this spillover will determine the extent to which the real effects of a monetary expansion are dampened. We return to this question later in this chapter. The third limitation concerns the absence of any dynamics. This limitation is important not only in respect to the price adjustment that we just noted but also for the adjustment of trade flows. The existence of adjustment lags implies the possibility that monetary policy in the short run may fail to be expansionary.

THE PORTFOLIO BALANCE MODEL

The Mundell-Fleming model emphasizes the high substitutability between domestic and foreign assets. Capital mobility is perfect so that the slightest deviation of interest rates from the world level unleashes unbounded incipient capital flows. An alternative formulation emphasizes a more limited substitutability between domestic and foreign assets and introduces the level of the exchange rate as a variable that, along with asset yields, helps achieve balance between asset demands and asset supplies.[4] The model concentrates on asset markets but can readily be extended to include the allocational effects of exchange rates in affecting the current account.

Consider now the basic model as shown in equations (1.11)–(1.13) and Figure 1-3. In equation (1.11) we show the condition of monetary equilibrium where W denotes nominal wealth and where $\phi(r,r^*)$ is the fraction of wealth people wish to hold in the form of domestic money:

$$M = \phi(r,\, r^*)W \qquad \phi_r,\, \phi_{r*} < 0. \tag{1.11}$$

Equilibrium in the market for domestic asset requires that the existing supply, X, equal the demand:

$$X = \psi(r,\, r^*)W \qquad \psi_r > 0;\, \psi_{r*} < 0, \tag{1.12}$$

where $\psi(r,\, r^*)$ is the desired ratio of domestic assets to wealth. The ratio is assumed to increase with the own rate of return and to decline with the return on foreign assets. Equations (1.11) and (1.12), together with the wealth constraint,

$$W = M + EF + X,$$

imply an equilibrium condition in the market for net external assets;

$$EF = (1-\psi - \phi)W = \rho(r, r^*)W \quad ; \quad \rho_{r*} > 0, \rho_r < 0, \qquad (1.13)$$

where F denotes net holdings of foeign assets measured in terms of foreign exchange. Note that since net external assets can be negative, ρ can be negative. We assume that assets are substitutes, so that asset demands respond positively to their own yield and negatively to yields on alternative assets.

In Figure 1-3 we show the money and domestic asset market equilibrium schedules for given stocks of each of the assets. Along MM the domestic money market is in equilibrium. Higher interest rates reduce money demand so that equilibrium requires a depreciation and thus a rise in the domestic currency value of foreign assets and hence wealth. The exchange rate thus plays a balancing role by affecting the valuation of assets. Along XX the domestic asset market

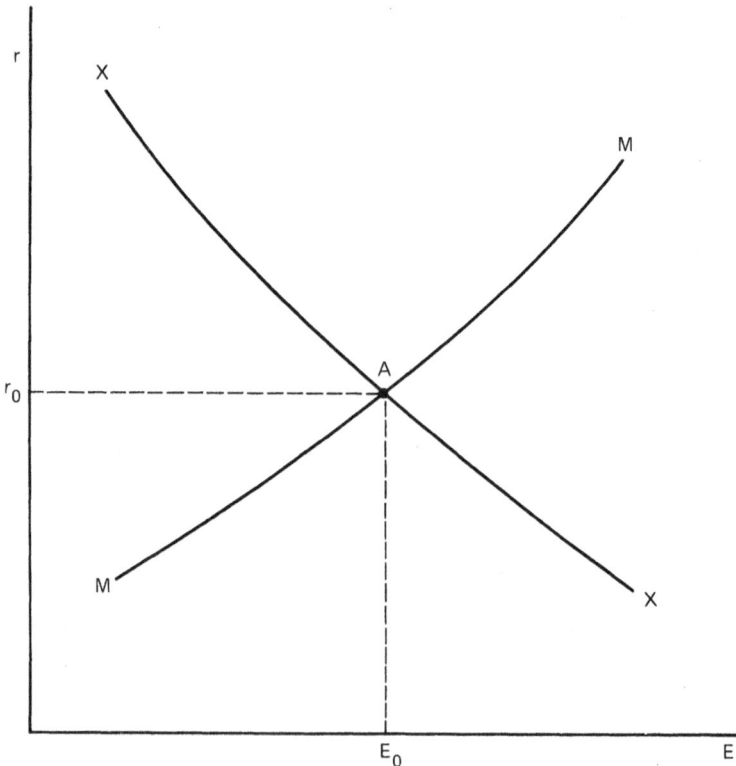

Figure 1-3.

is in equilibrium. Higher interest rates raise the demand for domestic assets and thus require an appreciation to reduce wealth and asset demand thus restoring equilibrium.

We want to establish next the effect of changes in foreign interest rates, changes in domestic money or net external assets. In terms of Figure 1-3, an increase in the foreign interest rate creates an excess supply of domestic money and domestic securities, thus shifting the *MM* schedule down and to the right and the *XX* schedule up and to the right. Without question, the equilibrium exchange rate depreciates.

Consider next an increase in the domestic money stock. At the initial equilibrium there will be an excess supply of money and an excess demand for domestic (and foreign) securities. Accordingly, the *MM* schedule will shift down and to the right while the *XX* schedule shifts down and to the left. It is readily established that the net effect is unambiguously a depreciation of the exchange rate.[5]

Finally we consider an increase in net external assets. Now both the money market and the domestic security market schedules shift to the left. They will shift in the same proportion, as inspection of equations (1.11) and (1.12) together with the wealth constraint will reveal. Accordingly, the equilibrium exchange rate appreciates in proportion to the increase in foreign assets.

The implications of the portfolio balance model are summarized in equation (1.14), which shows the reduced form equation for the equilibrium exchange rate:[6]

$$E = E(r^*, M, X, F); E_{r^*} > 0; E_M > 0; E_X \gtrless 0; E_F < 0. \quad (1.14)$$

Furthermore since equation (1.14) is homogeneous in domestic nominal money and securities, we can rewrite the equation as:[6]

$$E = \gamma(r^*, X/M) \frac{M}{F}. \quad (1.14)$$

In this form we emphasize that the equilibrium exchange rate depends on relative asset supplies. In particular, an increase in domestic nominal assets—money and securities—relative to external assets will lead to an equiproportionate depreciation. This homogeneity property is, of course, desirable since it corresponds to an ongoing, neutral inflation process.

The portfolio balance model draws attention to the substitution possibility between domestic and foreign assets. Domestic and foreign securities are no longer perfect substitutes, and accordingly, their relative supplies determine, along with the nominal money stock, equilibrium interest rates and the exchange rate. A link with the current account is established by virtue of the fact that external assets are acquired over time through the current account surplus. Accordingly, as Kouri (1976a, 1976b) and others have emphasized, the current account determines the evolution of the exchange rate over time. In particular, a current account surplus that implies accumulation of net external assets leads to an appreciating exchange rate.

The model remains a partial equilibrium representation in two important respects. First, we do not consider the interaction between financial markets, the exchange rate, goods markets, and the current account. Second, we do not allow for any expectational effects.

What makes this model potentially attractive for the analysis of exchange rate questions is the direct relation between asset market disturbances and movements in exchange rates. It extends the monetary model because we do not have to rely on shifts in money demand or supply as sole determinants of exchange rate movements but rather can consider shifts between domestic and foreign assets— for example, as motivated by expectations.

EXPECTATIONS AND EXCHANGE RATE DYNAMICS

We have so far concentrated on models of the exchange rate that are largely static and that do not emphasize the role of expectations. We extend the analysis now to questions of dynamics and to the place of expectations. The role of expectations is central to exchange rate determination and, therefore, to policies under flexible exchange rates. The spot exchange rate is almost entirely dominated by the course that the public expects it to take in the near future. These expectations, of course, are influenced by the structure of the economy and by institutional features such as indexing or systematic policy responses. In this section we will first review a fairly general model of exchange rate expectations and dynamics and then extend the analysis to discuss the idea of a virtuous and vicious circle.[8]

Expectations

We return to the assumption of perfect capital mobility to establish a relationship between interest rates, current exchange rates, and expected exchange rates. With perfect capital mobility, asset holders would find themselves indifferent between holding domestic or foreign assets provided they carry the same yield—that is, provided the interest differential matches the anticipated rate of depreciation:

$$r-r^* \cong (\bar{E}/E - 1), \tag{1.15}$$

where $r-r^*$ is the interest differential and where $(\bar{E}/E - 1)$ is the expected depreciation of the domestic currency, which is defined as the percentage excess of the expected future spot rate, $\bar{E}$, over the current spot rate, E. We can rewrite equation (1.15) to yield an equation for the spot rate:

$$E = \frac{\bar{E'}}{1 + r-r^*}. \tag{1.15'}$$

Equation (1.15′) is central to a correct interpretation of exchange rate movements. It argues that movements in the spot rate are due either to changes in interest differentials, given expectations, or to changes in expectations over the future course of exchange rates. Specifically, an increase in our interest rate will lead to an appreciation. The anticipation of depreciation, given interest rates, will lead to an immediate depreciation in the same proportion.

We close the model of exchange rate determination with a theory of nominal interest rates and a theory of how exchange rate expectations are formed. This is the point where our model ties in with the earlier theories. Thus we can appeal, for example, to the Keynesian model to argue that interest rates are determined by income, the terms of trade, and the real money stock. Suppose the foreign interest rate is given. The domestic interest rate, using the condition of money market equilibrium as implicit in an LM schedule, will depend on income and real money:

$$r = r(M/P, Y). \tag{1.16}$$

The expected future or long-run equilibrium exchange rate, $\bar{E}$, can be written as a function of the terms of trade, σ, and of long-run price levels, $\bar{P}/\bar{P}^*$.

$$\bar{E} = \sigma(\quad) \frac{\bar{P}}{\bar{P}^*} = \sigma(\quad) \frac{\pi \bar{M}}{\pi^* \bar{M}^*}, \tag{1.17}$$

which in turn are proportional to long-run money stocks $\bar{M}$, $\bar{M}^*$, with the factors of proportionality, π and π^*, determined by exogenous real variables. Substituting equations (1.16) and (1.17) in equation (1.15′) gives us a reduced form equation for the equilibrium exchange rate:

$$E = \frac{\sigma(\quad)(\pi\bar{M}/\pi^*\bar{M}^*)}{1 + r(M/P,\ Y) - r^*} = E(\sigma,\ M/P,\ Y;\ \pi,\ \pi^*,\ \bar{M},\ \bar{M}^*). \quad (1.18)$$

What are the implications of our model for exchange rate determination and monetary policy? The analysis is helped by Figure 1-4. The schedule QQ shows the equilibrium exchange rate of equation (1.18) for given long-run money stocks, terms of trade, and price levels and a given foreign interest rate.

The QQ schedule is downward sloping, since, given money, a higher price level—say a move to point A'''—raises the equilibrium interest

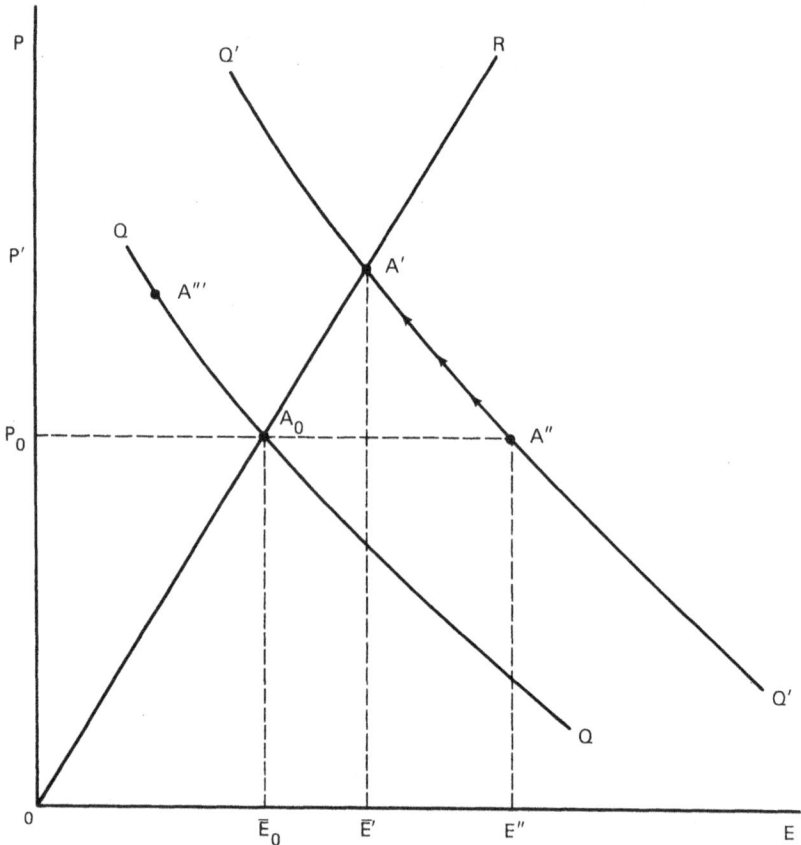

Figure 1-4.

rate at home and thus creates a differential in favor of the home country. To offset the differential, the spot rate must appreciate—E must decline—to the point where the anticipated rate of depreciation matches the interest differential.

How will a permanent increase in the money stock work itself out in this framework? An increase in money in the long run, with all prices flexible, will increase prices and exchange rates in the same proportion. This implies that the QQ schedule shifts out to $Q'Q'$ and that in the final long-run equilibrium, we will be at point A', with all real variables unchanged. In the short run, though, an increase in nominal money is an increase in the real money stock. Prices are unlikely to jump, and therefore, a lower rate of interest is required for the public to hold the higher real money stock. With a decline in interest rates there will be an incipient capital outflow until the exchange rate has depreciated enough to create the anticipation of appreciation exactly at the rate of the interest differential. This is true at point A'' where the exchange rate has depreciated beyond its new long-run level. This "overshooting" of exchange rates is an essential counterpart of permanent monetary changes under conditions of short-run price stickiness and perfect capital mobility.

By how much will exchange rates overshoot? That depends on the nature of the price adjustment process. If prices rise very rapidly because interest response of money demand is low and that of goods demand is high or because demand is highly responsive to relative prices—then the overshooting will tend to be small. Conversely, if the adjustment process of prices is slow, then the overshooting is large.

The adjustment, following the impact effect of an increase in money, is shown in Figure 1–4 by the movement along $Q'Q'$. The exchange rate has depreciated, thus making domestic goods more competitive. Interest rates at home have declined, thereby raising demand. Both factors work to put upward pressure on our price level. Prices will rise, real money declines, and interest rates rise back up until the new long-run equilibrium at A' is reached.

Virtuous and Vicious Cycles[9]

The framework we have laid out here helps understand a controversy that has developed about the working of a flexible rate system. It has been argued that flexible rates make inflation stabilization more difficult in soft currency countries and easier in hard currency countries. The reason is that monetary policy, through the rapid reaction of exchange rates and through overshooting, exerts rapid inflationary pressure in expanding countries and inflation dampening in relatively tight countries. Monetary policy becomes quite possibly ineffective if one recognizes that the inflationary pressure of depreciation is quite soon translated into domestic price increases. These price increases limit the gain in competitiveness from a depreciation. In these circumstances monetary policy is primarily inflationary; it has very little, if any, effect on real aggregate demand. All that would happen is that renewed attempts at stimulating aggregate demand would translate into increasing inflation rather than more employment.

What institutional factors would check or enhance such an ostensibly unstable process? It has been argued with force that the virtuous and vicious cycle is entirely a matter of monetary determination. Unless monetary policy validates the depreciation, it will ultimately undo itself. There can be little disagreement with this conclusion, except that it is fundamentally irrelevant as an observation about policy. The relevant policy setting is one where widespread indexation, for example, will immediately translate depreciation into wage and price inflation with the consequence of growing unemployment if the central bank fails to accommodate through further monetary expansion. The central bank may in practice have very little power to stop this inflationary process, and the right starting point is incomes policy, not monetary policy. At the same time it is, of course, true that the prospect of an effective stabilization program will immediately receive the side benefit of an appreciation and a consequent bonus in terms of inflation reduction.

A CRITICISM OF THE MONETARY MODEL

A serious criticism of the monetary approach would start from the recognition that PPP does not hold as any direct test will show. Therefore an equation like (1.6), which explicitly relies on PPP, cannot be derived or expected to hold. This leaves expectations as the only direct link between exchange rates and the monetary sector. The argument returns us to equation (1.15'), written for convenience of logs:[10]

$$e_t = {}_t\bar{e}_{t+1} - {}_t d_{t+1}, \qquad (1.15')$$

where the prefix denotes the time at which expectations are formed and where ${}_t d_{t+1}$ denotes the one period interest differential starting at time t.

We now want to sketch what the implications for empirical testing of an expectations-based approach would be. For that purpose we subtract from equation (1.15′) last period's exchange rate:[11]

$$e_{t-1} = {}_{t-1}\bar{e}_{t+1} - {}_{t-1}d_{t+1},\tag{1.19}$$

where ${}_{t-1}d_{t+1}$ is the two period interest differential:

$$e_t = e_{t-1} + ({}_t\bar{e}_{t+1} - {}_{t-1}\bar{e}_{t+1}) - {}_t d_{t+1} + {}_{t-1}d_{t+1}\tag{1.20}$$

$$= e_{t-1} + \epsilon_t + {}_{t-1}d_t - \eta_t.$$

The explanation for our equilibrium exchange rate as written here will rely on the rational use of information. I will argue that today's equilibrium exchange rate is equal to last period's adjusted for the one period interest differential that prevailed between last period and this period. The remaining determinants of the exchange rate are white noise or fresh news or unanticipated events. They represent respectively the change in the expected future spot rate between last period and this period, ϵ_t, and the reassessment of the one period interest differential starting today — that is, news about the term structure, η_t.[12]

The emphasis on exchange rate movements as embodying new information is of course an essential aspect of assets market theories of the exchange rate. This is particularly recognized in the work by Mussa (1976, 1977).

In this formulation the exchange rate will depreciate today relative to its previous level for one of three reasons:

1. The depreciation was anticipated and already reflected in the one period interest differential ${}_{t-1}d_t$, which in this case would have been positive.
2. There is news about interest rates. The one period differential starting today, had been incorrectly predicted, and the reassessment of the interest differential leads to a depreciation in the one period rate, which, starting today, is above the rate that was implicit in last period's two period differential. An unanticipated increase in interest rates with unchanged expectations about future exchange rates will lead to an appreciation of the spot rate.
3. The last piece that leads to a change in the exchange rate is news about next period's equilibrium exchange rate. Here again we look solely at a change in expectations due to new information. It is apparent that rationality requires that ϵ and η be serially uncorrelated.[13]

This model of the equilibrium exchange rate draws attention to the right variables in an exchange rate equation. The right variables, in addition to the lagged rate and the one period differential and change of differential, are the unanticipated components of the variables that systematically affect exchange rates. Thus an unanticipated, permanent increase in money will depreciate the exchange rate in the same proportion if interest rates remain unaffected and more than proportionately if interest rates transitorily decline. A change in the terms of trade, with unchanged price trends and output, will immediately depreciate the exchange rate in the same proportion.

From the perspective of the monetary approach, this formulation suggests that we need both a structural model that will tell us about long-term determinants of exchange rates and the dynamics of the economy and we need a model of the unanticipated component of the exogenous variables. The model differs, of course, from the monetary approach since the latter could be written as:

$$e_t = e_{t-1} + a_0 \Delta(m-m^*) - a_1 \Delta(y-y^*) + a_2 \Delta(r_S - r_S^*), \qquad (1.6'')$$

where the Δ denotes first differences. In contrast to equation $(1.6'')$, we have in equation (1.20) the unanticipated components of these first differences, but we have in addition other structural determinants of exchange rates as they arise in a world not bound by strict PPP. To implement an equation like (1.20), the procedure clearly parallels work on interest rates or output determination where the implications of rational expectations have started to be tested.

CONCLUDING OBSERVATIONS ABOUT MONETARY POLICY AND EXCHANGE RATES

Monetary policy under flexible rates and high capital mobility works not only by affecting the interest-sensitive components of aggregate demand but also by increasing net exports. Expansionary monetary policy will depreciate the exchange rate and thereby, at least temporarily, improve our competitiveness.

Will expansionary monetary policy improve the current account? The gain in competitiveness that is at least transitorily gained by an expansionary monetary policy will no doubt by itself improve net exports and thus add to aggregate demand. There is, however, a potentially offsetting increase in imports arising from the domestic expansion in demand due to lower interest rates and thus higher investment and consumption spending. The net effect on the current account remains uncertain, since it depends on the relative magnitudes of the decline in interest rates and the response of aggregate demand to interest rates and the composition of spending to relative prices. It is certainly not a foregone conclusion (except when interest rates cannot decline at all from the world level) that monetary expansion and depreciation must improve the current account. To the extent, though, that the interest rate effects affect construction in the first place, one would not expect the adverse absorption effects on the current account to arise early compared to the relative price effects.

Monetary policy has an immediate effect on exchange rates. A change in the nominal quantity of money in the short run is a change in the real quantity of money that will bring about a change in interest rates. With changed interest rates and unchanged expectations, spot rates have to move to maintain yields in line internationally. If monetary policy affects exchange rate expectations, then the exchange rate adjustments have to be even more pronounced.

The instability or volatility of exchange rates arises from two sources. The first is the very low interest elasticity of money demand, which implies that fluctuations in the demand or supply of money produce large fluctuations in interest rates and therefore require large movements in exchange rates to maintain yields internationally. The second source is instability in the exogenous variables—there is plenty of news.

Movements in exchange rates affect the level of import prices directly and spill over into consumer, wholesale and producer prices. The extent and speed of this spillover is an essential question from the perspective of monetary policy. While the increase in import prices is helpful in establishing a gain in competitiveness, it of course hurts from a point of view of inflation. The more rapid and the more substantial the spillover of import prices into domestic prices, the more inflationary is monetary policy and the less effective it is with respect to aggregate demand.

The empirical evidence indicates that the changes in real exchange rates and competitiveness induced by nominal exchange rate movements persist for a considerable length of time. The reaction of trade flows and direct investment to these changes in relative prices are, however, slow to come about so that the net export channel cannot be counted upon as one of the more rapid responses to monetary policy.

Having reviewed in a broad manner the implications of theory and evidence for the role of monetary policy under flexible rates, we conclude with another aspect of the same question: To what extent do monetary factors account for the ongoing depreciation of the dollar? There is a worrying temptation, in this connection, to look to monetary factors as the dominant explanation. Thus the *Wall Street Journal* in a continuing public education effort has reminded us once more:

> And surely the price of the dollar depends on supply and demand for the dollar. It declines because the Federal Reserve supplies more dollars than are demanded. For all the talk of swap networks, gold sales and so on, the *only* way the decline will be reversed is for the Fed to constrict the supply of dollars.[14]

Table 1-1 summarizes monetary growth rates for M_1 for some of the major industrialized countries and the United States. The table also shows the behavior of the effective dollar exchange rate. Note that for the last five quarters, the dollar has been depreciating, although U.S. monetary growth has been among the lowest. Note in particular German monetary growth, which surely must be reckoned high. No doubt the lesson of the monetary approach—the exchange rate is the relative price of two monies—must have been overlooked.

If monetary factors do not account for the full extent of the depreciation, what factors should we look to for an explanation? Of course, we should remember that real factors do have an impact

Table 1-1. Monetary Growth and Depreciation (percent annual rates).

| | Monetary Growth | | | | |
	Germany	*Japan*	*U.K.*	*U.S.*	*Effective $ Rate*
1976	10.3	14.2	11.4	5.1	-5.0
1977	8.3	7.0	21.5	7.1	1.1
1977 I	12.6	4.2	13.4	7.2	—
II	6.0	-3.0	15.9	8.6	2.7
III	12.7	16.9	29.5	8.3	2.7
IV	10.3	7.0	29.7	7.7	10.0
1978 I	25.3	9.7	17.3	6.3	13.2
II	6.5	13.2	n.a.	10.3	5.7

Note: The quarterly data show quarter-to-quarter changes at annual rates. The last column shows the annual rates of change of the effective dollar exchange rate. A minus sign indicates an appreciation of the dollar.

Source: Federal Reserve Bank of St. Louis Review, International Financial Statistics, and OECD Economic Outlook.

on exchange rates. Suppose a given trend of monetary policies in the United States and abroad and therefore a given trend of prices. Suppose now that a current account deficit arises and that there is no expectation that it will close in the near future of itself. A change in the terms of trade will be required to restore competitiveness and thus help achieve full employment current account balance. A deterioration of our terms of trade, of course, with a given path of prices will require a depreciation of the exchange rate.

Now let me argue why I believe this story to be the major explanation for the dollar depreciation. I see two main reasons for a "structural" U.S. current account deficit. One is the medium-term reduced growth rates in other industrialized countries, in particular Japan and Germany. This implies that with unchanged U.S. growth (I take it a 3.5–4 percent growth path will be maintained) and given the evidence on U.S. and foreign income elasticities in trade, there will be continuing if not growing imbalance.

The second and possibly more important reason is the growing competitiveness of less developed countries (LDCs) in manufacturing trade. These countries have achieved substantial industrialization in their domestic markets and have to look to the world market for continuing growth. They have already shown impressive performance in the U.S. market, as evidenced by the fact that their share in our manufactured imports in the last five years has risen from 15 to more than 20 percent. I suspect that this trend will be substantially accelerated as the large European and Japanese direct investment in these countries starts to bear fruit. The U.S. market will increasingly prove to be the testing ground for newcomers' export drives. The resulting effect for our current account is unquestionably a deterioration unless we manage to outpace with new products and innovations the rate at which the rest of the world imitates U.S. techniques.

At present there is no evidence of a restructuring of the economy toward a dynamic, trade-oriented stance. Accordingly, there is no surprise that the market should anticipate deteriorating terms of trade and ongoing depreciation. The anticipation of course translates into an immediate depreciation; and the depreciation presents a conflict. It is directly and immediately inflationary and to that extent interferes seriously with an attempt to contain inflation. At the same time, though, it contributes to a restoration of U.S. competitiveness and thus helps maintain or increase aggregate demand. Since the medium-term deterioration in the terms of trade is largely inevitable, it is important not to interfere with the depreciation but rather to concentrate on a more basic macroeconomic reorientation toward fiscal restraint for an improvement in the current account combined with monetary and fiscal policies conducive to investment and growth.

SUMMARY

We have reviewed a wide spectrum of exchange rate theories. There is little purpose in endorsing one particular formulation, since each of these models seeks to capture a special effect and thus is more or less suitable for a particular instance of policy analysis. Some models view the place of the exchange rate mainly in its short-term effects on competitiveness and its long-term role in keeping in line prices internationally. Monetary and portfolio models assign importance to exchange rate movements through valuation effects; exchange rate movements change the real value of the money stock or the relative supplies of domestic and foreign assets.

If a choice has to be made between models, then I do see a difference between Quantity-Theory-oriented models that leave for the exchange rate the purely passive role of keeping the current stock of real balances just right and expectations-oriented asset market models in which the current level of the exchange rate is set primarily by reference to its anticipated path. In this latter perspective, changes in current rates bring about an adjustment dynamics the details of which depend on the differential speeds of adjustment in goods and money markets, where the adjustments that are taking place are quite possibly directed toward events that have not yet materialized but are already anticipated.

Monetarist models, of course, also recognize the importance of expectations. In those models, however, the spot rate is influenced by the effect of anticipated depreciation on real money demand. The anticipation of depreciation would reduce real money demand, thus raising the price level, and would therefore, via PPP, lead to a depreciation of the exchange rate. The extent of the depreciation depends on the interest responsiveness of money demand. By contrast, in the present model the anticipation of depreciation leads directly, as of given prices and interest rates, to an equiproportionate depreciation of the spot rate.

From the perspective of monetary policy, these two strands of modeling differ quite radically. The Quantity Theory model assumes quite literally that prices are fully, instantaneously flexible. It thus cannot have any use for monetary policy, except perhaps to stabilize the price level in the face of money demand fluctuations. All other models, of course, share a macroeconomic—as opposed to monetarist—persuasion where monetary policy works more or less because the central bank can move the real money stock. In this perspective exchange rates become a vehicle for monetary policy. One of the chief channels of monetary policy is the direct effect of money on interest rates and on the exchange rate and thereby on relative prices and aggregate demand. The empirical problem is of course whether this link makes price adjustment more rapid or, to put it differently, whether flexible rates make the Phillips curve steeper.

The theoretical framework and the empirical evidence (not presented here) allow us to form some tentative conclusions about the determination of exchange rates and the scope for monetary policy under flexible rates. The conclusions must remain tentative because the theory itself remains very much in flux—much as the domestic counterpart in macroeconomics—and because the empirical evidence is only starting to come in and to receive proper scrutiny. With these caveats in mind, here are some conclusions.

A first conclusion must concern the "right" model of exchange rate determination. I take the evidence, theoretical and empirical, to reject the monetary approach in the narrow way in which it has been empirically implemented. The portfolio approach is important because it draws attention to the current account, but the empirical work remains largely to be done. My own preference remains with an extended Mundell-Fleming model that recognizes the determination of exchange rates in assets markets, the differential speeds of adjustment of assets and goods markets, and the central role of expectations of the future exchange rate in influencing the current rate. PPP in this model is a long-run tendency, although the terms of trade may have to change secularly to accommodate biased growth patterns.

NOTES

1. For extensive reviews see Officer (1976), Frenkel and Johnson (1978), and the collection of essays in May 1978 issue of the *Journal of International Economics*.

2. The literature of the monetary approach has predominantly used the forward premium rather than the interest differential. See, for example, Frenkel and Clements (1978). The theoretical rationale is, I believe, the idea that the relevant substitution is between domestic and foreign monies rather than between money and bonds. For a further discussion see Abel et al. (1979).

3. The condition of goods market equilibrium is: $Y = A(r, Y) + C(EP^*/P, Y, Y^*)$, where $A(\ )$ denotes aggregate spending by domestic residents and C is the trade balance. We solve the equation for the exchange rate to obtain equation (1.9).

4. Portfolio balance models as discussed here have been developed among others by Boyer (1977), Dornbusch (1975), Dornbusch and Fischer (1978), Flood (1976), Henderson and Girton (1977), Kouri (1976a, 1976b), Branson (1977), and Porter (1977).

5. Using equations (1.11) and (1.12) along with the definition of wealth, we have:

$$dE/dM = \frac{1}{F} \frac{\psi_r(1-\phi) + \psi\phi_r}{\phi\psi_r - \psi\phi_r} = \frac{1}{F} \frac{\psi_r\rho + \psi(\psi_r + \phi_r)}{\phi\psi_r - \psi\phi_r} > 0,$$

which is positive on our assumption of substitution.

6. The effect of an increase in domestic securities on the equilibrium exchange rate is ambiguous.

7. To derive equation (1.14'), we note that taking the ratio of equations (1.11) and (1.12) and solving for the equilibrium interest rate we have: $r = h(r^*, X/M)$. From equation (1.13) and the wealth definition we obtain:

$$E = \frac{\rho}{1-\rho}(M/F + X/F) = (M/F)\frac{\rho}{1-\rho}(1 + X/M).$$

Substituting the equilibrium interest rate $r = h(\quad)$ yields equation (1.14'), where

$$\gamma(r^*, X/M) \equiv \frac{\rho(r^*, h(r^*, X/M)}{1 - \rho(r^*, h(r^*, X/M)}(1 + X/M).$$

8. This section draws on Dornbusch (1976a).

9. The virtuous and vicious cycle has been discussed by, among others, Krugman (1977), Sachs (1978), Basevi and de Grauwe (1977) and Willett (1978).

10. Equalizing the expected return from an investment at home and abroad we have the following relation between the dollar returns:

$$(1+r^*)\overline{E}/E = (1+r),$$

where $\overline{E}$ is the exchange rate at which we anticipate to convert foreign exchange earnings. We can rewrite this equation as: $E = \overline{E}(1+r^*)/(1+r)$ or, taking logs, $e = \bar{e} - d$, where $d \equiv \log(1+r)/(1+r^*) \simeq r - r^*$.

11. For subsequent reference we also define the log of the two period interest rate starting last year: $_{t-1}d_{t+1} \equiv {}_{t-1}d_t + {}_{t-1}v_{t+1}$, where $_{t-1}v_{t+1}$ is the expected one period rate differential between t and $t+1$, expectations being formed at $t-1$. With these definitions we can define the term $\eta \equiv {}_{t}d_{t+1} - {}_{t-1}v_{t+1}$ as the unanticipated change in the one period interest rate. The term $\epsilon_t \equiv {}_t\bar{e}_{t+1} - {}_{t-1}\bar{e}_{t+1}$ represents new information about the future exchange rate.

12. A closely related question, the efficiency of the forward market, has been extensively tested by running regressions of the form $e_t = a_o + a_1 f_{t-1}$

+ u_t where f_{t-1} is the forward rate at t-1. The test involves the joint hypothesis of $a_o = 0$ and $a_1 = 1$ (see Levich 1978). The focus of interest here, of course, is that the serially uncorrelated innovations should be explained in terms of a structural model.

13. Since η_t is observable, there may be a temptation to run an equation $e_t = e_{t-1} + {}_{t-1}d_t + \eta_t + \epsilon_t$, treating ϵ_t as the error term. The procedure is not appropriate, since the revision of interest rates is likely to be correlated with ϵ_t—as the case of unanticipated money, for example, makes clear.

14. See *Wall Street Journal*, "The Counsel of Surrender," August 30, 1978.

REFERENCES

Abel, A.; R. Dornbusch; J. Huizinga; and A. Marcus. 1979. "Money Demand During Hyperinflation." *Journal of Monetary Economics*.

Artus, J. 1976. "Exchange Rate Stability and Managed Floating: The Experience of the Federal Republic of Germany." *IMF Staff Papers*, July.

Basevi, G., and P. De Grauwe. 1977. "Vicious and Virtuous Circles." *European Economic Review* 10.

Bilson, J. 1978a. "The Monetary Approach to the Exchange Rate: Some Empirical Evidence." *IMF Staff Papers*, March.

———. 1978b. "Rational Expectations and the Exchange Rate." In J. Frenkel and H.G. Johnson, eds., *The Economics of Exchange Rates*. Reading, Mass.: Addison-Wesley, 1978.

———. 1978c. "The Current Experience with Floating Exchange Rates: An Appraisal of the Monetary Approach." *American Economic Review*, May.

Black, S. 1977. *Flexible Exchange Rates and National Economic Policy*. New Haven: Yale University Press.

Boyer, R. 1977. "Devaluation and Portfolio Balance." *American Economic Review*, March.

Branson, W. 1977. "Asset Markets and Relative Prices in Exchange Rate Determination." *Sozialwissenschaftliche Annalen* I.

Branson, W.; H. Halttunen; and P. Masson. 1977. "Exchange Rates in the Short Run." *European Economic Review* 10.

Deppler, M.C., and D.C. Ripley. "The World Trade Model: Merchandise Trade." *IMF Staff Papers*, March.

Dooley, M., and P. Isard. 1978. "A Portfolio Balance Rational Expectations Model of the Dollar-Mark Rate." Board of Governors of the Federal Reserve. Unpublished.

Dornbusch, R. 1976a. "Expectations and Exchange Rate Dynamics." *Journal of Political Economy*, December.

———. 1976b. "Capital Mobility, Flexible Exchange Rates and Macroeconomic Equilibrium." In E. Claassen and P. Salin, eds., *Recent Issues in International Monetary Economics*. New York: American Eleesevier.

———. 1975. "A Portfolio Balance Model of the Open Economy." *Journal of Monetary Economics*, May.

Dornbusch, R., and S. Fischer. 1978. "Exchange Rates and the Current Account." Massachusetts Institute of Technology. Unpublished.

———., and J. Frenkel. 1979. *International Economic Policy: Theory and Evidence.* Baltimore: Johns Hopkins University Press.

Fleming, J.M. 1962. "Domestic Financial Policies under Fixed and Flexible Rates." *IMF Staff Papers*, November.

Flood, R. 1976. "Asset Trading, Exchange Rate Determination and Exchange Rate Dynamics." London School of Economics. Unpublished.

Frankel, J. 1979. "On the Mark." *American Economic Review*, September.

Frenkel, J. 1976. "A Monetary Approach to the Exchange Rate: Doctrinal Aspects and Empirical Evidence." *Scandinavian Journal of Economics* 2.

———. 1978. "Purchasing Power Parity." *Journal of International Economics*, May.

Frenkel J., and K. Clements. 1978. "Exchange Rates in the 1920's: A Monetary Approach." University of Chicago. Unpublished.

Frenkel, J., and H.G. Johnson. 1978. *The Economics of Flexible Exchange Rates.* Reading, Mass.: Addison-Wesley.

Girton, L., and D. Roper. 1977. "A Monetary Model of Exchange Market Pressure Applied to the Postwar Canadian Experience." *American Economic Review*, September.

Goldstein, M., and M.S. Khan. 1978. "The Supply and Demand for Exports: A Simultaneous Approach." *Review of Economics and Statistics*, May.

Henderson, D. 1978. "The Dynamic Effects of Exchange Market Intervention Policy: Two Extreme Views and a Synthesis." Board of Governors of the Federal Reserve. Unpublished.

Henderson, D., and L. Girton. 1977. Central Bank Operations in Foreign and Domestic Assets under Fixed and Flexible Exchange Rates." In P. Clark, et al. eds., *The Effects of Exchange Rate Adjustments.* Washington, D.C.: Government Printing Office.

Hodrick, R. 1978. "An Empirical Analysis of the Monetary Approach to the Determination of the Exchange Rate." In J. Frenkel and H.G. Johnson, eds., *The Economics of Exchange Rates*, Reading, Mass.: Addison-Wesley.

Hooper, P. 1978. "The Stability of Income and Price Elasticities in U.S. Trade." International Finance Discussion Papers, No. 119. Board of Governors of the Federal Reserve.

Humphrey, T. 1978. "The Monetary Approach to Exchange Rates: Its Historical Evolution and Role in Policy Debates," *Economic Review* (Federal Reserve Bank of Richmond), July–August.

Isard, P. 1978. *Exchange Rate Determination: A Survey of Popular Views and Recent Models.* Princeton Studies in International Finance, No. 42. Princeton, N.J.: Princeton University.

Kohlhagen, S.M. 1978. "The Behavior of Foreign Exchange Markets—A Critical Survey of the Empirical Literature." New York: New York University, Series in Finance and Economics.

Kouri, P. 1976a. "The Exchange Rate and the Balance of Payments in the Short Run and in the Long Run: A Monetary Approach." *Scandinavian Journal of Economics* 2.

———. 1976b. "Foreign Exchange Market Stabilization and Speculation under Flexible Exchange Rates." University of Stockholm. Unpublished.

———. 1975. "The Theory of Exchange Rates." Doctoral dissertation, Massachusetts Institute of Technology.

Kouri, P., and J. de Macedo, 1978. "Exchange Rates and the International Adjustment Process." *Brookings Papers on Economic Activity* 1.

Kravis, I., and R. Lipsey. 1978. "Price Behavior in the Light of Balance of Payments Theory." *Journal of International Economics*, May.

Krugman, P. 1977. "Essays on Flexible Exchange Rates." Doctoral dissertation, Massachusetts Institute of Technology.

Laidler, D. 1977. "Expectations and the Behavior of Prices and Output under Flexible Exchange Rates." *Economica*, November.

Levich, R. 1979. "On the Efficiency of Markets for Foreign Exchange." In R. Dornbusch and J. Frenkel, eds., *International Economic Policy: Theory and Evidence*. Baltimore: Johns Hopkins University Press.

Mundell, R.A. 1968. *International Economics*. New York: Macmillan.

Mussa, M. 1977. "Exchange Rate Uncertainty: Causes, Consequences and Policy Implications." University of Chicago. Unpublished.

———. 1976. "The Exchange Rate, the Balance of Payments and Monetary and Fiscal Policy under a Regime of Controlled Floating." *Scandinavian Journal of Economics* 2.

Niehans, J. 1977. "Exchange Rate Dynamics with Stock/Flow Interaction." *Journal of Political Economy*, December.

Officer, L. 1976. "Purchasing Power Parity Theory of Exchange Rates: A Review Article." *IMF Staff Papers*.

Porter, M. 1977. "The Exchange Rate and Portfolio Equilibrium." Monash University. Unpublished.

Rodriguez, C. 1978. "The Role of Trade Flows in Exchange Rate Determination: A Rational Expectations Approach." Columbia University. Unpublished.

Sachs, J. 1978. "Wage Indexation, Flexible Exchange Rates and Macroeconomic Policy." Harvard University. Unpublished.

Sargen, N. 1977. "Exchange Rate Flexibility and Demand for Money." *Journal of Finance*, May.

Schadler, S. 1977. "Sources of Exchange Rate Variability: Theory and Empirical Evidence." *IMF Staff Papers*, July.

Wall Street Journal. 1978. "The Counsel of Surrender." August 30.

Whitman, M. 1975. "Global Monetarism." *Brookings Papers* 3.

Willett, T. 1978. *Floating Exchange Rates and International Monetary Reform*. Washington, D.C.: American Enterprise Institute.

✳ *Chapter 2*

Floating as Seen from the Central Bank*

Henry C. Wallich
*Member, Board of Governors
of the Federal Reserve System*

Floating rates are discussed usually—and properly—from a general point of view. In this chapter, the approach taken will be that of a central banker. It is hoped that, in this way, some contribution can be made to a subject, the discussion of which has by now fallen into a fairly familiar pattern. At the same time, it hardly needs to be said that the occupational biases and preconceptions of central bankers are by no means monolithic.

Differences are bound to exist among views held in central banks of small countries and large countries, in reserve currency countries and nonreserve currency countries, in countries with an experience of strong currencies and of weak currencies, and in developed and developing countries. Analytical approaches will also be colored according to whether floating rates are implicitly compared with a well-working fixed rate system or with a badly working fixed rate system and by whether foreign exchange controls are regarded as a readily acceptable alternative or not. In addition, most central bankers probably would do well to admit to some bias in favor of hard money and strong currencies. Finally, central bankers are necessarily concerned about how the floating rate system affects the role of the central bank. I shall pick up the discussion at this point.

---

*The views expressed are those of the author and do not necessarily reflect those of the staff or any other member of the Federal Reserve Board.

POLICY FREEDOM

Floating exchange rates have given central banks, or the governments within which individual central banks may have a greater or lesser degree of freedom, the technical means of conducting independent monetary policies. Under a truly fixed rate system, money creation and extinction had to reflect the need to monetize balance of payments surpluses and deficits. Interest rate policy had to be geared in good part, although not totally, to the need to keep surpluses and deficits, including capital movements, within manageable limits. Under the floating rate system, the volume of money can be controlled without regard to the balance of payments, provided the monetary authorities are prepared to accept the consequences for the exchange rate. Interest rates, therefore, can likewise be "controlled" instead of the money supply, subject to some degree of compatibility with the expected rate of inflation. Thus, under the floating regime, many central banks found it possible and desirable to adopt money supply targets.

Substantively, the policy freedom bestowed by floating rates, as has often been noted, has been disappointingly limited. There are several reasons. First, analysts seem to have underrated the degree of policy freedom that the fixed rate system derived from the absence of a "bottling up" effect. Expansionary or contractionary policies could be pursued for a while because fixed rates permitted the country to export its inflation or unemployment and to import stability. Floating rates bottle up the effects of national policy within the domestic economy. Excess domestic demand, or a demand shortfall, tend immediately to be reflected in a movement of the exchange rate that has domestic price and income consequences.

Perhaps this development could not have been clearly foreseen prior to the onset of floating. The Bretton Woods system, after all, rested on the assumption that exchange rates should change only under conditions of fundamental disequilibrium. Minor disequilibria were to be ridden out, with reliance on reserves and IMF credit. It might have been supposed that the financial markets under floating would have taken a similar attitude and would have been ready to finance disequilibria other than fundamental ones without significant exchange rate changes. This the markets have not done, although the markets have been very ready to supply credit to monetary authorities who wanted to support their exchange rates. In the absence of managed floating aimed at effective rate stabilization, therefore, exchange rates have often if not always quickly reflected payments imbalances and changes in rates of inflation.

Second, exchange rates frequently have overshot purchasing power parity rates or almost any hypothetical longer run equilibrium rates. More will be said about this later. Markets seem to have extrapolated the effects of expansionary or contractionary policies into the distant future and moved rates sharply. "Rational expectations," which in the domestic goods market imply an implausibly high degree of price flexibility, seem to have worked only too well in the foreign exchange field.

Third, the impact of exchange rate movements on domestic prices seems to have been underestimated. Particularly for the United States, these effects revealed themselves to be surprisingly large, principally because of the impact of exchange rate fluctuations upon the prices of domestic import- and export-competing goods and because of subsequent real demand and wage-price effects. This has given rise to the phenomenon of so-called vicious and virtuous circles, in which exchange rate depreciation feeds back on domestic inflation, which in turn feeds back upon the exchange rate. It seems to be a matter of semantics whether one applies this description or epithet to cases where the real exchange rate remains constant—that is, where the nominal exchange rate moves with the domestic-foreign inflation differential. One could reserve it, alternatively, to the case of overshooting of equilibrium rates in some sense. In either case, there is an effect present that under fixed rates can be postponed so long as the fixed rate lasts.

Furthermore, the world's views of inflation have gradually been changing. The Phillips curve as a locus of long-run equilibria permitting a choice between different trade-offs of inflation and unemployment has been widely given up. The perception of the consequences of inflation has advanced, in the minds of governments that may not have thought so previously, from that of a minor nuisance to that of a major problem. Thus, policy leeway for stimulative action has become severely restricted, particularly for countries whose inflation is high already. The counterpart of this limitation of domestic policy freedom under floating has been the experience that floating does not substantially shield a country from events abroad.

Finally, the experience of vicious and virtuous circles has led to a polarization of countries that under fixed rates did not occur to the same extent. This seems, in part, to have happened because exchange rates have been determined very predominantly by the state of the current account rather than of the capital account. Thus, countries with "strong"—that is, rising—currencies have been those that had current account surpluses. Those with "weak"—that is, falling—currencies have had current account deficits. This was not preordained. One could have visualized, for instance, that countries with strong anti-inflationary policies would have had high interest rates that would have attracted capital and driven up their exchange rates. They might then have found themselves suffering current account deficits. The opposite might have happened in countries with low interest rates and declining currencies. Given that the speed of adjustment is higher in asset markets than in goods markets, this would not have been an implausible prediction. Reality has gone the other way. Countries with strong currencies have had large surpluses, perhaps because they have intervened sufficiently to keep their currencies from rising to the point of choking off their exports and strongly stimulating imports. These problems have been aggravated by the experience noted above that floating does not substantially shield a country from most economic events abroad, any more than it bestows substantive (as opposed to technical) policy independence.

Polarization among countries, in turn, has given rise to schemes of international coordination involving locomotive countries and cabooses or convoys, with attendant international recriminations. All this is a far cry from the idyllic vision of harmless and constructive economic nationalism under floating exchange rates where each country does its own thing in a context of free trade and without damage to its neighbors.

Disenchantment with the degree of policy independence provided by floating rates has numerous implications. One of them is the recognition that a country has relatively little to lose from voluntarily surrendering some of its remaining policy independence by forming a stable currency area jointly with other countries. What it gains in so doing, of course, are some of the benefits of exchange rate stability. What may keep a country from entering such a group, such as the snake or the European Monetary System, is not so much the desire for and belief in its ability to carry out independent policies, but the possibility that it may be unable to merge and coordinate its policies, especially its rate of inflation, with those of the group.

For the United States as a reserve currency country, other implications of limited policy freedom are evident. As a reserve currency country, the United States has not normally been under the same balance of payments discipline and consequent policy constraints as most other countries. Under the fixed rate system, however, the United States was severely constrained with respect to freedom to move its exchange rate, since that was determined by the dollar peg of other countries. Floating rates have to some extent relieved the United States of this "*n*th currency" role. Nevertheless, the continued reserve currency role of the dollar imposes constraints upon the United States that are not necessarily inherent in a floating dollar as such. Instability in the value of the dollar makes the dollar a less desirable reserve asset and less desirable also as a trading and investment currency for private users. Under floating rates, therefore, the world role of the dollar adds one more reason to the many that make it advisable for the United States to pursue policies conducive to a strong dollar. Floating has, if anything, increased the weight of balance of payments discipline upon the United States.

The question has often been asked whether the signal and disciplinary effects emanating from falling reserves under fixed rates are more powerful than those emanating from a falling exchange rate under floating. Historically, the fear of an exchange crisis often has powerfully motivated countries to adopt measures that were politically difficult. Under a floating system, a country is spared such pressures. On the other hand, the damage foreseeable from a falling exchange rate also has been severe enough at times to trigger major policy action. The answer quite likely depends in part on the speed with which an exchange rate moves. A slow decline may have little energizing effect, whereas a sudden sharp drop may stimulate action.

DISAPPOINTING ADJUSTMENT

Current account imbalances have been protracted under the floating system, especially the surpluses of the countries with strong currencies. If this is an indictment, it should be directed to any form of exchange rate change as a means of correcting imbalances, rather than to floating as a means of bringing about such changes. Perhaps the thought that clean floating would produce rapid current account adjustments arose from the expectation that in the absence of official reserve transfers, the current account must necessarily balance. But private capital movements can, of course, sustain a current account disequilibrium indefinitely and, in the case of developing countries, which are structural capital importers, ought in fact to do so. There seems to be nothing mysterious about slow adjustment in response to exchange rate changes. Goods markets are known to clear less rapidly than assets markets. There is a J-curve effect that takes some months to overcome. Income effects are more powerful than price and exchange rate effects and in cyclical situations often dominate. The magnitude of exchange rate effects has been explored empirically, though not always conclusively. There have been the well-known schools of price elasticity optimists and pessimists, and it is not clear that floating has added a great deal to our understanding of these matters.

There are some aspects of floating, however, that do bear specifically on the speed and magnitude of adjustment. One is the need to distinguish clearly between nominal and real exchange rates, in each case focusing upon an effective (e.g., trade-weighted) rate. Large changes in nominal rates may be quite consistent with small or zero changes in real rates. This, for instance, was the observation of the Managing Director of the International Monetary Fund, Johannes Witteveen, at the Fund's Manila meeting in October 1976, after three and one-half years of generalized floating experience. Without changes in real rates, adjustment cannot be expected to flow from floating.

If the equilibrating effects of exchange rate movements are indeed slow and small, this is an argument, if anything, in favor of a permanently fixed rate system. Adjustments would then have to be made in the old-fashioned way by controlling inflation, slowing down the growth of income, and reorienting the structure of the economy toward better balance of payments equilibrium.

Under floating rates there may be a tendency for real rates to remain stable. Policy action to drive down a floating rate could be regarded as inconsistent with the principles of Article IV of the Fund Agreement and at odds also with the common law injunction against "aggressive" intervention—that is, "driving" a rate in the direction in which it is already going. Under a fixed rate system, sharp sudden changes in real rates are possible, and they can set in motion strong equilibrating tendencies. This will be the case, in any event, if such rate changes are accompanied by appropriate macropolicies, which have often been lacking. A gradual movement of a floating rate, whether in nominal or real terms, may not energize a government into strong action in the same manner.

Finally, balance of payments adjustment for countries whose exchange rates move up and down may be asymmetrical. Prices and wages are sticky downward but not upward. A drop in the exchange rate is quickly translated into higher wages and prices. A subsequent rise in the exchange rate, for whatever reasons, does not reverse the preceding inflation, although it presumably will slow it. The net effect is more inflation, which in turn works against balance of payments adjustment.

OVERSHOOTING AND
MANAGED FLOATING

Rate movements have been wide and reversals frequent. There is some danger, to be sure, of being overimpressed by observed fluctuations. Effective rates change less than bilateral rates; real rates generally change less than nominal rates. Even so, frequent reversals even of real rates have occurred and raise questions about the efficiency of the process. Wide movement and reversals have contributed to the widespread impression that floating rates tend to overshoot. The theoretical possibility—indeed, probability—of overshooting has been demonstrated. Asset markets clear faster than goods markets. The rates required for clearing of asset markets may imply a wider move than those required for equilibrium in goods markets, because during the interval before goods prices have reached their equilibrium levels, excess supplies of or demands for money and securities are likely to arise.

Diagnosing the magnitude of rate movements is difficult. Effective weighted average rates depend on the choice of bilateral versus multilateral weighting, and real rates depend upon the choice of a price index. For some countries, these choices make substantial differences. This is the case, for instance, for the choice of bilateral versus multilateral weights in the U.S. effective rate, as well as with respect to the number of countries included in the weighting. For Japan, the choice of price index very materially affects the real valuation of the yen.

The equilibrium rate with respect to which overshooting may occur and toward which the market must ultimately be assumed to move remains vague in concept and practice. Forward premia have been poor, albeit unbiased, predictors of future spot rates. Forward rates simply have, for the most part, reflected relative interest rates. The process of current account adjustment is so long that market participants must make allowance for all kinds of exogenous events, many of them unforeseeable. Many market participants, including commercial banks, have only a limited ability to take positions reflecting their longer run hunches, in part as a result of bank regulation and changes in accounting practices. Very short-run-oriented actions, on the other hand, such as postponement and acceleration of trade payments, can quickly generate enormous capital movements. In the case of the United States, a shift in these leads and lags by one week on payments connected with total current account activity of about $350 billion annually would amount to $7 billion.

Specifying an equilibrium rate, cyclically adjusted and perhaps moving on a trend to allow for income differences and differences in income elasticities of imports and exports, to say nothing of estimating future inflation and capital movements, remains as difficult under floating as it was under fixed rates. Given this great uncertainty of rate expectations, there is a tendency on the part of the market as well as of policymakers to assume that whatever rate prevails is about right and then, after it has changed somewhat, or even appreciably, to assume that it is still right. If in the stock market, on conspicuous occasions, such as 1929 or 1974, analysts have been unable to arrive at plausible or sustainable evaluations of the present value of future cash flows discounted from here to eternity because of some short-run or cyclical event, it is not surprising that students of the exchange market should have similar difficulties. The best they can hope to do is to diagnose when a rate is seriously wrong but hardly when it is right.

Wide fluctuations and reversals have raised questions, in particular, about the merits of clean floating. Although clean floating has not yet become a dirty word, the simple faith that the market is always right has been shaken. Intervention, therefore, seems appropriate not only to counter disorder in the narrowest short-run sense, but also to correct or prevent conditions that with some degree of confidence can be diagnosed as excessive. This does not mean to say, of course, that intervention will be successful. The amounts that the market can mobilize are larger than the resources of the authorities. In 1977 and the early part of 1978, the market decisively defeated various national authorities in their efforts to prevent a rise in their currencies against the dollar. Intervention is most likely to be successful when it not only comes at a time when currency movements have become extreme, but is accompanied also by actions that convince the market of a shift in basic economic policies. The market, to be sure, may not be governed in a short-run sense by fundamentals. But over time it must be expected to be, even though its interpretation of these fundamentals may be shaky.

Management of floating with any purpose other than that of countering disorder runs the risk of very quickly coming into conflict with the interests of other countries. Small countries are less exposed to this risk than are large ones, and the United States is exposed most of all. Fears of competitive depreciation obsessed the framers of Bretton Woods. Fear of inflation and particularly of rising oil prices could lead to competitive appreciation.

Individual countries may well have current account objectives.

Historically, many industrial countries have acted as if the spirit of mercantilism was not yet altogether extinct. So long as there are countries willing to import capital, especially among the developing countries, the current account objectives of industrial countries need not be irreconcilable. But such current account objectives are better implemented by policies facilitating capital outflows and allowing exchange rates to adjust to these flows than by exchange market intervention.

THE ROLE OF THE CENTRAL BANK

Monetary policy was partly paralyzed under fixed rates; it has gained strength under floating. That does not mean that central banks as institutions were powerless under fixed rates or that they have become strong under floating. More nearly the opposite seems to have been the case. During the 1960s, central bankers derived influence from their ability to confront their domestic authorities with the danger of a currency crisis. Aided by the discipline of the balance of payments, they often were able to gain acceptance for their recommended policy courses. Under floating, the danger of crisis has diminished, although not disappeared. For some countries it seems to have been replaced with the near certainty of a continuing malaise. The latter is less persuasive on behalf of policies that central bankers consider sound. This shift is quite apparent in the general role played during the 1970s by finance ministers and central bankers, the ascendancy of the ministers undeniably increasing.

Exchange rates in most countries are in the hands of the political authority, running from the legislature to the chief of state to the minister of finance. The strong political nature of exchange rates decisions buttresses this relationship, even though it may not make for better decisions. Exchange market intervention to counter disorder belongs more plausibly in the hands of central bankers, with their closer contact with the financial markets. However, it should be noted that political control of the exchange rate can become a means of controlling monetary policy even in countries where the central bank has a degree of independence from the executive power. By requiring the central bank to defend an exchange rate that implies changes in money supply and interest rates, monetary policy can become subordinated to exchange rate objectives under managed floating, as, of course, it must be under a fixed rate system.

One of the defenses of central banks against such influences has been the establishment of money supply targets. These impose a certain discipline that can serve as a substitute for the discipline exerted in the past by a fixed rate. Hereafter, as international interdependence mounts, it is likely to be the broad discipline of the balance of payments, rather than that of a fixed exchange or money growth rate, that will most effectively back up central banks when they seek support for their policies.

Chapter 3

Analysis of Short-Run Exchange Rate Behavior: March 1973 to November 1981*

Michael P. Dooley
International Monetary Fund
Jeffrey R. Shafer
The Federal Reserve Bank of New York

The variability of exchange rates among currencies in recent years has been a prominent and troublesome feature of the international monetary system. In this chapter we evaluate two popular views of exchange rate determination that offer alternative explanations for this experience.

The *price dynamics* view emphasizes the role of perceived trends in the formation of traders' expectations. The resulting exchange rate path is only loosely related to fundamental factors and is interpreted in terms of price runs, bandwagons, and technical corrections.

The *efficient markets* view emphasizes the volatility of the economic environment in recent years. The resulting exchange rate path reflects frequent revisions in expectations for factors such as current account balances and rates of inflation. According to this view exchange rates do not follow patterns that could be the basis for profitable private position-taking or the basis for government intervention in exchange markets.

In this chapter we examine daily exchange rate data from March 1973 to November 1981 in order to determine which view of exchange rate determination is more consistent with experience under floating rates. We find that paths for exchange rates do seem to follow patterns and that simple trading rules based on readily available

*The authors wish to acknowledge the contribution of Alice Loftin of the Federal Reserve Board staff, who gathered the data and performed the calculations. Teizo Taya provided helpful comments on an earlier draft. The views expressed herein are solely those of the authors and do not necessarily represent the views of the Federal Reserve Bank of New York or the Federal Reserve System.

information about past exchange rate changes would have yielded substantial profits. This finding casts considerable doubt on a simple efficient markets model.

Two interpretations of the statistical results are possible. First, exchange markets may have been dominated by participants whose behavior is determined by the price dynamics of the market. The behavior of these market participants has led to patterns in exchange rates over time that are unrelated to fundamental factors and that could have been profitably exploited. The failure of either private or official market participants to take advantage of these opportunities would suggest that the floating rate system could benefit from institutional changes that encourage speculative positions based on this information.

A second interpretation is that these profit opportunities reflect changes in the equilibrium rates of return on assets denominated in different currencies. The possibility that expected rates of return can diverge by substantial and variable margins would also have important implications for our understanding of the floating exchange rate system. This would suggest, for example, that analyses of monetary policies, exchange market intervention policies, current account imbalances, or other factors that might alter equilibrium expected rates of return will provide a better understanding of the behavior of exchange rates.

TWO VIEWS OF EXCHANGE RATE DETERMINATION[1]

Exchange rates among major foreign currencies have experienced considerable short-run variability since the inception of generalized floating exchange rates in March 1973. Exchange rate movements of individual foreign currencies against the U.S. dollar of 0.5 percent or more in a single day have been frequent; movements of 2 percent or more have occurred on a few occasions. Moreover, while the variability of daily exchange rates has changed since 1973, there has been no consistent reduction over time. One set of explanations offered for the variability of exchange rates is in terms of the price dynamics of the market. The price dynamics view emphasizes the role of perceived price trends in the formation of exchange traders' expectations. Expectations based on "fundamental factors" are said to be "weakly held," and hence traders are unwilling to take large positions on the basis of them. The resulting exchange rate path is interpreted in terms of price runs, bandwagons, and technical corrections.

The origins and implications of the price dynamics view are elaborated in the next section.

Another explanation offered for this great (by historical standards) exchange rate variability is that the international monetary system has been subjected to frequent, severe shocks—rampant world inflation, the fall of governments, oil crises, deep and widespread recession, change in exchange controls, and more. These shocks, it is argued, have resulted in frequent revisions of expectations for future exchange rates. Under this view expectations are subject to frequent revision on the basis of small pieces of information, but the market for foreign exchange is "efficient" in taking into account whatever information is available. A weak form of the efficient market hypothesis is that all information contained in the past history of exchange rates is reflected in the current rate. Under this hypothesis bandwagons do not occur, and any attempt to profit from projected trends will fail to yield more than a normal rate of return.

In this chapter an analysis of exchange rates presented in Dooley and Shafer 1976 is extended in order to judge which view of exchange rate determination is more consistent with experience since March 1973. In the 1976 paper several well-known statistical tests were applied to the sequence of daily spot exchange rates for eight foreign currencies over the first 25 months of floating exchange rates. The conclusion was that substantial evidence existed that exchange markets did not behave according to the predictions of a weak efficient market model.[2]

In the past few years a large number of empirical studies have been conducted employing similar and more sophisticated techniques.[3] A common thread in this literature has been the argument that for many reasons a sequence of prices formed in a "speculatively efficient" market might not follow a martingale process.[4] This qualification was also a major element in the theoretical section of Dooley and Shafer 1976. However, they argued that it was unlikely, on the basis of an informal assessment of the size and nature of the profit opportunities, that such departures would be evident in a foreign exchange market that was speculatively efficient.

If foreign exchange markets were weakly efficient, spot exchange rates would follow a submartingale or supermartingale (depending on whether the exchange rate is expressed as x or $1/x$) if countries have different inflation rates and/or if equilibrium rates of return on assets denominated in various currencies are different. We account for the predictable component of changes in daily spot exchange rates by adjusting all exchange rate series for overnight Eurocurrency interest rate differentials or the best available alternative. We assume that any predictable exchange rate changes remaining in the data are not due to equilibrium differences in expected rates of return. We do not need to assume that equilibrium returns are constant but only that they move together across countries. Since we assume that equilibrium rates of return are the same on assets that differ only in their currency denomination, we are testing a joint hypothesis: that expected returns are identical and that exchange rate forecasts are weakly efficient. It is not possible to test market efficiency without putting some restriction on the behavior of expected returns since any time dependence in an exchange rate series can be "explained," or more accurately "defined," *ex post* as reflecting equilibrium rates of return. Nor is it useful to posit that "risk" generates whatever equilibrium returns are needed to ensure that the efficiency hypothesis is impossible to reject. In this study we test the joint hypothesis that equilibrium expected returns are identical across Eurocurrency assets and that exchange rate forecasts are weakly efficient. Other types of restrictions based on models of equilibrium rates of return might be called for if this simple and most obvious restriction leads to a rejection of the joint hypothesis. Since a joint hypothesis is being tested, it can only be concluded that one or both of the hypotheses is not supported by the data. We leave it to further research to determine whether the results are more likely due to the variability of equilibrium rates of return or a lack of efficient speculative activity.

The most surprising finding in Dooley and Shafer 1976 was that simple trading rules yielded substantial profits from March 1975 through October 1975 even when careful account was taken of opportunity costs, in terms of interest rate differentials, and transactions costs. An obvious limitation of this finding is that it is likely that several of the large number of possible trading rules would be profitable purely by chance over the short time then available. This chapter presents out-of-sample results for the same trading rules as well as other statistical tests for October 1975–November 1981. In order to provide results for the samples of about equal length, statistics for the two halves of the "post–1975" sample are also reported. If the profitability of these rules in the earlier time period was due to chance or if the structure of time dependence of exchange rates has changed over time, it would be extremely unlikely that the same rules would continue to yield comparable profits. The profitability of trading rules and the results of other statistical tests changed very little in the out-of-sample time period. The conclusion, therefore, is that exchange rates have continued to behave in ways that provide substantial potential for profit.

At a minimum the results suggest that a simple model of exchange rate determination that assumes both speculative efficiency and risk neutrality is not supported by the data. Finally we outline possible explanations for the failure of this model. In particular, further research might focus on an attempt to explain how and why equilibrium rates of return vary over time.

THE PRICE DYNAMICS VIEW

The price dynamics view asserts that prices in speculative markets follow predictable patterns. Several hypotheses concern the behavior of market participants that creates these patterns. Probably the oldest explanation is the "greater fool" hypothesis (MacKay 1841). According to this hypothesis speculators are not concerned with the factors that determine the long-run equilibrium price of a stock, a commodity, or, in the case of exchange markets, a currency. No price is too high as long as a greater fool will pay a higher price tomorrow. Once the price begins to move in one direction, it is argued, a speculative fever will keep pushing the price in that direction as long as the madness of the crowd is expected to last. The speculation feeds on itself.

The "bandwagon" hypothesis is a variant of the greater fool hypothesis. According to this hypothesis a small set of market leaders are known, or thought, to have more accurate information concerning the factors that will affect future prices. When this set of market participants buys or sells, generating a price change, a signal is provided to other market participants to jump on the bandwagon. The followers are thought generally to overshoot the new equilibrium price. The price dynamics implied by this hypothesis, therefore, involves successive changes in one direction followed by partial reversals. To quote a prominent banker-economist:

> Once a currency begins to fall, then the other banks join in the selling pressure, pushing the currency down further. The momentum can gather ground very quickly as the market trend becomes self-fulfilling assuming that no institutions are willing to take the opposite view. And many banks have concluded (quite correctly in the short term) that by following the pack it is easy to pick up profits; or, if they do not respond to the market movement they are exposed to the danger of serious currency losses. It is only when a currency has fallen (or risen) by a very great amount that the pressure of selling (or buying) stops and is reversed. (Bell 1974)

The alleged existence of the bandwagon effect has also given rise to the suspicion that exchange rates have been manipulated by a bank or syndicate that allegedly takes a position to get a bandwagon rolling, then later jumps off the bandwagon after having earned a handsome profit.

Price dynamics interpretations surfaced repeatedly in the spring of 1973 when the dollar fell very sharply against European currencies, again in the winter as the dollar subsequently appreciated, and yet again during successive swings in dollar exchange rates, particularly vis-à-vis the Deutsche mark and the Swiss franc, in 1974 and 1975. In the first instance, the statement was frequently heard, as the dollar reached successive new lows, that the dollar had fallen to "ridiculously low" levels, levels "unjustified . . . on any reasonable assessment of the outlook for the U.S. [balance-of-] payments position" (Coombs 1973). Traders were reported generally to believe the dollar to be fundamentally undervalued but were unwilling to "buck the market" in the short run and indeed found themselves jumping on the bandwagon for the short-term ride. Such market commentary has reappeared from time to time, notably during the decline in the dollar in 1978 and during the 1981 appreciation of the dollar.

If exchange markets are characterized by price dynamics behavior, there is a clear role for central bank participation in exchange markets. By acting in a more rational manner than private speculators, the central bank could reduce the deviations in market rates from equilibrium rates and make profits at the expense of speculators. Moreover, this could be accomplished with no net change in the average reserve position of the central bank over longer periods. On the other hand, if exchange rates do not follow predictable patterns, with markets efficiently appraising and adjusting to new information, central bank intervention that was triggered by price movements and that did not result in permanent changes in international reserves would at best not change noticeably the evolution of exchange rates. The central bank would in this case supplant some of the activity of private market participants. At worst, central bank intervention would introduce noticeable trends into the evolution of exchange rates and create opportunities for alert private market participants to profit from speculating against the central bank. A dramatic example of this outcome was seen in the final years of the fixed parity system.

THE EFFICIENT MARKETS HYPOTHESIS

An alternative to the price dynamics interpretation is that exchange rate changes are best described as being formed in an efficient market. In a large number of studies of prices in markets for equities and for commodities futures, the efficient market characterization has been found to be more consistent with the data than the price dynamics characterization. (A number of these studies are collected in Cootner 1964.) A strong version of the efficient market hypothesis is that a large and competitive group of market participants have access to *all* information relevant to the formation of expectations about future prices. As a result at any time all relevant information is discounted in the present price.

Under the strong efficient market hypothesis, the history of past price changes is only one of the types of information that is fully exploited. A weaker version of the efficient market hypothesis holds that, although not *all* information is available to a large number of market participants, any information in past price movements is known to a sufficient number of market participants so that profitable speculation based on such information is impossible. For example, if serial correlation existed in a price series, the recognition of this pattern would generate speculative positions that would break up the pattern.

The weak efficient market hypothesis is consistent with the existence of some kinds of nonprice information to which only a few market participants are privy and on the basis of which those participants may take profitable positions. On the other hand positions taken on the basis of inside information must be small enough that they do not affect the price and in that way signal other market participants that conditions have changed. If it were normal, as the proponents of the bandwagon hypothesis argue, for bullish information to diffuse slowly among market participants with the result that there were a slowly shifting demand schedule and a slowly rising price, one would only have to watch prices to know that other participants in the market knew something and that it was a good time to buy. Those investors who watched price patterns carefully would find price rises followed by price rises and would bid for a currency as soon as they saw a rise in its price. The result of this process would not be a gradual price increase that overshoots the new equilibrium but an abrupt price change that might be too large or too small in an individual case but that on average would move the price immediately to the new equilibrium. For if price changes tended to be taken too far, price watchers would take positions to profit on the consistent "technical corrections," and this action would tend to eliminate the overshooting.

The efficient market hypothesis is associated with the empirical hypothesis that forward prices for a given value data follow a martingale. A martingale is defined as a statistical process in which the expected value of successive changes are independent of all previous changes. For the efficient market hypothesis to hold, the next price change must not depend on past changes in any way that could lead to unusually profitable position-taking based on such a dependence.

We shall first consider a full set of conditions that would generate a martingale in the price of a futures contract for a given value date. This path for futures prices is then related to paths for spot exchange rates. We then consider several qualifications that can be expected to cause deviations of a martingale but that are consistent with the weak efficient market hypothesis.

Sequences of Futures Exchange Rates for a Given Value Date

If there is a competitive group of risk-neutral market participants whose combined resources are large relative to the size of the market, whose objectives are to maximize the expected dollar values of their portfolios, and to whom the study of price information is costless, the sequence of prices over time of a futures contract for the *same specified date in the future* will follow a martingale.[5] This proposition can be illustrated by considering the sequence of prices on a contract to receive foreign currency on September 30. On September 15 the rate on a futures contract for delivery on September 30 must be exactly equal to the rate that is expected to prevail in the spot market on September 30. The expected rate for September 30 reflects full utilization of any information contained in past quotations for value on September 30. Investors, who are assumed to take any fair bet, would offer to buy any amount of the currency forward if their expectation for the September 30 spot rate were above the futures rate. There would be an excess demand for the currency in the forward market. Similarly, any futures rate above the expected future spot rate would be associated with excess supply. Equality must also hold between the futures rate for September 30 on September 15 and the futures rate expected to occur for September 30 on September 16. If not, investors could buy or sell currency for delivery on September 30 and plan to cover on September 16 with an expected profit. There would be an excess demand or supply of future delivery of a currency on September 15. Therefore, equilibrium requires that the expected change in the futures rate between September 15 and 16 be zero, regardless of the level of the rate on September 15. On September 16 the actual futures rate will, in general, have changed as new factors affect the market. These factors could not have been predictable, however. The futures rate on September 16 will be exactly equal to the new spot rate that is expected for September 30. The expected future spot rate changes in response to information that is known on September 16 that had not been known on September 15. The same argument applies to each successive day until September 30—each day the futures rate changes to reflect new expectations about the spot rate on September 30, but in each case the expected change in the futures rate is zero. The resulting sequence of prices on successive days for value on a specified future date is a martingale.[6]

Sequence of Spot Exchange Rates

The statistical work in this chapter is based on changes in spot exchange rates rather than on successive futures quotes for the same value date. Interest arbitrage will lead to the equality of covered yields on available instruments of identical payment risk denominated in different currencies. The annualized forward premium on a foreign currency must therefore equal the amount by which the nominal interest rate on assets denominated in that currency falls short of the nominal interest rate on dollar assets.

As an example, assume that equilibrium in international asset markets requires an expected rate of return on three-month Deutsche mark assets that is equal to the rate of return expected on three-month U.S. dollar assets. Assume further that the three-month nominal interest rate on DM is 2 percent above the comparable dollar rate. Equilibrium would then require an expected depreciation of the mark of 2 percent per year vis-à-vis the dollar. The spot exchange rate will be 0.5 percent above the spot rate expected to prevail in three months. Expected daily exchange rate changes will have a nonzero mean; in this case the mean will be about 0.006 percent. An expected depreciation will, of course, mean that consecutive changes in spot exchange rates will follow a submartingale even if the market is efficient.

All of the statistical tests reported have been performed on changes in daily exchange rates that have been adjusted for overnight Eurocurrency interest rate differentials or the best available alternative. Thus we have fully accounted for the predictable component of successive changes in daily spot exchange rates due to differences in interest rates.

Sequences of Spot Exchange Rates When Expected Rates of Return Are Not Identical

An important qualification to the model just outlined is that market participants may not, in fact, take large forward positions for arbitrarily small discrepancies between the futures rate and a consensus expected spot rate. For any of several reasons—risk aversion, limited resources, legal limitations on capital movements, or divergent expectations among market participants combined with any of the other reasons—a larger expected gain is required to induce individuals to hold larger open positions. That is, net positions denominated in different currencies are imperfect substitutes for one another. Under these conditions both expected rates of return and spot exchange rates adjust to clear the market for net assets of all maturities of all currencies. A holder of a futures contract has a net asset position in one currency and a net liability position in another. The expected rate of return on this contract, which is the annualized percentage difference between the expected future spot rate and the forward rate, will be equivalent to the return from holding a security of the same maturity as the forward contract in the currency in which one is long and a liability of the same maturity in the currency in which one is short. If a higher expected rate of return is required on foreign currency assets than on dollar assets in order for outstanding supplies of foreign currency assets and dollar assets to be willingly held, the futures rate for the foreign currency will be less than the expected future spot rate by an amount that, when annualized, will be equal to the required premium on the rate of return on foreign currency assets. Successive revisions of expectations concerning what spot rate will prevail on the value date will still have an expected value of zero, but imperfect substitutability and related considerations could lead to predictable daily price changes in spot rates of as much as 0.003 percent for every 1 percent difference in expected rates of return required to have stocks of assets denominated in different currencies willingly held.[7]

A finding that sequences of spot exchange rates, adjusted for nominal interest rate differentials, have predictable trends can be interpreted as a rejection of one or both parts of the joint hypothesis. Either information available in past price changes is not being utilized efficiently, or equilibrium differentials in rates of return due to exchange risk or other factors are quantitatively important determinants of the behavior of exchange rates. Other factors that might account for differences in equilibrium rates of return include transactions costs, which although small are not zero in exchange markets. Obtaining information and analyzing it are costly. The risks of doing business in exchange markets involve credit risk as well as the risk of exchange rate changes. Capital controls could cause real interest rate differentials, and controls were in effect for some countries during the period under consideration. Finally, if central banks enter the market to smooth exchange rate changes with sufficient resources to at times outweigh private market participants, they could introduce unusually long runs of exchange rate changes in one direction. Central bank intervention that is large relative to private position taking in exchange markets and that is motivated by other objectives may introduce other systematic patterns in rate changes.

STATISTICAL EVIDENCE ON THE BEHAVIOR OF EXCHANGE RATES

Summary of Tests

Three sets of tests were designed to detect exchange rate behavior that is inconsistent with the weak efficient market-identical real interest rate hypothesis. The tests were performed on daily noon bid rates for foreign currencies in the New York market. Changes in the logs of exchange rates were adjusted for overnight Eurocurrency interest rate differentials or the best available alternative and, where appropriate, transactions costs in both foreign exchange markets and Eurocurrency markets.[8] Dollar prices for the currencies of Belgium, Canada, France, Germany, Italy, Japan, Netherlands, Switzerland, and the United Kingdom were tested for the period March 13, 1973, to September 5, 1975, and September 8, 1975, to November 6, 1981. The evidence from the 1975 sample period was reported in Dooley and Shafer 1976 and is reproduced with minor improvements here.[9] The post-1975 sample provides out-of-sample tests of the statistical evidence reported in the 1976 paper.

In order to provide an intuitive sense of the power of the tests, all of the tests carried out on the exchange rate data were also carried out on series constructed using computer-generated pseudorandom variables. Four series that follow martingales with identically distributed error terms (random walks) were constructed. Four additional series were created that obey the following equation:

$$X_t - X_{t-1} = \alpha (X_{t-1} - X_{t-2}) - \beta (X_{t-1} - \overline{X}) + \epsilon_t , \quad (3.1)$$

where X_t is the logarithm of the hypothetical exchange rate on day t and the ϵ_t are independent, identically, normally distributed random variables with mean zero. This equation is intended to characterize two types of behavior. For values of α between zero and one the hypothetical exchange rate series will exhibit inertia; that is, the exchange rate change today will include a fraction of yesterday's change as well as a new unpredictable component. For values of β between zero and one the hypothetical series will exhibit mean regressiveness, that is, the exchange rate will be pulled back toward its

Table 3–1. Parameter Values of Pricing Dynamics Paths.

Path	α	β
A_1, A_2	.3	.01
B_1, B_2	.1	.15

"normal" level whenever unpredictable forces move it away. The martingale hypothesis implies that both α and β are zero. Table 3–1 gives the assumed parameter values for the hypothetical price dynamics paths.

The first set of tests for time dependence of exchange rate changes is based on the sample autocorrelations of changes in the logarithms of exchange rates adjusted for overnight Eurocurrency interest rate differentials for lags up to twenty days. Tests were performed on the autocorrelations taken as a whole and on the values of individual correlations. The price dynamics view suggests that changes in exchange rates should be correlated with previous changes. This is true of the hypothetical series that obey Equation (3.1) and of first differences of more complicated autoregressive-moving-average processes. An absence of autocorrelation would indicate that at least this information has been fully exploited by market participants. If changes in the logarithms of exchange rates were stationary and had a normal distribution, the absence of correlations would be a necessary and sufficient condition for intertemporal independence. If the changes are not stationary or are not normally distributed, the possibility exists for profitable information that is not reflected in autocorrelations to be hidden in prices; however, the absence of autocorrelations would rule out the most obvious and the most likely departures from randomness.[10]

A second set of tests examines whether the sequence of signs of exchange rate changes can be distinguished from the sequence of signs that would be generated by tossing a fair coin.[11] The sequence of signs of changes in an exchange rate need not correspond to a coin-tossing experiment for there to be no *useful* information in the history of past prices—a high probability of an outcome of a particular sign may correspond to a low absolute change so that the expected value of any exchange rate change is zero. On the other hand a sequence of signs could be generated by a fair coin, while gains were possible from knowing about the relative magnitudes of positive and negative changes. These qualifications notwithstanding, tests on the lengths of runs are potentially valuable because they distinguish between the behavior of exchange rates that would be likely in a weakly efficient market and behavior that is hypothesized to characterize exchange rates in the price dynamics view—a prevalence of sustained runs (that is, bandwagons) up or down. We report the results of a formal test of the hypothesis that the total number of runs in an exchange rate series could have been generated by tossing a fair coin. We also consider the incidence of runs of unusual length.

A third set of tests was conducted on the profitability of a class of trading rules, so-called filter rules,[12] which are profitable if there are bandwagons in exchange markets. An investor following an X percent filter rule starts the investment period with no position in either currency. On each day following the beginning of the period, the investor compares the current exchange rate with previous rates within the period. If the current rate exceeds the lowest previous rate by X percent, that previous rate is identified as a trough. When a trough is identified, the investor borrows the currency that has depreciated at the Eurocurrency overnight offer rate for that day, sells this currency at the bid foreign exchange rate for the currency that has appreciated, and invests the proceeds at the appropriate Eurocurrency overnight bid rate for that day. If a trough is initially identified, the investor rolls the position over daily until a peak is identified. A peak is identified when the exchange rate falls by X percent from the highest rate following the trough. When a peak is identified, the investor first squares his position by selling the currency held at the offer exchange rate and pays off the loan. The investor then borrows the currency, which has now depreciated since the most recent peak, and sells it at the bid exchange rate for the relatively stronger currency.[13] At the end of the investment period all loans are paid off and, if the remaining assets are greater than zero, the investment strategy is profitable. The profits and losses are expressed as annual rates of return on the size of the position. For example, if the speculator maintains a $1 short- or long-term position for one year and has at the end of that period $0.10, he is said to have earned 10 percent per annum by following the trading rule.[14]

Transactions costs in the markets that we are considering are fully captured by bid-ask spreads both in the foreign exchange markets and in the Eurocurrency credit markets. Bid rates for foreign exchange contracts averaged about 0.1 percent (0.05 percent for the United Kingdom) lower than offer rates over the time period considered while Eurocurrency interest rates were bid at about 0.25 percent less than offered over the period.

A sufficiently exhaustive set of tests would certainly contain one that would lead to rejection of the hypothesis of randomness for a set of truly random sequences. Our list is long enough so that one should not put much weight in isolated results. The results of the tests on the pseudorandom series serve to remind us of this. However, as reported in Dooley and Shafer 1976 the tests of the auto-correlations taken as a whole, the frequency of positive autocorrelations and the profitability of the filter trading rules constitute departures from the martingale hypothesis that cast considerable doubt on the weak efficient market-identical real interest rate hypothesis. The same tests for the longer out-of-sample period strongly reinforced our earlier conclusions.

Results

The autocorrelation evidence is summarized in Tables 3-2 and 3-3. Sample autocorrelations were calculated for each exchange rate and for the random walk and price dynamics paths for lags up to 20 business days. We tested the first 20 autocorrelations, taken as a whole, in order to determine the adequacy of the martingale model for describing exchange rate changes using a X^2 test. The Q statistic reported in Table 3-2 is large when the absolute values of the sums of the autocorrelations is large. The critical value for Q indicates the

Table 3-2. Values of $Q+$ Statistics for Exchange Rates and Random Walk Paths.

		Post-1975 Sample		
	1975 Sample	*All*	*1/2*	*2/2*
Belgium	35.86	40.48[a]	52.44[a]	21.86
Canada	37.49	48.68[a]	46.14[a]	40.56[a]
France	35.29	40.27[a]	46.41[a]	24.45
Germany	32.35	45.38[a]	32.71	37.24
Italy	33.46	89.5[a]	206.6[a]	38.60[a]
Japan	21.59	48.85[a]	52.03[a]	36.92
Netherlands	45.65[a]	43.40[a]	43.10[a]	32.00
Switzerland	28.83	33.12	26.89	45.75[a]
United Kingdom	39.21[a]	44.01[a]	27.90	32.00
RW #1	12.97	22.61	37.48	25.18
RW #2	14.13	16.12	12.93	16.10
RW #3	29.84	21.32	21.12	30.79
RW #4	24.55	17.14	16.35	15.12
PDP A_1	30.84	68.04[a]	60.50[a]	47.40[a]
PDP A_2	27.65	50.87	32.06	32.85
PDP B_1	36.96	58.19[a]	38.81[a]	44.54[a]
PDP B_2	39.51[a]	67.50[a]	38.10[a]	45.81[a]

[a]Significant at 1 percent level, critical value = 37.6

$$Q = \sum_{i=1}^{20} a_i^2 * N,$$

where N = number of observations;
a_i = sample autocorrelation of lag i = 1, | ..., 20; and
Q is distributed as a chi-squared variable with 20 degrees of freedom.

Table 3-3. Number of Positive Autocorrelations.

	1975 Sample	Post-1975 Sample		
		All	1/2	2/2
Belgium	16	13	12	12
Canada	13	14	16	11
France	18	13	10	11
Germany	17	11	11	11
Italy	15	13	11	14
Japan	11	14	14	11
Netherlands	15	13	11	11
Switzerland	10	13	8	13
United Kingdom	12	13	14	12
RW #1	7	11	10	14
RW #2	12	9	10	11
RW #3	11	10	5	14
RW #4	10	11	9	11
PDP A_1	5	6	6	9
PDP A_2	5	4	5	8
PDP B_1	7	4	3	7
PDP B_2	5	5	6	7

probability of rejecting the martingale model when it is the true model. For the 1975 sample the martingale model can be rejected for two of the nine countries at the 99 percent confidence level. For the longer post-1975 sample the martingale model can be rejected for eight of the nine countries. The Q statistics generated for the known random walk paths are clearly smaller than those generated by the exchange rate data and the price dynamics paths.

In Dooley and Shafer 1976 we observed that sample autocorrelations from subperiods of the 1975 sample showed little apparent stability over time. This property of exchange rate data is again evident in the post-1975 sample. As shown in Table 3-2, there are clear differences in the Q statistics in the two halves of our post-1975 sample but no consistent pattern over time. A possible interpretation of this evidence is that, although the sample autocorrelations are significant over short time intervals, the patterns have changed too rapidly to permit unusually profitable speculation based on this information.

The stability of sample autocorrelations, however, is not a necessary condition for the existence of useful information, although it would be sufficient. Although the pattern of sample autocorrelations changed in each subperiod studied, a prominent feature of these statistics, noted in our earlier paper, was the preponderance of positive values. As shown in Table 3-2 this has remained a striking feature of the sample autocorrelations for exchange rates. There is only one sample period (for the Swiss franc in the first half of the post-1975 sample) for which there are fewer than ten positive sample autocorrelations.

A comparison of the signs of sample autocorrelations for the exchange rate data with that for the price dynamics simulations makes it clear that the processes are different. Negative sample autocorrelations predominate for the price dynamics paths. Nevertheless, the strength of the processes in the exchange rate data—that is, the magnitude of the moving average parameters—appears to be comparable to that of the price dynamics processes.

As reported in Dooley and Shafer 1976, the price dynamics simulations provide the basis for a further observation. The pattern of sample autocorrelations for a given currency is unstable over different sample periods. However, considerable instability also occurs among the subperiods of the two runs of each price dynamics case. Therefore, we do not consider the instability of the sample autocorrelations to be a very strong indication of instability of patterns in exchange rates. Since the distribution of the sample autocorrelations depends on the theoretical autocorrelations, a direct test of stability based on the sample autocorrelations is not possible.

The second test involved the sequences of signs of exchange rate changes. It provides only isolated evidence of nonrandom behavior. A formal test was performed to determine whether the total number of runs occurring in each sample was consistent with the hypothesis that the changes were independent. The Z-test statistic is a standard normal variable computed from the following formula (Siegel 1958), where n = number of runs, n_1 = positive changes, and n_2 = negative changes.

$$Z = \frac{r - \dfrac{2n_1 \, n_2}{n_1 + n_2} + 1}{\left[\dfrac{2n_1 \, n_2 \, (2n_1 \, n_2 - n_1 - n_2)}{(n_1 + n_2)^2 \, (n_1 + n_2 - 1)}\right]^{1/2}} .$$

A positive value of Z indicates that the number of runs in the sample exceeds the expected number for a random ordering. A negative value for Z indicates fewer than the expected number of runs. The hypothesis of random ordering may not be rejected with 95 percent confidence if the value of Z lies in the critical region; $-1.96 < Z > 1.96$. The results of this test for the actual exchange rates are reported in Table 3-4. They show that, with the exception of Italy, the hypothesis of randomness cannot be rejected for any country,

Table 3-4. Test on Number of Runs.

Country	1975	Post-1975
Belgium	-1.89	-1.07
Canada	-1.87	-1.22
France	-0.59	0.25
Germany	-1.25	0.69
Italy	-2.60	-3.80
Japan	-1.66	-0.88
Netherlands	-1.32	-0.33
Switzerland	-1.32	0.18
United Kingdom	-1.31	0.55

although the absolute values for many of the standard normal variables are large.

During the entire 8-1/2 year period there are only two instances of runs of exchange rate changes in the same direction that are too long to have occurred by chance. In the first episode, as reported in Dooley and Shafer 1976, the Belgian franc and the German mark appreciated against the U.S. dollar on 15 and 16 consecutive days, respectively. In the second, the Italian lira appreciated against the dollar on forty consecutive days. The probability of a run of S or larger, conditional on the total number of runs, R, is

$$Pr\left(s > s_c \mid R\right) = .5^S R .$$

The numbers of runs for the entire sample are clustered in the vicinity of 1,000. The probability of obtaining a run of fifteen days or more is about 0.03, conditional on there being 1,000 runs, while the probability of a forty-day run is very small. This gives a crude indication of the probability of these events under the null hypothesis.

We looked closely at the rise of the German mark on sixteen consecutive days, which coincides with the fifteen-day rise of the Belgian franc, and we found that during this episode, which occurred in December 1973 and January 1974, dollar/mark intervention was larger and more sustained than at any other time during the period covered by the 1975 sample. Although an important objective of intervention during this period was to adjust reserve levels, it appears that this episode was a successful example of leaning against the wind and thereby spreading what would otherwise have been an abrupt exchange rate adjustment over a four week period. The total change in the dollar/mark rate over this period was 10.6 percent. The amounts of intervention were largest at the end of the period. On days near the end of the period when there was no intervention, exchange rate changes were large with over one-half the total rate change taking place on two days.

An even longer run was reached for the Italian lira during the post-1975 sample, and it is interesting to note that in many respects the episodes are similar. This positive run of forty days, which occurred during April–August 1977, is an extraordinarily unlikely event under the null hypothesis. As with the case discussed before, this was a time during which the Italian government was rebuilding reserves following a long period of pressure on lira exchange rates. From the end of April to the end of August 1977, foreign exchange reserve assets rose by about $4 billion, from $3.3 billion to $7.2 billion, while the lira appreciated gradually against the dollar by about 5 percent. In this episode the interest rate adjustment played an important role in sustaining the run of positive changes, since there were a few days on which the unadjusted exchange rate declined by small amounts. However, in such cases the decline was less than would have been expected given the high level of interest rates in Italy relative to the United States.[15] This appears to be another example of successful smoothing of rate changes by unusually large intervention activities. It is interesting to note that in each of the unusually long runs we have identified the government was increasing its reserve assets, a situation in which private speculators might be uncertain as to the quantity of reserves that the government would be willing to accumulate.

The results of the third set of tests, the filter trading rules, are reported in Table 3–5. The filter rules embody the price dynamics hypothesis that turning points in price series are followed by trends and that turning points can be identified by filtering out "small" reversals in exchange rates. The persistence of a trend is sometimes said to depend on the underlying psychology in the market. On individual days there are likely to be reversals or technical corrections, but these small reversals do not signal a shift in the psychology of the market. The definition of "small" reversals is of course arbitrary, and we have tested filters ranging from 1 to 25 percent.

The results presented in Table 3–5 have several striking characteristics. First, the remarkable profits reported in Dooley and Shafer 1976 for the 1, 3, and 5 percent filter remained clearly in evidence for the post-1975 sample. For example, the 1 percent filter for the French franc would have yielded a 17 percent annual rate of return over the first 2–1/2 years of floating exchange rates and 12 percent for the 6-year period ending in late 1981. On the other hand the largest filter showed consistent losses. These are based on only a few

Table 3-5. Filter Rules—Annual Percentage Profits and Losses Adjusted for Interest Rate Differentials.

		0.01	0.03	0.05	0.10	0.15	0.20	0.25	Var × 10⁻⁵
Belgium	1975	10.17	13.49	14.35	3.55	-7.42	-7.97	-12.05	3.88
	Post-1975	5.58	2.54	3.04	3.07	3.19	0.64	-0.91	3.48
	Post-1975, first half	4.11	-2.83	5.52	5.36	3.55	1.85	0.71	1.74
	Post-1975, second half	8.78	5.88	2.28	3.63	8.98	0.01	-3.53	5.19
Canada	1975	-0.72	-0.93	-2.57	0	—	—	—	0.18
	Post-1975	4.95	1.62	1.33	3.71	3.08	2.26	-1.34	0.57
	1/2	2.93	0.20	-0.79	0	—	—	—	0.60
	2/2	8.02	3.37	4.20	4.06	2.64	0.76	0	0.54
France	1975	17.31	12.15	21.85	10.03	-1.51	-0.90	-6.02	4.20
	Post-1975	5.93	5.53	2.11	-0.89	-2.49	-0.12	-2.43	3.18
	1/2	-0.64	-1.16	-2.99	-2.23	-6.46	0	—	1.83
	2/2	12.13	11.30	5.11	0.44	3.22	.008	-2.57	4.52
Germany	1975	5.71	6.42	11.65	-6.10	-8.30	-16.54	-26.17	4.85
	Post-1975	5.77	5.36	5.79	3.62	3.08	0.22	-1.42	3.44
	1/2	4.98	-0.08	5.14	6.11	4.76	3.72	2.43	1.85
	2/2	10.74	9.82	6.91	3.43	6.91	-1.23	-3.66	5.00
Italy	1975	6.51	5.57	-1.66	0.29	-1.69	-3.55	0	—
	Post-1975	3.72	4.08	5.86	-0.09	7.76	12.90	12.72	3.07
	1/2	7.14	6.08	4.19	-8.35	14.36	13.54	12.55	2.54
	2/2	4.81	5.65	10.52	5.43	6.91	3.14	0.80	3.60
Japan	1975	3.89	5.29	2.56	-2.95	1.00	0	—	1.96
	Post-1975	13.08	7.62	7.28	10.83	5.46	0.64	-1.07	3.60
	1/2	15.45	9.17	15.48	14.27	11.89	10.34	8.74	2.04
	2/2	17.28	9.41	5.31	14.64	6.34	-1.20	-2.68	5.11

(Table 3-5. continued overleaf)

Table 3-5. continued

		0.01	0.03	0.05	0.10	0.15	0.20	0.25	Var × 10⁻⁵
Netherlands	1975	17.06	13.20	2.91	.54	-10.85	-18.89	-4.42	3.87
	Post-1975	9.85	4.37	3.03	3.57	3.77	.48	-2.07	4.45
	1/2	4.24	1.82	2.32	4.80	4.00	2.44	1.29	1.68
	2/2	16.05	6.38	2.83	3.71	7.51	-1.07	-4.66	5.20
Switzerland	1975	10.44	-0.11	8.00	2.26	-6.78	-16.13	13.04	6.24
	Post-1975	7.54	10.27	3.3	5.62	4.79	3.34	1.12	5.64
	1/2	11.09	11.87	1.97	6.07	9.95	10.65	9.30	4.79
	2/2	8.19	13.13	7.55	8.18	5.58	7.38	-8.80	6.45
United Kingdom	1975	8.88	10.32	3.06	-1.06	3.50	0.82	0	1.48
	Post-1975	11.46	7.57	4.32	4.77	3.09	0.44	-2.66	3.32
	1/2	11.12	11.11	7.68	5.01	-0.22	-3.11	-6.69	2.28
	2/2	12.58	3.93	0.12	3.19	3.35	-0.49	-4.98	4.35
RW #1	1975	-14.15	-3.60	0.00	1.90	-0.43	0	0	
	Post-1975	-0.01	4.65	-0.92	-0.33	-1.24	-3.53	-5.49	
	1/2	0.45	-3.07	-2.78	-4.06	-1.45	-3.08	0	
	2/2	-2.43	12.97	2.13	1.27	-5.97	-2.77	-3.93	
RW #2	1975	3.74	9.15	14.07	3.04	0.26	-6.45	0.88	
	All	-3.06	-1.92	-4.44	0.68	-2.74	-2.66	0	
Post-1975	1/2	-0.69	-2.27	-9.58	0.14	-4.81	0	0	
	2/2	-4.88	-2.51	-1.08	-1.38	-0.67	-3.27	0	
RW #3	1975	-2.39	-0.53	3.16	2.00	0.2	-1.61	0	
	All	3.78	14.78	3.59	6.98	9.36	8.24	3.48	
Post-1975	1/2	-6.72	6.59	3.06	-2.17	0.98	-0.32	-0.53	
	2/2	16.19	20.12	17.71	4.53	13.52	11.65	9.80	

RW #4	1975	6.315	-1.79	4.28	-8.64	-1.32	0	0	0
	All	-1.44	-1.75	2.37	2.91	4.86	4.37	3.88
Post-1975	1/2	0.00	-1.23	2.75	2.59	3.61	2.37	1.13
	2/2	-3.35	-2.24	0.81	6.58	1.60	0.80	0
PDP #1	1975	-25.93	-22.29	-4.11	0	0	0	0
	All	-18.41	-15.95	-6.65	0	0	0	0
Post-1975	1/2	-10.13	-22.52	-11.22	0	0	0	0
	2/2	-26.41	-9.79	-3.28	0	0	0	0
PDP #2	1975	-17.98	-17.46	-2.73	0	0	0	0
	All	-21.51	-16.86	-3.66	0	0	0	0
Post-1975	1/2	-13.65	-17.37	-4.80	0	0	0	0
	2/2	-28.65	-17.24	-2.22	0	0	0	0
PDP #3	1975	-17.42	-15.38	-1.69	0	0	0	0
	All	-11.26	-21.49	-4.64	0	0	0	0
Post-1975	1/2	-16.35	-22.59	-5.11	0	0	0	0
	2/2	-5.19	-19.76	-3.25	0	0	0	0
PDP #4	1975	-17.80	-18.47	-4.59	0	0	0	0
	All	-22.64	-21.69	-2.76	0	0	0	0
Post-1975	1/2	-22.74	-19.31	-2.13	0	0	0	0
	2/2	-22.10	-22.04	-3.50	0	0	0	0

transactions, but they do suggest that large swings in exchange rates tended to be systematically reversed during the sample period.

Perhaps more surprising is the fact that there is no pattern of declining profitability over time. In the 1976 paper we reported that the profitability of the trading rules seemed to decline toward the end of the sample period. But this pattern was not in evidence for the post-1975 sample. For example, the 1 percent filter for Canada, Germany, Japan, and the United Kingdom showed greater profits in the post-1975 sample as compared to the 1975 sample. In six of nine countries the profitability of the 1 percent filter was greater in the second half of the post-1975 sample than in the first half of the post-1975 sample. Although there are several exceptions, some relationship appears to exist between the variability of exchange rates, as measured by the variance of daily changes in logs, and the profitability of the filter rules in different periods. This phenomenon is most apparent for Belgium, France, Germany, and the Netherlands, where a large increase in the variability in the second half of the post-1975 sample is associated with a dramatic increase in the profitability of the 1 and 3 percent filters.

As with our other tests, the filters were applied to random and simulated price dynamics paths with the same variance as the average for the exchange rates. One can see in Table 3-5 that for the random number paths the 1 and 3 percent filters were unprofitable more than half the time as would be expected due to transactions costs. The second half of the post-1975 sample for RW#3 is a notable exception. This sample was also noteworthy in that it showed 14 positive autocorrelations and a relatively large Q statistic. This is a valuable reminder that such rules will occasionally be profitable by chance. For the larger filters, profits appear more frequently since the number of transactions, and hence the total transactions costs, is smaller. The range of gains and losses demonstrates the sizable potential for windfall gains and losses that exists when prices are as volatile as exchange rates were during the sample period.

Our generated price dynamics paths generally show losses substantially greater than those from the random paths. This suggests that if these price dynamics paths were accurate models of actual exchange rate changes, profits or smaller losses could be made by reversing the filter rule—that is, the foreign currency would be purchased when a trough is observed and sold after a peak. Since the filters were profitable for actual exchange rates, the losses shown for the price dynamics paths suggest that they are based on a wrong model of exchange rates.

WHERE MATTERS STAND

Substantial evidence just presented leads us to reject the martingale model for changes in spot rates adjusted for nominal interest rate differentials. The profitability of the filter rules further suggests that the deviations from a martingale are important and that exchange markets for many currencies either were not efficient in the use of price information or differences in equilibrium rates of return were large and variable during the sample period. We have some pieces of evidence with which to begin a characterization of the price dynamics of exchange markets, but clearly more work is required before we have an understanding of exchange rate behavior that would lead to policy prescriptions, such as either to intervene more in specified ways or to eliminate intervention as it has been carried out up to now.

Central bank intervention may have at times been an important factor in exchange markets during this period. In both our 1976 paper and the present chapter we have identified the longest sustained runs in exchange rates with periods when substantial intervention tended to resist the direction of movement of the exchange rate. However, we were able to identify only two episodes in a very large sample. We do not know how much of the deviation of exchange rates from rates that would prevail in efficient markets should be ascribed to intervention.

Capital controls, under which price information may be correctly appraised while investors are unable to profit from it, have been present during the period. The United States, however, has had no capital controls since January 1974. Moreover, extraterritorial markets have made positions in controlled currencies available to investors for most of the currencies we have studied. Inefficiency in exchange markets would imply that the "Euro" market facilities were not fully exploited by investors and additional factors would be needed to explain the foregone opportunities. Although fixed capital controls as a barrier to position-taking provide a poor candidate for the cause of unexploited price information, changing capital controls could be a source of shifts in effective currency demands that overwhelmed the capacity of the market to assimilate them in a short period of time. However, most capital control changes have been defensive and have tended to reduce rather than increase the position-taking required for the market to clear. The effect of capital control changes on exchange rates during this period must be studied directly before a judgment can be made as to their role in causing exchange rate paths to deviate from a martingale.

The empirical results may be explained, in part, by the existence of only a small pool of funds that have been actively managed for short-term profit in exchange markets. The volume of transactions in the markets is many billions of dollars per day, with large and often discrete shifts in demand associated with trade payments and long-term investment flows. Many of the largest nongovernment participants—the major international banks and multinational firms—have been generally conservative in taking exposed short-term foreign exchange positions. The views of governments and central banks have probably contributed to this behavior. Regulation has often inhibited or restricted the growth of participation by others. As a result, the market may not be deep enough for the size of the shocks to which it has been subjected.

The lack of position-taking in exchange markets may be due to risks other than those of rate changes. Most important is the credit risk implicit in any foreign exchange contract. The Herstatt failure in June 1974 resulted in a marked drop in foreign exchange market activity as market participants grew wary of credit risks. This decline in activity could have resulted in less efficient exchange markets.

The absence of any apparent reduction in the profitability of the filter rules over time might suggest that differences in equilibrium rates of return, rather than inefficient use of information, are responsible for failure of the joint hypothesis. It would not have been surprising if exchange markets in the early part of the floating dollar period were quite different from the theoretical model in which participants have a long history of observations to draw on. Patterns could persist for some time before they would be recognized as such. The persistent profitability of rules based on readily available information is more difficult to understand. While we have no grounds for believing that such information is efficiently incorporated into forecasts of exchange rates, it seems likely that the more fruitful direction for future research is to test less restrictive models of equilibrium rates of return on assets denominated in different currencies.

NOTES

1. This section and the next two are drawn largely from Dooley and Shafer 1976.

2. A weak efficient market is one in which information contained in historical prices is fully reflected in current prices, so that unusual profits cannot be gained through an investment strategy based on this information. See Fama 1965.

Similar statistical results for this sample period, but different interpretations, can be found in Cornell and Dietrich 1978 and Logue, Sweeney, and Willett 1978. Further evaluation of these results is presented in Sweeney 1982.

3. For a survey see Levich 1979. A feature of the majority of these papers is that the error structure of longer maturity forward exchange rates has been studied rather than the sequence of spot exchange rates. As explained later the procedure used in this chapter is equivalent as long as the differential in overnight Eurocurrency rates utilized here to adjust changes in daily spot exchange rates are equal to forward exchange rate premiums or discounts. Several studies have shown that interest parity conditions hold quite closely for longer maturities, and there is no reason to doubt that this is true of overnight data. Changes in daily exchange rates adjusted for nominal interest rate differentials under our assumptions are sequences of forecast errors. This seems to be the best data set available, and it avoids the need for complex statistical procedures for dealing with the error structure of longer maturity forward exchange rates. Procedures for dealing with these problems are discussed in Hansen and Hodrick 1980.

4. See Bilson 1981. A martingale is a statistical process in which the expected value of successive changes is independent of all previous changes. That is, a sequence of random variables, X_i, that has the property that $E(X_{n+1} \mid X_n, \ldots X_1) = X_n$ for all n is said to be a martingale. If $E(X_{n+1} \mid X_n, \ldots X_i \leq (\geq) X_n)$ for all n it is said to be a submartingale (supermartingale).

5. For a proof of this proposition see Samuelson 1965.

6. Note that this result holds even if fundamental determinants of exchange rates such as current account imbalances are themselves serially correlated. A predictable change in a determinant of exchange rates does not alter the information available to forecast the exchange rate on a given future date.

7. More formally we define a time series of rates of return $Z_{j,\,t+1} = r_{j,\,t+1} - E(\tilde{X}_{j,\,t+1} \mid \phi_t)$ where $r_{j,\,t+1}$ is the difference in the equilibrium or market rates of return of dollar and Deutsche-mark-denominated assets, $X_{j,\,t+1}$ is a time series of changes in logs of daily exchange rates adjusted for overnight Eurocurrency interest rate differentials (the tilde indicates that $X_{j,\,t+1}$ is a random variable at t), E is the expectations operator, and ϕ is an information set. If the sequence $(Z_{j,\,t+1})$ is a fair game, that is if $E(\tilde{Z}_{j,\,t+1} \mid \phi_t) = 0$, the market is said to be efficient with respect to the information set (ϕ). In this chapter $r_{j,\,t+1}$ is assumed to be always equal to zero.

8. The sample autocorrelations were calculated on changes in *logarithms* of prices in order to obtain a distribution of changes that was symmetrical. The advantages of analyzing logarithms of speculative prices are discussed in Fama 1965. A consequence of using logarithms is that the results are the same whether one measures the dollar price of foreign currency or the foreign currency price of the dollar as the exchange rate. Slightly different results for absolute changes may be obtained when one measures the exchange rate each way. As a practical matter, however, the difference between absolute changes, percent changes, and log changes are very small for daily data.

9. The important difference is that all of the statistical tests reported in this chapter are based on exchange rate series that have been adjusted by nominal interest rate differentials.

10. In Dooley and Shafer 1976 evidence was presented that the hypothesis that daily exchange rate changes are normally distributed can be rejected. A comparison of sample density functions with the density function for normal distribution revealed that the tails of the distribution of the changes in logarithms of exchange rates are too fat. Fat tails, which were first focused on by Mandelbrot (1963), appear to be the rule for speculative prices. We explored whether the fat tails were symptomatic of a stable distribution with infinite variance for speculative price changes, as Mandelbrot hypothesized, by examining the behavior of daily, weekly, and monthly exchange rate changes. If daily changes are drawn from any stable distribution with infinite variance, the distribution of changes over longer periods would look no more normal than daily changes. On the other hand, if daily changes are independent draws from any finite variance distribution, the central limit theorem assures that changes over long time periods will be normally distributed. A comparison of sample distributions showed a clear tendency for longer differencing intervals to better fit the normal distribution. The fact that logarithms of daily exchange rate changes seem to have finite variance distributions allows classical statistical theory to be used to evaluate the sample autocorrelations.

11. These tests do not depend upon knowledge of the distribution of daily exchange rate changes.

12. Alexander (1961) first tested the profitability of rules of this type on common stock prices.

13. If interest parity holds for forward exchange rates (and there is substantial evidence that it does), this process is equivalent to selling either dollars or foreign currency in the forward market.

14. The opportunity costs associated with a filter rule are difficult to identify. The investor does not directly forego income since the asset and liability positions generated by the rule are largely offsetting. However, it is probable that both the expected value and the variability of the investor's wealth will be altered by the positions generated by trading rules. A full evaluation of this problem would require, at a minimum, a calculation of the mean and variance of the profits generated by the filter rule over various holding periods—a task well beyond our computer budget. See Grossman and Shiller 1981 for a discussion of a similar problem; see Praetz 1979 and Sweeney 1982 for discussions of filter profits as compared to buy and hold strategies.

15. We do not have a reliable series for Eurocurrency or domestic overnight interest rates for Italy. We used a three-month forward premium as a proxy for the overnight interest rate differential. A spot check of several days during April–August 1977, however, shows that, on days for which data are available for overnight domestic interest rates, the forward premium is a good proxy and would not effect the measure of runs in adjusted exchange rates.

REFERENCES

Alexander, Sidney S. 1964. "Price Movements in Speculative Markets: Trends or Random Walks, No. 2." In *The Random Character of Stock Market Prices*, ed. Paul H. Cootner. Cambridge, Mass.: MIT Press.

_____. 1961. "Price Movements in Speculative Markets: Trends or Random Walks." *Industrial Management Review* 2 (May): 7-26.

Bell, Geoffrey. 1974. "Fifteen Months of Floating: A View from London." Presented at the Williamsburg Conference, May 17-18.

Bilson, John F.O. 1981. "The Speculative Efficiency Hypothesis." *Journal of Business* 54 (July): 435-52.

Coombs, Charles A. 1973. "Treasury and Federal Reserve Foreign Exchange Operations." *Federal Reserve Bulletin* (September): 622-40.

Cootner, Paul H., ed. 1964. *The Random Character of Stock Market Prices.* Cambridge, Mass.: MIT Press.

Cornell, W.B., and Dietrich, J.K. 1978. "The Efficiency of the Market for Foreign Exchange Rate." *Review of Economic and Statistics* 60 (February): 111-20.

Dooley, Michael P., and Shafer, Jeffrey R. 1976. "Analysis of Short-Run Exchange Rate Behavior: March 1973 to September 1975." International Finance Discussion Paper 123, Federal Reserve Board, Washington, D.C.

Fama, Eugene F. 1970. "Efficient Capital Markets: A Review of Theory and Empirical Work," *Journal of Finance* (May): 383-417.

_____. 1965. "The Behavior of Stock Market Prices." *Journal of Business* (January): 34-105.

Grossman, Sanford J., and Shiller, Robert J. 1981. "The Determinants of the Variability of Stock Market Prices." *The American Economic Review* 71 (May): 222-27.

Hansen, Lars Peter, and Hodrick, Robert J. 1980. "Forward Exchange Rates as Optimal Predictors of Future Spot Rates: An Econometric Analysis." *Journal of Political Economy* 88 (October): 829-53.

Levich, Richard M. 1979. "On the Efficiency of Markets for Foreign Exchange." In *International Economic Policy, Theory and Evidence*, ed. R. Dornbusch and J.A. Frenkel. Baltimore: Johns Hopkins University Press.

Logue, D.E.; R.J. Sweeney; and T.D. Willett. 1978. "Speculative Behavior of Foreign Exchange Rates during the Current Float." *Journal of Business Research* 6: 150-74.

MacKay, Charles. 1841. *Extraordinary Popular Delusions and the Madness of Crowds.* London: Richard Bently.

Mandelbrot, Benoit. 1963. "The Variations of Certain Speculative Prices." *Journal of Business* 36 (October): 394-419.

Praetz, P.D. 1979. "A General Test of a Filter Effect." *Journal of Financial and Quantitative Analysis* 14 (June): 385-94.

Samuelson, Paul A. 1965. "Proof That Properly Anticipated Prices Fluctuate Randomly." *Industrial Management Review* (Spring).

Siegel, Sidney. 1958. *Nonparametric Statistics.* New York: McGraw-Hill.

Sweeney, R.J. 1982. "Intervention Strategy: Implications of Purchasing Power Parity and Tests of Exchange-Market Efficiency." In *International Monetary System under Stress*, ed. J. Dreyer. Washington, D.C.: American Enterprise Institute.

✳ *Chapter 4*

Exchange Rate Determination: Some Old Myths and New Paradigms

David Bigman*
The Hebrew University of Jerusalem

The revolution that occurred in the international monetary order in the 1970s with the advent of the generalized floating system, the development of international banking, and the swift and sweeping changes in national monetary policies also revolutionized thinking about exchange rates and the balance of payments. The elasticity and absorption approaches that dominated international trade theory in the 1950s and 1960s were completely abandoned in favor of the monetary approach and a revived version of the purchasing power parity (PPP) doctrine. However, as evidence has accumulated that the monetary approach cannot offer a complete theory of exchange rate determination, efforts have shifted in recent years toward development of an integrated approach.

The purpose of this chapter is to illuminate the landmarks along this journey. The main theories put forward in the late 1970s and early 1980s are reviewed and examined in light of the evidence of ten years experience with the float and in view of the controversies that unavoidably emerged. Considerable attention is given to recent thinking and the evidence on the PPP doctrine. The importance of this doctrine lies not only in its being an essential building block in the monetary approach, but even more in its application by many countries as the most important guide in their exchange rate policy.

The fundamental tenets of the old and new approaches to exchange rate determination and the concepts of flow and stock equilibrium are presented first, both for an ordinary currency and for a

*I am grateful to Yoav Kislev and Teizo Taya for helpful comments.

reserve currency. Next the theory, evidence, and policy implications of PPP are considered. A short-run version of this doctrine that takes into account the time dimension in every trade and financial transaction is then given. Finally the main monetary models advanced in the late 1970s and early 1980s are reviewed and some concluding remarks offered about the direction of future research.

EXCHANGE RATE: FLOW AND STOCK EQUILIBRIUM

Traditional writings in the theory of international trade and finance have focused on the role of exchange rates in balancing the flow of foreign currency demanded by domestic residents in order to purchase goods and assets abroad with the flow of foreign currency supplied by foreigners who purchase goods and services in the domestic market (see, e.g., Robinson 1937; Machlup 1949; Haberler 1949). The exchange market was treated in essentially the same manner as the market for any ordinary commodity: Demand and supply schedules of foreign exchange were derived from the corresponding demand and supply schedules for imports and exports; the equilibrium exchange rate is the price that balances the demand for and supply of foreign currency.

A textbook exposition of the process of exchange rate determination is presented in Figure 4-1. Demand and supply schedules of foreign exchange are plotted as a function of the exchange rate (defined as the domestic price of a unit of foreign currency). The intersection of the *dd* and the *ss* curves determines both the equilibrium exchange rate and the equilibrium volume of trading in the foreign exchange market. The demand for foreign currency, like all ordinary demand functions, is a decreasing function of the exchange rate. The supply of foreign currency need not be an increasing function of the foreign exchange, however, since it depends not on the physical volume of exports but on the amount of money earned on account of these exports. If foreign demand for domestic exports is highly inelastic, the volume of exports may well rise with a rise in the exchange rate (that is, a devaluation of the domestic currency) but the *value* of the foreign currency earned would actually decline. Suppose that the current exchange rate is below the equilibrium rate. At this rate demand for foreign currency exceeds supply, and, in the absence of offsetting capital inflow, the central bank will lose its foreign exchange or gold reserves. If the domestic currency is devalued to E^*, the deficit in the balance of payments would be eliminated and equilibrium restored. In cases in which the supply curve of foreign ex-

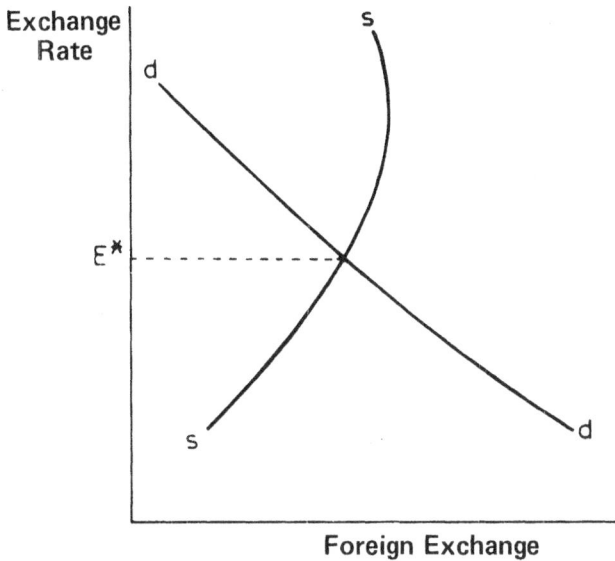

Figure 4-1. Exchange Rate Determination — Flow Equilibrium.

change is negatively sloped, it is possible that the equilibrium is unstable. An attempt by the central bank to raise the price of the foreign currency may only contribute to increase the deficit. The stability of the foreign exchange market depends on the magnitudes of the demand elasticities for imports; the stability condition is specified by the well-known Marshall–Lerner condition.

The 1970s witnessed a full-force revival of the monetary or the asset market approach to the balance of payments and exchange rate determination. The principal tenet of this approach is that the exchange rate is determined not by balancing *flow* demands and *flow* supplies of foreign currencies, but rather by balancing demands for and supplies of *stocks* of assets denominated in foreign currencies. The forces that determine the exchange rate in the asset markets are thus fundamentally different from the forces that balance flow demand and supplies. In particular the *expected* yield on foreign-currency-denominated financial assets relative to the expected yield on domestic financial assets plays a pivotal role in determining the exchange rate.

The exchange rate determined in the asset markets is a short-run equilibrium rate as these markets tend to be cleared rather rapidly. This rate need not balance flow demands and supplies, however. Nevertheless certain forces within the economy will not allow this equilibrium rate to persist unless the trade account is also in balance. The long-run equilibrium would thus be reached only when the exchange rate balances both stock and flow demands and supplies for foreign currencies. The stock/flow interaction was widely discussed in the 1970s (see, e.g., Kouri 1980 and 1976; Neihans 1977; Calvo and Rodriguez 1977; McKinnon 1979). Figure 4-2 offers one such presentation. The left-hand side of the figure is simply a reflection of Figure 4-1, and E^* is the flow equilibrium exchange rate. The right-hand side describes the demand for and supply of stock of financial assets denominated in foreign currency. The demand for foreign assets is calculated under the assumption that interest rates and the expected future exchange value of the foreign currency remain unchanged—in other words, that the expected (or covered) yield on foreign-currency-denominated assets remains unchanged. Suppose, as illustrated in Figure 4-2, that a *stock* equilibrium is established at the exchange rate E_0, above the flow equilibrium rate E^*. At this rate domestic production exceeds domestic absorption and the cur-

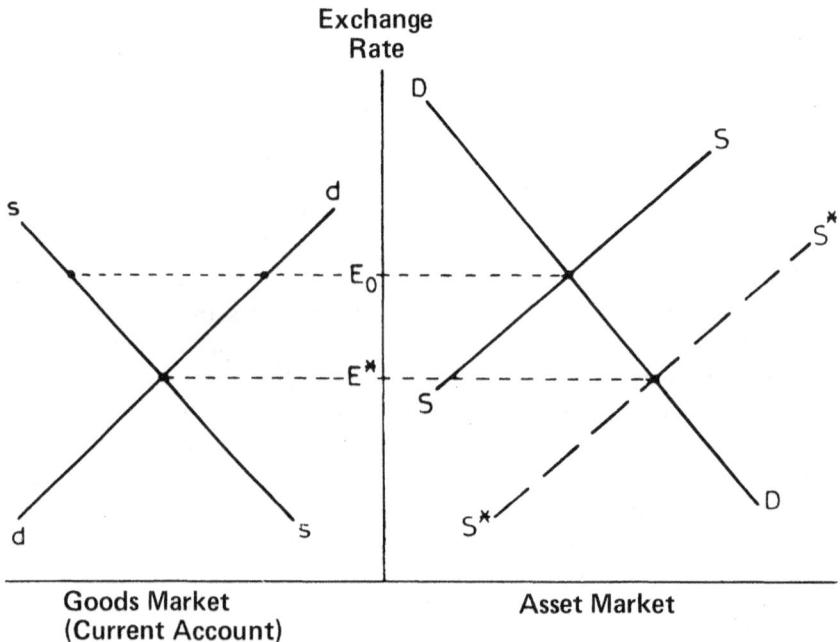

Figure 4-2. Exchange Rate Determination—Stock and Flow Equilibrium.

rent account is in surplus. The trade surplus leaves the residents of the home country with a larger stock of foreign financial assets, thereby shifting the supply curve in the stock market leftward. This in turn will cause the exchange rate to decline—the domestic currency appreciates—thereby reducing the previous disparity in the relative competitive position of the country and lowering the balance-of-payments surplus. The process will continue until all the trade surplus is eliminated and the equilibrium exchange rate E^*, which equilibrates both flow and stock demands and supplies, is established.

This analytical framework can be utilized to highlight certain important aspects concerning an international reserve currency. For this purpose, let the left-hand side of Figure 4–3 denote the goods market in the reserve currency country and let the right-hand side denote the *world* demand and supply of stock of financial assets denominated in the *domestic* (reserve) currency. The *DD* curve in Figure 4–2 denotes the domestic demand for foreign-currency-denominated assets, which is the same as the domestic *supply* of domestic (re-

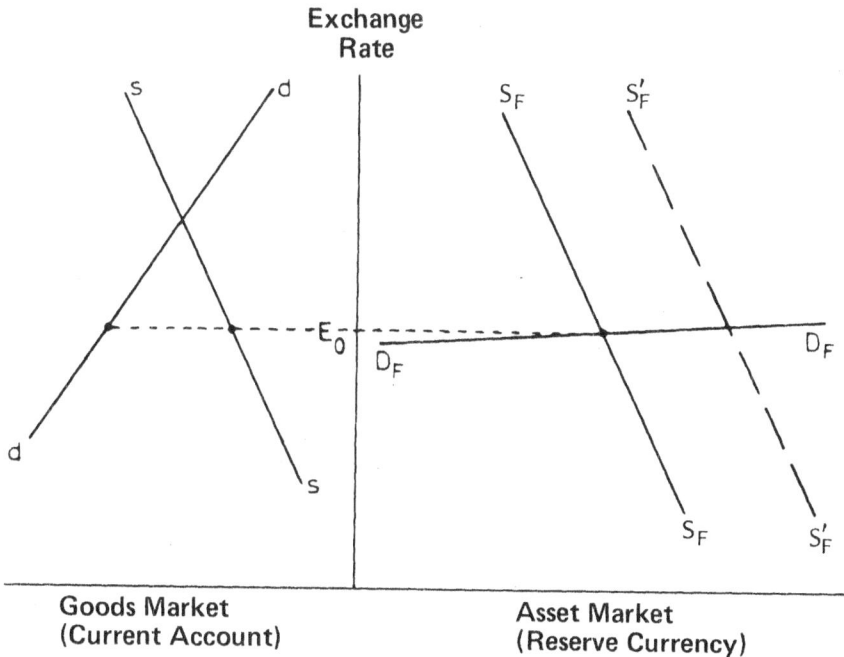

Figure 4–3. Exchange Rate Determination of a Reserve Currency — Stock and Flow Equilibrium.

serve)-currency-denominated assets, denoted by $S_F S_F$ in Figure 4-3. Similarly, the SS curve in Figure 4-2 denotes the supply of foreign assets, which is the same as the foreign demand for reserve-currency-denominated assets, denoted by $D_F D_F$ in Figure 4-3.[1]

A unique feature of a reserve currency is that it is widely accepted in all countries and its use in international transactions is far wider than its use by the reserve currency country for its own foreign receipts or payments. In terms of the diagram, therefore, this would mean that the demand schedule $D_F D_F$ of foreign residents for the reserve-currency-denominated assets is highly elastic, as illustrated in Figure 4-3. Suppose for example that a stock equilibrium exchange rate is established at E_0, where the current account is in deficit. The resulting increase in the liabilities of the country to residents of other countries will cause the stock of reserve currency assets to rise and the stock supply schedule $S_F S_F$ to shift rightward. However, since the foreign demand for these assets is highly elastic (and so long as there is no change in expectations regarding the *future* exchange value of the reserve currency), the rise in the *stock* of reserve currency financial assets will not have a noticeable effect on its *current* exchange value. Hence the mechanism by which the long-run equilibrium is established in an ordinary country (illustrated in Figure 4-2) will require massive shifts in supply to reach a new equilibrium in the case of a reserve currency country.

The process by which the reserve currency adjusts to its long-run flow equilibrium level is, however, markedly different from that for an ordinary currency. A trade deficit of the reserve-currency country will lead to a rise in the stock of reserve-currency-denominated assets of its trading partners, which in turn will cause a monetary expansion in the foreign countries, which (unless fully sterilized) will trigger an inflationary process in these countries. This in turn will erode the relative competitive position of these countries and cause the existing trade imbalance of the reserve-currency country to diminish. In this case the flow demand and supply schedules dd and ss in the goods market of the reserve-currency country will shift as domestic demand for the inflated foreign goods declines while foreign demand for the more competitive domestic goods rises, and thus the flow equilibrium exchange rate will adjust to the stock equilibrium rate. It should also be noted that, in the absence of capital flows, a certain current account deficit in the reserve currency country is *not* inconsistent with long-run equilibrium. This deficit and the resulting increase in the stock of international reserves would furnish the needs for additional financial assets in the world market associated with the growth in the volume of trade.

The demand curve for reserve-currency-denominated assets may shift if any change occurs in the covered yield on these assets for foreign holders—that is, if either the nominal interest rate differential or the *expected* future exchange value of the reserve currency changes. If, for instance, foreign traders expect the reserve currency to depreciate at a rate not offset by the interest rate differential, it means that they anticipate losses on their reserve holdings. To protect themselves they may shift out of the reserve currency assets; the demand curve $D_F D_F$ may thus shift *upward* (in view of the *anticipated* losses they would maintain the same stocks of the reserve-currency-denominated assets only if their *current* price is lowered), thereby causing an actual depreciation of the reserve currencies.

This model, although highly stylized, illustrates the crucial role of expectations in affecting exchange rate movements, especially in the short run. It can also explain several phenomena experienced by the exchange markets in the 1970s. In 1977 and even more so in 1978, the U.S. dollar lost ground sharply against most leading currencies. The decline of the dollar was largely attributed to the mounting deficit in the U.S. balance of payments, which totaled about $15 billion in each of the two years. These deficits were added to an existing stock of $600 to $700 billion held outside the United States. The deficits themselves, therefore, represent an increase of a mere 0.25 of 1 percent in the stock of dollar reserve assets. In itself such an increase could not possibly lead to a fall of 19 percent in the exchange value of the dollar against (a weighted basket of) other currencies from mid-1977 to the end of October 1978 had there not been a significant shift in demand. The U.S. current account deficit was an important cause of a shift in demand, however, because it created expectations that the exchange value of the U.S. dollar would decline in the future. As traders shifted out of dollar assets into "strong" Eurocurrency assets, they prompted the actual decline in the exchange value of the dollar, thereby ensuring their self-fulfilling expectations.

PURCHASING POWER PARITY

The PPP doctrine is an essential building block in the monetary or asset-market approach. The modern treatment of the PPP originates in the works of Cassel in the 1920s. From the advent of the float in 1973 there was renewed interest in the PPP theory, motivated by the belief that with some caveats the equilibrium exchange rate is determined by the PPP relation and that, if left to float freely, the exchange rate will tend to that equilibrium. Less than a decade later, however, a great deal of disillusionment was being expressed with respect to the usefulness of this concept and even its very validity has been questioned. Jacob A. Frenkel summarized the facts, observing that "During the 1970s short-run changes in exchange rates bore little relationship to short-run differentials in national inflation rates, and frequently, divergencies from purchasing power parities have been cumulative" (1981b: 145). A number of theoretical studies have echoed this skepticism, questioning the basic premises which underlie the PPP hypothesis at the micro- as well as the macroeconomic level.

After presenting briefly the basic structure (or structures) of the PPP doctrine, this section takes stock of the relevance, applicability, and usefulness of the doctrine in view of recent writings in exchange rate theory and of the evidence accumulated during the 1970s. (For a thorough review of the PPP doctrine and the early theoretical and empirical studies of this subject, see Officer 1976.)

The PPP hypothesis has two versions. The absolute version states that the equilibrium exchange rate equals the ratio of domestic to foreign prices; the relative version relates changes in the exchange rates to changes in the two price levels. Commodity arbitrage assures that exchange rates will not deviate from their parity level. If commodity prices should deviate from their parity level, leaving an international price discrepancy, then traders, seeking the least expensive source for their purchases, will switch to the market where their buying power is highest. If the markets are internationally coordinated, commodity arbitrage should, therefore, ensure that the price of homogeneous commodities will be the same in all countries, after accounting for transaction and transportation costs. At the individual commodity level this hypothesis has been termed "the law of one price." In a regime of fixed exchange rates, the doctrine implies, in the words of H.G. Johnson, that a "country's price level is pegged to the world price level and must move rigidly in line with it" (1972: 234). In a regime of floating exchange rates, as traders switch to the market where they can secure the highest purchasing power for their money, they increase their demand for the currency of that market, thereby raising the exchange value of that currency until it is brought in line with its parity level.

Even its most ardent proponents, including Cassel himself, did not regard the PPP as the sole determinant of the exchange rate. They allowed for other explanatory variables and for random disturbances as well. For example, trade restrictions that apply at different rates to different products, government intervention in the exchange markets, speculative pressures, and long-term capital movements may all divert the exchange rate from its PPP. Despite its limitations, however, even the most fervent critics of the theory recognize what Officer has termed "its residual validity" (1976: 24). Haberler for one noted that the PPP calculation, if cautiously used, has considerable diagnostic value since "under normal circumstances . . . the PPP theory holds in an approximate fashion in the sense that it would hardly be possible to find under such circumstances a case where an equilibrium rate is, say, 15–20 percent off purchasing power par" (1961: 51).

In addition, several empirical studies examined the hypothesis that prices of individual commodities tend to be equalized across regions and countries as traders seek spatial arbitrage opportunities (Isard 1977; Richardson 1978; Genberg 1978; Grennes, Johnson, and Thursby 1978). But, by and large the evidence presented in these works was unfavorable to the law of one price. Isard examined price behavior for Standard International Trade Classification (SITC) commodity categories as disaggregated as four and five digits. His results did not give support to the hypothesis that prices of homogeneous commodities should differ only by the transportation costs. Richardson refuted the law of one price for 22 narrowly defined primary products using U.S. and Canadian price data. Grennes, Johnson, and Thursby found that even for narrowly defined products such as wheat the evidence is not favorable to the law of one price. On these grounds Isard concluded that "the denial of the law of one price in this context—at the most disaggregated product level for which price data can be readily matched—provides a strong presumption that it is impossible to assemble available data into aggregate price indexes which can be expected to obey the law of one price" (1977: 943).

At the disaggregate product level, deviations from the law of one price may be the result of product differentiation, information costs, product aggregation, and data problems. One such problem was illustrated by Magee (1978), who noted that commodity arbitrage is undertaken on the basis of the *expected* exchange rates and prices. Perfect arbitrage should ensure that the expected price of homogeneous goods, when denominated in the same currency, should be the same across countries. In contrast, the *measured* PPP is with respect to prices that prevail at the date that the shipments arrive, even though they were contracted for at some prior date. Since both the expected exchange rate and the prices at the contracting date may differ from their levels at the date that the shipments arrive, the expected PPP may differ from the measured PPP. Magee proves that this may lead to a spurious autocorrelation in the deviations from

PPP, which is by no means an indication that the market is in some sense inefficient.

Nevertheless, the law of one price should be expected to hold in international trade only within substantial margins. Even internal trade within a country is subject to some price disparities, and travelers may sometimes find that the price of gasoline differs among different stations along the same road. The unique features of trade between countries are likely to augment price disparities further. Barring these qualifications, it is still a fact that PPP with respect to individual tradable commodities is essentially a trivial truism of arbitrage, because the economic forces operating freely within the economy will prevent consistent, large, or prolonged deviations from the PPP. The main thrust of the PPP doctrine does not apply, however, to individual commodities but to the aggregate of all commodities; it does not apply to the individual price of a tradable product but to the price index of all products.

The basic premise underlying the PPP hypothesis at the aggregate level is that people exchange monies at a rate that represents their overall buying power. The *value* of each currency is determined fundamentally by its purchasing power (defined as the inverse of the price level). The *exchange value* of the currency is thus determined by its *relative* purchasing power (defined as the ratio between the price levels). The exchange rate as the relative price of two monies is determined by the purchasing power of money in the domestic market relative to its purchasing power in the foreign market. This specification of the PPP hypothesis suggests that the price indices applied to the purchasing power of money in each economy should be at the highest possible level of aggregation. This was indeed the approach advocated by Cassel and later on by Keynes.

Nevertheless, much of the controversy concerning the PPP centered on the question of what the appropriate level of product aggregation is, and whether the index should be broad enough to incorporate nontraded goods. In Cassel's view, the price levels used to define the PPP should be the *general* price levels of the countries, representing prices of all goods and services available for purchase. He particularly emphasized that price indices limited to traded goods are unsuitable (see, e.g., Cassel 1925: 18). Keynes held the same view, and in his criticism of the British exchange rate policy in the 1920s he argued against the use of the wholesale price index (WPI), because it is heavily weighted with tradable goods, a too narrow selection to measure the appropriate price index. Keynes held the view that for individual traded goods the PPP calculation is merely a truism. Therefore, parity calculations based on price indices of traded goods come close to the actual exchange rate, which, in turn, results in a spurious verification of the theory. Only when the price index used was wide enough to include nontraded goods might there be "just that degree of discrepancy in the 'verifications' to make the theory seem *prima facie* interesting" (1930: 74). (See Office 1976: 13-16 and Frenkel 1976: 201-4 for a review of these and other views.)

Another view, advocated by Heckscher, Pigou, and Viner, among others, held that the appropriate price index should pertain to traded goods only. They emphasized the role of commodity arbitrage in determining the equilibrium exchange rate. In Ohlin's view no price *index* is relevant and only individual commodity prices should be analyzed: "Foreign exchange rate have nothing to do with the wholesale commodity price *level* as such but only with individual prices" (1967: 290). This view holds that the equilibrium exchange rate reflect spatial arbitrage from which nontraded goods should be excluded and the equilibrium exchange rate should be determined by flow demand and supply of tradable goods. In contrast, the asset-market approach holds that the equilibrium exchange rate is determined by stock demand and supply of financial assets. It advocates a broader price index as an appropriate measure of the purchasing power of money and thus of the exchange value of two monies.[2]

Dornbusch and Krugman made the observation that "Under the skin of any international economist lies a deep-seated belief in some variant of the PPP theory of exchange rate" (1976: 540). Nevertheless, the hypothesis that the exchange rate tends to move in the direction that will offset movements in relative price *levels* has been widely challenged on both theoretical and empirical grounds. Samuelson (1964) emphasized that this hypothesis can be seriously incorrect as a general proposition about actual or equilibrium exchange rates in cases where real changes alter the *relative* price structure within a country. Balassa (1964) pointed out that growth process tends to change relative prices in a way that may introduce a systematic bias between the exchange rate and the PPP. Balassa argued that since productivity growth tends to be concentrated in the traded goods sector, their prices tend to fall relative to the prices of nontraded goods. But with prices of traded goods being equalized across countries, an increase in the relative price of nontraded goods would make the domestic currency seem overvalued relative to PPP.

A simple analytical framework that may illustrate this argument was employed by Dornbusch (1976b). Assume that prices of traded goods are fully arbitraged so that PPP (in its absolute version) holds; that is,

$$P_T = E\, P_T^* ,$$

where P_T denotes the price of traded goods, E the exchange rate, and an asterisk the foreign country. Next, assume a relation between traded goods prices and the price level in each country given by

$$P_T = \theta\, P \quad \text{and} \quad P_T^* = \theta^*\, P^* .$$

Logarithmic derivation of these relations therefore yields

$$\hat{E} = (\hat{P} - \hat{P}^*) + (\hat{\theta} - \hat{\theta}^*) , \qquad (4.1)$$

where a "hat" over a variable indicates a percentage change. The first term in equation (4.1) represents the pure inflation effect; the second term shows the impact of real changes associated with changes in the relative price structure. Dornbusch formalized the corresponding equation for the cost-parity relation given by

$$\hat{E} = (\hat{W} - \hat{W}^*) + (\hat{\omega}^* - \hat{\omega}) + (\hat{\theta} - \hat{\theta}^*) , \qquad (4.2)$$

where $\hat{W}$ measures the wage inflation rate and $\hat{\omega}$ the real wage change stemming, for example, from productivity growth. Hence a relatively high rate of productivity growth in the home country would tend to be reflected in an appreciation of its currency.

Jones and Purvis (1981) focus on structural characteristics of the economy that may cause the equilibrium exchange rate to deviate from the PPP rate. In their analysis they assume full arbitrage of traded goods so that the law of one price applies to them and hence $\hat{E} = \hat{P}_T - \hat{P}_T^*$. They further assume that traded goods require the application of domestic value-added prior to being consumed. The change in the price of the *final* product[3] will therefore reflect both the change in the price of the traded intermediate products *and* the change in the price of domestic value added. In countries having different economic structures, $\hat{\theta}$ is likely to be different from $\hat{\theta}^*$, so that changes in prices of domestic value added differ. In that case P/P_T will change relative to P^*/P_T^* and $(\hat{P} - \hat{P}_T^*)$ will therefore differ from $\hat{E}$.

Real factors that may cause the equilibrium exchange rate to deviate from its PPP rate should not be regarded as an objection of the PPP doctrine, however, since, as Neihans (1981) has pointed out, this doctrine does not deny the effects of real factors on the exchange rate in the same way that the quantity theory of money does not deny the effects of real factors on the money demand function. Neihans shows, however, that even in the case of purely monetary disturbances there is no reason for the equilibrium exchange rate to correspond to PPP: Money creation through foreign exchange purchases would depress traded-goods prices relative to domestic prices, thereby leaving the exchange rate overvalued relative to its PPP; money creation through an increase in domestic debt would, on the other hand, have the opposite result on prices, leaving the exchange rate undervalued relative to its PPP.

While expressions of surprise at the tendency for the law of one price to operate reflect a quite substantial underestimation of the "residual validity" of the theory, expressions of despair at the "collapse" of the PPP doctrine reflect a prior overestimation of its applicability. A more useful approach would be to recognize the factors that may cause cumulative divergencies between the exchange rate and the PPP rate and take them into account in the analysis of exchange rate determination.

PURCHASING POWER PARITY AS A GUIDE FOR EXCHANGE RATE MANAGEMENT

Purchasing power parity has been, and still is, widely used as a guide for exchange rate policy on the grounds that it is the equilibrium toward which the exchange rate will converge over time. The crawling peg, where the crawl is determined by PPP calculations, is the most rigid version of this hypothesis. The argument in favor of exchange rate management emphasizes the need for central bank intervention in order to stabilize inherently unstable exchange market. In the absence of any exchange rate intervention, so the argument goes, the rates are highly volatile: Speculators tend to ride the waves, thus further destabilizing the exchange market. Exchange rate management via announced or de facto target rates, for example, provide private traders and speculators with an anchor for their expectations, thus encouraging them to act in a stabilizing manner. A PPP rule for exchange rate management, so the argument goes, would secure that the anchor for the chain of expectations will indeed be sought in the fundamentals that ultimately determine the equilibrium exchange rate.

Proponents of a more explicit formula for the exchange rate policy also mention the volatility and unpredictability of government policies, particularly monetary policies, which all too often become the main source of instability in the economy. Recourse to a pre-determined formula, although reducing government discretion in its exchange rate policy, may remove one source of instability associated with misjudgments or shortsightedness, which is sometimes characteristic of monetary policies. Others would argue that a PPP rule would moderate if not eliminate the phenomenon of exchange rate overshooting of its long-run equilibrium level as an effect of monetary disturbance. Such overshooting may drive the economy into a vicious circle of depreciation and inflation. In contrast, if the exchange rate is pegged to PPP or at least not allowed to deviate too much from it, then the degree of overshooting will be much smaller.

Those against a PPP-based exchange rate policy, on the other hand, would argue that this policy, especially in its crawling peg form, must also determine the choice of monetary policy. Even though there might be some latitude for independent domestic credit policy over the short run (which largely depends on the strictness with which the PPP rule is followed), the very choice of some kind of pegging arrangement deprives the government of its ability to conduct an independent monetary policy. For a variety of reasons, however, many governments, disillusioned or skeptical about the performance of their independent monetary policies, have elected to renounce part of their monetary freedom in favor of an exchange rate pegging arrangement aimed at providing greater coherence to their balance-of-payments policy (and possibly also to their monetary policy).

The question still remains whether even for these countries a PPP rule is the appropriate one. The most serious objection raised against adoption of a PPP-based intervention strategy is that it amounts to fixing the relative price of nontraded goods. The review of the PPP hypothesis in the preceding section emphasized that the equilibrium exchange rate will *not*, in general, follow the PPP when real disturbances alter relative prices. The theoretical literature mentions productivity differentials (Balassa) and different technologies (Jones and Purvis) as possible reasons for a consistent bias in the PPP as a measure of the long-run equilibrium exchange rate.

In the 1970s however we witnessed powerful examples of real disturbances, specifically wide changes in the relative prices of certain primary products and a few other tradable goods, of which oil is the most obvious example. Paradoxically, failure to take these real changes into account would enhance rather than depress exchange rate and domestic price instability. Genberg offered the following illustration of a policy-induced vicious circle.

Suppose that equilibrium requires an increase in the relative price of non-traded goods and therefore an increase in the domestic price level relative to the domestic price of foreign exchange for any given value of the foreign price level. If the authorities ignored this need for real adjustment they would interpret the increase in the domestic price level as signalling a depreciation of the target value of the home currency and, hence, a need to intervene in the foreign exchange market by selling the domestic currency. This would depreciate the market rate towards the new target exchange rate, but the implied increase in the money supply would increase the domestic price level by the same proportion. The latter increase would in turn signal a further depreciation of the target exchange rate, a new round of intervention-monetary expansion, etc. (1980: 98–99).

A simple illustration can be given via equation (3.1). Suppose, for simplicity that real changes have left the relative price of traded goods unexchanged; that is, $(\hat{P}_T - \hat{P}_T^*) = 0$, in which case there should not be any change in the equilibrium exchange rate. If the exchange rate policy follows the PPP rule, however, that is, $\hat{E} = (\hat{P} - \hat{P}^*)$ then the real structural change will nonetheless bring a change in the exchange rate equal to $\hat{E} = (\hat{\theta}^* - \hat{\theta})$, which can be quite different from zero, thereby shifting the exchange rate away from its equilibrium level. The potential bias associated with the PPP rule may be further augmented because, in the short run, even monetary disturbances are nonneutral. A monetary shock may alter relative prices between traded and nontraded goods for several months or even years. This change in relative prices may induce authorities that intervene daily in the exchange markets to shift the exchange rate in the direction implied by the measured PPP, without taking into account the real changes that are only temporary. By so doing the authorities may augment the exchange rate fluctuations, destabilize the economy, and, as was pointed out by Neihans (1978), transform temporary disturbances into permanent inflation.

The primary conclusion emerging from this analysis is that the PPP rule may be detrimental to the very objectives that it attempts to achieve. The PPP rule may increase rather than reduce exchange rate fluctuations, destabilize rather than stabilize the economy. Nevertheless, once the residual validity of the PPP hypothesis is acknowledged after its limitations are recognized, this rule can be useful for determining whether the exchange rate has deviated "too much" from its equilibrium level and for establishing "reasonable" boundaries for exchange rate movements.

THE LAW OF ONE PRICE AND COMMODITY
ARBITRAGE IN THE SHORT RUN[3]

The failure of the PPP hypothesis to explain exchange rate movements in the 1970s was attributed in part to real factors that caused
persistent and protracted deviations of the exchange rates from their
PPP values. In Frenkel's view "the experience during the 1970s illustrates the extent to which real shocks (oil embargo, supply shocks,
commodity booms and shortages, shifts in the demand for money,
differential productivity growth) result in systematic deviations from
purchasing power parities" (1981: 67). To a large measure these
deviations were, however, attributed to short-run factors such as
interest rate movements and direct interventions in the exchange
markets that were especially powerful in the latter part of the 1970s.

The short-run factors do not refute the applicability of the PPP,
namely that commodity arbitrage should equate the price of homog-
enous commodities across internationally integrated markets after
allowing for transaction and transportation costs. Nevertheless, even
for individual traded goods the usual PPP specification in either its
absolute or its relative forms is suitable only for the long run, whereas
in the short run additional considerations must enter that take into
account time and space dimensions in commodity arbitrage. These
considerations include the financial aspects of any trade transaction
and the uncertainties existing with respect to future prices and future
exchange rates during the time from contract to delivery.

Magee (1978) demonstrated that even if complete *ex ante* PPP
holds in internationally traded goods, substantial deviations may be
revealed from the *measured* PPP, which takes the actual price at the
time of delivery rather than the expected price at the time of the
contract. Artus (1978) made a similar point with respect to the PPP
value of the aggregate price index and the long-run equilibrium exchange rate. The distinction between expected and actual PPP is an
important factor in the short-run formulation of the law of one price
being developed here. The other important factors are financial evaluation of the time involved in international transactions and an explicit account of the different options open to traders for carrying
out their transactions.

In formulating the short-run version of the law of one price, we
shall follow the specific considerations of traders and arbitragers in
carrying out trade of financial transactions between countries. In
these transactions they are exposed to two types of risk: exchange
risk and price risk. The price risk exists even when the purchasing

price is fixed at the time the contract is made, because the prices at the time of delivery, when the product is sold to domestic consumers, are still unknown (and so also are its production costs). Traders have several choices for protecting themselves against these risks, including forward trading and appropriate hedging. They still have to take a position about the future values of prices and the exchange rate before deciding whether these arrangements are indeed worth their while, however. In what follows we shall consider the alternative arrangements for carrying out a foreign trade transaction and calculate the *expected* purchasing power (EPP) of a unit of the home currency for each. For simplicity of the presentation, it is assumed that all payments are made at the time of delivery and that the money allocated for these payments is invested until delivery in financial instruments in the home country or abroad—according to the highest expected yield. In practice traders do not have to mobilize the money prior to the actual payments, but the investment alternative must be considered as a benchmark for comparison.

Alternative 1. Buy the product abroad; buy the foreign currency in the spot market at the time that the contract is made; invest the money until delivery in foreign financial instruments. The expected purchasing power is given by the following equation:

$$EPP_1 = \frac{1/E \cdot (1 + r^*)}{P^*e} \quad ,$$

where E denotes the exchange rate (the domestic price of a foreign currency), asterisk denotes the foreign country, superscript e denotes the expected value, and r denotes the interest rate for the appropriate maturity.

Alternative 2. Buy the product abroad; buy the foreign currency in the forward market; invest the money until delivery in domestic financial instruments. The expected purchasing power is given by

$$EPP_2 = \frac{1/E \cdot (1 + r)/(1 + m)}{P^*e} \quad ,$$

where $m = (F - E)/E$ is the forward discount on the domestic currency and F is the appropriate forward rate.

Alternative 3.   Buy the product abroad; buy the foreign currency in the spot market at the time of delivery; invest the money until delivery in domestic financial instruments. The expected purchasing power is given by

$$\text{EPP}_3 = \frac{1/E \cdot (1 + r)/(1 + h)}{P^*e} \quad ,$$

where $h = (E^e - E)/E$ is the expected rate of depreciation of the home currency and E^e is the expected exchange rate at the time of delivery.

Alternative 4.   Buy the product in the domestic market; invest the money until delivery in foreign financial instruments; buy the foreign currency in the spot market (both at the time of the contract and at the time of delivery). The expected purchasing power is given by

$$\text{EPP}_4 = \frac{(1 + r^*)(1 + h)}{P^e} \quad .$$

Alternative 5.   Buy the product in the domestic market; invest the money until delivery in domestic financial instruments. The expected purchasing power is given by

$$\text{EPP}_5 = \frac{(1 + r)}{P^e} \quad .$$

Although there are several other alternatives, the five presented suffice for drawing the main conclusions from this analysis. Toward that end a short-run equilibrium in the money market is defined as a state in which the various investment alternatives are equally profitable. A short-run equilibrium in all markets will be restored when all options for carrying out the financial *and* the commercial transactions are equally profitable.

When the money markets are in short-run equilibrium, different investment alternatives involving the same trade activity should yield the same rate of return per unit of domestic currency. In this case alternatives 1–3 are equally profitable and alternatives 4 and 5 are equally profitable. In the case of alternatives 1–3, for instance, the product is purchased in the foreign market and the alternatives differ only in regard to the financial investment decision and the decision about purchase of the foreign exchange.

Alternatives 1 and 3 as well as 4 and 5 differ only in regard to the investment decision. Short-run equilibrium in the money market implies, by definition, that each pair yields the same return. Equating either EPP_1 to EPP_3 or EPP_4 to EPP_5 yields the (uncovered) interest rate parity condition,

$$(1 + r^*) (1 + h) = (1 + r) \quad . \tag{4.3}$$

In words, the expected return on investments in foreign financial instruments would be equally profitable as investments in domestic financial instruments if the money markets are in equilibrium.

Equating EPP_1 to EPP_2 yields the covered interest rate parity condition:

$$(1 + r^*) (1 + m) = (1 + r) \quad . \tag{4.4}$$

Alternatives 2 and 3 involve the same trading and the same investment decisions and differ only in the decision about the foreign exchange transaction. *Efficiency* of the foreign exchange market should guarantee that the two alternatives are equally profitable, yielding the condition,

$$m = h \iff F = E^e \quad . \tag{4.5}$$

In words, efficiency of the exchange market assures that the forward exchange rate is an unbiased estimate of the expected spot rate.

The foregoing conditions are the well-known conditions of financial arbitrage. The more interesting condition is the one emerging from commodity arbitrage, however. For that, alternatives having different trading decisions must be compared. Equating EPP_1 to EPP_5 yields the following condition for the determination of the exchange rate associated with commodity arbitrage:

$$E = \frac{P^e / (1 + r)}{P^{*e} / (1 + r^*)} . \tag{4.6}$$

In words, under perfect commodity arbitrage the exchange rate would be equal to the *present value* of the *expected* purchasing power of the two monies (discounted to the contracting date). Writing the expected price as $P^e = P(1 + \pi)$, where π is the expected rate of inflation, condition (4.6) can be rewritten as

$$E = \frac{\dfrac{P(1 + \pi)}{(1 + r)}}{\dfrac{P^*(1 + \pi^*)}{(1 + r^*)}} \ . \tag{4.7}$$

Equating either EPP_2 or EPP_3 to EPP_5 yields

$$h = m = \frac{P^e}{EP^{*e}} - 1 \ .$$

Hence, following the relative version of the PPP implies that with respect to *changes* in the expected exchange rate or the forward premium or discount:

$$h = m \approx \pi - \pi^* \ . \tag{4.8}$$

In words, the forward discount on the domestic currency measures its expected rate of depreciation, which is also an approximation of the expected inflation rate differential. Expectations in this analysis are defined as *stationary* when the home and the foreign countries are expected to have the same rate of inflation, that is, when $\pi = \pi^*$ (which need *not* be zero). It is easy to verify that under stationary expectations $m = h = 0$, $E = E^e = F$, and $r = r^*$. Hence if $\pi = \pi^*$ equation (3.7) is reduced to

$$E = \frac{P}{P^*} \ . \tag{4.9}$$

Hence, if expectations are constant, the conventional formulation of the PPP will be an appropriate approximation of the equilibrium exchange rate. If the *real* interest rates in the two countries are equal so that $(1 + r)/(1 + \pi) = (1 + r)/(1 + \pi^*)$, then (4.7) would be reduced to (4.9). Hence, a sufficient condition for the equilibrium exchange rate to be equal to the relative price ratio is the equality of the *real* interest rates in the home and the foreign countries. Only in these cases does the law of one price imply that the price of homogeneous commodities should be equal in different countries after allowing for transportation costs. If countries are expected to have different rates of inflation or if real interest rates differ across countries, as certainly was the case during the 1970s (see Chapter 11, by George von Furstenberg),[*] then commodity arbitrage should not be expected to equalize the exchange rate to the relative price ratio either at the aggregate level or even at the disaggregate level of individual commodities.

THE MONETARY MODELS

The monetary models are in many respects an offspring or a more advanced formulation of the PPP despite some fundamental differences that will be discussed below. A basic principle underlies the monetary or asset market approach: exchange rates are determined by relative demands and supplies of *stocks* of financial assets rather than flow of goods and services. The monetary model, in the version put forward by Frenkel (1976) and Bilson (1979, 1978), assumes that domestic and foreign goods and interest bearing assets are perfect substitutes and that prices are flexible also in the short run; thus PPP always holds. Under these assumptions the model then focuses on stock demands and supplies of national monies. Frenkel has stated these principles as follows: "Being a relative price of two assets (moneys), the equilibrium exchange rate is attained when the existing stocks of the two moneys are willingly held. It is reasonable, therefore, that a theory of the determination of the relative price of two moneys should be stated conveniently in terms of the supply of and the demand for these moneys" (1976: 201). The monetary model associated with these assumptions has two basic building blocks: One is PPP, which, under flexible prices and a perfectly integrated international market, should hold at all times, and the other is national money demand functions assumed to be stable functions of a limited number of aggregate economic variables. Analytically the monetary model consists of the following two sets of equations: PPP and "Cagan" type of money demand functions for home and foreign countries. The latter is given by

$$\frac{M}{P} = K \cdot e^{-\epsilon i} \cdot Y^{\eta} \quad , \text{ and}$$

$$\frac{M*}{P*} = K* \; e^{-\epsilon * i *} \; Y*^{\eta *} \tag{4.10}$$

where Y denotes the national income. The issue of choice of index involved with the functional specification of the PPP has been re-

[*] "Exchange Rate and Trade Instability" 1983, Bigman and Taya.

solved (or brushed off) by "treating the 'true' price index as an unobservable variable whose ratio, for any two countries, is defined by the exchange rate" (Bilson 1978: 51). Assume the following specification of PPP:

$$E = \frac{P}{P*} \quad . \tag{4.11}$$

Substituting equation (4.10) into equation (4.11) and assuming identical money demand functions for the home and the foreign countries yields a solution for the exchange rate, given in a logarithmic form by

$$e = (m - m*) + \epsilon(i - i*) - \eta(y - y*) \quad , \tag{4.12}$$

where the lower case letters denote the logarithms and asterisks the foreign country. In a fully flexible exchange rate regime, a rise in the home country money supply would lead to an equiproportional rise in the exchange rate, i.e., a depreciation of the home currency, leaving unchanged the relative prices denominated in terms of the home country currency, and thus having no real effect. The interest rate differential represents the relative cost of holding the two currencies compared with holding other financial assets. Under the interest rate parity condition, which should hold if financial assets of different countries are perfect substitutes, together with the Fisher condition, the interest rate differential would reflect the expected inflation rate differential between the two countries. Hence a rise in the domestic interest rate relative to the foreign interest rate would reflect expectations for a rise in the domestic inflation rate, which would lower the exchange value of the domestic currency in the future. This shift in expectations in turn would immediately lower the current demand for the domestic currency and lead to its actual depreciation. In short this model envisages a *positive* relation between the exchange rate and the interest rate (or a *negative* relation between the exchange value of the domestic currency against foreign currencies and the interest rate).

Frankel (1979) noted, however, that if prices are sticky in the short run, changes in the domestic interest rates would reflect changes in the tightness of the monetary policy. A rise in the domestic interest rate relative to the foreign rate would then reflect a contraction in the domestic money supply relative to the foreign money supply without a matching fall in prices. The higher interest rate in the home country should therefore attract foreign demand for the home country financial assets, which would cause the domestic currency to appreciate. This Keynesian view thus envisages a *negative* relation between the exchange rate and the interest rate.

Under the assumption of sticky prices, Frankel assumed that the exchange rate can adjust only gradually to its equilibrium value at a rate given by

$$h = -\theta(e - \bar{e}) + (\pi - \pi^*) \quad, \tag{4.13}$$

where $\bar{e}$ denotes the long-run equilibrium exchange rate and h denotes the expected rate of depreciation, which in integrated money markets should reflect the inflation rate differential and thus be equal to the interest rate differential. This in turn yields the interest rate parity condition given by

$$h = i - i^* \tag{4.14}$$

Combining equations (4.13) and (4.14) and assuming the long-run equilibrium rate to be equal to the PPP rate, that is,

$$\bar{e} = \bar{p} - \bar{p}^* \quad, \tag{4.15}$$

yields the following expression for the current exchange rate:

$$e = (\bar{p} - \bar{p}^*) - \frac{1}{\theta}[(i - \pi) - (i^* - \pi^*)] \quad. \tag{4.16}$$

The expression in the square brackets on the right-hand side of equation (4.16) denotes the *real* interest rate differential. Note that this specification is essentially identical to the one in equation (4.7) with a unitary adjustment elasticity. Put differently, Frankel's model is essentially a more general formulation of the short-run version of the PPP. Combining the latter equation with the conventional money demand functions such as (4.10), yields the following expression for the current exchange rate:

$$e = (m - m^*) - \eta(y - y^*) - \frac{1}{\theta}(i - i^*) + (\frac{1}{\theta} + \epsilon)(\pi - \pi^*) \quad. \tag{4.17}$$

The Frankel-Bilson monetary model is a special case of Frankel's model in which θ, the speed of adjustment, is infinite, assuming also that in the long run:

$$(i - i^*) = (\pi - \pi^*) \quad.$$

Even earlier versions of the monetary model recognized, however, the possibility of temporary deviations of the current exchange rate from the PPP rate owing to short-run factors such as "news" or interest rate differentials. Bilson (1978) proposed a short-run version of the monetary model where the PPP specification allows for short-run deviation and is given by

$$e_t - (p_t - p_t^*) = \alpha_0 + \alpha_1 (i - i^*) + \alpha_2 [e_{t-1} - (p_t - p_t^*)] \quad . \quad (4.18)$$

Frenkel (1981a) emphasized the role of expectations and news as the key factors affecting exchange rates in the short run. He concluded that "in periods which are dominated by 'news' which alters expectations, exchange rates are likely to be more volatile, and departures from purchasing power parities are likely to be the rule rather than the exception" (1981a: 667). In Chapter 6 of another book* McNelis and Condon examine the structural stability of exchange rate models. They tested the hypothesis of time-varying parameters and concluded that changes in the coefficient were closely synchronized with changes in economic policy rules. Dornbusch (1980) found PPP to be entirely inappropriate for explaining exchange rate behavior in the short run. His analysis indicates that "Not only does the short-term exchange rate deviate from a PPP path, but there are also cumulative deviations from that path that show substantial persistence" (p. 146). Models based on the PPP hypothesis are likely therefore to be misleading and thus, in Dornbusch's view, offer "an unsatisfactory theory of exchange rate determination" (p. 151). In his seminal work, Dornbusch (1976) offered an exchange rate model that removes the PPP restrictions. The details of that model are well known by now and need not be repeated here. For the purpose of this review it should suffice to present the final specification of the exchange rate equation that emerges from the model. This equation can be written in the following general form:

$$e = a_0 + a_1 (m - m^*) + a_2 (y - y^*) + a_3 (i - i^*) \quad . \quad (4.19)$$

Dornbusch and Fischer (1980) later extended the analysis to introduce the role of the current account. This was done by assuming that demand for home goods depends not only on income and the terms of trade but also on wealth, where the change in real wealth is equal to the current account. Hooper and Morton (1980) also incorporated the effects of the current account and examined an exchange rate determination model that leads to a reduced-form equation similar

---

*"Exchange Rate and Trade Instability" 1983, Bigman and Taya.

to equation (4.19) but adds terms measuring the current account effects.

Despite the rapid progress in the thinking about exchange rate behavior and the intensive interest that the subject has enjoyed in recent years, it still seems that no satisfactory theoretical model has yet been developed. Meese and Rogoff, who tested the various exchange rate models, concluded that "a random walk model would have outperformed all the other models as a predictor of the logarithm of major-country exchange rates during the 1970s" (1981:1). They gloomily observed therefore that "the broader implications of the results concern the failure of the structural models to predict or even explain exchange rate behavior out-of-sample" (p. 1). Part of the problem is due to the fact that structural relations and parameter values that have been estimated by Meese and Rogoff under one set of policies have been used to predict exchange rate behavior under a completely different set of policies. Nevertheless it can hardly be debated. Exchange rate theory will have to advance in the years ahead in order to provide a more satisfactory understanding.

CONCLUDING REMARKS

The evidence in the late 1970s and early 1980s indicates that the monetary models that were developed in these years still inadequately present a complete theory of exchange rate determination. Most compelling is the evidence against the simple version of PPP. The collapse of purchasing power parities during the 1970s has broad implications not only for the validity of the monetary models that assume PPP but even more so for the desirability of a PPP rule in exchange rate policy. This latter implication is of special importance for the monetary authorities in many countries that still gauge the behavior of their exchange rate on the basis of a PPP rule.

The evidence against PPP should not strip the theory of its residual validity, however. The economic forces that would prevent "excessive" deviations of the current exchange rate from the PPP rate are still in operation even though it may now take more time for their effect to be revealed. Commodity and financial arbitrage, the feedback effect from exchange rates to domestic prices, speculative expectations that are strongly influenced by inflation rate differentials, and exchange rate policy that is often guided by relative prices remain strong economic forces that will drive the exchange rate and the PPP rate along the same time trend. Future modeling efforts are certain to concentrate on constructing a more sophisticated version of the hypothesis, taking into account both short-run (but still predictable) variations and long-run biases associated with structural changes. One direction for such extensions was offered in the preceding section, where a short-run version of the PPP hypothesis is developed. It shows that the conventional version will hold valid only in a world of stationary expectations. While it may be appropriate for the very long run, the stationary assumption is clearly unsuitable for the short run, especially during the years of upheaval that followed the advent of the float.

Disenchantment with simple monetary models has led to renewed interest in the role of the current account. At this stage, however, the exact form in which the current account affects the exchange rate has not yet been sorted out. The feedback effect of exchange rates on the current account must also be reckoned with, and in this connection the J-curve effect may pose a special problem. The effect of the current account on exchange rate expectations may also be important; indeed at times it may dominate the direct effects on wealth or on money demand and supply. Expectations concerning the future course of the exchange rate may be affected by a current account deficit for a variety of reasons. Basically both traders and the monetary authorities regard a deficit as an indication that the exchange rate is not in equilibrium. Traders are therefore likely to assume that "the market"—the collective opinion of *all* traders— may regard the deficit as signaling future depreciation of the currency of the deficit country. By taking precautionary measures, including shifting altogether from that currency, they may make their expectations self-validating. But traders may also expect the monetary authorities to intervene in the exchange market to deliberately depreciate the currency to correct the trade imbalance. Again, traders are likely to take appropriate measures to protect themselves against currency losses, thereby immediately affecting the market.

The 1970s were hectic years not only for the exchange rates but also for exchange rate theories. Old theories deemed highly appropriate in the 1920s and later in the 1950s and 1960s collapsed in the 1970s, and many new theories were put forward. Much work remains to be done, however, before exchange rate behavior can be satisfactorily explained and predicted. The rapid and highly unstable developments in the international financial markets during the decade of the 1970s make the task extremely difficult. The breakdown of the Bretton Woods arrangement, followed by the oil crisis in the early 1970s, propelled massive changes in the structure of the world financial markets and in the mechanism of world trade and payments.

International banking in general, and the Eurocurrency market and forward trading arrangements in particular, gained prominence during those years. At the same time, the quadruple rise in oil prices and the wide price gyrations of many other primary products triggered massive structural changes in the pattern of world production and consumption. In addition, the years 1977 and 1978 were largely dominated by the massive trade imbalances. Exchange rate movements during these years, notably the sharp decline of the U.S. dollar and the rise of the Deutsche mark and the Japanese yen, were mostly directed at reducing these imbalances. These years and even more so the year 1979 marked also growing government intervention in the exchange markets to restore stability and to counter "undesirable" exchange rate movements. The years 1980–1982 were dominated by high and extremely volatile interest rates that appeared to be the driving force of exchange rate movements.

Obviously no exchange rate theory can be expected to be entirely satisfactory under such volatile circumstances. At the same time, however, we cannot content ourselves by saying, to paraphrase Einstein: if the evidence does not agree with the theory, well then it's too bad for the evidence.

NOTES

1. $D_F D_F$, the foreign demand for the reserve-currency-denominated assets, is upward sloping as a function of E because, for foreign residents, the price of the reserve currency in terms of their domestic currency is $1/E$.

2. This view dates back to Ricardo, who stated that "In speaking of the exchange and the comparative value of money in different countries, we must not in the least refer to the value of money estimated in commodities in either country. The exchange is never ascertained by estimating the comparative value of money in corn, cloth or any commodity whatever but by estimating the value of the currency of one country, in the currency of another" (1821: 128). Quoted also in Frenkel 1976: 204.

3. To avoid the index number issue Jones and Purvis assume a single-product economy.

4. This section draws on Bigman 1978.

REFERENCES

Artus, J.R. 1978. "Methods of Assessing the Long-run Equilibrium Value of an Exchange Rate." *Journal of International Economies* 8 (May): 277–99.

Balassa, B. 1964. "The Purchasing Power Parity Doctrine: A Reappraisal." *Journal of Political Economy* 72: 584–96.

Bigman, D. 1978. "Exchange Rate Determination in the Short-Run."

DM/78/48, International Monetary Fund, Washington, D.C.

Bilson, J.O. 1979. "The Deutsche Mark/Dollar Rate: A Monetary Analysis." In *Policies for Employment, Prices and Exchange Rates*, ed. K. Brunner and A.H. Meltzer. Carnegie-Rochester Conference Series on Public Policy, vol. 11. Amsterdam: North Holland.

_____. 1978. "Monetary Approach to the Exchange Rate—Some Empirical Evidence." *IMF Staff Papers* 25: 48-75.

Brillembourg, A. 1976. "Purchasing Power Parity and the Balance of Payments: Some Empirical Evidence." *IMF Staff Papers* 24: 77-99.

Calvo, G., and C. Rodriguez. 1977. "A Model of Exchange Rate Determination under Currency Substitution and Rational Expectations." *Journal of Political Economy* 85 (June).

Cassel, G. 1925. "Rates of Exchange and Purchasing—Power Parity." *Skandinaviska Kerditaktieholaget Quarterly Report* 55-58.

Caves, D.W., and E.L. Feige. 1980. "Efficient Foreign Exchange Markets and the Monetary Approach to Exchange-Rate Determination." *American Economic Review* 70: 120-34.

Cornell, B. 1977. "Spot Rates, Forward Rates and Exchange Market Efficiency." *Journal of Financial Economics* 5: 55-65.

Dornbusch, R. 1980. "Exchange Rate Economics: Where Do We Stand." *Brookings Papers on Economic Activity* 1: 143-85.

_____. 1976a. "The Theory of Flexible Exchange Rate Regimes and Macroeconomic Policy." *Scandinavian Journal of Economics* 78: 255-75.

_____. 1976b. "Expectations and Exchange Rate Dynamics." *Journal of Political Economy* 84: 1161-76.

Dornbusch, R., and S. Fischer. 1980. "Exchange Rates and the Current Account." *American Economic Review* 70: 960-71.

Dornbusch, R., and P. Krugman. 1976. "Flexible Exchange Rates in the Short-Run." *Brookings Papers on Economic Activity* 3: 537-75.

Driskill, R.A., and S.M. Sheffrin. 1981. "On the Mark: Comment." *American Economic Review* 71: 1068-74.

Ellis, H.S., and L.A. Metzler, eds. 1949. *Readings in the Theory of International Trade*. Philadelphia: Balkiston.

Frankel, J. 1979. "On the Mark: A Theory of Floating Exchange Rates Based on Real Interest Differentials." *American Economic Review* 69: 610-22.

Frenkel, J.A. 1976. "A Monetary Approach to the Exchange Rate: Doctrinal Aspects and Empirical Evidence." *Scandinavian Journal of Economics* 78: 200-24.

Frenkel, J.A. 1981a. "Flexible Exchange Rates, Prices, and the Role of "News": Lessons from the 1970's." *Journal of Political Economy* 89: 665-705.

_____. 1981b. "The Collapse of Purchasing Power Parities during the 1970's." *European Economic Review* 16: 145-65.

Frenkel, J., and H. Johnson, eds. 1978. *The Economics of Exchange Rates*. Reading, Mass.: Addison-Wesley.

Genberg, H. 1981. "Purchasing Power Parity as a Rule for a Crawling Peg." In *Exchange Rate Rules*, ed. J. Williamson. New York: St. Martin's Press.

_____. 1978. "Purchasing Power Parity under Fixed and Flexible Exchange Rates." *Journal of International Economics* 8: 247-76.

Grennes, T.; P.R. Johnson; and M. Thursby. 1978. "Some Evidence on the Nebulous Law of One Price." A paper presented at the Southern Economic Association Meeting, November 1978, Washington, D.C.

Haberler, G. 1961. *A Survey of International Trade Theory.* International Finance Section, Special Papers in International Economics, rev. ed. no. 1, Princeton University, Princeton, N.J.

_____. 1949. "The Market for Foreign Exchange and the Stability of the Balance of Payments: A Theoretical Analysis." *Kyklos* 3: 193-218.

Harris, R.G., and D.D. Purvis. 1981. "Diverse Information and Market Efficiency in a Monetary Model of the Exchange Rate." *The Economic Journal* 91: 829-47.

Helliwell, J.F. 1979. "Policy Modeling of Foreign Exchange Rates." *Journal of Policy Modeling* 1: 425-44.

Hooper P., and J. Morton. 1980. "Fluctuations in the Dollar: A Model of Nominal and Real Exchange Determination." International Finance Discussion Paper 168, Board of Governors of the Federal Reserve System, Washington, D.C., October.

Isard, P. 1977. "How Far Can We Push the Law of One Price?" *American Economic Review* 67: 942-48.

Johnson, H.G. 1972. "The Monetary Approach to the Balance of Payments." In *Further Essays in Monetary Economics.* London: George Allen and Unwin.

Jones, R.W., and D.D. Purvis. 1981. "International Differences in Response to Common External Shocks: The Role of Purchasing Power Parity." A paper presented at the Fifth International Conference of the University of Paris-Dauphine on Money and International Monetary Problems, June 1981.

Keynes, J.M. 1932. *Essays in Persuasion.* New York.

_____. 1930. *A Treatise on Money.* Vol. 1, London.

Kindleberger, C.P. 1973. *International Economics.* 5th ed. Homewood, Ill.: Richard D. Irwin.

Kohlhagen, S.W. 1978. "The Behavior of Foreign Exchange Markets—A Critical Survey of the Empirical Literature." Monograph 1978-3, Monograph Series in Financial Economics, Graduate School of Business Administration, New York University, New York.

Kouri, P. 1980. "Monetary Policy, The Balance of Payments, and the Exchange Rate." *The Functioning of Floating Exchange Rates: Theory, Evidence, and Policy Implication,* ed. D. Bigman and T. Taya. Cambridge, Mass.: Ballinger Publishing Co.

_____. 1976. "The Exchange Rate and the Balance of Payments in the Short Run and in the Long Run: A Monetary Approach." *Scandinavian Journal of Economics* 78, no. 2.

Machlup, F. 1949. "The Theory of Foreign Exchanges." In *Readings in the Theory of International Trade,* ed. H.S. Ellis and L.A. Metzler. Philadelphia: Balkiston.

Magee, S. 1978. "Contracting and Spurious Deviations from Purchasing Power Parity." In *The Economics of Exchange Rates,* ed. J. Frenkel and H. Johnson, Reading, Mass.: Addison-Wesley.

McKinnon, R.I. 1979. *Money in International Exchange.* New York: Oxford University Press.

Meese, R., and K. Rogoff. 1981. "Empirical Exchange Rate Models of the Seventies: Are Any Fit to Survive?" International Finance Discussion Paper 184, Board of Governors of the Federal Reserve System, June 1981.

Metzler, L.A. 1948. "The Theory of International Trade." In *A Survey of Contemporary Economics*. Homewood, Ill.: Richard D. Irwin.

Murphy, R.G., and C. Van Duyne. 1980. "Asset Market Approaches to Exchange Rate Determination: A Comparative Analysis." *Weltwirtschaftliches Archive* 116: 627–56.

Mussa, M. 1979. "Empirical Regularities in the Behavior of Exchange Rates and Theories of the Foreign Exchange Market." In *Policies for Employment, Prices and Exchange Rates*, ed. K. Brunner and A.H. Meltzer, Carnegie-Rochester Conference Series on Public Policy. Amsterdam: North-Holland.

_____. 1976. "The Exchange Rate, the Balance of Payments and Monetary and Fiscal Policy under a Regime of Controlled Floating." *Scandinavian Journal of Economics* 78: 229–48.

Neihans, J. 1981. "Static Deviations from Purchasing-Power Parity." *Journal of Monetary Economics* 7: 57–68.

_____. 1978. "Purchasing-Power Parity under Flexible Rates." In *Issues in International Economics*, ed. P. Oppenheimer. Stocksfield: Oriel Press, pp. 255–72.

_____. 1977. "Exchange Rate Dynamics with Stock/Flow Interaction." *Journal of Political Economy* 85: 1245–57.

Officer, L.H. 1976. "The Purchasing Power Parity Theory of Exchange Rates: A Review Article." *IMF Staff Papers* 23: 1–60.

Ohlin, B. 1967. *Interregional and International Trade*. Rev. ed. (1st ed., 1933). Cambridge, Mass.: Harvard University Press.

Ricardo, D. 1821. *Principles of Political Economy and Taxation*, London. Also edited by E.C. Conner, New York: Kelly, 1911.

Richardson, J.D. 1978. "Some Empirical Evidence on the Law of One Price." *Journal of International Economics* 8: 341–51.

Robinson, J. 1937. "The Foreign Exchanges." In *Essays in the Theory of Employment*, New York, ch. 1. (Reprinted in H.S. Ellis and L.A. Metzler, eds.).

Samuelson, P.A. 1974. "Theoretical Notes on Trade Problems." *Review of Economics and Statistics* 46: 145–54.

Williamson, J. 1981. *Exchange Rate Rules*. New York: St. Martin's Press.

✳ *Chapter 5*

The J-Curve, Stabilizing Speculation, and Capital Constraints on Foreign Exchange Dealers

Ronald I. McKinnon*
Stanford University

What financial conditions must hold for private speculation to stabilize the foreign exchange market? In this chapter the highly favorable circumstances where monetary disturbances are presumed to be absent are considered; the focus is on the financial service functions that covered interest arbitrageurs and (speculative) foreign exchange dealers provide to (nonspeculative) merchants. All participants are subject to explicit wealth or portfolio balance constraints in their holding of money and bonds, with exports invoiced in the home currency of the exporter so as to generate the familiar J-curve effect. Even when exchange rate expectations are regressive, it will be shown that the conditions for a floating exchange rate to be stable are quite stringent and depend heavily on private capital flows being unrestricted and otherwise highly mobile internationally to a degree that may seem implausible to many observers.

In the 1970s and 1980s fluctuations in exchange rates among currencies of the great industrial countries have been unexpectedly large. Moreover, there is no indication that the system is "settling down" as traders and central banks gain more experience with (managed) floating since it began early in 1973. Indeed 1981 was a year of particularly virulent changes with sharp net appreciation of the dollar, net depreciation of many European currencies, and fairly erratic movements in the position of the Japanese yen.

*I would like to thank John Cuddington and Michael Michaely for their helpful comments.

101

Much of this instability can be explained by unanticipated monetary shocks that create short-run portfolio imbalances and drive exchange rates much more than any long-run need to balance international commodity flows would suggest. These overshooting effects of unexpected changes in national money supplies have dominated the literature on the subject and were a central theme of the preceding volume, *The Functioning of Floating Exchange Rates*, edited by Bigman and Taya (1980). In addition new evidence from the 1970s suggests that the relative international *demands* for national monies are becoming increasingly unstable (Miles 1978; Arrango and Nadiri 1981; Brittain 1981; McKinnon 1982, 1981).

What agency should be responsible for offsetting the foreign exchange consequences of these monetary disturbances? In a fiat money system the central bank has the basic responsibility to alter the supply of the national money to accommodate shifting demand. Private speculators, who have no control over national monetary policies, have neither the resources nor information to compensate for substantial monetary imbalances. It would be entirely inappropriate to expect stabilizing speculation by private banks, multinational enterprises, and individuals to smooth the foreign exchange consequences of portfolio shifts in the demand for or supply of national monies.

For the analytical purposes of this chapter, therefore, let us put aside the important monetary issue by simply assuming that (1) national money supplies are given and well known and (2) there is no international currency substitution on the demand side—that is, no arbitrary shifts in portfolio preferences from one national money to another associated with political uncertainty or changed expectations regarding future inflation. Then, under these highly favorable monetary conditions for exchange stability, the question is asked: Will the supply of stabilizing speculation by foreign exchange dealers (and other speculators) be "sufficient" to compensate for inherent instability of foreign exchange purchases and receipts by merchants on current account associated with the familiar J-curve effect?

THE INSTITUTIONAL FRAMEWORK

Writings on this subject have been peculiarly disembodied from the actual institutions of international exchange. The modern literature began with Milton Friedman's (1953) seminal suggestion that speculators, if they were not to lose money, must on average buy when the price of foreign exchange is low and sell when it is high, thereby stabilizing the foreign exchange market—or any other market for that matter. Under the ground rules of the peculiar literature that followed in the 1950s and 1960s (summarized by Stern (1973)), where various protagonists tried to construct counterexamples to Friedman's proposition, foreign exchange was disembodied and treated as if it were any ordinary flexibly priced commodity like wheat or copper. (Surprisingly, the monetary considerations alluded to before did not enter either pro or con.) Whether private financial speculation was stabilizing or destabilizing was debated under the tacit but incorrect presumption that a market-clearing exchange rate could exist in the absence of stabilizing speculation. Such reasoning made it easier to justify exchange controls on capital account in order to prevent "destabilizing" hot money flows.

Only in the 1970s did writers (Magee 1973; Williamson 1973) begin to take seriously the fact that foreign exchange payments and receipts on current account had, in the short run, their own peculiar source of instability: the J-curve effect associated with the common practice of merchants invoicing industrial or processed goods in the home currency of the exporter (Grassman 1973). Recent theoretical investigations are now directly incorporating the destabilizing effects of this differential currency invoicing in trade among industrial countries, thus divorcing the analysis from the earlier (false) analogies of flexibly prices markets for wheat or copper denominated in a single currency. In McKinnon (1979: ch. 7) a model is presented showing that the market for foreign exchange is completely unstable in the absence of dealer speculators.

The analytical gap that remains, however, is the treatment of the financial side of the commodity transactions that constitute the J-curve. Several authors have specified supply functions for speculative capital flows based on anticipated exchange rate movements (Britton 1970; Driskill and MacCafferty 1980; and Levin 1980) but did not relate their speculative asset functions to the money and bond holdings of either merchants or foreign exchange dealers. The capital constraints on various market participants were not made explicit. Other attempts to introduce a more complete model of portfolio balance have been seriously incomplete. Niehans (1977) supplies a model with only foreign and domestic monies but no bonds, whereas Driskill's (1981) model has individuals holding only domestic money and foreign bonds—so that selling "bonds" abroad avoids foreign exchange risk. No distinctions were made among various classes of market participants.

In this chapter, in contrast, an effort is made to model the financial constraints, risk aversion, and institutional framework within which operate the principal agents in the foreign exchange market:

speculative foreign exchange dealers, nonspeculative merchants, and covered interest arbitrageurs. The analysis is confined to two countries where all foreign exchange payments and receipts are cleared through (intermediated by) the commercial banking system.

At least as far as day-to-day trading is concerned, *foreign exchange dealers*, namely the foreign exchange departments of large commercial banks, are the main source of speculative capital. They have virtually unique access to the wholesale interbank market among the major convertible currencies of the industrial countries and can transact more cheaply than other potential speculators. In practice, foreign exchange dealers are significant holders of non-interest-bearing working balances of domestic and foreign currencies, which they hold in differing proportions according to expected exchange rate movements. Each commercial bank, however, strictly limits its foreign exchange exposure: the amount of risk capital that it commits to holding open foreign exchange positions—an important ingredient in the portfolio balance model to be developed below. Moreover, I assume they have well-formed and regressive expectations of the normal level of the exchange rate, deviations from which are expected to be temporary. Assuming this high degree of speculator confidence in the long-run stability of the (nominal) exchange rate is only plausible if monetary disturbances are suppressed—as per the strong assumptions made previously.

Speculative dealers are distinguished from *nonspeculative merchants*, who have passive stationary expectations regarding the exchange rate expected to prevail in the future: today's term structure of forward exchange rates is the best guess of what tomorrow will bring, although variance in the exchange rate is understood to be substantial. Merchants specialize in commodity manufacture and trade, the source of their main profit flow. They are averse to taking a net open position in foreign exchange and hedge foreign obligations back into the domestic currency (their preferred monetary habitat) unless it is costly or inconvenient to do so. Domestic merchants hold only domestic cash balances, and foreign merchants hold only foreign cash balances—unlike dealers, who have well-defined portfolio preferences for both. Merchants hold bonds mainly in the domestic currency and hold some foreign currency bonds (or borrow abroad) only when the net interest differential is favorable for doing so. Finally, merchants are manufacturers of Hicksian "fix-price" goods invoiced in the home currency of the country where the product is manufactured. Thus the export price is fixed in domestic currency for finite intervals over which the exchange rate may move, setting the stage for the J-curve. This commonly observed invoicing practice is consistent with the assumption that merchants are "nonspeculative" and that the domestic currency is their preferred habitat (McKinnon 1979: ch. 4).

Unlike dealers and merchants who are subject to important wealth and portfolio balance constraints, *covered interest arbitrageurs* (CIAs) are not limited by balance sheet considerations because, by definition, they do not bear exchange risk. Although kept in a separate analytical category, such CIAs are also likely to be large commercial banks with easy access to the interbank market for foreign exchange for moving covered interest-bearing funds from one country to another; but they could also include nonbank corporations with excess liquidity. Their demand for non-interest-bearing cash is zero, and risk-free entry into this business provides a perfectly elastic supply of arbitrage capital to align covered interest rates across countries. Thus the interest rate parity theorem is assumed to hold exactly as seems to be true empirically if one compares interbank rates of interest in the Eurocurrency markets (Aliber 1973). By allowing an active forward market to exist and by unifying the spot and forward markets for foreign exchange, CIAs greatly reduce the need for stabilizing speculative capital, that is, for speculators to take risky open positions in foreign exchange.

ON APPROXIMATELY AGGREGATING THE POSITIONS OF MERCHANTS IN THE SPOT AND FORWARD EXCHANGE MARKETS

Consider first the problem of aggregating merchants and covered interest arbitrageurs in country A into a single analytical entity that responds homogeneously and predictably to changes in the foreign exchange rate. Not only do merchants in A order their banks (dealers) to make spot payments in currency B on their behalf, but they also purchase currency B in an active forward market, which spans all terms to maturity, in order to hedge against future changes in the exchange rate. A's merchants may buy B's currency one month, three months, or six months hence in order to roughly offset normal commercial credits that give the buyer one month, three months, or six months to pay. Fortunately, because of covered interest arbitrage, this potentially bewildering array of dated demands for foreign exchange on any given trading day can be treated *as if* it were all telescoped into the spot market.

Consider the role of the covered interest arbitrageur, or CIA, in country A, who by definition never takes an open position in bonds denominated in B's currency. However, CIAs from country A can buy bonds denominated in B's currency provided that they sell B's currency forward at the same terms to maturity; CIAs from country B can do the converse. Hence the free two-way flow of short-term capital is dominated by CIAs from both countries precisely because they avoid exchange risk. This arbitrage then aligns the term structure of forward exchange rates with the relative interest rates on the two countries' bonds.

More precisely, suppose R_f^{30}, R_f^{60}, R_f^{90} are the forward rates for thirty, sixty, and ninety days, etc.; and i^{30}, i^{60}, i^{90} are the interest rates of the corresponding term to maturity. R_s is the prevailing spot exchange rate: currency A/currency B. Then, from the interest rate parity theorem (IRPT):

$$R_f^{30} \simeq R_s \frac{(1 + i_a^{30})}{(1 + i_b^{30})}$$

$$R_f^{60} \simeq R_s \frac{(1 + i_a^{60})}{(1 + i_b^{60})} \tag{5.1}$$

$$R_f^{v} \simeq R_s \frac{(1 + i_a^{v})}{(1 + i_b^{v})} \quad , \text{where } v \text{ is any arbitrarily given term.}$$

Among convertible currencies, relations such as (5.1) have proven very robust empirically (Aliber 1973) if one considers interbank deposit and lending rates of interest. Covered interest arbitrage, then, emerges as the key force unifying flow demands and supplies for foreign exchange over all terms to maturity. For example, if merchants in country A purchase 30 days forward 100 units of currency B, CIAs automatically transmit this 100-unit purchase of foreign exchange to the spot market as if the merchants had purchased spot exchange directly.

To see this more clearly, rewrite the first equation in (5.1) to be

$$\frac{R_f^{30}}{R_s} (1 + i_b^{30}) \simeq (1 + i_a^{30}) \quad . \tag{5.2}$$

Consider now a CIA resident in country A who is anxious to avoid taking an open position in B's currency but wants to exploit covered interest differentials. The right-hand side of equation (5.2) represents the returns from investing one unit of currency A in a bond maturing in thirty days, whereas the left-hand side represents the covered yield from shifting one unit of currency A to a thirty-day bond denominated in currency B; and there is no incentive to move capital when the two sides balance. Now suppose the merchant in A "disturbs" the market *ex ante* with an order to buy 100 units of currency B in thirty days. This order generates incipient upward pressure on R_f^{30}. The CIA then sees a bit of daylight, as the left-hand side of (5.1) slightly exceeds the right-hand side; the arbitrageur purchases currency B *spot* (to invest in interest-bearing bonds) and covers by selling it thirty days forward to the merchant. CIAs act as financial intermediaries by buying foreign exchange spot to cover the melange of forward purchases—at various terms to maturity—made by merchants. Hence by using CIAs as financial agents, merchants behave as if they had a well-defined flow demand for foreign exchange that is confined to the spot market.

One further problem remains in aggregating the foreign exchange positions of merchants over all terms to maturity. Can the relative prices of spot and forward foreign exchange be assumed to be fixed? From equations (5.1), the margin of variation between R_s and R_f^v is confined to changes in interest differentials. For a given R_s, therefore, it can be assumed that merchants ignore any increases (or decreases) in R_f^v when determining *the current flow of imports and exports*. R_s itself, relative to given domestic currency prices, provides sufficient information for merchants to determine how much merchandise to buy or sell on world markets. That is, gross profits in merchandising the international flow of goods and services are not substantially influenced by such "small" changes in R_f^v vis-à-vis R_s. Thus the aggregation of the (flow of) dated demands for foreign exchange by merchants is only a useful approximation.[1]

THE J-CURVE

Using this method of aggregation, let Z_a denote the total flow demands by A's merchants to obtain country B's goods; and let Z_b be the flow demand by merchants in B for A's goods. Assume further that both countries are industrialized and produce only Hicksian fixprice goods: heterogeneous manufactures that are brand (and country) specific. Over the relevant short run, each country's exports are invoiced in the home currency and these invoice prices are invariant to unexpected exchange rate changes and shifts in the volume of new orders. One can think of the initial response to any increase in Z_a to be a drawing down of commodity inventories by producers in

B. With fixed domestic prices in B, therefore Z_a can then also be interpreted as the equilibrium flow demand for currency B by importers in A, and Z_b is also the flow demand for currency A by B's importers.

With these passive output responses by exporters, let us specify how merchant importers react to changes in the exchange rate in adjusting the flow of payments for current imports and in determining new import commitments. What is the nature of the functions $Z_a(R_s)$ and $Z_b(R_s)$ as they evolve through time? At the initial spot exchange rate $\overline{R}_s$ (representative of all terms to maturity) suppose the two-way flow of payments by merchants between A and B is exactly balanced. Now a small unanticipated increase in the exchange rate R_s occurs; A's currency depreciates slightly relative to B's. Taken by surprise, merchants respond via the by now conventional J-curve effect (Magee 1973) in four stages:

1. During very short periods of *currency contract*, neither commodity prices nor amounts traded can be adjusted, but bills under old contracts must be paid as they become due. Because uncovered importers in A must now pay more domestic currency for a unit of foreign exchange, A's current account goes into deficit and B's into surplus.

2. After *pass through*, newly contracting importers in both countries see the altered domestic currency equivalents of commodity price quotations fixed in foreign currency, but they do not have time to alter the traditional flow of goods purchased. In particular, importers in A must pay more domestic currency per unit imported without the possibility of ex ante hedging. This effect also adds to the trade deficit.

3. In the intermediate period of *quantity adjustment*, domestic buyers now alter quantities purchased in response to the changed pass through prices for imports seen in domestic currency. Importers in A contract their purchases, and importers in B expand theirs. These adjustments reduce the trade deficit of A and reduce the surplus of B.

4. Only in the long run are *invoice prices* in the domestic currency of the exporter adjusted to the new exchange rate, so as to further lower A's import costs and raise those of B—and push the system further back toward balanced trade.

Clearly, phases (1) and (2), currency contract and pass through, are the relevant short run for asking if a market made up of nonspeculative merchants—traders in fix-price commodities—could themselves stabilize the market. By definition, this is a period of time suffi-ciently short (days or weeks) over which the flow demand for B's goods (and effective payments in B's currency) by merchants in A does not respond at all to changes in R_s and vice versa. Under these circumstances the flow demand by merchants in A for B's currency is completely inelastic as its price in terms of currency A rises. Con-sidering only these current payments flows, without other financial adjustment by speculators or by merchants on capital account, the foreign exchange market is indeed inherently unstable. The task now is to consider what other financial adjustments are likely to occur.

SHORT-RUN CASH-BALANCE ADJUSTMENTS BY MERCHANTS IN RESPONSE TO AN UNANTICIPATED EXCHANGE RATE FLUCTUATION

Consider now the circular flow of production and foreign payments in both countries and how any disturbance in R_s influences the cash balance positions of merchants during the periods of currency con-tract or pass through. Invoice prices of goods produced in country A are fixed in currency A, and similarly with country B. The period is sufficiently short that production and employment levels have been predetermined in both countries, and final flow demands for physical goods—including imports—are fixed. What is *not* predetermined is the floating exchange rate R_s and the payments flows for imports (by merchants in each country) that vary with R_s.

The Hicksian fix-price assumption conveniently allows the output of each country to be treated as if it were a single good, although the cost of imports in domestic currency will vary with the exchange rate. Hence the circular flow of production and consumption in country A, measured in terms of its own currency, is simply

$$E_a + Z_b - R_s Z_a = Y_a \ , \tag{5.3}$$

where Y_a is the fixed output in A and E_a is the total flow of expen-diture (in A's currency) for domestic output and imports. Z_b is the fixed flow of exports to B, and Z_a is the physical flow of imports from B.

Suppose now we start off with exactly balanced trade at the equi-librium exchange rate $\bar{R}_s$:

$$Z_b = \bar{R}_s Z_a \quad \text{and} \quad E_a = Y_a \ . \tag{5.4}$$

In specifying the portfolio demands for domestic money and bonds, let us consolidate merchants with all domestic transactors except speculative dealers. These domestic "merchants" (broadly defined) hold no foreign (non-interest-bearing) cash balances, and initially we assume that they hold no foreign currency bonds, an assumption that is relaxed later on. For merchants in country A of given total financial wealth W_m^a divided between money M_m^a and bonds B_m^a , the resulting target stock asset demand functions are

$$M_m^a = M_m^a \underset{+\quad-\quad+}{(Y_a, i_a, W_m^a)} , \qquad (5.5)$$

$$B_m^a = B_m^a \underset{+\quad+\quad+}{(Y_a, i_a, W_m^a)} , \qquad (5.6)$$

$$W_m^a = M_m^a + B_m^a , \qquad (5.7)$$

where the superscript a refers to the currency of denomination, and the subscript m to merchant. There is a similar set of portfolio demands by merchants in country B for financial assets denominated in B's currency:

$$M_m^b, B_m^b, \text{ and } W_m^b .$$

The stationary equilibrium in the balance of payments (equation (5.4)) implies that target stocks of money and bonds in both countries are at their desired levels as described by equations (5.5)–(5.7). No premium or discount exists on currency A over currency B so that $R_f^v = R_s$ at all terms to maturity. Because $R_s = \bar{R}_s$, the actual spot rate is at its normal level, and covered interest arbitrage implies that $i_a^v = i_b^v$ at all terms to maturity.

In this otherwise stationary state of bliss, suppose now R_s is disturbed above $\bar{R}_s$ by $\triangle R_s$. A's currency depreciates slightly relative to B's. This disturbance is purely financial, say a random but temporary capital outflow from A to B.

What happens to the cash balance positions of merchants in country A and in country B? Within this very short time horizon of currency contract and pass through, I assume that cash balances are the primary contingency reserve against unanticipated flows of profits or losses. (Over a larger time horizon, merchants may well consider discrete purchases or sales of bonds.) Because of the unanticipated depreciation of currency A, the costs of any new imports by merchants in country A rise above their net earnings from exports, and vice versa for merchants in B. The losses to merchants in A would be minimized (as would the profits of merchants in B) had they covered forward 100 percent of old contracts coming due before the unexpected increase in R_s occurred (Witte 1980). If we assume that merchants continue to cover forward 100 percent of new contracts during pass through after this exchange rate change, then the ongoing *ex-ante* rate of decrease in cash balances of merchants is simply the measured trade deficit of country A:

$$\dot{M}^a_m = \dot{W}^a_m = Z_b - R_s Z_a = -\Delta R_s Z_a < 0 \ . \qquad (5.8)$$

Correspondingly, with symmetrical 100 percent forward covering abroad, the rate of cash balance accumulation by B's merchants is

$$\dot{M}^b_m = \dot{W}^b_m = Z_a - Z_b / R_s = \Delta R_s Z_a / R_s > 0 \ . \qquad (5.9)$$

At the new exchange rate R_s, the releasing of A's currency by merchants in A (equation (5.8)) is just equal to the accumulation of B's currency by merchants in B, both of which are just equal to the trade imbalance as measured in each country's balance of payments statistics in the pass through phase of the J-curve.

If merchants in both countries had not covered forward 100 percent, however, then A's merchants would suffer additional capital losses as old contracts came due and had to be paid off at the less favorable exchange rate—and B's merchants would garner additional capital gains. With less than full forward covering, equations (5.8) and (5.9) tend to understate the rate of change in cash balance positions of both groups of merchants. To capture this effect while avoiding a complex specification of the exact time profile of when old uncovered contracts become due, define a forward covering parameter $\rho \geqq 1$ such that

$$\dot{M}^a_m = -\rho \cdot \Delta R_s \cdot Z_a < 0 \ , \qquad (5.8')$$

and

$$\dot{M}^b_m = \rho \Delta R_s \cdot Z_a / R_s > 0 \ ; \qquad (5.9')$$

$\rho = 1$ corresponds to symmetrical 100 percent hedging by both groups of merchants and $\rho > 1$ indicates less than full forward covering. The financial strain (change in cash balance positions) on merchants is greater—possibly much greater—when the exchange rate changes discretely and unexpectedly and when they have not covered forward.[2]

Because nonspeculative merchants in A and B will not hold each other's currencies, for equations (5.8$'$) and (5.9$'$) to be consistent some other financial agents must simultaneously be purchasing non-interest-bearing cash balances denominated in A's currency from A's merchants and selling B's currency to B's merchants. Otherwise R_s would increase further without limit. If government intervention by either central bank is ruled out, then this task of balancing the two cash balance positions of merchants to dampen or prevent further depreciation of A's currency naturally devolves on *dealer speculators.* Indeed, stabilizing the exchange rate in the periods of currency contract and pass through is equivalent to dealers purchasing currency A according to

$$\dot{M}_d^a = - M_m^a > 0 \qquad\qquad (5.10)$$

and simultaneously releasing currency B according to

$$\dot{M}_d^b = - \dot{M}_m^b < 0 \quad , \qquad\qquad (5.11)$$

in order to accommodate merchants. Otherwise no determinate exchange rate could exist.

FOREIGN EXCHANGE DEALERS, REGRESSIVE EXPECTATIONS, AND THE RISK-FREE PORTFOLIO OF WORKING CASH BALANCES

What then induces dealers to absorb currency A and release currency B? Of course, they expect to make a profit from R_s returning to its normal level $\overline{R}_s$ in the "near" future. Thus the strong assumption that dealer expectations are regressive is being imposed. This mode of behavior is quasi-rational insofar as dealers are ultimately proved to be correct because national money supplies remain unchanged, as do the long-run underlying export and import functions. However, dealers do not behave as if they knew the equations of motion of the system: They do not speculate on further movements of R_s away from $\overline{R}_s$ as if they had full knowledge of the time path of R_s.

If dealer speculators were consolidated into a single analytical entity, what is the nature of the aggregate wealth constraint on their foreign exchange exposure? Remember that their primary business is money changing—not speculation—and that they combine two country-specific components:

1. The foreign exchange departments of commercial banks based in country A. I assume that a definite share of the bank's operating capital is allocated to its money changing activities and that strict limits are placed on the open positions that may be taken in currency B.
2. The foreign exchange departments of commercial banks in country B, which are subject to a similar capital constraint and restriction on taking an open position in currency A.

In order to function effectively as dealers, each class of banks must hold non-interest-bearing working balances in the other country's currency. Let M_d^a denote working cash balances in currency A held by B's dealers and M_d^b denote working balances in currency B held by A's dealers. For a given flow of imports and exports requiring payments to be serviced, and for $R_s = \overline{R}_s$ so that no net change in the exchange rate is expected, there will exist "normal" desired levels for M_d^a and M_d^b, as denoted by $\overline{M}_d^a$ and $\overline{M}_d^b$ respectively.

Moreover, in this normal position, each class of dealers will minimize its exposure to exchange risk by an offsetting forward transaction. Dealers from A sell M_d^b of currency B in the forward exchange market to achieve approximately 100 percent forward cover, and dealers in B sell approximately 100 percent of M_d^a of currency A forward. Alternatively, dealers could cover themselves forward by buying or selling short-term foreign currency bonds to each other, as is done in interbank trading in Eurocurrency deposits. As long as covered interest arbitrage is unrestricted, selling foreign exchange forward in thirty days for domestic currency is equivalent to borrowing in foreign exchange now with repayment required in thirty days. The important point is that dealers collectively offset their own foreign exchange risks to a considerable extent by taking opposite positions in the forward market. For analytical purposes these risk offsets allow dealers from both countries to be consolidated into a single entity.

Consider the interesting special case where $R_s = \overline{R}_s$ and current payments for imports and exports by merchants are exactly balanced. The equilibrium forward exchange rate R_f, should also be equal to $\overline{R}_s$ because the spot exchange rate is not expected to move one way or the other. But forward purchases and sales by dealers will only be exactly balanced at $R_f = \overline{R}_s$ if the values of their working cash balances in foreign currency are identical, that is, if

$$\overline{R}_s \cdot \overline{M}_d^b = \overline{M}_d^a \quad . \tag{5.12}$$

Equation (5.12) described the consolidated dealers' *risk-free portfolio*. If they arrange their financial affairs so that working balances of currency B held by dealers in A are (approximately) equal to working balances of currency A held by dealers in B, then neither party need bear exchange risk. Their forward purchases and sales exactly offset at $R_f = \overline{R}_s$. In contract, if $\overline{R}_s \overline{M}_d^b > \overline{M}_d^a$, then the forward exchange rate will be forced down *ex ante* by the net excess forward sales of currency B (that is, $R_f < \overline{R}_s$), and dealers in A will be forced to pay an "insurance" premium to those in B. Because it is assumed here that international money changers work within very narrow margins of profitability, $\overline{M}_d^b$ would be adjusted downward and $\overline{M}_d^a$ adjusted upward to achieve the risk-free portfolio, as described by equation (5.12). If one could obtain comparable confidential financial data from the foreign exchange departments of commercial banks, equation (5.12) describes an empirically testable proposition. Here, I simply adopt the risk-free portfolio, associated with stationary equilibrium in the foreign exchange market, as a *working hypothesis*: dealers in country A hold cash balances in foreign currency equal to that held by dealers in B when the spot exchange rate is not expected to move.

Equation (5.12) suggests a convenient method of introducing wealth or capital constraints into dealer behavior. Given the balanced flow of trade between the two countries and equal "normal" holdings of working balances of foreign exchange, let us suppose each country's dealers receive approximately the same allocation of capital or same "line of credit" from the senior management of the bank. The opportunity cost of holding non-interest-bearing cash balances is the forgone interest, while the benefits (apart from speculative capital gains) are the implicit or explicit brokerage fees earned from money changing. Let W_d^a denote the consolidated dealer wealth denominated in currency A. We may treat consolidated dealers as if they allocated all their wealth between working balances of currencies A and B.

$$W_d^a = M_d^a + R_s M_d^b \quad . \tag{5.13}$$

But at the balance point or risk-free portfolio, exactly half their wealth is allocated to each currency:

$$\frac{1}{2} \; \overline{W}_d^a \; = \; \overline{M}_d^a \; = \; \overline{R}_s \, \overline{M}_d^b \quad . \tag{5.14}$$

How does the demand for either currency vary when $R_s \neq \overline{R}_s$? Combining the balance-sheet condition (5.14) with the assumption of regressive expectations, ϕ is the demand function by dealers for non-interest-bearing cash balances denominated in currency A:

$$M_d^a \; = \; \frac{1}{2} \; \overline{W}_d^a \; \phi \, (R_s - \overline{R}_s) \quad \text{where} \quad \phi \, (0) \; = \; 1 \quad \text{and} \quad \phi' >) \quad . \tag{5.15}$$

As R_s increases above $\overline{R}_s$, dealers confidently expect it to return to its norm. They absorb more currency A into their portfolios in exchange for currency B. The reverse would be true if R_s dips below $\overline{R}$: dealers then come to expect an appreciation of currency B which they acquire by releasing currency A. Thus, the demand for currency B is just the obverse of the ϕ function in equation (5.15) and is plotted as the function γ in Figure 5-2 below where $\overline{W}_d^b = \overline{W}_d^a / R_s$. This duality can be seen better if the wealth constraint on dealers is rewritten in a slightly different form:

$$R_s \, (M_d^b - \overline{M}_d^b) \; = \; - \, (M_d^a - \overline{M}_d^a) \quad . \tag{5.16}$$

From equation (5.16), as M_d^a increases because $R_s > \overline{R}_s$ so does M_d^b decrease. Away from the balance point, however, dealers collectively begin to bear exchange risk. For example, if $M_d^a > R_s M_d^b$, dealers will try to sell forward more of currency A than of currency B, thus depressing the forward price of currency A relative to the spot rate expected to prevail in the future. This expected loss on their forward contracts induces some of them to hold the excess cash balances of currency A without forward cover, on which there is now the expectation of capital gains when $R_s > \overline{R}_s$. As a consolidated group, dealers have now taken on the role of speculators by incurring exposure in currency A.

Figures 5-1 and 5-2 give the reader a more vivid portrayal of dealer willingness to incur exchange risk by holding unbalanced portfolios of non-interest-bearing cash balances. In Figure 5-2, the demand by dealers for currency A in terms of currency B is highly

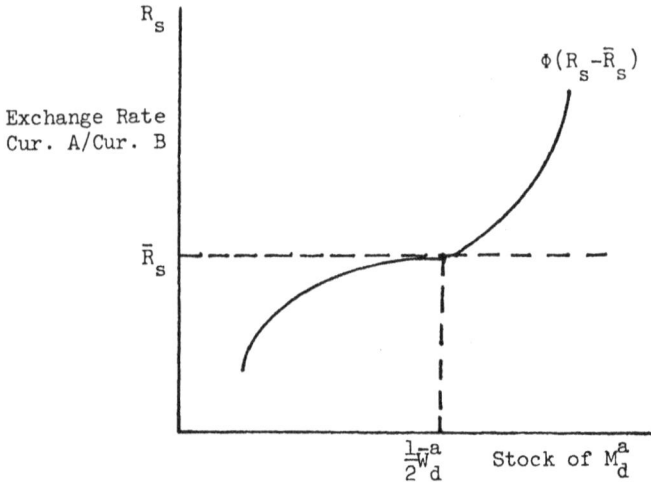

Figure 5-1.   Dealer Demand for Working Balances of Currency A.

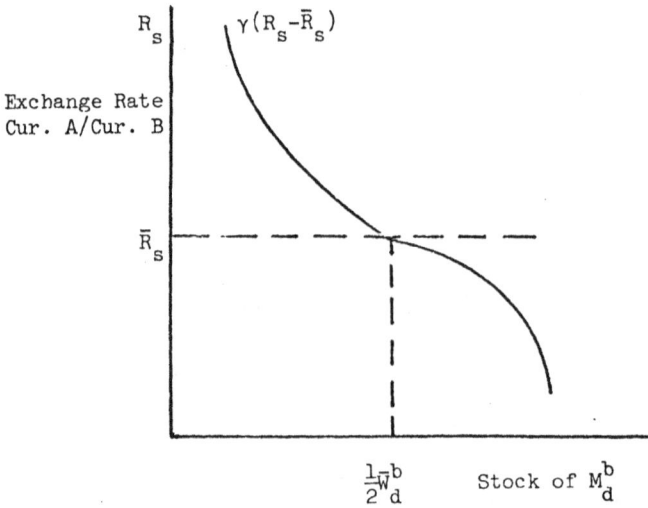

Figure 5-2.   Dealer Demand for Working Balances of Currency B.

elastic in the neighborhood of the balance point. Outside this neighborhood, however, rather large deviations of R_s from $\overline{R}_s$ are required to reward dealers for holding more currency A and less currency B, or vice versa.

Why have we not explicitly considered dealer holdings of bonds or other interest-bearing term deposits in response to expected exchange rate changes? First, dealers may shuffle their portfolios of interest-bearing term deposits in the two currencies as an alternative to contracting in the forward exchange market, as suggested. Secondly, and more fundamentally, interest rates are sensitive to anticipated exchange rate fluctuations and are closely tied to forward exchange rates by covered interest arbitrage as will be described. Thus holders of foreign currency bonds are given a fair bet on the future exchange rate if they hold to maturity, and they have much less reason than unprotected moneyholders to reshuffle their portfolios of interest-bearing securities in response to expected exchange rate changes. Thus in deriving the market-clearing exchange rate below, I first concentrate only on cash balance adjustments between dealers and merchants.

EXCHANGE-RATE EQUILIBRIUM IN THE SHORT RUN WHERE ONLY CASH BALANCES ADJUST

Let us derive the path for the exchange rate that equilibriates the demand for and supply for currency A. The problem has been set up symmetrically between the two countries so that the same path balances the demand for and supply of currency B. Consider how dealers vary their working balances of currency A, against holdings of currency B, in response to a moving exchange rate $\dot{R}_s$. Differentiate equation (5.15) with respect to time to get

$$\dot{M}_d^a = \frac{1}{2} \, \overline{W}_d^a \, \phi' \, \dot{R}_s > 0 \ . \tag{5.17}$$

As R_s moves further above $\overline{R}_s$, dealers acquire more of currency A because, with their regressive expectations, they expect currency A to appreciate back to its "normal" level. In contrast, from the J-curve effect, A's merchants are releasing currency A at a rate equal to $-\rho \triangle R_s Z_a$ according to equation (5.8'). Imposing the balance condition that $\dot{M}_d^a = -\dot{M}_m^a$ for money market equilibrium, we combine equations (5.8') and (5.17) to get

$$\dot{R}_s = \frac{\rho \triangle R_s \cdot Z_a}{\frac{1}{2} \overline{W}_d^a \, \theta'} > 0 \quad \text{where} \quad \triangle R_s = R_s - \overline{R}_s \ . \tag{5.18}$$

Even with dealers in the market, the system is locally unstable in this short run. Given the impetus of the discrete unexpected increase in R_s above $\overline{R}$ as denoted by $\triangle R_s$, the exchange rate will continue to move upward although dealers are absorbing currency A into their portfolios in a stabilizing fashion. Only if R_s is exactly at its norm $\overline{R}_s$ does R_s have zero velocity.

However, dealers in particular and short capital flows in the interbank market in general slow the rate at which R_s is moving away from $\overline{R}_s$ in several important ways. First, the parameter ρ is inversely related to the degree of forward covering by merchants. The more complete forward covering is, the less releasing of currency A by merchants, and hence the lower is $\dot{R}_s$. But the cost of taking a forward position depends heavily on having covered interest arbitrageurs moving short-term capital freely between the two countries, as explained previously.

Secondly, the level of dealer wealth relative to the flow of trade is roughly measured by $\overline{W}_a^d/Z_a$. The greater this relative wealth is, the more stable the exchange rate is in the short run. If the foreign exchange departments of the commercial banks are kept on a tight rein by their managements because of exchange rate instability experienced in the past, or if the country's central bank directly limits or monitors the foreign exchange exposure that commercial banks undertake,[3] the effect is equivalent to reducing $\overline{W}_d^a$ and making the market less stable: The velocity of $\dot{R}_s$ is greater.

Thirdly, the stability of the market depends heavily on ϕ', which is a rough measure of the confidence with which dealers expect R_s to return to $\overline{R}_s$. As long as the underlying monetary conditions are stable as we posited above, ϕ' should be substantial: dealers should respond elastically to exchange rate changes by unbalancing their portfolios in favor of currency A and reducing B in order to accommodate merchants and stabilize the market. But the presumption of underlying monetary stability is critical for these expectation effects to be favorable and is not well grounded in recent experience.

In summary, immediately following an unexpected exchange rate change where merchants are confined to adjusting only their cash balance positions, at most dealer-speculators can be expected to hold the fort, to prevent the exchange rate from moving farther away from equilibrium too quickly. Alone, the actions of dealers will not turn the exchange rate back toward equilibrium. For that, some further stabilizing force is required beyond the short time horizon within which a floating exchange rate seems naturally very volatile.

But will the flows of imports and exports not themselves adjust in a stabilizing fashion over a somewhat longer time perspective? If dealers hang on long enough, that is, slow the velocity of $\dot{R}_s$ away from equilibrium, merchants should respond by quantity and invoice price adjustment—the last two phases of the J-curve described. Aside from the conventional concerns about time lags and the sluggishness of merchants adjusting commodity flows, there is a more fundamental welfare concern. Should small random perturbations in R_s, which are substantially magnified by the J-curve effect, be allowed to set in train substantial real adjustments in the physical flow of commodities? In an "efficient" international financial system, one hopes that random perturbations in R_s wash out rather quickly without substantial real adjustment costs that are not warranted by any permanent changes in the flow of capital from one country to the other.

THE BOND MARKET, INTEREST RATES, AND INTERMEDIATE-RUN ADJUSTMENT

Further domestic bond-market transactions by merchants, transmitted internationally by covered interest arbitrageurs, are capable of greatly ameliorating the situation. This is true even in an intermediate-run horizon still sufficiently short that commodity market adjustments remain impractical (and undesirable). Let us continue to assume that real expenditure and invoice prices in domestic currencies are all given. In this intermediate run after the movement in R_s above $\overline{R}$, suppose merchants in country A try to recoup their depleted cash positions by selling bonds in the domestic capital market, whereas merchants in B wish to exchange their excess cash balances for interest-bearing bonds in B's capital market. Moreover, we go beyond the foregoing algebraic specifications and allow dealers to consider buying or selling interest-bearing bonds.

How do interest rates behave as R_s moves above $\overline{R}_s$? Under a floating exchange rate, what is intriguing about the appropriate capital-market adjustment in the "deficit" country A is that its interest rate should *fall*. Similarly the short-term interest rate in the "surplus" country B should *rise*. These movements in interest rates are just the opposite of the "classical" interest adjustments that are appropriate for a fixed exchange rate or a gold-standard regime. Therefore, it would seem important to understand the underlying mechanism.

The key difference from the classical adjustment mechanism is the presumed (temporary) rise in R_s above $\overline{R}_s$ under floating rates. Because dealers have regressive expectations that $\overline{R}_s$ is indeed the norm, then any forward exchange rate of arbitrary term, say R_f^v, must be trapped between R_s and $\overline{R}_s$. That is

$$R_s > R_f^{30} > R_f^{60} \ldots \ldots R_f^v > \overline{R}_s \quad . \tag{5.19}$$

Near-term forward rates are close to R_s, whereas more distant futures are closer to $\overline{R}_s$. Besides holding currencies spot, dealers are free to take forward positions at any term to maturity, as per the foregoing analysis of dealer-speculators. Hence, forward exchange rates must reflect these expectations.

With this structure of forward rates and virtually perfect covered interest arbitrage between the two countries, interest rates must conform. From equation (5.1), interest rates in country A are forced down and those in B are forced up. Having $i_a^v < i_b^v$ simply reflects the expected decline of R_s (appreciation) of currency A back to its normal rate of exchange. As long as expectations in both countries adjust simultaneously, no capital need actually flow between the two for interest rates to adjust to the point where the forward exchange rate provides an unbiased estimate of the expected future spot exchange rate.

Of fundamental importance in this intermediate run, therefore, is that the lower interest rate in country A and higher rate in B help restore equilibrium in the money markets of both countries. The lower interest rate in A induces A's merchants to increase their demand for money and *sell* more bonds than they otherwise would. The reverse is true with higher interest rates in B. Merchants in B are more prone to release their cash balances and buy bonds, despite their greater wealth holdings. Thus, although interest rates adjust in the opposite direction from what might be appropriate under fixed exchange rates, they do tend to make it easier for merchants to rebalance their portfolios. This rebalancing takes some of the pressure off dealers as will be shown. An unwary central banker who was using the wrong model in the "deficit" country A might be unduly upset by the fall in A's interest rates.

What are the implications of these bond-market transactions for relieving the capital constraint or foreign exchange exposure of (consolidated) dealers? Consider first the case where merchants will only buy or sell bonds in their home currency. In country A bond sales will brake the decline in interest rates described. If bonds were sold directly to dealers, this would allow them to get rid of their excess of non-interest-bearing demand deposits of currency A in favor of interest-bearing bonds, thus relieving their capital constraint to some extent. However, since the bonds purchased are also denominated in currency A, it will not relieve dealers of their net exposure in A's currency. With international capital mobility thus limited, interest rates in A will be bid up, at least incipiently, beyond what future exchange rate changes would seem to warrant, and this provides further net incentives for dealers to hold the bonds.

The reverse set of transactions would be occurring in country B. Merchants would sell their excess cash balances back to dealers whose normal stocks of currency B are depleted, and at the same time acquire bonds or promissory notes (denominated in currency B) from dealers. The net bonded indebtedness of consolidated dealers in currencies A and B combined would not change significantly, but their working cash position would be better balanced across the two currencies. However, dealers' net foreign currency exposure—long in currency A and short in B—would be unaffected. Thus having merchants adjust their cash position through sales of bonds denominated in their domestic currencies relieves dealers of some financial strain but does not relieve them of bearing the full burden of foreign currency exposure. With the capital constraints they face, dealers would still be unlikely to smooth fluctuations adequately in the exchange rate.

Let us now completely relax the portfolio inhibitions on merchants described by equation (5.6), where their borrowing and lending is confined to the domestic currency. Suppose merchants could buy and sell bonds, denominated in either currency, directly among themselves. Moreover, they become sophisticated investors who were now willing to bear exchange risk. They compare interest rates on bonds denominated in different currencies to expected exchange rate movements. No longer do we distinguish between speculative dealers and nonspeculative merchants, who always hedge against foreign exchange risk as best they can. However, the more sophisticated merchants still use dealers for money changing.

With these inhibitions on merchants (broadly defined) removed, the short-run and intermediate-run problems of exchange instability from the J-curve are largely resolved. As R_s is disturbed above $\bar{R}_s$ and merchants in A lose cash balances (denominated in currency A) and those in B are surfeited with cash (denominated in currency B), then A's merchants would naturally sell bonds (denominated in either currency) to B's merchants using dealers as pure money changers. This automatic pressure for capital to flow into A from B would directly stabilize the exchange rate (prevent R_s from rising further or even reversing it) while allowing dealers to rebalance their cash positions without incurring significant foreign currency exposure. Because merchants from either or both countries are willing to bear the foreign exchange risk, capital constraints on dealers are no longer a significant impediment to securing exchange stability. As long as the underlying monetary and trade conditions are known and understood to be stable, the J-curve "problem" is largely ameliorated.

In conclusion, local exchange market instability associated with the J-curve is only a problem if capital is imperfectly mobile such that some important participants—say merchants—are unwilling to bear exchange risk; or, as is often the case, governments restrict domestic nationals other than authorized foreign exchange dealers from freely lending to or borrowing from foreigners (McKinnon 1979: ch. 1). In the latter case the capital constraint on dealers is virtually certain to be sufficiently binding that a floating exchange rate would be expected to move very erratically in the absence of official intervention.

Note that even if capital is "perfectly" mobile internationally, the need for some goods market adjustment—in response to the random perturbation in R_s—cannot be entirely eliminated. The net wealth position of merchants (broadly defined) in country A will contract, and that of merchants in B will increase. Domestic absorption and imports will contract in country A and will expand in country B, in the "quantity" and "invoice price" adjustment phase of the J-curve. With a high degree of international capital mobility, however, R_s will be kept close to $\overline{R}$ such that these wealth changes in the currency-contract and pass through phases will be minimal.

CAPITAL CONTROLS AND EXCHANGE STABILITY: THE REGULATORY DILEMMA

In helping the beleaguered garrison of dealer-speculators clear current payments for imports and exports under floating exchange rates, the importance of free international movements of short-term capital should now be readily apparent. Unfortunately, this point is not generally recognized by international institutions or national governments who grew up with the "hot" money flows associated with the old adjustable-peg system of setting exchange rates, whereby governments were bearing much of the exchange risk. In defining members' "convertible"—currency obligation under Article VIII, the International Monetary Fund does not require that foreign capital flows be free of restraint. With the major exceptions of the United States and the Federal Republic of Germany, over most of the postwar period and the very recent capital-account liberalizations in Britain and Japan, most national authorities impose strict controls on holding foreign assets by domestic nations, albeit with more freedom granted to authorized commercial banks. In such circumstances a floating or no-par system might be expected to suffer exchange rate instability magnified by the J-curve effect. Governments will be continually tempted to intervene to become dealer-speculators themselves in order to provide the system with more risk capital.

Should we conclude that floating exchange rates would function better if all controls on capital flows among the industrial countries were abolished? The argument for doing so rests heavily on the assumption of monetary stability, which was made at the beginning of this chapter. If each government controls its national money supply to secure price level stability, and consequently little incentive exists for international currency substitution—where individuals and firms switch their liquid asset portfolios from one country to another—then the complete elimination of exchange controls would seem to be warranted. But the evidence alluded to earlier suggests that international currency substitution is becoming more pronounced, for both political and economic reasons, especially among potential reserve-currency countries following (even slightly) divergent monetary policies. In a floating exchange rate regime, therefore, capital controls are often viewed as a technique for stabilizing the demand for the national money and insulating domestic interest rates from those prevailing abroad, even though they upset the efficiency of the clearing of international payments on current account.

The resolution of this regulatory dilemma is beyond the scope of this chapter. In McKinnon 1982, a scheme for the international harmonization of monetary policies is suggested under which the case for eliminating all capita-account restrictions becomes unambiguous. Exchange rate stability within a narrow band is a natural consequence of such harmonization, and, of course, the J-curve effect then disappears. Private capital flows naturally offset trade deficits or surpluses. The opportunity cost, and it may not really be a cost, is that the industrial countries with convertible currencies give up national autonomy in the monetary sphere.

NOTES

1. As John Cuddington pointed out to me, a completely fixed interest differential would require variable national money supplies. Here, however, we want to rule out (shifting) large differentials based on anticipated divergences in national monetary policies in the future. Thus this assumption that relative interest rates move within a "small" range is valid if national money supplies are understood to be constant, so that expected future exchange rate movements are inherently limited.

2. Note that less than 100 percent forward covering is likely in practice. If we go back to a narrow definition of "merchants," that is, only those directly engaged in foreign trade, they normally hold inventories of imported goods that may well be revalued when the exchange rate changes. These capital gains or losses on inventories are then simply passed on to domestic customers. In these

circumstances optimal hedging against currency risk by the foreign-trade merchants dictates that their future foreign currency payments be less than 100 percent covered (McKinnon 1979: ch. 4). Then A's domestic transactors as a group—"merchants" broadly defined—find their cash balance position diminishing as per equations (5.8′) with $\rho > 1$.

3. In McKinnon (1976), the case is made that there is an inherent conflict in the motivation of central banks in regulating the foreign exchange exposure of commercial banks in a floating exchange rate regime. On the one hand the authorities want to guard against commercial bank failure because they are the custodians of the domestic money supply; hence the authorities wish to limit all banking risks including foreign exchange exposure. On the other hand a floating exchange rate system really requires that commercial banks commit substantial risk capital to their foreign exchange operations if undue exchange rate instability is to be avoided. This ambivalent regulatory behavior is an important reason why the supply of risk capital for foreign exchange speculation may well be inadequate.

REFERENCES

Aliber, Robert E. 1973. "The Interest Rate Parity Theorem: A Reinterpretation." *Journal of Political Economy* 81 (November/December): 1453-57.

Arrango, Sebastian, and M. Nadiri. 1981. "Demand for Money in Open Economics." *Journal of Monetary Economics* 7, 1 (January): 69-84.

Bigman, David, and Teizo Taya. 1980. *The Functioning of Floating Exchange Rates: Theory, Evidence and Policy Implications.* Cambridge, Mass.: Ballinger.

Brittain, Bruce. 1981. "International Currency Substitution and the Apparent Instability of Velocity in Some Western European Economies and in the United States." *Journal of Money, Credit, and Banking* (May): 135-55.

Britton, A.J.C. 1970. "The Dynamic Stability of the Foreign Exchange Market." *Economic Journal* (March): 91-96.

Driskill, Robert. 1981. "Exchange Rate Overshooting, the Trade Balance and Rational Expectations." *Journal of International Economics* 11 (August): 361-78.

Driskill, Robert, and Stephen McCafferty. 1980. "Speculation, Rational Expectations, and Stability of the Foreign Exchange Market." *Journal of International Economics* 10 (February): 91-102.

Friedman, Milton. 1953. "The Case for Flexible Exchange Rates." In *Essays in Positive Economics.* Chicago: University of Chicago Press, pp. 157-203.

Grassman, Sven. 1973. "A Fundamental Symmetry in International Payments Patterns." *Journal of International Economics* 3 (May): 105-6.

Levin, Jay S. 1980. "Devaluation, the J-Curve, and Flexible Exchange Rates." *The Manchester School* (December).

Magee, Stephen P. 1973. "Currency Contracts, Pass Through, and Devaluation." In Brookings Papers in Economic Activity, vol. 1, pp. 303-25.

McKinnon, Ronald I. 1982. "Currency Substitution and Instability in the World Dollar Standard." *American Economic Review* (June): 320-33.

_____. "The Exchange Rate and Macroeconomic Policy: Changing Postwar Perceptions." *Journal of Economic Literature* 19. June: 531-57.

_____. 1979. *Money in International Exchange: The Convertible Currency System.* New York: Oxford University Press.

_____. 1976. "Floating Foreign Exchange Rates 1973-74: The Emperor's New Clothes." In *Carnegie-Rochester Conference Series on Public Policy*, vol. 3, pp. 79-114.

Miles, Marc. 1978. "Currency Substitution, Flexible Exchange Rates, and Monetary Independence." *American Economic Review* (June): 428-36.

Niehans, Jürg. 1977. "Exchange Rate Dynamics and Stock/Flow Interaction." *Journal of Political Economy* 85 (December): 1245-58.

Stern, Robert. 1973. *The Balance of Payments.* Chicago: Aldine Press.

Williamson, John. 1973. "Another Case of Profitable Destabilizing Speculation." *Journal of International Economics* 3 (February): 77-84.

Witte, Willard. 1980. "Trade Hedging and the Dynamic Stability of the Foreign Exchange Market." *Quarterly Journal of Economics* 94 (February): 15-30.

❋ *Chapter 6*

Monetary Policy, The Balance of Payments, and The Exchange Rate

Pentti J.K. Kouri
New York University and
Yale University

INTRODUCTION

This chapter develops and extends the portfolio equilibrium model of the open economy to explain the behavior of the exchange rate. In line with the modern asset market view, the foreign exchange market is viewed as an efficient speculative market dominated, in the short run, by speculation and capital account transactions rather than by payments flows associated with merchandise trade. In particular, the short-run equilibrium value of the exchange rate is determined together with other asset prices by conditions of equilibrium between the demands for and the supplies of different assets.

The long-run equilibrium value of the exchange rate is determined by the conditions of stationary state equilibrium (it is assumed that there is no growth). One of these conditions is that the current account balance is equal to zero. Thus the traditional textbook model of the exchange rate emphasizing the trade account is one of the building blocks of the dynamic theory of exchange rate determination developed in this chapter.

There are several dynamic processes that are involved in the adjustment from short-run equilibrium to long-run equilibrium: time lags in the response of aggregate demand and trade flows to changes

This is a substantially revised version of a paper given at the conference on The Monetary Mechanism in Open Economies in Helsinki in August 1975.

in financial variables, such as interest rates and exchange rates, slow adjustment of prices and wages to variations in aggregate demand, accumulation of assets over time, and revision of expectations over time. For this reason the dynamics of the flexible rate regime is much harder to model than the determination of either short- or long-run equilibrium.

This chapter focuses on two aspects of the dynamics of exchange rate behavior: the accumulation of foreign assets (or decumulation as the case may be) through the current account on the one hand, and the dynamics of exchange rate expectations on the other. In this respect the chapter extends the dynamic model of exchange rate behavior developed in Kouri (1976).

This formulation brings out the similarities between the stock market on the one hand and the foreign exchange market on the other. The short-run equilibrium value of the exchange rate corresponds, in this analogy, to the demand price of capital, while the long-run equilibrium value of the exchange rate corresponds to the supply price of capital. In the same way that a discrepancy between the demand price of capital and the supply price of capital (Tobin's q-ratio) gives rise to capital accumulation (or decumulation) that eventually restores equality between the two, deviation of the exchange rate from its long-run equilibrium value gives rise to foreign investment (or disinvestment) through current account surpluses (or deficits).

One important implication of the dynamic model developed in this chapter is the relationship between the rate of change of the exchange rate and the current account: the exchange rate appreciates (relative to its trend) whenever the current account is in surplus, and depreciates whenever the current account is in deficit.

Another implication of the model concerns the volatility of exchange rates. In the old textbook model of the foreign exchange market the concern was that 'elasticities' would be so small that small changes in import or export demand would give rise to large movements in the exchange rate. Friedman (1956) argued that speculators would stabilize the exchange rate against reversible disturbances. The consensus view amongst the proponents of flexible exchange rates was that the free market would produce smooth and predictable changes in the exchange rate.

The asset market model implies in contrast that shifts in asset preferences and in future expectations, only weakly anchored to "fundamentals" that can be verified in the short run, can give rise to "large" and unpredictable changes in exchange rates. Indeed, also in this respect, the behavior of exchange rates is likely to resemble the behavior of other speculative prices, such as equity prices and commodity prices. The behavior of exchange rates since the beginning of generalized floating has been consistent with this implication of the asset market model.

Even if relative price elasticities of trade flows are very high, the exchange rate need not be stable, as implied by the textbook partial equilibrium model. This is because the domestic price level is not determined independently of the exchange rate. Indeed, in the limiting case of instantaneous purchasing power parity the domestic price level is determined by the exchange rate (given world prices), and thus becomes equally volatile and sensitive to disturbances.

The experience of some countries, Germany and Switzerland in particular but also to some extent the United States, in recent years brings out this new aspect of inflation that has become relevant with the flotation of exchange rates: a much larger share of prices are now determined in speculative auction markets.

This introduces a new and difficult problem for monetary policy. Monetary policy has a direct effect on prices through the exchange rate mechanism, but it is unlikely that monetary policy can be used in a predictable way to control the exchange rate short of pegging the rate. The market responds to policy measures differently depending on whether it perceives these measures to be permanent or transitory. Furthermore, the market responds to anticipated, rather than implemented, policy changes. Policies that have been correctly anticipated—or discounted—in advance have little noticeable effect when they are actually implemented. In the jargon of the "efficient market" literature, only new information, or "surprises," give rise to large changes in the exchange rate.

Indeed, trying to manage the exchange rate may be as difficult as trying to control the price of equity by means of monetary policy. This is particularly the case when the stock of privately held assets available for speculation is large relative to reserves that central banks have available for intervention, as in the case for the U.S. dollar today.

This chapter proceeds from these general considerations to develop a formal model of exchange rate determination. The following section develops a short-run model of exchange rate and interest rate determination and discusses the impact effects of different types of monetary policies and disturbances. Next, a dynamic model of exchange rate determination and current account adjustment is developed with emphasis on the implications of rational expectations. The model is an extension of Kouri (1976). The chapter concludes with a brief summary.

The details of the mathematical analysis are left out, since the derivations are quite straightforward if occasionally tedious.

THE ASSET MARKET MODEL OF EXCHANGE RATE DETERMINATION

In this part we review and extend the prototype asset market model of exchange rate determination in the short run.[1] The model is a straightforward application of the general equilibrium approach to monetary theory (Tobin 1969) to the monetary problems of the open economy.

The model differs from the monetarist model of exchange rate determination[2] in that it does not assume that all other assets but monies are perfect substitutes. Therefore it is necessary to specify the demands for and the supplies of all assets and not only monies in the analysis of the determination of equilibrium in financial markets. In the monetarist model, there is only one instrument of monetary policy—the supply of money. In the asset market, or portfolio equilibrium, model one can distinguish between different types of monetary policies, such as domestic open market operations on the one hand and foreign exchange market intervention on the other. These policies are identical in their effects only in the limiting case of perfect substitutability between domestic and foreign securities.

To focus on the essentials, we assume in this chapter, following Henderson and Girton (1977) and Kouri and Porter (1974), that there are only three assets—money, bonds, and foreign assets.[3] This abstraction retains the essential features of a mere complicated portfolio equilibrium model as long as interest focuses on balance of payments adjustment rather than on real growth and capital accumulation.[4]

The supply of money is controlled by the central bank, while the stock of domestic bonds consists of short-term government securities. Foreign residents are assumed not to hold any domestic assets.

We assume that the demand for money function is of the standard "liquidity preference" form:

$$\frac{M^d}{P} = L(r, y) = \frac{M^s}{P}, \qquad (6.1)$$

where

$$M^d = \text{demand for money,}$$

$$M^s = \text{supply of money,}$$

$$P = \text{domestic price deflator,}$$

$$r = \text{domestic nominal interest rate, and}$$

$$y = \text{domestic real income.}$$

We treat real income as exogenous in the short-run analysis but recognize the effect of the exchange rate on the price deflator:

$$P = h(ep^*, p), \tag{6.2}$$

where

$$ep^* = \text{price of foreign goods in domestic currency, and}$$

$$p = \text{price of domestic output.}$$

The central bank can change the supply of money discretely at any moment either through intervention in the domestic bond market or through intervention in the foreign exchange market:

$$M^s = M_0 + (B^{cb} - B_0^{cb}) + e(F^{cb} - F_0^{cb}), \tag{6.3}$$

where

$$M_0 = \text{stock of money at the initial moment,}$$

$$B^{cb} - B_0^{cb} = \text{the central bank's purchase of domestic bonds, and}$$

$$F^{cb} - F_0^{cb} = \text{the central bank's purchase of foreign exchange.}$$

The demand for domestic-currency-denominated bonds is a function of interest rates, the expected rate of depreciation of the domestic currency, real income, and real value of marketable wealth:

$$\frac{B^d}{P} = B\left(r, r^* + \pi_e, y, \frac{A}{P}\right) = D(r, r^* + \pi_e)\frac{A}{P}$$

$$- L(r, y) = \frac{B^s}{P}, \tag{6.4}$$

where

$$B^d = \text{demand for domestic-currency-denominated bonds,}$$

B^s = supply of domestic-currency-denominated bonds,

$D(\ )$ = total demand for domestic assets,

A = value of marketable wealth in domestic currency, and

π_e = expected rate of change of the price of foreign currency.

The specifications of the money demand and bond demand equations imply that the total demand for domestic-currency-denominated assets does not depend on its distribution between money and bonds.[5]

The net supply of domestic bonds to be held by the private sector is equal to the total stock of government securities, less holdings of the central bank.

$$B^s = B^t - B^{cb}, \tag{6.5}$$

where

B^t = total stock of government debt.

In order that the asset demand functions satisfy the wealth constraint, the demand for foreign assets must be of the form:

$$F^d \frac{e}{P} = F(r, r^* + \pi_e)\frac{A}{P} \equiv (1 - D(r, r^* + \pi_e))\frac{A}{P} = F^s \frac{e}{P}, \tag{6.6}$$

where

F^d = demand for foreign assets in foreign currency, and

F^s = supply of foreign assets.

The supply of foreign assets available to the private sector is equal to the total stock of foreign assets acquired through past surpluses in the current account, less holdings of foreign assets by the central bank:

$$F^s = F^t - F^{cb}, \tag{6.7}$$

where

F^t = cumulative sum of past current account surpluses or deficits.

The portfolio choice of the private sector must, at each point in time, satisfy the wealth constraint,

$$M^d + B^d + eF^d \equiv A \equiv M_0 + B_0 + eF_0. \tag{6.8}$$

This balance sheet constraint implies the following familiar restrictions on the partial derivatives of the asset demand functions:

$$L_i + B_i + F_i = 0, \tag{6.9.1}$$

for $i = r, r^* + \pi_e, y$, and

$$L_i + B_i + F_i = 1, \tag{6.9.2}$$

for $i = A/P$.

The balance sheet constraints for the domestic private sector and for the central bank imply together Walras' law for the financial markets:

$$(M^d - M^s) + (B^d - B^s) + e(F^d - F^s) \equiv 0. \tag{6.10}$$

There are thus only two independent equilibrium conditions sufficient to determine the exchange rate and the interest rate. It is useful to note from equation (6.10) that the ex ante stock deficit in the balance of payments is not equal to the ex ante excess supply of money but rather to the total ex ante excess supply of domestic assets—money and bonds. It is therefore a mistake to attribute currency depreciation resulting from excess supply of domestic currency to spend on foreign assets necessarily to ex ante excess supply of domestic money over the demand to hold it.

Short-run Equilibrium in the Foreign Exchange Market

In this section we analyze the determination of equilibrium in the foreign exchange market assuming that the central bank pegs the domestic interest rate. It follows from Walras' law (equation 6.10) that when the foreign exchange market is in equilibrium, the total demand for domestic assets equals the total supply of domestic assets. Therefore, we can write the equilibrium condition for the foreign exchange market in the form:

$$\frac{eF^s}{D^s} = f(r, r^* + \pi_e), \tag{6.11}$$

where

$$f = F(r, r* + \pi_e)/D(r, r* + \pi_e).$$

This form is convenient because it does not involve the initial holdings of assets.[6] For each value of the exchange rate, the ratio on the left-hand side can range between plus and minus infinity, as F^s and D^s range from plus to minus infinity. It is possible in principle that both F^s and D^s are negative, implying that the private sector is a net debtor in both domestic and foreign currency and therefore has a net stock of financial liabilities rather than of assets.[7]

Available empirical evidence suggests that there is no reason to constrain F^s or D^s to be of any particular sign.[8] There is a problem, however, if either F^s or D^s is negative: from equation (6.11) there need not exist any equilibrium with stationary expectations for arbitrary interest rates r and $r*$. The same problem also arises if either D or F are zero or if domestic and foreign securities are perfect substitutes.

The solution to this problem is the endogeneity of the expected rate of change of the exchange rate, π_e—in particular, its dependence on the level of the exchange rate. We assume in this section that exchange rate expectations are regressive around the expected long-run equilibrium value of the exchange rate:

$$\pi_e = \theta(e, \bar{e}), \tag{6.12}$$

where $\bar{e}$ = expected long-run equilibrium value of the exchange rate; $\theta_e < 0$, $\theta_{\bar{e}} > 0$, $\theta_e \to +\infty$ as $e \to 0$, and $\theta_e \to -\infty$ as $e \to \infty$; and $\theta(\bar{e}, \bar{e}) = 0$.

The determination of equilibrium in the foreign exchange market can now be analyzed with the aid of Figure 6-1. The FF schedule plots the demand for foreign assets relative to the stock of domestic assets as a function of the exchange rate. It is downward sloping because an increase in the price of foreign currency reduces the expected rate of depreciation or, as the case may be, increases the expected rate of appreciation. The supply side is represented by a straight line starting from the origin, such as $0f_1$, drawn for given supplies of domestic and foreign assets (D^s and F^s respectively). Equilibrium obtains at A_1 with the exchange rate equal to e_0 and the relative share of foreign assets equal to f_0. An increase in the supply of foreign assets rotates the $0f$ ray to the left (from $0f_0$ to $0f_1$), while a reduction in the stock of foreign assets rotates the $0f$ ray to the right. The $0f_2$ ray in Figure 6-1 illustrates the case

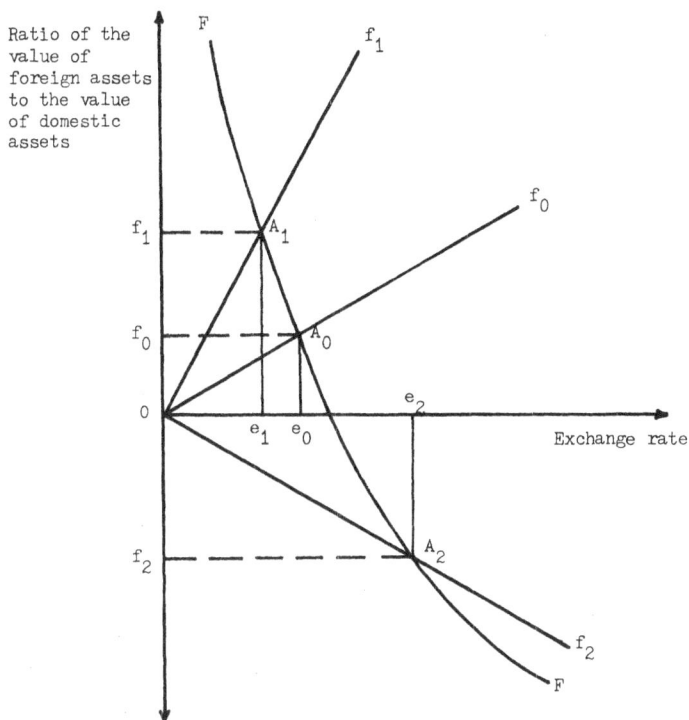

Figure 6-1. Equilibrium in the Foreign Exchange Market.

of a negative stock of foreign assets. Changes in the supply of domestic assets shift the $0f$ ray by the same amount as equiproportionate changes in the supply of foreign assets but in the opposite
direction. The FF schedule in turn shifts with changes in interest
rates and in long-run exchange rate expectations. In the limiting case
of perfect substitutability between domestic and foreign securities,
assumed in Dornbusch (1976), the equilibrium yield differential
between domestic and foreign securities no longer depends on the
relative supply of the two assets, and therefore the FF schedule
becomes vertical: the equilibrium exchange rate is that rate that
makes the expected rate of depreciation equal to the interest rate
differential.[9]

Simultaneous Determination of the Exchange
Rate and the Interest Rate

In this section we study how the exchange rate and the domestic interest rate [10] are simultaneously determined and how they
are affected by various policies and disturbances. It was established

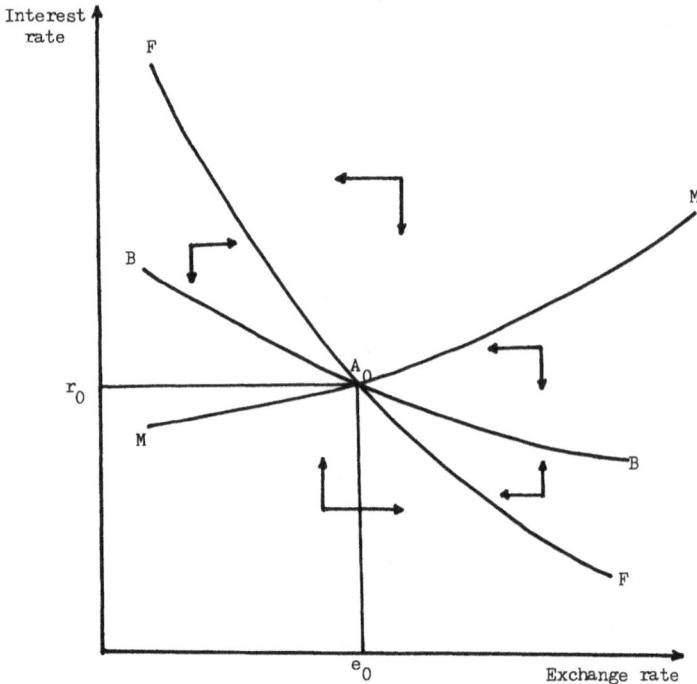

Figure 6-2. Simultaneous Determination of the Exchange Rate and the Interest Rate.

in the previous section that an increase in the domestic interest rate appreciates the domestic currency. The *FF* schedule in Figure 6-2, which represents equilibrium in the foreign exchange market, illustrates this relationship. It is defined by equations (6.11) and (6.12). Limiting the analysis to continuous changes in the underlying variables, we may solve these equations in terms of rates of change, to obtain:

$$\hat{e} = -\frac{e}{f + f_{r*}\epsilon_e} \, d(F^s/D^s) - \frac{f_r}{f + f_{r*}\epsilon_e} \, dr \qquad (6.13)$$

$$+ \frac{f_{r*}}{f + f_{r*}\epsilon_e} \, dr* + \frac{f_{r*}\epsilon_e}{f + f_{r*}\epsilon_e} \, \hat{\bar{e}}, \cdot$$

where

$$\hat{e} = \frac{de}{e}$$

$$f_r = -\partial f/\partial r,$$

$$f_{r^*} = \partial f/\partial (r^* + \pi_e), \text{ and}$$

$$\epsilon_e = \partial \theta /(\partial e/e).$$

We note that the slope of the *FF* schedule, as well as the magnitudes of shifts in its location, depend on the elasticity of exchange rate expectations, ϵ_e.

The second crucial relationship is the condition of equilibrium between the demand for and the supply of money, illustrated by the *MM* schedule in Figure 6-2. It is upward sloping because an increase in the price of foreign currency increases the price level and therefore the demand for money, thus requiring an offsetting increase in the domestic interest rate.[11] In terms of proportionate changes the equation of the *MM* schedule is:

$$dr = -\frac{1}{\ell_r}\hat{M}^s + \frac{1 - h_e}{\ell_r}\hat{p} + \frac{m}{\ell_r}(\hat{e} + \hat{p}^*) + \frac{\ell_y}{\ell_r}\hat{y}, \qquad (6.14)$$

where

$$\ell_r = -(\partial L/L)/\partial r,$$

$$\ell_y = (\partial L/L)/(\partial y/y), \text{ and}$$

$$h_e = (\partial h/h)/(\partial (ep^*)/(ep^*)).$$

Note that the *MM* schedule becomes steeper as the interest elasticity of the demand for money increases and as the elasticity of the domestic price level with respect to the domestic currency price of foreign goods (m) increases. The short-run equilibrium values of the interest rate and the exchange rate are determined by the intersection of the *FF* and the *MM* schedules at A_0. Because of Walras' Law the *BB* schedule representing equilibrium in the domestic bond market (equation 6.4) goes through the point of intersection of these two schedules. The *BB* schedule may be downward or upward sloping depending on the strength of the exchange rate effect on money demand. In any case it is less steep than the *FF* schedule.

In analyzing shifts from one equilibrium position to another any two of the three schedules can be used. The short-run dynamics of interest rate and exchange rate adjustment are, however, governed by the *FF* and *BB* schedules, as indicated by the arrows in Figure 6-2. It is assumed there that the interest rate changes as a function of excess demand for domestic credit (excess supply of domestic bonds) and the exchange rate as a function of stock excess demand for foreign exchange. It is easy to establish that with these rules of price adjustment, short-run equilibrium in financial markets is stable. It will be assumed in this chpater that the adjustment to short-run equilibrium is instantaneous: as time passes financial markets stay continuously in equilibrium although prices are changing because of changes in asset demands and supplies.

We next apply the model to study the effects of changes in asset supplies brought about either by monetary policy, a current account surplus, or a budget deficit. Three types of monetary policy can be distinguished. First, the central bank can engage in a traditional open market operation, which involves the purchase of domestic bonds with domestic money. In Figure 6-3, this is shown as a shift of the *MM* schedule to the right with no change in the location of the *FF* schedule. The domestic interest rate declines from r_0 to r_1 while the domestic currency depreciates from e_0 to e_1. Second, the central bank can increase the supply of money by intervening in the foreign exchange market. This is shown in Figure 6-4 as a shift of the *MM* schedule with no change in the location of the *BB* schedule. The shift of the *MM* schedule in Figure 6-4 is drawn to be the same as the shift in Figure 6-3. It is clear that foreign exchange market intervention has a weaker effect on the interest rate and a stronger effect on the exchange rate than intervention in the domestic bond market (compare points A_2 and A_1 in Figure 6-4). The effects would be the same only if domestic and foreign bonds were perfect substitutes, in which case the *BB* and the *FF* schedules would coincide. This is the assumption that is typically made, either implicitly or explicitly, in monetarist models of exchange rate determination.

A third type of monetary policy that we may consider is foreign exchange market intervention by a "stabilization fund" that borrows the funds that it needs to support the exchange rate. Such intervention would leave the *MM* schedule unchanged, since it would not affect the supply of money, and instead would shift the *FF* and the *BB* schedules. Figure 6-5 illustrates the effects of a sale of domestic currency in the foreign exchange market by the stabilization fund, which has obtained the funds by issuing domestic bonds in the amount of the foreign currency purchase. The effect of this policy is to depreciate the domestic currency and to increase the domestic interest rate. Under certain conditions—namely, if the interest rate parity holds—this type of foreign exchange market intervention is identical in its effects to intervention in the forward exchange market.[12] The same effects on the exchange rate and on the interest rate could also be obtained by changing the currency composition of government debt.

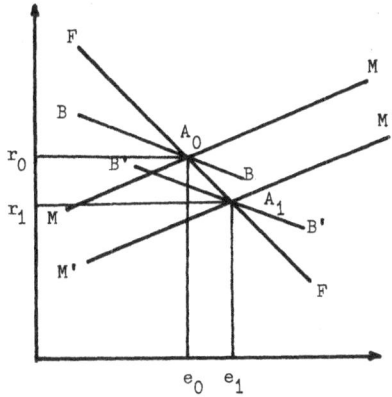

Figure 6-3. Domestic Open Market Operation.

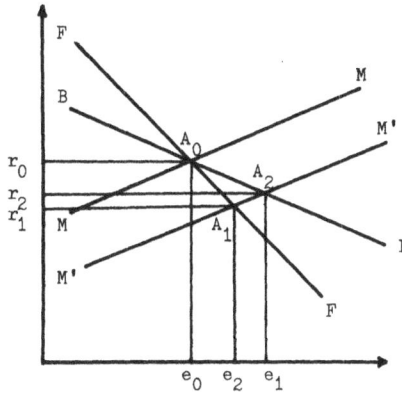

Figure 6-4. Intervention in the Foreign Exchange Market.

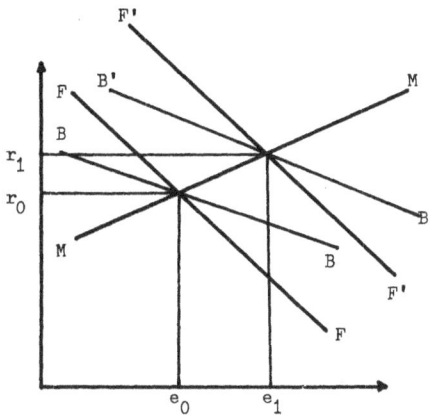

Figure 6-5. Exchange of Domestic Bonds for Foreign Assets: Intervention in the Forward Market.

Because of Walras' law there are, in general, only two independent instruments of financial policy, and in the limiting case of perfect substitutability between domestic and foreign securities, only one—the supply of money.

Apart from changes in monetary policy, equilibrium in financial markets changes from one period to the next as a result of asset accumulation. A budget deficit increases the supply of domestic assets and thus shifts the FF schedule to the right: with no change in the supply of money the interest rate increases, while the domestic currency depreciates in the foreign exchange market. A current account deficit has exactly the same effect: in the absence of intervention it also shifts the FF schedule to the right, thus increasing the domestic interest rate and depreciating the domestic currency. These effects play a crucial role in the process of adjustment to long-run equilibrium in the balance of payments.

The asset market model implies that the exchange rate does not fully offset changes in the foreign price level in the short run. An increase in the foreign price level leaves the FF schedule unchanged, holding expectations constant, and shifts the MM schedule to the right in the same proportion. The domestic currency appreciates, but by a smaller proportion. Therefore, domestic price level increases, and with constant money supply, the equilibrium interest rate also increases.

Probably the single most important explanation of short-term exchange rate movements is the volatility of exchange rate expectations. Figure 6-6 illustrates the effects of a speculative shift out of "domestic currency." The shift is assumed to be from domestic bonds to foreign bonds. Thus the FF and the BB schedules shift to the right, to $F'F'$ and $B'B'$ respectively in Figure 6-6, with no change in the MM schedule.[13] The central bank has several options to deal with this situation. One is to do nothing, in which case the domestic currency would depreciate to e_1 and the interest rate would increase to r_1. Another is to support the exchange rate at e_0 by means of intervention in the spot market without sterilization. In that case new equilibrium would obtain at A_2 with interest rate r_2. Yet another alternative is not to intervene in the foreign exchange market at all, but instead to support the exchange rate at e_0 by means of "tight money." In that case, an even higher interest rate, r_3 in Figure 6-6, would be required. A fourth alternative is a policy of intervention with complete sterilization. This policy, which amounts to forward market intervention, or intervention by a steri-

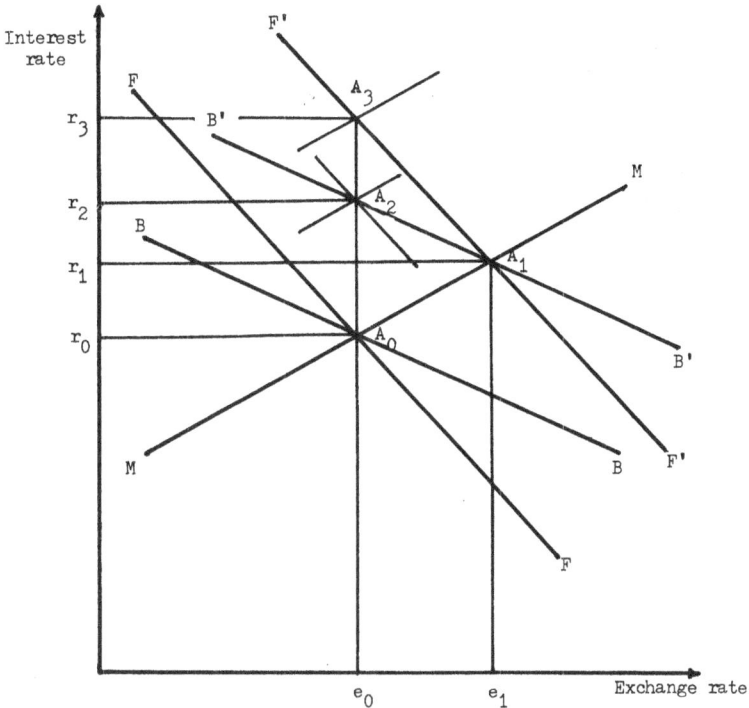

Figure 6-6. A Speculative Disturbance.

lization fund of the type discussed above, leaves both the interest rate and the exchange rate unchanged in the event of the speculative disturbance and therefore dominates the other alternatives. Needless to say, any intervention in support of the exchange rate will be successful over time only if the central bank is correct in assuming that the disturbance is indeed "purely speculative," and is not justified by changes in the underlying "fundamentals." Other alternatives for dealing with speculative capital movements are taxes or restrictions on capital movements or the establishment of a dual foreign exchange market.[14]

The Reduced Form Exchange Rate Equation

We conclude this part with a discussion of the reduced form exchange rate equation, solved from equations (6.13) and (6.14). This equation is the flexible rate counterpart of the capital flow equation developed and estimated in Kouri and Porter (1974):

$$\hat{e} = -\frac{e}{f + mf_r + \epsilon_e f_{r*}} d(F^s/D^s) + \frac{f_r/\ell_r}{f + mf_r + \epsilon_e f_{r*}} \hat{M}^s$$

$$-\frac{(1-m)f_r/\ell_r}{f + mf_r + \epsilon_e f_{r*}} \hat{p} - \frac{mf_r/\ell_r}{f + mf_r + \epsilon_e f_{r*}} \hat{p}*$$

$$-\frac{\ell_y f_r/\ell_r}{f + mf_r + \epsilon_e f_{r*}} \hat{y} + \frac{f_{r*}}{f + mf_r + \epsilon_e f_{r*}} dr*$$

$$+\frac{\epsilon_e f_{r*}}{f + mf_r + \epsilon_e f_{r*}} \hat{\bar{e}}.$$

(6.15)

This equation is empirically testable and has already been estimated in terms of levels by Branson, Halttunen, and Masson (1978) and by Porter (1977). The results suggest that the privately held stock of foreign assets is indeed an important variable in explaining fluctuations in the exchange rate. It is likely, however, that the coefficients of equation (6.15) are highly unstable because of the variability of f. Dornbusch's (1976) model is a special case of this equation, obtained as f_r and f_{r*} approach infinity. In the limiting case we have:[15]

$$\hat{e} = \frac{1}{m + \ell_r \epsilon_e} \hat{M}^s - \frac{(1-m)}{m + \ell_r \epsilon_e} \hat{p} - \frac{m}{m + \ell_r \epsilon_e} \hat{p}*$$

$$-\frac{\ell_r}{m + \ell_r \epsilon_e} \hat{y} + \frac{\ell_r}{m + \ell_r \epsilon_e} dr* + \frac{\ell_r \epsilon_e}{m + \ell_r \epsilon_e} \hat{\bar{e}}.$$

(6.16)

The monetarist exchange rate equation is obtained from the reduced form equation of the portfolio equilibrium model by assuming that domestic and foreign securities are perfect substitutes and by assuming instantaneous price flexibility and purchasing power parity.[16] In that case, $\hat{e} = \hat{p} - \hat{p}*$, and equation (6.16) further simplifies into:

$$\hat{e} = \frac{1}{1 + \epsilon_e \ell_r} (\hat{M}^s - \hat{p}*) - \frac{\ell_y}{1 + \epsilon_e \ell_r} \hat{y} + \frac{\ell_r}{1 + \epsilon_e \ell_r} dr*$$

$$+\frac{\epsilon_e \ell_r}{1 + \epsilon_e \ell_r} \hat{\bar{e}}.$$

(6.17)

The portfolio equilibrium model does not provide a complete theory of exchange rate determination because most of the explanatory variables are endogenous, except in the very short run. And even in the short run, the endogenous nature of exchange rate expectations is crucial.

There are several complementary ways of closing the model. One is to assume, as Mundell and Fleming, that prices are completely rigid and also to neglect asset accumulation. In that case the model would be closed by adding a dynamic *IS* schedule that would allow for time lags in the response of aggregate demand and output to changes in the exchange rate and in the interest rate.

An alternative is to abstract from time lags in the transmission from financial variables to aggregate demand, as well as from asset accumulation, and instead to allow for sluggish adjustment of prices to variations in aggregate demand. This is, of course, the approach taken in Dornbusch (1976). Third, one may focus on the dynamics of asset accumulation and balance of payments adjustment at the cost of considerable simplification of price and output adjustment. This is the approach taken in Kouri (1975, 1976) and further pursued in this chapter. Ideally one would like to combine all the relevant dynamic elements, but that is impossible in the framework of a tractable analytical model. An important contribution in this respect is, however, Henderson (1977), who combines asset accumulation with disequilibrium price adjustment.

ASSET ACCUMULATION AND THE DYNAMICS OF THE EXCHANGE RATE

In this part we extend the asset market model of exchange rate determination to analyze the dynamic effect of different types of monetary policies and disturbances on the exchange rate and on the balance of payments. We assume price flexibility and continuous market clearing and instead focus on the dynamics of asset accumulation and expectations formation, extending the model developed in Kouri (1976).

For the purposes of this analysis in this section, we assume that the purchasing power parity holds. Therefore, the domestic price level is determined by the purchasing power parity equation:

$$P = p = ep^* = e, \qquad (6.18)$$

where p^* is set equal to one for convenience. The price level is thus completely determined in the asset markets in the short run.

Regarding the asset markets, we assume that the foreign exchange market stabilization fund is a department of the government rather than of the central bank. The money supply is equal to the central bank's stock of government securities, and the total stock of domestic assets, D^s, is equal to the total stock of government debt. The two equilibrium conditions are accordingly:

$$\frac{M^d}{P} = L(r,y)\frac{M^s}{P} = \phi\frac{B^g}{P} \quad \text{(cf. equation 6.1), and} \qquad (6.19)$$

$$F^d = f(r - \pi, r*)\frac{B^g}{P} = F^s = F^t - F^g \text{ (cf. equation 6.11),} \quad (6.20)$$

where

$\pi = \pi_e$ = expected rate of inflation,

ϕ = ratio of the money stock to the total stock of government debt, and

F^g = government held stock of foreign assets.

These two equations determine the real value of government debt, B^g/P, and the nominal interest rate r, as functions of the supply of foreign assets, F^s, monetary policy, ϕ, the foreign interest rate $r*$, the expected rate of inflation π, and domestic real income y:

$$\frac{B^g}{P} = b(F^t - F^g, \phi, r*, \pi, y); \qquad (6.21)$$
$$\quad\;\; (+) \quad\; (-)\,(-)\;\,(-)\,(+)$$

$$r = i(F^t - F^g, \phi, r*, \pi, y). \qquad (6.22)$$
$$\quad (-) \qquad (-)\,(+)\;\,(+)\,(+)$$

The signs given in the parentheses are the signs of the partial derivatives.

The monetarist model of exchange rate determination is a special case of the model defined by equations (6.19) and (6.20). It is obtained from this model by assuming that domestic and foreign securities are perfect substitutes in which case equation (6.20) collapses to the Fisher parity equation, $r = r* + \pi$, which is one of the building blocks of the monetarist model. With imperfect substitutability, assumed in this chapter, the stock of foreign assets becomes a determinant of the domestic interest rate as well as of the domestic price level. Even if the supply of money is constant, and the demand for money stable, the price level can be unstable if the demand for foreign securities is not stable.

The *PP* schedule in Figure 6–7 plots the real value of government debt as a function of the supply of foreign assets to the private sector, as defined by equation (6.21). This schedule is drawn for a particular value of π, the expected rate of inflation. Short-run portfolio equilibrium obtains at point A_0. This is as far as the static asset market model goes. To go further we need to specify how the stock of foreign assets changes over time and how expectations are formed.

Given the assumption that all domestic goods are internationally traded and face infinitely elastic demand, the current account is simply the difference between national disposable income and total

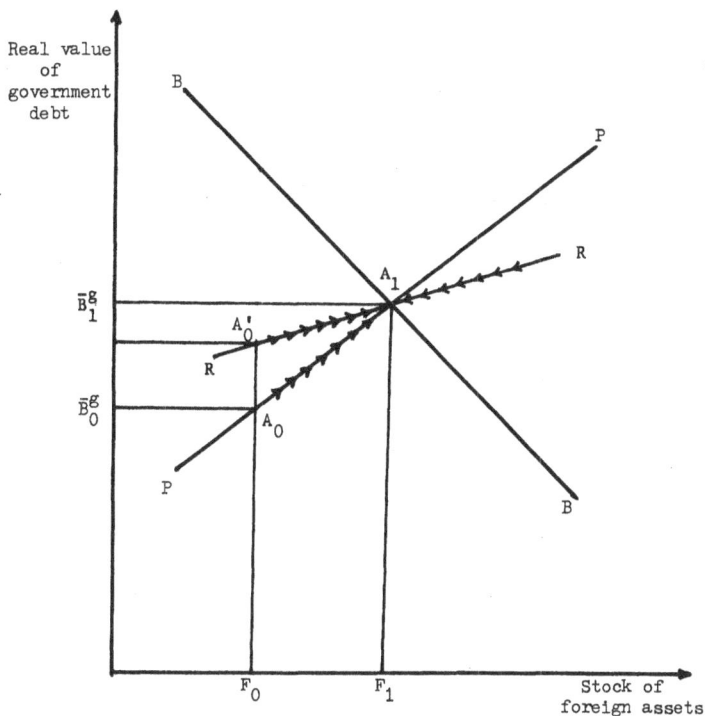

Figure 6–7. Stationary State Equilibrium.

domestic absorption:

$$\dot{F}^t = CB = y + r*F^t - G - C, \qquad (6.23)$$

where

$$CB = \text{current account surplus,}$$
$$y + r*F^t = \text{national disposable income,}$$
$$G = \text{government consumption, and}$$
$$C = \text{private consumption.}$$

Private consumption is a function of permanent private disposable income and expected domestic and foreign real interest rates. Disposable income is equal to national income plus real interest earnings on foreign assets and government securities, less net tax payments to the government:

$$y^d = y + r*F^s + (r - \pi)\frac{B^s}{P} - \pi\frac{M^s}{P} - T, \qquad (6.24)$$

where T = net tax payments to the government. Taxes are assumed to be lump sum taxes. The government also faces a budget constraint, given below:[17]

$$\frac{\dot{B}^g}{P} = \mu\frac{B^g}{P} = BS = T - r\frac{B^s}{P} + r*F^g - G, \qquad (6.25)$$

where

$$\mu = \text{rate of growth of nominal public debt, and}$$
$$BS = \text{budget surplus.}$$

It is assumed that the central bank reimburses the government all of its interest earnings on government securities. We assume further that the government fixes the rate of growth of nominal debt, μ, and real government expenditure, G, and adjusts net tax revenue as required by the budget constraint. Substituting from equation (6.25) into the private sector's budget constraint we obtain then:

$$y^d = y + r*F^t - G + (\mu - \pi)\frac{B^g}{P}. \qquad (6.26)$$

Thus deficit financing increases private disposable income only as long as the rate of growth of nominal debt is greater than the expected rate of inflation π. In long-run stationary equilibrium the two must be the same. Permanent private disposable income is accordingly:

$$\tilde{y}^d = y + r^* F^t - G, \tag{6.27}$$

where

$$\tilde{y}^d = \text{permanent private disposable income.}$$

Consumption is a function of expected real interest rates and permanent income:

$$C = C(r - \pi, r^*, \tilde{y}^d). \tag{6.28}$$
$$(-) \ (-)$$

The marginal propensity to consume out of permanent income is assumed to be greater than one: otherwise both consumption and the stock of foreign assets would increase without limit for given real interest rates.[18] This is, of course, a familiar stability condition in dynamic portfolio balance models. In the Metzlerian model, however, only the marginal propensity to consume out of interest income is assumed to be greater than one, while the marginal propensity to consume out of noninterest income is assumed to be less than one.[19] Substituting the consumption function in equation (6.23), we obtain the current account or capital flow equation:

$$\dot{F}^t = y + r^* F^t - G - C(r - \pi, r^*, y + r^* F^t - G). \tag{6.29}$$

Note that an increase in the domestic interest rate increases the current account surplus and thus causes an outflow of capital. In contrast, an increase in the foreign interest rate may either increase or decrease the current account surplus depending on the relative strengths of the income effect on the one hand and the substitution effect on the other.

The dynamic model is now defined by equations (6.19), (6.21), and (6.29). To complete it we need to specify how expectations are formed. We shall consider two alternatives: first, static expectations with π always equal to μ, and second, rational expectations with π equal to the actual rate of inflation:[20]

$$\pi = \frac{\dot{P}}{P}. \tag{6.30}$$

The Stationary State

In the short run the stock of foreign assets is given; only its valuation can change. In the long run it adjusts through surpluses and deficits in the current account. In this section we study the determinants of the long-run asset positions. The following section analyzes the process of adjustment to long-run stationary equilibrium.[21]

The stationary state solution is obtained from equations (6.19), (6.21), and (6.29) by setting $\dot{F}^t$ equal to zero and π equal to μ.

The determination of long-run stationary equilibrium is illustrated in Figure 6-7. The *PP* schedule is the portfolio equilibrium schedule. It is drawn for π equal to μ. The *BB* schedule represents long-run equilibrium in the balance of payments. It is downward sloping because a reduction in the real money stock reduces the domestic interest rate, and thus reduces saving and the long-run equilibrium stock of foreign assets.

Long-run equilibrium obtains the Figure 6-7 at point A_1 where the *PP* and *BB* schedules intersect. Assuming stationary expectations, adjustment to long-run equilibrium takes place along the *PP* schedule as indicated by the arrows. Along this path the current account is in surplus while the rate of inflation is below the long-run rate of inflation, μ. The assumption that the marginal propensity to consume out of permanent income is greater than one ensures the stability of the adjustment process, even in the absence of any effect of foreign asset accumulation on the domestic interest rate.

The adjustment path with rational expectations is illustrated by the *RR* ray:[22] the initial price level is lower than with static expectations because of the anticipated future appreciation of the domestic currency relative to trend. The assumptions of the model imply that there exists a rational expectations solution, although the difficult problem concerning how the market ever gets on this path of course remains.

Comparative Dynamic Exercises

In this part we put the dynamic model to use and study the response patterns to different types of monetary policies. We consider three types of monetary policies in particular: a change in the money-debt ratio (ϕ); a change in the supply of foreign assets, F^s, with no change in the money-debt ratio; and a change in the rate of growth of nominal debt (μ) with no change in the money-debt ratio.

The nonneutrality of changes in the supply of money with outside debt is well known (Metzler 1951) and it arises because future tax liabilities are not perfect substitutes with currently held government debt (Barro 1977) in private portfolios. In the portfolio model developed above, there is no offsetting of future tax liabilities in the private sector's demand for government securities, although government bonds do not add to the private sector's permanent disposable income.

Figure 6-8 illustrates the response to an income in the money-debt ratio. The economy is initially in equilibrium at A_0 with real value of government debt equal to $\bar{B}_0^g$ and the stock of foreign assets equal to F_0. As ϕ increases, the BB schedule shifts down in exactly the same proportion. The PP schedule also shifts down but by a smaller amount. Therefore, both the real value of government debt and the stock of foreign assets are lower in the new long-run equilibrium position at A_1. Domestic interest rate will also be lower in this new equilibrium. With static expectations adjustment takes place along the $P'P'$ schedule, after an initial jump from A_0 to A_0'. With rational expectations, the adjustment takes place along the $R'R'$ ray after an initial jump from A_0 to A_0''.

In both cases, expansionary monetary policy leads to a current

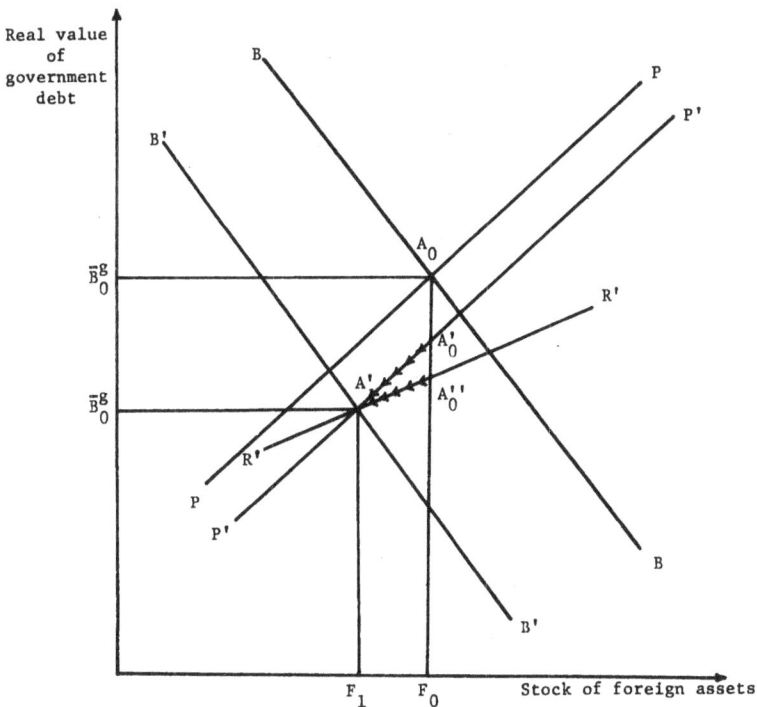

Figure 6-8. Increase in the Money-Debt Ratio.

account deficit, and thus an inflow of capital. As long as the current account is in deficit, the domestic currency depreciates relative to its trend.

Another nonneutrality result which is well known from the literature on monetary growth models (Tobin 1955) is the effect of changes in the rate of monetary expansion. In the present model an increase in the rate of monetary expansion, with no change in the money-debt ratio, reduces the real rate of interest and therefore reduces both the real value of domestic assets and the stock of foreign assets, because the effect of the reduction of the real interest rate on saving (shift of the *BB* schedule) dominates the substitution effect (shift of the *PP* schedule). This is in contrast with some of the models of money and growth, in which inflation increases the stock of real capital because of the dominance of the substitution effect.

Figure 6–9 illustrates the pattern of response to a permanent reduction in monetary expansion to zero. There is an immediate

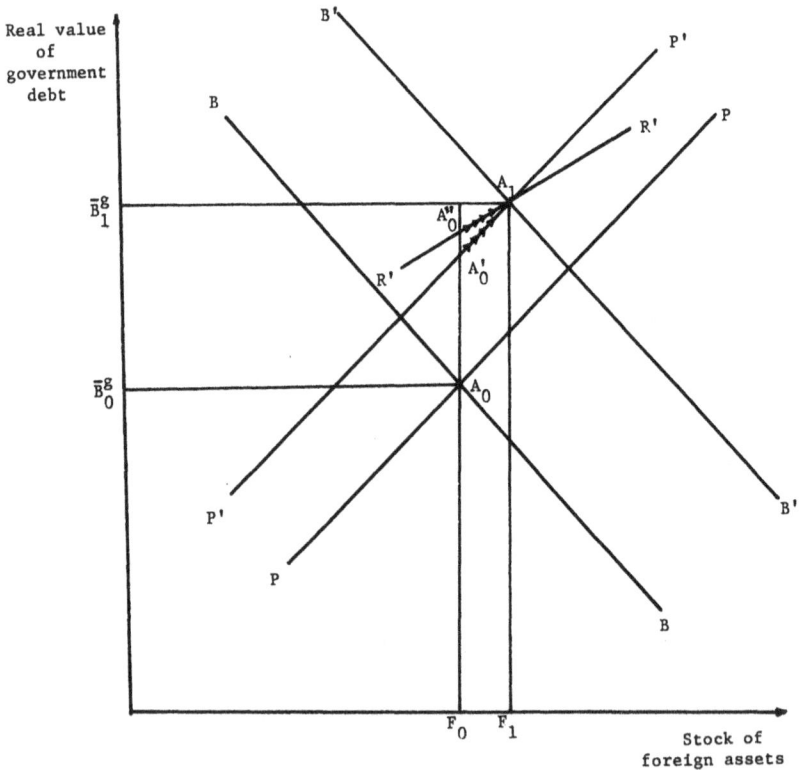

Figure 6-9. Reduction in the Rate of Monetary Expansion.

appreciation of the domestic currency from A_0 to A_0'' (with rational expectations). The nominal interest rate decreases while the real interest rate increases, thus producing a surplus in the current account. Supported by the current account surplus, the exchange rate continues to appreciate until new long-run equilibrium is reached at A_1 with a higher real value of government debt as well as a higher stock of foreign assets. This example is interesting in view of the behaviour of the German mark and the Swiss franc since early 1977.

An increase in the nominal stock of government debt brought about by government purchase of foreign exchange with no change in the money-debt ratio increases the price level in the same proportion in the long run. In the short run, however, the price level overshoots its long-run equilibrium value. This is illustrated in Figure 6-10. The foreign exchange market is initially in equilibrium at A_0 with real value of government debt equal to $\bar{B}_0^g$ and the stock of foreign assets equal to F_0. As the government purchases foreign exchange the stock available to the private sector is reduced to F_1.

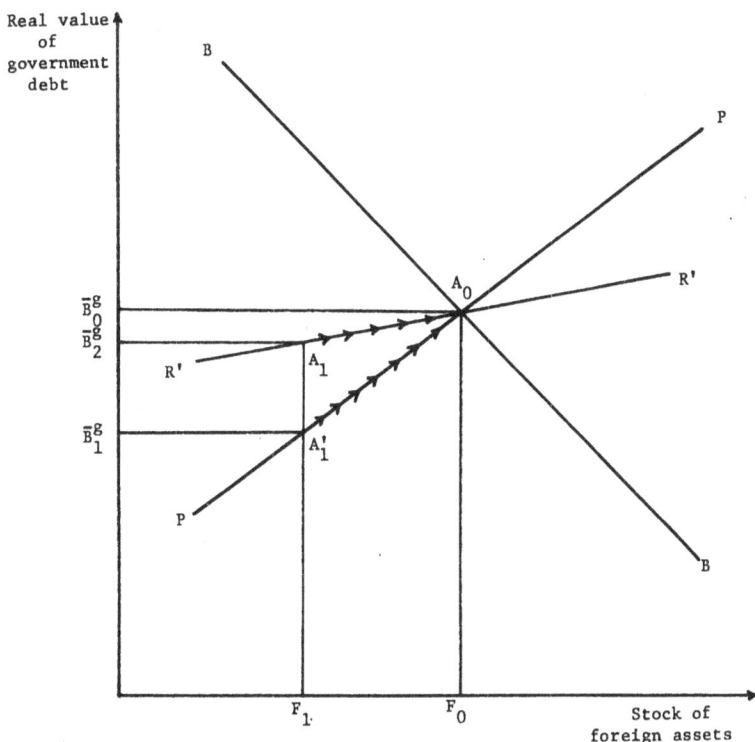

Figure 6-10. Foreign Exchange Market Intervention.

Despite the increase in the nominal value of government debt, the real value of government debt decreases, either to A_1 (static expectations) or to A_2 (rational expectations). Long-run neutrality is established as the market adjusts back to the same long-run equilibrium at A_0 through appreciation and current account surpluses.

The second point concerns the distinction between anticipated disturbances on the one hand, and unanticipated disturbances on the other. As an efficient speculative market the foreign exchange market responds immediately to all anticipated policies and disturbances even if they are expected to occur in the future. When the disturbances actually occur there is no noticeable jump in the exchange rate if the market has been correct in its expectation: the event has been "discounted" in advance.

In fact this type of anticipatory behaviour can give rise to apparently counterintuitive patterns of response. We conclude with one such example. Suppose that the market comes to expect a "helicopter rain" of money and bonds, such that that money-debt ratio would not be affected. If this disturbance occurred immediately, it would have no real effects: the price level would increase in the same proportion. When the disturbance is anticipated to occur in the future, there will, however, be real effects. It is clear that the exchange rate cannot jump at the known date when the"helicopter rain" actually occurs: because the disturbance is anticipated speculators would make infinite profits. Therefore, the jump in the price level must occur immediately. This means that the real money stock must decrease and therefore that the nominal interest must increase. The real value of domestic assets must also decrease and therefore the real interest rate on domestic assets must decrease in order that the foreign exchange market remains in equilibrium. Therefore, the exchange rate must continue to depreciate after the initial jump in order for the market to remain in rational expectations equilibrium. The decline of the real interest rate turns the current account into a deficit. Thus an anticipated future "rain of money" causes currency depreciation and a weakening of the current account immediately. When the "rain" actually occurs, the price level cannot jump, and therefore the real money stock and the real value of government debt must, paradoxically, increase in the same proportion when the supply of nominal debt is increased. For the financial markets to remain in equilibrium, the nominal interest rate must decrease and the real interest rate increase at that time. The current account must accordingly move into a surplus and the exchange rate must begin to appreciate. Eventually the market will converge back to the same long-run equilibrium position, in which the neutrality of money again holds.

This argument establishes the pattern of response illustrated in Figure 6-11. The market is initially in equilibrium at A_0, and suddenly comes to expect a helicopter rain of money and bonds at some future date. The exchange rate jumps immediately bringing the real value of government debt down to A_0'. Thereafter exchange rate depreciation continues to reduce the real value of government debt while a deficit in the current account reduces the stock of foreign assets. When the nominal supply of debt is increased at A_1 there is no jump in the price level; therefore the real value of government debt increases in the same proportion to A_1'. After the disturbance the exchange rate begins to appreciate while the current account moves into a surplus: the economy converges back to the same long-run equilibrium position at A_0 along the RR schedule.

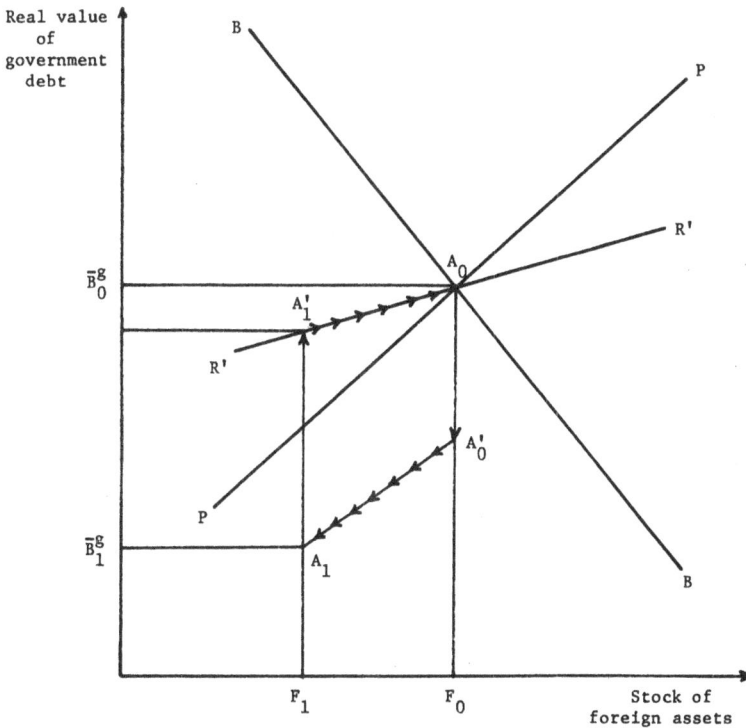

Figure 6-11. Anticipated "Helicopter Rain" of Money and Bonds.

CONCLUDING REMARKS

This chapter has developed a dynamic theory of exchange rate determination that formalizes the idea that the foreign exchange market is, like the stock market, an "efficient speculative market."

In short-run analysis the theory views the exchange rate as one of the many prices that equilibrate the demands for and the supplies of different types of financial assets. Monetary policy can affect the exchange rate by changing the mixture of asset supplies to be held by private wealth holders. In contrast with the monetarist model, the more general portfolio model developed in this chapter distinguishes between different types of monetary policies such as foreign exchange market intervention on the one hand, and domestic open market operations on the other. Volatility of exchange rate expectations becomes a potential source of exchange rate instability in the portfolio equilibrium model, even when the demand for and the supply of money are stable. This is yet another implication that distinguishes the portfolio equilibrium model from the monetarist model.

The emphasis on capital account transactions is appropriate in short-run analysis when potential shifts in asset positions are large relative to current account flows. Over a slightly longer time horizon, however, the cumulative effect of current account surpluses and deficits on the distribution of asset holdings, and therefore on the equilibrium value of the exchange rate must be recognized.

The second part of this chapter develops a stylized dynamic model that emphasizes the association between the current account and the exchange rate. The reason why there is a close relationship between the exchange rate and the current account is that a surplus (or deficit) in the current account implies a transfer of net wealth from foreign residents to domestic residents, ceteris paribus. As long as spending patterns and patterns of asset holdings differ, such wealth transfer cannot be effected without continuous changes in market clearing prices, including the exchange rate. This chapter abstracts from an important aspect of the process of current account adjustment, namely the effect of the wealth transfer on the equilibrium real exchange rate by assuming that the purchasing power parity holds.[23] Instead, the chapter focuses on the effect of wealth transfers on equilibrium asset prices, such as the nominal exchange rate and the interest rate. These effects arise—in the case of a small open economy facing an exogenous world interest rate—with a constant nominal money stock as long as domestic and foreign securities are not perfect substitutes in the portfolios of either domestic or foreign wealth holders. To emphasize this point the model assumes that foreign investors hold no domestic-currency-denominated assets, while domestic residents are risk averse and regard domestic- and foreign-currency-denominated securities as imperfect substitutes. In such case, a current account surplus, or deficit, continuously perturbs portfolio equilibrium thus requiring continuous exchange rate and interest rate adjustment.

This dynamic association between the current account and the exchange rate is only one aspect of exchange rate dynamics in the model. The other is the dynamics of expectations. To formalize the idea that the foreign exchange market is an informationally efficient speculative market the model assumes rational expectations. A number of comparative dynamic exercises further illustrate the differences between the monetarist and portfolio equilibrium approaches to exchange rate analysis, even in a model that assumes purchasing power parity: there is not simple one-to-one relationship between the nominal money stock and the nominal exchange rate.

The purchasing power parity assumption of the second part of the chapter needs, of course, to be abandoned in any empirical application of the portfolio equilibrium approach. Also, the sluggishness of price and output adjustment, in contrast with the high speed of adjustment in financial markets, is a feature that must be incorporated in any model that seeks to account for the behaviour of the flexible exchange rate system. Since the short-run model developed in the first part of the chapter does not make any of these restrictive assumptions, it can be a building block of more realistic models as well.

NOTES

1. This section draws on Kouri (1975). Other relevant references are Black (1973, 1977), Branson (1979), Dornbusch (1976a), Flood (1979), Henderson and Girton (1977), Kouri (1976, 1978), Kouri and de Macedo (1978), McKinnon (1978), Niehans (1977), Porter (1977), Tobin and de Macedo (1979), and Turnovsky (1977).

2. Frenkel (1976), Mussa (1976), Bilson (1979). Other papers developing and applying the monetarist model of exchange rate determination are contained in Frenkel and Johnson (1978). Dornbusch (1976a) extends the monetarist model by allowing for sluggish price adjustment in the goods market.

3. Porter (1977) extends the model to include equity claims on real capital. Dornbusch (1976b) develops a portfolio equilibrium model with money and real capital.

4. Tobin and de Macedo (1979) develop a model with money, bonds, foreign assets, and capital.

5. For a justification of this formulation see Kouri (1977) and Fama and Farber (1979).

6. For a recent application of this model of the foreign exchange market see Black (1979), and Bruno and Sussman (1979).

7. I am indebted to Kari Puumanen of the Bank of Finland for pointing out the relevance of this case for Finland, where firms have a large foreign debt and the government, acting as a financial intermediary in housing and industry, is a net creditor of the domestic private sector in domestic currency while being a debtor in foreign currency. Puumanen's unpublished work suggests the potential instability of the flexible rate regime in this environment.

8. Branson finds in his empirical work that the stock of foreign claims held by the German private sector became negative as a result of massive central bank intervention. For an early reference to this work see Branson, Halttunen and Masson (1978). On this issue see, too, Porter (1978). De Macedo encounters the same problem in his work on Portugal (de Macedo, 1979).

9. It is determined by the equation: $\theta(e, \bar{e}) = r - r^*$. Frankel (1979) extends this model to allow for secular inflation and currency depreciation. In that case it is the real rather than the nominal interest rate differential that is relevant in explaining short-run fluctuations in the exchange rate.

10. When we talk about the domestic interest rate, we refer to the short-term interest rate abstracting from the problem of the term structure of interest rates.

11. Branson (1979) and Henderson and Girton (1977) introduce wealth as an argument in the demand for money function. The wealth effect of exchange rate changes can go either way depending on whether domestic residents are debtors or creditors in foreign currency.

12. On this point see Henderson and Girton (1977).

13. In the monetarist model a disturbance of this type could not occur because domestic and foreign securities are perfect substitutes. A shift "out of domestic currency" must always mean a shift in the demand for money or in the *MM* schedule.

14. The advantages and disadvantages of these alternatives are evaluated in Fleming (1974).

15. Dornbusch (1976) in fact assumes that $h_e = 0$, implying that the interest rate is determined independently of the exchange rate and of exchange rate expectations in the short run.

16. Frenkel and Johnson (1978).

17. Recent work on fiscal policy by Christ, Solow and Blinder, Tobin and Buiter, Branson and others has emphasized the budget constraint of the government. For an up-to-date survey of this work see Christ (1979).

18. For a derivation of this consumption function from a model of optimum saving with variable time discount see Uzawa (1968).

19. See, for example, Dornbusch and Fischer (1979).

20. Because the price level has a trend, we work with the real value of government debt, B^g/P' in the dynamic analysis. The rate of change of this variable

is $\mu = \dot{P}/P$ or the difference between the secular rate of inflation and the actual rate of inflation.

21. The seminal contribution on the portfolio balance, or stationary state, approach is Mckinnon and Oates (1966). See also McKinnon (1969). There is an analogue to the short-run and long-run models of open economies in closed economy models of fiscal policy emphasizing the government budget constraint. For an up-to-date survey of this work see Christ (1979).

22. For a detailed derivation of the rational expectations solution and a discussion of problems with it, see Kouri (1976).

23. The relationship between the current account and the real exchange rate is investigated in Dornbusch and Fischer (1979), Calvo and Rodriguez (1977), and Kouri (1975, 1978).

REFERENCES

Barro, R. 1977. "Are Government Bonds Net Wealth." *Journal of Political Economy* (November/December).

Bilson, J. 1979. "The "Vicious Circle" Hypothesis." *IMF Staff Papers* 26, no. 1 (March).

Black, S. 1979. "The Analysis of Floating Exchange Rates and the Choice Between Crawl and Float." Unpublished manuscript.

———. 1977. *Floating Exchange Rates and National Economic Policy.* New Haven: Yale University Press.

———. 1973. *International Money Markets and Flexible Exchange Rates.* Princeton: Princeton Studies in International Finance.

Branson, W. 1979. "Exchange Rate Dynamics and Monetary Policy." In *Inflation and Employment in Open Economies*, edited by A. Lindbeck. North Holland Publishing Co.

Branson, W.; H. Halttunen; and P. Masson. 1978. "Exchange Rates in the Short Run: The Dollar/Deutschemark Rate," *European Economic Review.*

Bruno, M., and Z. Sussman. 1979. "Floating vs. Crawling: Israel 1977–79 in Hindsight." Unpublished manuscript.

Calvo, G. and C. Rodriguez. 1977. "A Model of Exchange Rate Determination under Currency Substitution and Rational Expectations," *Journal of Political Economy* 85. (June).

Christ, C. 1979. "On Fiscal and Monetary Policies and the Government Budget Restraint." *American Economic Review* (September).

De Macedo, J.B. 1979. "Portfolio Diversification and Currency Inconvertibility: Three Essays in International Monetary Economics." Ph.D. dissertation, Yale University.

Dornbusch, R. 1976a. "Expectations and Exchange Rate Dynamics." *Journal of Political Economy* 84, no. 6 (December).

———. 1976b. "Capital Mobility, Flexible Exchange Rates and Macroeconomic Equilibrium," In *Recent Issues in International Monetary Economics*, edited by E. Claassen and P. Salin. North Holland.

Dornbusch, R., and S. Fischer. 1979. "Exchange Rates and the Current Account." Unpublished.

Fama, E., and A. Farber. 1979. "Money, Bonds and Foreign Exchange." *American Economic Review* (September).

Fleming, J.M. 1974. "Dual Exchange Markets and Other Remedies for Disruptive Capital Flows." *IMF Staff Papers* 21, no. 1 (March): 1-17.

Flood, R. 1979. "An Example of Exchange Rate Overshooting." *Southern Journal of Economics* (July).

Frankel, J.A. 1979. "On the Mark: A Theory of Floating Exchange Rates Based on the Real Interest Rate Differential." *American Economic Review* (September).

Frenkel, J. 1976. "A Monetary Approach to the Exchange Rate: Doctrinal Aspects and Empirical Evidence." *Scandinavian Journal of Economics* 78, no. 2.

Frenkel, J. and H.G. Johnson (eds.), 1978. *The Economics of Exchange Rates: Selected Studies.* Reading, Mass.: Addison-Wesley.

Friedman, M. 1956. "The Case for Flexible Exchange Rates," in *Essays in Positive Economics.* University of Chicago Press.

Henderson, D. 1977. "Dynamic Effects of Exchange Market Intervention Policy: Two Extreme Views and A Synthesis." Unpublished manuscript.

Henderson, D., and L. Girton. 1977. "Central Bank Operations in Foreign and Domestic Assets Under Fixed and Flexible Exchange Rates." In *The Effects of Exchange Rate Adjustments*, edited by P.B. Clark, D.E. Logue, and R.J. Sweeney. Washington, D.C.: U.S. Government Printing Office.

Kouri, P. 1978. "A Dynamic Partial Equilibrium Model of the Foreign Exchange Market." *Cowles Foundation Discussion Paper*, 510.

———. 1977. "International Investment and Interest Rate Linkages Under Flexible Exchange Rates." In *The Political Economy of Monetary Reform*, edited by R.Z. Aliber. New York.

———. 1976. "The Exchange Rate and the Balance of Payments in the Short Run and In the Long Run: A Monetary Approach." *Scandinavian Journal of Economics* 78, no. 2.

———. 1975. "Essays on the Theory of Flexible Exchange Rates." Ph.D. dissertation, M.I.T.

Kouri, P., and J. de Macedo. 1978. "Exchange Rates and the International Adjustment Process." *Brookings Papers on Economic Activity.*

Kouri, P., and M.G. Porter. 1974. "Portfolio Equilibrium and International Capital Flows." *Journal of Political Economy* 82 (May-June).

McKinnon, R. 1969. "Portfolio Balance and International Adjustment," in R. Mundell and A. Swoboda (eds), *Monetary Problems of the International Economy*, Chicago: Chicago University Press, Chapter 4.

———. 1978. "Instability of Exchange Rates: A Qualified Monetary Interpretation." Unpublished manuscript.

McKinnon, R., and W.E. Oates. 1967. "Implications of International Economic Integration for Monetary, Fiscal, and Exchange Rate Policy, Princeton Studies in International Finance, No. 16, Princeton University, International Finance Section.

Metzler, L. 1951. "Wealth, Saving and the Rate of Interest." *Journal of Political Economy* (April).

Mussa, M. 1976. "The Exchange Rate, The Balance of Payments, and Monetary and Fiscal Policy under a Regime of Controlled Floating." *Scandinavian Journal of Economics* 78, no. 2 (May).

Niehans, I. 1977. "Exchange Rate Dynamics with Stock Flow Interaction." *Journal of Political Economy* (December).

Porter, M.G. 1977. "Exchange Rates and Portfolio Equilibrium." Unpublished manuscript.

Tobin, J. 1969. "A General Equilibrium Approach to Monetary Theory." *Journal of Money, Credit and Banking* 1 (February).

———. 1955. *"A Dynamic Aggregative Model."* Journal of Political Economy. (April).

Tobin, J.; and J. de Macedo. Forthcoming. "The Short-Run Macroeconomics of Floating Exchange Rates: An Exposition." In *Flexible Exchange Rates and the Balance of Payments: Essays in Memory of Egon Sohmen*, edited by J. Chipman and C.P. Kindleberger.

Turnovsky, S. 1977. *Macroeconomic Analysis and Stabilization Policy.* Cambridge: Cambridge University Press.

Uzawa, H. 1968. "Time Preference, the Consumption Function, and Optimum Asset Holdings." In *Value, Capital, and Growth. Papers in Honour of Sir John Hicks*, edited by J.N. Wolfe. Edinburgh: Edinburgh University Press; and Chicago: Aldine Publishing Co.

✳ *Chapter 7*

The Demand for International Reserves under Pegged and Flexible Exchange Rate Regimes and Aspects of the Economics of Managed Float*

Jacob A. Frenkel
University of Chicago and
National Bureau of Economic Research

INTRODUCTION

One of the striking features characterizing the international
monetary system since the early 1970s has been the continued use of international reserves even though, legally, the system
has been characterized as a flexible exchange rate regime. In this
chapter I analyze the interrelationship between the determinants
and patterns of reserve holdings and the international monetary
system. The opening section contains an empirical analysis of the
demand for international reserves. In this context I analyze the differences in behavioral patterns of developed and less-developed
countries. The next section deals with the empirical question of the
timing at which the system moved from pegged to floating rates. The
interest in this question stems from the belief that timing of changes
in economic behavior need not correspond to, or be associated with,

*Previous drafts of this chapter were presented at the conference on "The
Economics of Flexible Exchange Rates," Institute for Advanced Studies, Vienna,
Austria, March 29–31, 1978, and at the Carnegie-Rochester Conference held
at Carnegie-Mellon University, November 18-19, 1977. I am indebted to Craig
Hakkio for helpful comments, suggestions, and efficient research assistance. In
revising the chapter, I have benefited from useful comments by Russell Boyer,
Kenneth Clements, Robert Hodrick, Edi Karni, and David Laidler. The present
version draws on Frenkel (1978); it extends the discussion by including a framework for the analysis of managed float and by modifying the definitions of the
measures of variability and scale that are used in the empirical work, which is
extended to cover the period up to 1977. This version corrects some errors in
the data for LDCs and incorporates more recent revisions of the IMF data
base.

the timing of changes in legal commitments. One of the conclusions emerging from the analysis is that the extent of the change in economic behavior (as far as the holding of international reserves is concerned) has not been as large as one might have predicted. Countries have preferred to move to a system of managed floating that is intermediate between the extremes of fixed rates and clean float. The fourth section provides a sketch of an analytical framework for the analysis of a managed float regime, while some concluding remarks and suggested extensions are contained in the final section.

THE DETERMINANTS OF THE DEMAND FOR INTERNATIONAL RESERVES

Earlier studies of the demand for reserves considered the variability of international receipts and payments as an important argument in the demand function (e.g., Kenen and Yudin 1965; Clower and Lipsey 1968; Archibald and Richmond 1971). In addition, it has been suggested that the demand function also depends on the propensity to import (e.g., Heller 1966; Kelly 1970; Clark 1970; Flanders 1971; Frenkel 1974a, 1974b, 1978; Hipple 1974; Iyoha 1976). These and other studies have recently been surveyed by Grubel (1971), Williamson (1973), Claassen (1974), and Cohen (1975).

The choice of a variability measure as an argument in the demand function stems directly from the role of international reserves in serving as a buffer stock accommodating fluctuations in external transactions. Consequently, it has generally been expected that the demand for reserves is positively associated with the extent of these fluctuations.

The rationale for the use of the propensity to import as an argument is more involved and stems from an application of the Keynesian priceless model of the foreign trade multiplier. According to that model, an external disequilibrium that is induced by a decline in export earnings could be corrected by a decline in output proportional to the multiplier. The cost of output adjustment could be saved if the monetary authorities are able to run down their stock of international reserves, thereby enabling them to finance the external deficit. Since the foreign trade multiplier (and thus the required output dampening due to the fall in exports) is inversely related to the marginal propensity to import, the popular approach argues that the cost of not having reserves, and hence the demand for reserves, is inversely related to the marginal propensity to import. In the absence of data on the marginal propensity to import, earlier empirical studies have replaced it by the ratio of imports to income—

that is, by the average propensity (typically referred to as the degree of "openness" of the economy). The coefficient of the average propensity to import frequently appeared with the "wrong" (positive) sign when used to estimate the demand for reserves.

Using an adjustment mechanism that emphasizes the role of relative prices, price level, and demand for money, it was previously shown (Frenkel 1974a) that under certain assumptions, the demand for reserves was expected to be associated positively with the average propensity to import. This association was shown to be consistent with data for the period 1963–1967 for both developed and less-developed countries (Frenkel, 1974b). A simplified derivation of the association between reserve holdings and the propensity to import is presented in Appendix A to this chapter. It is shown that the relationship between these two variables is, in general, not clear cut, although under some assumptions this relationship is expected to be positive. In the following cross-sectional estimates of the demand for international reserves, I have included, in addition to the above-mentioned variables, a scaling variable as one of the determinants of the demand.[1]

Cross-Sectional Estimates of the Demand for International Reserves

The empirical analysis includes data from twenty-two developed countries and thirty-two less-developed countries (LDCs) and covers the period 1963–1977. Appendix B to this chapter contains the list of countries and the definitions of variables used in the analysis. The classification of countries as developed and less developed is based on that of the IMF. The choice of countries and the period of analysis were determined by the availability of continuous series of data.[2] As indicated above, the demand function was assumed to depend on three variables: (1) a measure of variability of international receipts and payments denoted by σ (the value of σ for each year was estimated by computing the standard deviation over the previous fifteen years of the trend-adjusted annual changes of the level of reserves);[3] (2) a scaling variable measuring the size of international transactions represented by the level of GNP, Y (in the few cases where this was not available, it was replaced by gross domestic products, GDP); and (3) the average propensity to import, $m = IM/Y$, where IM denotes imports.

The functional form of the demand function was assumed to be:

$$\ell n\, R = \alpha_0 + \alpha_1 \ell n\, \sigma + \alpha_2 \ell n\, Y + \alpha_3 \ell n\, m + u, \qquad (7.1)$$

where u denotes an error term.

Tables 7-1 and 7-2 present for each year the cross-sectional ordinary least squares estimates of the demand for reserves by developed and less-developed countries. In all cases, the coefficients have the expected positive sign, and in most cases these coefficients are statistically significant at the 95 percent confidence level.

In summary it should be noted that the overall fit of the regressions reported in Tables 7-1 and 7-2 (as measured by the coefficients of determination R^2) is very satisfactory.[4] This point is noteworthy since these results pertain to cross-sectional estimates.

Table 7-1. Estimates for Developed Countries, N = 22 (standard errors in parentheses).

Year	Constant	$\ln \sigma$	$\ln Y$	$\ln m$	R^2	s.e.
1963	4.141 (0.701)	0.618 (0.211)	0.441 (0.214)	0.781 (0.271)	0.90	0.436
1964	4.243 (0.809)	0.608 (0.255)	0.399 (0.259)	0.738 (0.276)	0.88	0.480
1965	4.464 (0.916)	0.507 (0.294)	0.546 (0.292)	0.867 (0.314)	0.85	0.538
1966	4.448 (0.914)	0.596 (0.288)	0.506 (0.286)	1.042 (0.329)	0.86	0.540
1967	4.291 (0.899)	0.650 (0.280)	0.495 (0.270)	1.096 (0.316)	0.86	0.556
1968	4.254 (1.114)	0.570 (0.324)	0.582 (0.280)	1.019 (0.341)	0.85	0.587
1969	4.282 (0.940)	0.510 (0.269)	0.483 (0.239)	0.735 (0.298)	0.84	0.551
1970	4.006 (0.817)	0.569 (0.249)	0.446 (0.225)	0.627 (0.292)	0.85	0.534
1971	4.378 (0.771)	0.352 (0.242)	0.661 (0.230)	0.405 (0.303)	0.86	0.539
1972	3.568 (0.620)	0.733 (0.219)	0.209 (0.212)	0.265 (0.237)	0.90	0.425
1973	3.915 (0.667)	0.675 (0.272)	0.291 (0.248)	0.533 (0.283)	0.88	0.475
1974	3.171 (0.796)	0.803 (0.325)	0.257 (0.319)	0.676 (0.334)	0.87	0.533
1975	3.366 (0.944)	0.668 (0.348)	0.510 (0.298)	1.012 (0.414)	0.85	0.606
1976	3.226 (0.946)	0.809 (0.352)	0.330 (0.301)	1.088 (0.374)	0.84	0.588
1977	3.126 (0.616)	0.851 (0.219)	0.435 (0.195)	1.422 (0.236)	0.93	0.410

Table 7-2. Estimates for Less-developed Countries, N = 32 (standard errors in parentheses).

Year	Constant	$\ln \sigma$	$\ln Y$	$\ln m$	R^2	s.e.
1963	5.864 (0.684)	0.297 (0.174)	0.946 (0.204)	1.598 (0.280)	0.84	0.523
1964	5.751 (0.723)	0.241 (0.190)	0.955 (0.219)	1.491 (0.287)	0.80	0.553
1965	5.596 (0.647)	0.188 (0.179)	0.937 (0.197)	1.223 (0.263)	0.79	0.539
1966	4.924 (0.724)	0.380 (0.201)	0.734 (0.220)	1.129 (0.321)	0.73	0.627
1967	4.228 (0.851)	0.586 (0.223)	0.666 (0.254)	1.110 (0.399)	0.70	0.753
1968	4.611 (0.749)	0.425 (0.193)	0.791 (0.219)	1.101 (0.334)	0.74	0.684
1969	4.610 (0.754)	0.297 (0.204)	0.909 (0.224)	0.947 (0.305)	0.77	0.655
1970	4.281 (0.801)	0.293 (0.222)	0.913 (0.248)	0.784 (0.321)	0.76	0.719
1971	4.877 (0.829)	0.240 (0.235)	0.997 (0.256)	1.071 (0.312)	0.77	0.684
1972	5.036 (0.713)	0.269 (0.203)	0.964 (0.213)	1.062 (0.248)	0.83	0.592
1973	3.782 (0.612)	0.549 (0.187)	0.641 (0.193)	0.599 (0.204)	0.86	0.537
1974	2.882 (0.772)	0.703 (0.257)	0.400 (0.263)	0.292 (0.264)	0.78	0.700
1975	3.328 (0.665)	0.603 (0.205)	0.467 (0.236)	0.538 (0.276)	0.75	0.737
1976	3.615 (0.754)	0.462 (0.224)	0.696 (0.249)	0.545 (0.288)	0.74	0.807
1977	3.368 (0.802)	0.569 (0.255)	0.572 (0.301)	0.503 (0.298)	0.76	0.759

Of special interest is the good fit of the cross-sectional regressions for the last few years reported in Tables 7-1 and 7-2. During the latter years of the sample period, the international monetary system moved toward a greater flexibility of exchange rates. This move was expected to result in different as well as in less stable estimates of the parameters of the demand for reserves. Since, as will be shown below, the cross-sectional estimates seem to have remained stable (at least during the periods 1963-1972 and 1973-1977), more efficient estimates may be obtained by pooling the time series with cross sections.

Pooled Time Series and Cross-Sections:
Pegged versus Floating Exchange Rates

In order to examine the effect of the move to a regime of flexible exchange rates, I have divided the sample into two periods—the pegged exchange rate period (1963-1972) and the flexible exchange rate period (1973-1977). In the next section, I provide a formal justification for this division.

To the extent that the coefficients of the cross-sectional equations remained stable within each of the periods 1963-1972 and 1973-1977, one may obtain more efficient estimates by pooling the time series with the cross-sections. Table 7-3 contains the ordinary least squares (OLS) estimates of the pooled regression for both periods. In all cases the coefficients are positive and significant at the 95 percent confidence level.

I turn now to a comparison of the regression coefficients between developed and less-developed countries during the two periods. The first method used for this comparison was the dummy variables method as outlined by Gujarti (1970). According to this method, each and every coefficient was allowed to differ between developed and less-developed countries by including dummy variables pertaining to data for developed countries. The estimated coefficients of the dummy variables are reported in Table 7-4, where it is seen that for the first period the coefficients of the constant term, of income, and of the average propensity to import are significantly lower for developed countries while the coefficient of the variability measure is higher. For the latter period, however, the behavior of the two groups with respect to international reserves is much more similar. These estimates reveal a larger degree of economies of scale in the demand for reserves (as measured by the income elasticity) in de-

Table 7-3. Estimates for Pooled Time Series and Cross Sections (standard errors in parentheses).

Year	Group	Constant	$\ln \sigma$	$\ln Y$	$\ln m$	R^2	s.e.
1963-1972	DCs NOB = 220	4.129 (0.247)	0.593 (0.076)	0.467 (0.072)	0.760 (0.089)	0.86	0.504
1963-1972	LDCs NOB = 320	4.907 (0.226)	0.323 (0.062)	0.865 (0.067)	1.103 (0.092)	0.76	0.623
1973-1977	DCs NOB = 110	3.469 (0.366)	0.708 (0.139)	0.379 (0.125)	0.826 (0.147)	0.84	0.549
1973-1977	LDCs NOB = 160	3.356 (0.310)	0.572 (0.097)	0.532 (0.106)	0.434 (0.113)	0.77	0.696

Table 7-4. Tests for Difference Between Developed and Less-developed Countries (standard errors in parentheses).

Year	Estimated Dummies for Developed Countries				F-statistic for Chow-test
	Constant	$\ell n\ \sigma$	$\ell n\ Y$	$\ell n\ m$	
1963–1972	−0.778	0.270	−0.398	−0.343	5.069
	(0.353)	(0.104)	(0.104)	(0.133)	
1973–1977	0.113	0.136	−0.153	0.392	2.564
	(0.514)	(0.185)	(0.176)	(0.201)	

Note: The estimated dummies measure the differential values of the constant and the slope coefficients for developed countries from the corresponding estimates for LDCs. The F-statistics for the Chow-test correspond to the null hypothesis that the regression coefficients are the same for developed and less-developed countries. The relevant degrees of freedom for the two periods are $F(4, 532)$ and $F(4, 262)$, respectively. The null hypothesis is rejected since the values of the F-statistics exceed the critical values at the 95-percent confidence levels.

veloped countries than in LDCs. It is also apparent that the demand for reserves by LDCs is less sensitive to the variability measure than the demand by developed countries. The differences in the income elasticities may reflect differences in the character of the financial systems. The financial system in developed countries is more sophisticated than its counterpart in LDCs, thus entailing larger possibilities for economies of scale in reserve management. In addition, developed countries have a larger access to world capital markets and greater facilities for swap agreements.[5] The higher sensitivity of developed countries to the variability measure may reflect larger reluctance to cope with unexpected shocks by imposing trade controls and restrictions.[6] These differences have diminished significantly with the move toward greater flexibility of exchange rates.

The dummy variables method focuses on comparisons between individual coefficients. The second method that was employed in the comparison between developed and less-developed countries was that of the Chow-test following the procedure described by Fisher (1970). The results of this test are also reported in Table 7–4, where the F-statistics correspond to the null hypothesis that the OLS regressions in Table 7–4 do not differ from each other. The null hypothesis is rejected, since the values of the F-statistics exceed the critical values at the 95 percent confidence level. Thus, the Chow-test also leads to the conclusion that developed and less-developed countries reveal different behavior concerning the holdings of international reserves. It should be noted, however, that for the second period the statistical significance of the difference between the groups is marginal. It is of interest to explore in greater detail the patterns of the move to the floating rates regime, as implied by the characteristics of reserve holdings.

WHEN DID THE SYSTEM MOVE FROM PEGGED TO FLOATING RATES?

The analysis in the previous sections made a distinction between the periods 1963-1972 and 1973-1977. The presumption was that the evolution of the international monetary system from pegged exchange rates to floating exchange rates might have resulted in a structural change in the demand for international reserves. In the present section, I examine formally the timing and extent of the structural change following the method proposed by Quandt (1958, 1960).[7]

Consider a situation in which a structural change occurred at year t^* within the period $1, \ldots, T$ and assume that the demand for reserves corresponding to the two regimes (before and after t^*) can be characterized by two distinct regression equations like (7.2) and (7.3):

$$y_{nt} = x'_{nt}\beta_1 + u_{1nt}, \qquad t \leqslant t^*, \qquad (7.2)$$

$$y_{nt} = x'_{nt}\beta_2 + u_{2nt}, \qquad t > t^*, \qquad (7.3)$$

where u_{1nt} and u_{2nt} are the error terms that are assumed to be distributed as $N(0, \sigma_1^2)$ and $N(0, \sigma_2^2)$, β_1 and β_2 are the vectors of the regression coefficients corresponding to the two regimes, and $n = 1, \ldots, N$ denotes the countries (for the developed countries $N = 22$ and for the LDCs $N = 32$). The analysis of the timing of the structural change amounts to searching for the value of t^*. Quandt's method of estimating t^* involves the following: first, a maximization of the likelihood function (7.4) conditional on t^*:

$$L(y \mid t^*) = \left(\frac{1}{2\pi}\right)^{NT/2} \sigma_1^{-Nt^*} \sigma_2^{-N(T-t^*)}$$

$$\exp \left\{ -\frac{1}{2\sigma_1^2} \sum_{t=1}^{t^*} \sum_{n=1}^{N} (y_{nt} - x'_{nt}\beta_1)^2 \right.$$

$$\left. -\frac{1}{2\sigma_2^2} \sum_{t=t^*+1}^{T} \sum_{n=1}^{N} (y_{nt} - x'_{nt}\beta_2)^2 \right\}, \qquad (7.4)$$

where N denotes the number of countries and T denotes the number of years; and second, determination of the breakpoint $t*$ as the value that yields the highest maximum likelihood $L(y|t*)$. The application of this procedure to determining the breakpoint in the demand for reserves yields 1973 and 1972 as the estimates for $t*$ for developed and less-developed countries, respectively.

Based on these results, 1972 is used as the estimate of the breakpoint for both the developed and the less-developed countries, implying that the two subperiods are 1963–1972 and 1973–1977. This choice is based on the fact that while, for LDCs, 1972 seems to be an unambiguous estimate for the date of the structural change, the case for developed countries is less clear-cut; it is therefore assumed that, by analogy with the LDCs, the breakpoint for developed countries also occurred in 1972 (even though it should be noted that the choice between 1972 and 1973 is somewhat arbitrary). The validity of this assumption can be tested by applying the likelihood ratio test to the null hypothesis that no switch took place between 1972 and 1973. The likelihood ratio statistic is

$$\phi = \hat{\sigma}_1^{N\hat{t}*} \hat{\sigma}_2^{N(T-\hat{t}*)} / \hat{\sigma}^{NT},$$

where $\hat{\sigma}^{NT}$ is the estimated standard deviation of the residuals from the single regression estimated over the entire period 1963–1977.

According to the null hypothesis, $-2 \ln \phi$ is distributed χ^2 (5). The null hypothesis is rejected for both groups of countries. For the LDCs the value of $-2 \ln \phi$ is 26.6, while the corresponding value for developed countries is 37.8, both exceeding 15.1—the critical value at the 99 percent confidence level.[8] The practical implication is that for the purpose of estimation, data from the period 1963–1972 should not be pooled with those from the period 1973–1977 and that the structural change occurred by the end of 1972.

In addition to the above tests, one may also use a Chow-test to test for the equality of the regression coefficients between the two periods.[9] The resulting values of the F-statistics relevant for testing the null hypothesis are 9.45 for developed countries and 6.12 for LDCs—well above the critical values at the 99 percent confidence level. Thus, the Chow-test as well leads to the rejection of the null hypothesis. The overall inference is that the system has changed by the end of 1972. It is this conclusion that provides the rationale for the pattern of the intertemporal pooling that is employed in Tables 7–3 and 7–4.[10] It should be noted that even though, as a statistical matter, the system underwent a structural change, the extent of the change has not been large enough to make obsolete parameter estimates that are based on the period 1963–1972. In fact, forecasting reserve holdings during the period 1973-1977, based on parameter estimates from 1963-1972, yields extremely good predictions (for details see Frenkel 1978).

The interpretation of the relative stability of the patterns of reserve holdings is quite obvious: during the pegged rate regime the rate was adjustable rather than fixed and during the so-called floating rate regime the rate has been managed rather than free. Economic behavior seems to be more stable than legal arrangements. Central banks have revealed that their choice is for neither of the extreme exchange rate systems; rather, they have preferred the intermediate system of managed floating. Since managing the float requires international reserves, it seems relevant to analyze the determinants of the degree to which countries will attempt to manage the float.

A SKETCH OF A FRAMEWORK FOR THE ANALYSIS OF MANAGED FLOAT[11]

Earlier discussions of the optimal exchange rate regime centered around comparisons between fixed and flexible exchange rate systems. More recent explorations—originating with Mundell's contributions in the early 1960s—have shifted to the determination of optimal currency areas within which exchange rates are fixed and between which exchange rates are flexible. The following analysis of the optimal managed float recognizes that the spectrum of possibilities is broader and that the rate of exchange between any pair of currencies need not be entirely fixed or flexible, but rather that it might be some optimal mix of the two extremes. In what follows, I will sketch a simple analytical framework that highlights some of the determinants of the optimal degree of exchange rate flexibility. The analysis will emphasize the role of the stochastic structure of the various shocks that affect the economy, and its purpose is to suggest an additional set of variables that might be incorporated into the specification of the demand for international reserves under a regime of managed float.

Consider a small economy that is subject to two types of repetitive and serially uncorrelated shocks. These shocks, which are specified below in a manner similar to that of Fischer (1977), are referred to as real and monetary shocks.

Denote the supply of output by Y_t and let

$$Y_t = ye^{\mu}; \mu \sim N(-\sigma_{\mu}^2/2, \sigma_{\mu}^2), \tag{7.5}$$

where μ is a stochastic shock (the "real" shock) with a constant variance σ_μ^2. The mean of the distribution of the real shock is chosen to be $-\sigma_\mu^2/2$ so as to assure that the expected value of output equals y (permanent income).

The second shock arises from the monetary sector. Let the demand for nominal cash balances L_t be

$$L_t = kP_tY_te^\epsilon; \epsilon \sim N(-\sigma_\epsilon^2/2, \sigma_\epsilon^2), \qquad (7.6)$$

where k denotes the desired money-income ratio, P denotes the domestic price level, and ϵ denotes the stochastic shock to the demand for money (the "monetary" shock).

The domestic price level is linked to the foreign price through the purchasing power parity relationship. Thus

$$P_t = S_tP_t^*, \qquad (7.7)$$

where P_t^* denotes the foreign price level and S_t denotes the exchange rate (the price of foreign currency in terms of domestic currency). To simplify the analysis, it is assumed that foreign prices are fixed, (and thus it will be denoted henceforth as P^*), that purchasing power parity holds deterministically, and that μ and ϵ are independent.[12]

Assume that the flow demand for money ΔM^d corresponds to a stock adjustment process such that

$$\Delta M^d = \alpha(L_t - \bar{M}_t), \qquad (7.8)$$

where $\bar{M}_t$ denotes the money stock at the beginning of the period.

Using equations (7.5) and (7.7) we may express the demand for money (equation [5.6]) as

$$L_t = kS_tP^*ye^{\mu+\epsilon}. \qquad (7.9)$$

When the exchange rate is flexible, it will adjust so as to eliminate any stock disequilibrium in the money market, thus ensuring that $L_t - \bar{M}_t = 0$. Using equation (7.9), it follows that when the exchange rate is flexible,

$$kS_tP^*ye^{\mu+\epsilon} - \bar{M}_t = 0. \qquad (7.10)$$

The equilibrium exchange rate can be written as

$$S_t = (\bar{M}_t/kP^*y)e^{-(\mu+\epsilon)}, \qquad (7.11)$$

and the percentage change thereof is

$$\ell n\ S_t - \ell n\ S_{t-1} = \ell n\ (\bar{M}_t/kS_{t-1}P^*y) - (\mu + \epsilon). \qquad (7.12)$$

The other extreme system is the fixed exchange rate system, for which

$$\ell n\ S_t - \ell n\ S_{t-1} = 0. \qquad (7.13)$$

Using equations (7.12) and (7.13), we may define an index γ such that $0 \leqslant \gamma \leqslant 1$:

$$\gamma = (\ell n\ S_t - \ell n\ S_{t-1})/[\ell n\ (\bar{M}_t/kS_{t-1}P^*y) - (\mu + \epsilon)]. \qquad (7.14)$$

The coefficient γ characterizes the whole spectrum of exchange rate regimes. When $\gamma = 0$, the system is that of a fixed exchange rate, and when $\gamma = 1$, the system is that of a freely flexible exchange rate. An intermediate value of γ indicates an intermediate degree of exchange rate flexibility. We will refer to the coefficient γ as the coefficient of managed float—that is, the intervention index. From the policy perspective, the basic question is to determine the optimal value of γ and thus to determine the optimal degree of exchange rate flexibility.

In principle, if shocks were identifiable, the optimal policy would be to allow the exchange rate to correct monetary disturbances but not real disturbances.[13] We will assume, however, that information is incomplete and that during a given period only the joint outcome of the shocks $\mu + \epsilon$ is known but not the separate values of μ and ϵ. It is this lack of complete information that necessitates a second best policy of managed float.[14]

Assume that the objective is to minimize the losses due to imperfect information and that the policymaker wishes to minimize the quadratic loss function H:

$$\text{Minimize } H = E[c_t - E(Y_t)]^2, \qquad (7.15)$$

where c_t denotes the rate of consumption that, from the budget constraint, equals the rate of income minus the real value of additions to real cash balances:

$$c_t = Y_t - \frac{\Delta M}{P_t}. \qquad (7.16)$$

The previous relationships imply that

$$[c_t - E(Y_t)] = y(e^\mu - 1) - \alpha k y [e^{\mu+\epsilon}$$
$$- (\bar{M}_t/kS_{t-1}P^*y)^{1-\gamma} e^{\gamma(\mu+\epsilon)}] , \qquad (7.17)$$

and using equation (7.17) in equation (7.15) yields the loss function, which is to be minimized with respect to the intervention index γ.

The above analysis has not specified the value of the money stock $\bar{M}_t$ at the beginning of the period. It is assumed, following Fischer (1977), that at the beginning of each period the monetary authority changes the money supply so as to compensate for past disturbances according to

$$\bar{M}_t = kS_{t-1}P^*y. \qquad (7.18)$$

Substituting equation (7.18) in equation (7.17) and minimizing the loss function with respect to γ yield the following implications concerning the choice of the optimal degree of exchange rate flexibility:

1. In general, the optimal value of γ will be within the range $(0, 1)$, so that the optimal exchange rate regime will correspond to neither of the extremes of a completely fixed or a completely flexible rate regime.
2. The intermediate solution is more likely the higher is αk—the propensity to save out of transitory income.
3. When the only shocks to the system are real ($\sigma_\epsilon = 0$), the optimal solution is that of fixed rates ($\gamma = 0$); and conversely, when the only source of shocks is monetary ($\sigma_\mu = 0$), the optimal solution is that of freely floating rates ($\gamma = 1$).
4. The higher the variance of the monetary shock, the larger will be the optimal value of γ, while the higher the variance of the real shock, the lower will be the optimal value of γ. That is, high variance of real shocks, ceteris paribus, tends to raise the desirability of greater fixity of exchange rates and, conversely, for high variance of monetary shocks.

Table 7-5 contains the results of illustrative computations of the optimal degree of the intervention index γ for alternative values of αk—the propensity to save out of transitory income—and for alternative assumptions concerning the magnitudes of the various shocks. These results illustrate the above propositions.

The analysis in this section provides a simple framework for determining the optimal degree of exchange rate flexibility. It highlights the unique role of the stochastic structure of the economy and suggests, therefore, that the magnitude of and the relationship between these variables are among the determinants of the demand for reserves and should be incorporated into the analysis of the de-

Table 7-5. Optimal Managed Float for Alternative Values of Real and Monetary Disturbances and Saving Propensities.

σ_ϵ / σ_μ	$\alpha k = 0.5$					$\alpha k = 1$				
	0.01	0.03	0.05	0.07	0.09	0.01	0.03	0.05	0.07	0.09
0.01	0	0.80	0.92	0.96	0.98	0.50	0.90	0.96	0.98	0.99
0.03	0	0.47	0.69	0.80	0.87	0.10	0.50	0.74	0.85	0.90
0.05	0	0	0	0.33	0.53	0.04	0.27	0.50	0.67	0.77
0.07	0	0	0	0	0.25	0.02	0.16	0.34	0.50	0.63
0.09	0	0	0	0	0	0.01	0.10	0.24	0.38	0.51

mand for international reserves under a regime of managed float.

As a general comment on the analysis in this section, it should be noted that monetary policy and foreign exchange intervention are treated as close substitutes. In fact, as a first approximation, these two policies are indistinguishable. It is believed that this feature of the model is much closer to reality than would be the other extreme, in which monetary policy and foreign exchange policies are viewed as two independent policy instruments.

The special role of the exchange rate should also be noted. In the above framework, the exchange rate (and thereby the price level) is determined by considerations of asset market equilibrium. This characteristic is in accord with the recent developments of the asset market approach to the analysis of exchange rates.[15] An important limitation of the model is the absence of an explicit incorporation of an integrated world capital market that would reflect itself in the capital account of the balance of payments.

Finally, it should be noted that the present specification of the nature of the shocks is somewhat biased in favor of government intervention since the shocks have been presumed to originate from the instability of the private sector rather than from the actions of government policies. Furthermore, the concept of the optimal managed float and, thereby, the derived demand for international reserves were developed as a policy prescription for the monetary authorities. This was motivated by realism and could be rationalized in terms of the assumption that the monetary authorities possess superior information concerning its own actions as well as concerning the official holdings of international reserves. In principle, however, much of the optimal mix could also be performed by the private sector.

CONCLUDING REMARKS

This chapter has presented an analysis of the role of international reserves under a regime of pegged exchange rates and under a regime of managed float as well as evidence on the stability of the demand for reserves during the periods 1963-1972 and 1973-1977. It was shown that the demand for reserves by developed countries differs from that of less-developed countries and that the system underwent a structural change by the end of 1972. In view of the drastic changes in the international monetary system, the extent of the structural change (in particular with reference to the behavior of developed countries) has not been as large as one might have expected.[16] This finding led to the observation that economic behavior seems to be more stable than legal arrangements. The evidence suggests that countries have continued to hold and use international reserves. Likewise, countries have chosen to manage their exchange rates rather than let them float freely. From the policy perspective, it follows that the problems concerning the provision of international reserves and the discussions concerning the role of the IMF in this context are as relevant at present as they were in the past.[17] The chapter concluded with a sketch of a stochastic framework for the analysis of the optimal degree of managed floating.

The analysis in this chapter would benefit from several extensions. First, it was assumed that, during the sample period, countries were "on" their long-run demand functions. An extension would allow for a distinction between short-run and long-run demand functions and would examine the determinants of the speed of adjustment along the lines of Clark (1970). Second, an examination of the residuals from the estimated equations reveals the existence of persistent negative residuals for some countries (e.g., the United Kingdom and New Zealand) and positive residuals for others (e.g., Switzerland). An extension would refine the grouping of countries by allowing for country-specific factors. In this connection it would be of interest to test the hypothesis that countries behave so as to trade off large stocks of reserves for high speeds of adjustment; some preliminary results in Bilson and Frenkel (1979) are consistent with this hypothesis.

Third, the specification of the demand for reserves was assumed to remain unchanged as between the two exchange rate regimes. In principle, however, the specification of the demand for reserves during a regime of managed float should be derived from the analysis of the determinants of countries' decisions concerning the degree of optimal foreign exchange intervention (i.e., the optimal managed float). In the preceding section it was shown that the optimal degree of managed float depends on the details of the stochastic structure of the various shocks that affect the economy. It suggests, therefore, that these stochastic characteristics should be incorporated into the specification of the demand for reserves under a regime of managed float.[18]

Finally, the analytical framework underlying the literature on the demand for international reserves needs to be tied up with the framework underlying the literature on the monetary approach to the balance of payments. The monetary approach to the balance of payments emphasizes the considerations of monetary equilibrium and highlights the fact that when the monetary authorities peg the rate of exchange, they lose control over the nominal monetary stock. In many of the simplified versions of the monetary approach to the balance of payments, credit policies are viewed as the exogenous variable that, along with the path of the demand for money, determines (as a residual) the path of international reserves.[19] In this framework, little attention has been paid to incorporating into the analysis the possibility that the monetary authorities may have preferences concerning the composition of their assets.[20] These preferences are emphasized in the analytical framework underlying the demand for international reserves. In that literature, however, little attention has been paid to the conditions of monetary equilibrium. A useful extension would combine these two strands of analysis. In such an extension, credit policies would not be viewed as exogenous, but rather, international reserves and domestic credit would be determined jointly so as to satisfy simultaneously equilibrium in the money market as well as equilibrium in the composition of central banks' assets.

APPENDIX A: RESERVE HOLDINGS AND THE AVERAGE PROPENSITY TO IMPORT

In this appendix I derive the relationship between long-run holdings of international reserves and the average propensity to import. It is shown that in contrast with the implications of the simple foreign trade multiplier, the relationship is not a clear-cut one. Furthermore, it is shown that according to a specific interpretation of the "small country assumption," there exists a positive long-run relationship between openness (the average propensity to import) and reserve holdings.

Consider the following simple two goods model of a fully employed economy. The economy produces and consumes the quantities $[X_1, X_2]$ and $[x_1, x_2]$ respectively, and exports the first commodity. Nominal income (Y) is:

$$Y = P_1 X_1 + P_2 X_2,$$
(7A.1)

where P_1 and P_2 are the money prices of the two goods. Denoting a percentage change in a variable by a circumflex (e.g., $\hat{X} = dX/X$) and using the fact that for small changes $P_1 dX_1 + P_2 dX_2 = 0$ (the envelope theorem), one may write the percentage change in nominal income as:

$$\hat{Y} = \theta_1 \hat{P}_1 + \theta_2 \hat{P}_2,$$
(7A.2)

where

$$\theta_1 = \frac{P_1 X_1}{Y}; \theta_2 = \frac{P_2 X_2}{Y}, \text{ and}$$

$$\theta_1 + \theta_2 = 1.$$

In equation (7A.2), θ_i denotes the relative share in production of good i ($i = 1, 2$). Let consumer price level (P) be a linear homogeneous function of the money prices of goods with constant elasticities that are equal to the relative shares of expenditures on these goods in total expenditures. Thus:

$$\hat{P} = \beta_1 \hat{P}_1 + \beta_2 \hat{P}_2,$$
(7A.3)

where

$$\beta_1 = \frac{P_1 x_1}{Y}; \beta_2 = \frac{P_2 x_2}{Y}, \text{ and}$$

$$\beta_1 + \beta_2 = 1.$$

In equation (7A.3), β_i denotes the average propensity to consume good i (i = 1, 2). The following analysis is confined to the long run when expenditures are equal to income.

The real value of income in terms of the consumer basket is y = Y/P:

$$y = \frac{P_1 X_1 + P_2 X_2}{P}. \qquad (7A.4)$$

Using equations (7A.2) and (7A.3) in equation (7A.4), the percentage change in real income is

$$\hat{y} = (\beta_2 - \theta_2)(\hat{P}_1 - \hat{P}_2). \qquad (7A.5)$$

Equation (7A.5) emphasizes the fact that a change in the terms of trade (P_1/P_2) raises real income if the relative share in production of the good whose relative price has risen exceeds its relative share in consumption. In particular, since the second commodity is the imported good, $\beta_2 > \theta_2$, and thus, when $\hat{P}_1 - \hat{P}_2 > 0$, real income rises. Using the above notations, the average propensity to import is ($\beta_2 - \theta_2$).

The stock demand for nominal cash balances (M^d) is assumed to depend on the price level and on real income. This demand function is homogeneous of degree one in all prices:

$$M^d = PL(y). \qquad (7A.6)$$

The long-run holdings of international reserves by the monetary authorities is assumed to be an increasing function of the central bank's assets. For simplicity, it is assumed that in the long run, the money supply is proportional to the stock of reserves, as it is when the money multiplier is fixed and when the operations of the monetary authorities are confined to pegging the exchange rate. By an appropriate choice of units, the proportionality factor is set to equal unity. It should be noted, however, that the following qualitative results do not depend on this simplification.

At equilibrium the existing stock of cash balances (reserves) equals the desired stock:

$$R = PL(y), \qquad (7A.7)$$

where R denotes the stock of reserves.

The percentage change of equation (7A.7) is

$$\hat{R} = \hat{P} + \eta\hat{y}; \eta = (\partial L/\partial y)y/L, \qquad (7A.8)$$

where η denotes the income elasticity of the demand for real cash balances. Using equations (7A.3) and (7A.5) in equation (7A.8) yields

$$\hat{R} = \beta_1\hat{P}_1 + \beta_2\hat{P}_2 + \eta(\beta_2 - \theta_2)(\hat{P}_1 - \hat{P}_2). \qquad (7A.9)$$

Equation (7A.9) expresses the proportional change in reserves as a function of the proportional change in prices. The first two terms describe the effects of the change in the price level due to changes in its components, and the third term describes the effects of the change in real income due to a change in relative prices.

As can be seen from equation (7A.9), for any given price level (so that the sum of the first two terms in equation [7A.9] vanishes), the effect of a given change in the terms of trade on reserve holdings increases with $(\beta_2 - \theta_2)$. On these grounds alone one may expect to find a positive relationship between reserves and the average propensity to import. In general, however, the price level will also change, and therefore, in addition to the value of the parameters, the relationship depends on whether the changes are due to variations in the price of exportables or in the price of importables. It is in this sense that the effect of openness on reserve holdings is not a clear-cut one. However, if we adopt some variant of the "small country assumption" and assume that the price of importables (P_2) is given by the rest of the world, then equation (7A.9) can be written as:

$$\hat{R}/\hat{P}_1 = 1 - \beta_2 + \eta(\beta_2 - \theta_2), \qquad (7A.10)$$

which describes the effects of a given change in price on the holdings of international reserves.[21]

The effects of the magnitude of the average propensity to import on reserve holdings can be ascertained by differentiating equation (7A.10) with respect to $(\beta_2 - \theta_2)$. An increase in the average propensity to import could result from either a decline in the production of importables and/or from an increase in the consumption of importables. Thus, from equation (7A.10):

$$\left. \frac{\partial(\hat{R}/\hat{P}_1)}{\partial(\beta_2 - \theta_2)} \right|_{\beta_2 \,=\, \text{constant}} = \eta \qquad (7A.11)$$

$$\left. \frac{\partial(\hat{R}/\hat{P}_1)}{\partial(\beta_2 - \theta_2)} \right|_{\theta_2 \,=\, \text{constant}} = \eta - 1 \qquad (7A.12)$$

Equation (7A.11) states that for given consumption conditions the induced changes in international reserves (due to a given change in export price) are positively related to the average propensity to import. The smaller the production of importables, the larger will be the resulting change and thus the holdings of reserves. Equation (7A.12) states that for given production conditions, the induced changes in international reserves are also positively related to the average propensity to import if the income elasticity of the demand for money does not fall short of unity.[22] Cross-sectional differences in the average propensity to import reflect differences in both production and consumption shares. Since empirical studies on the demand for money suggest that, in general, η does not fall short of unity, one can expect reserve holdings to depend positively on the average propensity to import. Further, if the main differences among countries are in production patterns rather than in consumption patterns (as in the Heckscher-Ohlin model of international trade), equation (7A.11) implies that the positive association between reserves and the average propensity to import will be maintained as long as the income elasticity of the demand for money is positive. It should, however, be emphasized that the above conclusions have been derived for a specific interpretation of the "small country assumption" and for a specific assumption concerning the nature and origin of disturbances. In general, the relationship between reserve holdings and the average propensity to import depends on the nature and origin of disturbances and is not clear cut. Furthermore, the formulation in this appendix assumes that under a pegged exchange rate system, the operation of the monetary authorities are confined to pegging the rate and thus yielding a "passive" path of reserves along the lines described by the monetary approach to the balance of payments. Consequently, the term used was "reserve holdings" rather than "demand for reserves." An extension would modify the assumption concerning the operations of the monetary authorities and would allow for credit policies that are aimed at achieving the desired stock of international reserves.

APPENDIX B: LIST OF COUNTRIES AND DEFINITIONS OF VARIABLES

List of Countries[23]

Developed Countries	*Less-developed Countries*	
United Kingdom	Argentina	Jamaica
Austria	Brazil	Israel
Belgium	Chile	Jordan
Denmark	Columbia	Egypt
France	Costa Rica	Burma
Germany	Dominican	Sri Lanka
Italy	Republic	China
Netherlands	Ecuador	India
Norway	El Salvador	Korea
Sweden	Guatemala	Malaysia
Switzerland	Honduras	Pakistan
Japan	Mexico	Philippines
Finland	Nicaragua	Thailand
Greece	Panama	Ghana
Iceland	Paraguay	Sudan
Ireland	Peru	Tunisia
Portugal	Venezuela	
Spain		
Turkey		
Australia		
New Zealand		
South Africa		

Definitions of Variables

All data sources are from the IFS May 1979 tape obtained from the International Monetary Fund.

R—International reserves are measured in end of period 10^6 U.S. dollars. Reserves are defined as the sum of gold, SDRs, foreign exchange, and reserve position at the Fund. When reserves are reported in local currency, they were converted to U.S. dollars using the end of period exchange rate.

IM—Imports are reported as cif in local currency units. These figures were then converted to U.S. dollars using the period average exchange rate. The figures used are measured in 10^9 U.S. dollars.

GNP—GNP and GDP are reported in local currency units. These figures were converted to U.S. dollars using the period average exchange rate. The figures are measured in 10^9 U.S. dollars.

m—The average propensity to import was defined as the ratio of imports to GNP. When the latter was unavailable, GDP was used instead.

σ—The variability measure. To calculate the value of σ_T^2 for year T for a given country, the following regression was first run:

$$R_t = \alpha + \beta_T t + u \text{ over } t = T - 15, \ldots, T - 1,$$

and then using the estimated trend $\hat{\beta}_T$, σ_T^2 was defined

$$\sigma_T^2 = \sum_{t=T-15}^{T-1} (R_t - R_{t-1} - \hat{\beta}_T)^2 / 14$$

(except for 1963 for which, due to lack of data, σ_T^2 is based on the previous fourteen observations). Thus, σ^2 is defined as the variance of the trend-adjusted changes in the stock of international reserves. A plot of the time series of reserves revealed that the assumption of a linear trend seems more appropriate than that of an exponential trend.

NOTES

1. An additional variable that in principle should have been included in the list of the determinants of reserve holdings is the opportunity cost of holding reserves. In practice, a large fraction of international reserves is held in the form of short-term interest-bearing assets, and thus, the opportunity cost is the difference between the alternative yield and the rate of return on reserves. Previous studies faced serious difficulties in estimating this cost. Clark (1970) decided to exclude this variable from his estimation. Heller (1966) assumed that the cost was the same for all countries (5 percent). Kenen and Yudin (1965) used income per capita as a proxy and found that it had the "wrong" sign and was not significant. Kelly (1970) used, in addition to per capita income, the value of foreign assets and liabilities as proxies, but found that in all cases the latter appeared with the "wrong" sign, while in some cases the former had the "wrong" sign. Courchene and Youssef (1967) used the long-term interest rate as a proxy

and found that in five out of nine cases its coefficient was not significantly negative. All these attempts taken together provided the rationale for not including this variable in the estimating equations. For an incorporation of the rate of interest into a stochastic framework, see Frenkel and Jovanovic (1979).

2. From the list of countries for which data were available, two countries—Canada and the United States—were excluded from the analysis. Canada was excluded since it had a flexible exchange rate system during most of the period for which the variability measure was calculated. Since the discussion focuses on the behavior of countries as demanders of reserves, the exclusion of the United States as the main supplier seems justified. This relates to one of the limitations of the present approach of estimating the demand for reserves by means of a single regression equation. To the best of my knowledge, the potential difficulty of an identification problem is shared by all previous empirical studies of the demand for reserves.

3. A limitation of this measure is that actual changes in reserves need not provide an exact measure of the disturbance, since countries may use other policies. Kenen and Yudin (1965) and Heller (1966), who have used similar measures, have assumed that its estimates are not materially affected by national policies.

4. The estimates for LDCs in this chapter differ from those in Frenkel (1978) due to revisions and some errors in the data used in the previous paper. The errors, however, affected mainly the values of the constant terms without altering any of the basic qualitative results.

5. The interpretation of the estimates of the income elasticities as measuring economies of scale should be taken only as suggestive since the variability measure is not free of units and might therefore pick up some of the effect of size.

6. For further elaboration of these and other interpretations see Frenkel (1974b).

7. For this and other methods of analyzing switching regressions see Goldfeld and Quandt (1976: chs. 1, 4).

8. It should be noted that the application of this method to the problem at hand is not without conceptual difficulties since it requires differentiating the likelihood function with respect to t^*. It should also be noted that the analysis assumes that the structural change has taken place at a given point in time. An alternative approach would allow for a gradual evolution and would estimate regression equations with variable coefficients. For references and discussion of the properties of the distribution of $-2 \ln \phi$ see Goldfeld and Quandt (1976: ch.1).

9. In implementing the Chow-test, one pretends that t^* was known a priori. Goldfeld and Quandt (1976: ch.1) provide reference to evidence that the Chow-test yields satisfactory results.

10. The above discussion associated the structural change with the change in the exchange rate regime; it could of course reflect other (not necessarily unrelated) phenomena that occurred in the early 1970s, such as the oil crisis and the commodity price boom.

11. I am indebted to Michael Bazdarich for research assistance and suggestions concerning the material in this section. The material in this section draws on Frenkel (1976b).

12. A more elaborate analysis would allow for disturbances that originate from the foreign sector and that are allowed to be correlated with domestic shocks. Another extension would allow for possible short-run deviations from purchasing power parity, in which case, in the short run, changes in the exchange rate induce changes in relative prices. For a rationale for managed float that is based on this phenomenon see Mussa (1976); for recent empirical evidence on the short-run relationship between exchange rates and relative prices see Dornbusch and Krugman (1977). In a recent analysis of the optimal foreign exchange intervention, Boyer (1976) extends and applies Poole's framework (1970) to the problem at hand. Boyer assumes that real income is fixed and that the objective function is to minimize variability of prices.

13. For an analysis of this proposition see Fischer (1977).

14. The assumption of the lack of complete information has been used by Gray (1976) to analyze partial wage indexation.

15. See for example Dornbusch (1976), Frenkel (1976a), Kouri (1976), Mussa (1976), Bilson (1978), and Frenkel and Johnson (1978).

16. For analyses of the effects of the move to floating exchange rates on the demand for and the optimal provision of international reserves see Grubel (1976), Makin (1974), and Williamson (1976). For evidence on reserve use during the two regimes see Suss (1976), and for a comparison of the estimated coefficients in the Canadian case see Saïdi and Barro (1977) and for further evidence on structural change see Heller and Kahn (1978).

17. On this issue see, however, Haberler (1976).

18. On the relationship between the stochastic structure of the economy and the estimated coefficients see Lucas (1976).

19. See for example the various studies in Frenkel and Johnson (1976).

20. For an exception that incorporates the monetary authorities' reaction function into the analytical framework of the monetary approach to the balance of payments see Ujiie (1978).

21. Clearly, this variant of the "small country assumption" does not imply that the terms of trade are fixed, since the price of exportables is determined endogenously.

22. It was previously shown (Frenkel, 1974a) that in this case the positive association between reserve holdings and the average propensity to import will be maintained as long as η exceeds some critical number that is smaller than unity. The difference arises from the simplification adopted in the present analysis: the present analysis takes the change in export prices as being the exogenous disturbance while the previous analysis allowed export prices to be endogenously determined while taking changes in foreign demand as the exogenous factor. In the latter case, the average propensity to import will also determine (via the Marshall-Lerner condition) the effect of a given change in foreign demand on the price of exportables.

23. Classification based on the International Monetary Fund.

REFERENCES

Archibald, G.C., and J. Richmond. 1971. "On the Theory of Foreign Exchange Reserve Requirements." *The Review of Economic Studies* 38 (April): 245-63.

Bilson, John F.O. 1978. "Rational Expectations and the Exchange Rates." In *The Economics of Exchange Rates: Selected Studies*, ed. J.A. Frenkel and H.G. Johnson. Reading, Mass.: Addison-Wesley Publishing Company.

Bilson, John F.O., and Jacob A. Frenkel. 1979. "International Reserves and the Dynamics of Adjustment." University of Chicago. Unpublished.

Boyer, Russell S. 1976. "Optimal Foreign Exchange Market Intervention." University of Western Ontario. Unpublished.

Claassen, Emil M. 1974. "The Optimizing Approach to the Demand for International Reserves." *Weltwirtschaftliches Archiv* 3: 353-98.

Clark, Peter B. 1970. "Demand for International Reserves: A Cross-Country Analysis." *Canadian Journal of Economics* 3 (November): 577-94.

Clower, Robert, and Richard Lipsey. 1968. "The Present State of International Liquidity Theory." *American Economic Review* 57 (May): 586-94.

Cohen, Benjamin J. 1975. "International Reserves and Liquidity: A Survey." In *International Trade and Finance*, ed. Peter B. Kenen, pp. 411-51. Cambridge: Cambridge University Press.

Courchene, Thomas J., and G.M. Youseff. 1967. "The Demand for International Reserves." *Journal of Political Economy* 75, 4, pt. I (August): 404-13.

Dornbusch, Rudiger. 1976. "The Theory of Flexible Exchange Rate Regimes and Macroeconomic Policy." *Scandinavian Journal of Economics* 78, 2 (May): 255-75.

Dornbusch, Rudiger, and Paul Krugman. 1976. "Flexible Exchange Rates in the Short Run." *Brookings Papers on Economic Activities* 3: 537-75.

Fischer, Stanley. 1977. "Stability and Exchange Rate Systems in a Monetarist Model of the Balance of Payments." In *The Politcal Economy of Monetary Reform*, ed. R.Z. Aliber, pp. 59-73. Cambridge: Cambridge University Press.

Fisher, Franklin M. 1970. "Tests of Equality between Sets of Coefficients in Two Linear Regressions: An Expository Note." *Econometrica* 38: 361-66.

Flanders, M. June. 1971. "The Demand for International Reserves." *Princeton Studies in International Finance* 27: 1-50.

Frenkel, Jacob A. 1978. "International Reserves: Pegged Exchange Rates and Managed Float." In *Economic Policies in Open Economies*, ed. K. Brunner and A.H. Meltzer. Vol. 9 of the Carnegie-Rochester Conference Series on Public Policy. Supplementary Series to the *Journal of Monetary Economics* (July).

——. 1976a. "A Monetary Approach to the Exchange Rate: Doctrinal Aspects and Empirical Evidence." *Scandinavian Journal of Economics* 78, 2 (May): 200-24.

——. 1976b. "Comments on Exchange Rate Flexibility and Currency Areas." Paper presented at a conference on Money and International Monetary Problems, Martinique. Forthcoming in the Proceedings, E. Claasen and P. Salin (eds.) Exchange Rate Regimes and Currency Areas, Zeitschrift der Wirtschafts-messenschaften, 1978-79.

————. 1974a. "Openness and the Demand for International Reserves." In *National Monetary Policies and the International Financial System*, ed. R.Z. Aliber, pp. 289-98. Chicago: University of Chicago Press.

————. 1974b "The Demand for International Reserves by Developed and Less-Developed Countries." *Economica* 41, no. 161 (February): 14-24.

Frenkel, Jacob A., and Harry G. Johnson, eds. 1978. *The Economics of Exchange Rates: Selected Studies*. Reading, Mass.: Addison-Wesley.

————. 1976. *The Monetary Approach to the Balance of Payments*. London: Allen and Unwin, and Toronto: University of Toronto Press.

Frenkel, Jacob A., and Boyan Jovanovic, 1979. "Optimal International Reserves: A Stochastic Framework," Center for Mathematical Studies in Business and Economics, University of Chicago, Report no. 7918.

Goldfeld, Stephen M., and Richard E. Quandt, eds. 1976. *Studies in Nonlinear Estimation*. Cambridge, Mass.: Ballinger.

Gray, JoAnna. 1976. "Wage Indexation: A Macroeconomic Approach." *Journal of Monetary Economics* 2, no. 2 (April): 231-46.

Grubel, Herbert G. 1976. "The Optimum Supply of International Reserves in a World of Managed Floating." Paper presented at the Marcus Fleming Memorial Conference on The New International Monetary System, Washington, D.C., November.

————. 1971. "The Demand for International Reserves: A Critical Review of the Literature." *Journal of Economic Literature* 9 (December): 1148-66.

Gujarti, Damodar. 1970. "The Use of Dummy Variables in Testing for Equality between Sets of Coefficients in Linear Regressions: A Generalization." *The American Statistician* (Decmeber): 18-22.

Haberler, Gottfried. 1976. "How Important is Control over International Reserves?" Paper presented at the Marcus Fleming Memorial Conference on The New International Monetary System, Washington, D.C., November.

Heller, Robert H. 1966. "Optimal International Reserves." *Economic Journal* 76 (June): 296-311.

Heller, H. Robert, and Mohsin S. Kahn, 1978. "The Demand for International Reserves Under Fixed and Floating Exchange Rates," IMF *Staff Papers* 25, no. 4 (December): 623-49.

Hipple, F. Steb. 1974. "The Disturbances Approach to the Demand for International Reserves." *Princeton Studies in International Finance* 35 (May).

Iyoha, Milton A. 1976. "Demand for International Reserves in Less Developed Countries: A Distributed Lag Specification." *The Review of Economics and Statistics* 58, no. 3 (August): 351-55.

Kelly, Michael G. 1970. "The Demand for International Reserves." *American Economic Review* 60 (September): 655-67.

Kenen, Peter B., and Elinor B. Yudin. 1965. "The Demand for International Reserves." *Review of Economics and Statistics* 47 (August): 242-50.

Kouri, Pentti J.K. 1976. "The Exchange Rate and the Balance of Payments in the Short Run and in the Long Run: A Monetary Approach." *Scandinavian Journal of Economics* 78, no. 2 (May): 280-304.

Lucus, Robert E., Jr. 1976. "Econometric Policy Evaluation; Critique." In *Phillips Curve and Labor Markets*, ed. K. Brunner and A.H. Meltzer. Vol. 1 of the Carnegie-Rochester Conference Series on Public Policy. Supplementary Series to the *Journal of Monetary Economics*.

Makin, John H. 1974. "Exchange Rate Flexibility and the Demand for International Reserves." *Weltwirtschaftliches Archiv* 110, no. 2: 229–43.

Mundell, Robert A. 1968. *International Economics*. New York: Macmillan.

Mussa, Michael. 1976. "The Exchange Rate, the Balance of Payments, and Monetary and Fiscal Policy under a Regime of Controlled Floating." *Scandinavian Journal of Economics* 78, no. 2 (May): 229–49.

Poole, William. 1970. "Optimal Choice of Monetary Policy Instruments in a Simple Stochastic Macro-Model." *Quarterly Journal of Economics* 84 (May): 197–216.

Quandt, Richard E. 1960. "Tests of the Hypothesis that a Linear Regression System Obeys Two Separate Regimes." *Journal of the American Statistical Association* 55 (June): 324–30.

———. 1958. "The Estimation of the Parameters of a Linear Regression System Obeying Two Separate Regimes." *Journal of the American Statistical Association* 53 (September): 873–80.

Saïdi, Nasser, and Robert J. Barro. 1977. "Unanticipated Money Growth and Unemployment in Canada." University of Rochester. Mimeo.

Suss, Esther C. 1976. "A Note on Reserve Use under Alternative Exchange Rate Regimes." *IMF Staff Papers* 23, no. 2 (July): 387–94.

Ujiie, Junichi. 1978. "A Stock Adjustment Approach to Monetary Policy and the Balance of Payments." In *The Economics of Exchange Rates: Selected Studies*, ed. J.A. Frenkel and H.G. Johnson. Reading, Mass.: Addison-Wesley.

Williamson, John. 1976. "Generalized Floating and the Reserve Needs of Developing Countries." In *The International Monetary System and Developing Nations*, ed. D.M. Leipziger, pp. 75–86. Washington, D.C.: Agency for International Development.

———. 1973. "International Liquidity: A Survey." *Economic Journal* 83 (September): 685–746.

Chapter 8

Exchange Rate–Price Causality in the Recent Floating Period

Masahiro Kawai*
The Johns Hopkins University

INTRODUCTION

Since the final collapse of official parities in the spring of 1973, exchange rates of the major industrial countries have fluctuated widely. Rates of change of 1 percent a day, 5 percent a week, or 25 percent a year have not been uncommon. These apparently erratic movements of the rates have created the grave concern of disorderly market behavior and increased uncertainty among foreign exchange traders and national monetary authorities. For economic units who have future claims and/or obligations fixed in foreign currencies, exchange uncertainty has increased. For individual monetary authorities, price stabilization policies can be nullified in the face of unexpected fluctuations in the exchange rates.

This chapter attempts to detect the direction of causality between unanticipated fluctuations in exchange rates and unanticipated movements in relative prices (WPI and CPI) of the big ten countries (Belgrium, Canada, France, Germany, Italy, Japan, the Netherlands, Switzerland, the United Kingdom and the United States) in the present system (or nonsystem?) of floating exchange rates, using monthly data for the period of January 1975–December 1978.

Exchange rates and prices have bidirectional causal effects. First,

*The author is thankful to Bela Balassa, Louis Maccini, and Tom O'Toole for their suggestions and comments on an earlier version of the chapter. He has also benefited from conversations with Carl Christ in clarifying several issues involved in the chapter. He is, however, solely responsible for remaining errors and deficiencies.

consider the case of domestic currency depreciation under the usual assumption that all internationally traded goods are invoiced in foreign currency. Then domestic currency prices of traded goods would increase more or less proportionately to the rate of depreciation during the currency contract period, because trade contracts negotiated prior to the depreciation should be executed without changing the terms (Magee 1973, 1974). Higher costs of imported inputs may be passed on to prices of final outputs and may gradually induce higher prices of domestic inputs due to input substitution on the part of firms. Higher prices of imported consumption goods may raise prices of competing domestic consumption goods due to consumption substitution on the part of households. Higher prices of exported goods may stimulate exports and reduce domestic supply, causing prices of their domestic substitutes to rise.

On the other hand, changes in prices also lead to exchange rate changes. Suppose domestic inflation is created by, say, an exogenous monetary expansion. Then demand will be shifted away from domestic toward foreign goods, and the balance of trade will tend to worsen. The resulting excess demand for foreign exchange would put downward pressure on the value of the domestic currency. Foreign exchange traders who regard Purchasing Power Parity as the "normal" or long-run exchange rate would revise their expectations about the future rates (Kawai 1979b) and reshuffle their portfolios of various currencies, causing exchange rate changes. Thus causal relationships between exchange rates and prices may not be a priori obvious, but we expect them to exist.

There are at least three underlying focal points that encourage the present study of exchange rate–price causality. The first point is related to the Purchasing Power Parity (PPP) doctrine.[1] Under the flexible exchange rate system, if unanticipated changes in exchange rates are well associated with unanticipated changes in prices in such a way that PPP always holds, then exchange rate fluctuations per se do not imply risk for the economic units concerned (Kawai, 1979a). Hence an examination of the PPP relationship is particularly important under the floating system. In a number of regression analyses of PPP, authors have put either exchange rates or prices as dependent variables without fully justifying the form of regression equations.[2] A correct causality detection would rationalize one form of the PPP regression equation against the other.

Second, there is an issue of "vicious circle" and "virtuous circle" hypotheses. It has been argued that for some countries, unanticipated exchange rate fluctuations have caused changes in costs, wages, and general prices that have induced further exchange rate changes. This issue is technically one of the dynamic instability of the economic system; a small perturbation in prices or exchange rates from the stable equilibrium path will force the system continuously away from equilibrium.[3] In order to empirically examine the validity of the view that the floating exchange rate system is a source of instability of prices and exchange rates, due to a pass-through from exchange rates to domestic prices and a feedback from prices to exchange rates, causality detection is necessary.

Third, the effects of exchange rate changes on prices are of great concern for countries whose currencies are pegged—mostly less-developed countries. The reluctance of these countries to devalue their currencies in the face of severe balance of payments difficulties has stemmed from their fear that exchange rate devaluations might cause or aggravate inflation of domestic prices. If causality from exchange rates to prices is strongly observed in our investigation, this fear can be well supported.

In this chapter, "causality" is defined in the sense of Granger (1969) as explained in the next section. Based on Granger's concept, Sims (1972) has developed a unique procedure of causality testing: regress one prewhitened variable on past, current, and future values of another prewhitened variable as a two-sided distributed lag model, and test whether or not the coefficients of future values are significant as a whole.[4] Pierce (1977) and Pierce and Haugh (1977) have suggested a simpler technique along the line of Sims: cross-correlate the prewhitened variables, and examine whether or not the sample autocorrelation functions are significantly different from zero as a whole. Recently Hsiao (1978a; 1978b) has employed an alternative approach to causality detection: regress a stationary variable, say Y, on its own past values and on current and past values of another stationary variable, say X, and test whether or not the existence of X in the regression equation would improve the prediction of Y.

All of these past studies have conducted causality analysis within a two variable system, assuming that there is no third variable that affects the two variables to be investigated. However, if a third variable, say Z, affects X more quickly than Y, then X might spuriously appear to cause Y even though X and Y are in fact causally unrelated. In this case the two variable model would be seriously misleading. Although Sims has noticed this problem, his procedure or Pierce's cross-correlation technique does not seem capable of handling a three variable model. Hsiao has not considered a three variable system, but his approach can be readily extended to a more general n variable system. Hence, this chapter adopts and extends Hsiao's technique to detect exchange rate–price causality in a three variable framework.

The chapter has several important contributions. First, in detecting causality-feedback relationships, effective or trade-weighted exchange rates and relative prices (WPI and CPI) will be constructed. An advantage of using the concept of effective rates and effective relative prices is that there need not be any standard country and that the relative importance of one country to the other in a multilateral world can be efficiently captured by one index. Second, a linear filter is endogenously determined to stationarize the variables, which is required in causality analysis, and to eliminate the possible contemporaneous correlations among the prefiltered variables. This procedure enables us to focus on what is called "proper causality"—namely, the case where causal effects take at least one month to manifest themselves (Williams, Goodhart, and Gowland 1976). Third, autoregressive processes are specified in formulating the causal structure and the minimum final prediction error criterion suggested by Akaike (1969; 1970) is adopted in choosing the best autoregressive specification. Fourth, in order to avoid spurious causality relationships, a third variable, effective or trade-weighted relative money supply (narrowly defined), is introduced, and the three variable model is compared with the simpler two variable framework.

CAUSALITY AND FEEDBACK

Our first task is to define the concepts of "causality" and "feedback" both in formal and in operational or empirically testable ways. Let X, Y, and Z be stationary stochastic processes. Define $\bar{X}$, $\bar{Y}$, and $\bar{Z}$, as the sets of past values of X, Y, and Z, respectively. Let $\sigma^2(X|U)$ be the variance of the error series of the optimum, unbiased, least squares predictor of X using the set of information values U that may contain X, Y, Z, and their past values. Granger (1969) provides general definitions of "causality" and "feedback" in a two variable case that can be rephrased as:

Definition 1 (causality in the absence of the third variable): If $\sigma^2(Y|\bar{X},\bar{Y}) < \sigma^2(Y|\bar{Y})$, X is defined to cause Y. That is, if we are better able to predict Y by using the past values of X and Y than by using the past values of Y only, then we say that X causes Y. Causation from Y to X is similarly defined.

Definition 2 (feedback in the absence of the third variable): If

$\sigma^2(Y|\bar{X}, \bar{Y}) < \sigma^2(Y|\bar{Y})$ and $\sigma^2(X|\bar{X},\bar{Y}) < \sigma^2(X|\bar{X})$, feedback is said to occur.

Granger also defines "instantaneous causality" as the situation in which a given variable is better explained by including the current value of another variable than by excluding it. This chapter, however, does not consider "instantaneous causality" or "instantaneous feedback"; the causal effect is assumed to take at least one time period to manifest itself. As will be shown later, the variables generated will exclude the possibility of contemporaneous correlations among one another, which makes it possible for us to test "noninstantaneous causality" and "noninstantaneous feedback" relationships only.

In practice it is not usually possible to use completely optimum predictors. Therefore, we use only linear predictors, and the above definitions will be maintained throughout under the assumption of linearity. Let X_t and Y_t be two stationary time series. Consider the simple causal structure:

$$X_t = \sum_{j=1}^{m} \alpha_j X_{t-j} + \sum_{j=1}^{n} \beta_j Y_{t-j} + \gamma + u_{1t}, \qquad (8.1)$$

$$Y_t = \sum_{j=1}^{q} \theta_j X_{t-j} + \sum_{j=1}^{r} \lambda_j Y_{t-j} + \delta + u_{2t}, \qquad (8.2)$$

where γ and δ are constants and u_{1t} and u_{2t} are white noise disturbances. The definition of causality given above implies that Y causes X if X_t is better predicted by including Y_{t-j}s on the right-hand side of equation (8.1), that X causes Y if Y_t is better predicted by including X_{t-j}s in equation (8.2), and that a feedback relationship exists if both of these events occur. Granger (1969) shows that these operational definitions of causality and feedback are identical to the formal definitions introduced above.

In the case of three variables, one can speak of causality and feedback between X and Y conditionally on the presence of a third variable Z. Based on Granger's spectral analysis of the three variable case, the following formal definitions can be derived:

Definition 3 (causality in the presence of the third variable): If $\sigma^2(Y|\bar{X},\bar{Y},\bar{Z}) < \sigma^2(Y|\bar{Y},\bar{Z})$, then we say that X causes Y conditional on the presence of Z. Causation from Y to X conditional on Z is similarly defined.

Definition 4 (feedback in the presence of the third variable): If $\sigma^2(Y|\bar{X},\bar{Y},\bar{Z}) < \sigma^2(Y|\bar{Y},\bar{Z})$ and $\sigma^2(X|\bar{X},\bar{Y},\bar{Z}) < \sigma^2(X|\bar{X},\bar{Z})$, then feedback is said to exist conditionally on the presence of Z.

In practice, we specify our causal structure as:

$$X_t = \sum_{j=1}^{m} \alpha_j X_{t-j} + \sum_{j=1}^{n} \beta_j Y_{t-j} + \sum_{j=1}^{\ell} \epsilon_j Z_{t-j} + \gamma + u_{1t}, \quad (8.3)$$

$$Y_t = \sum_{j=1}^{q} \theta_j X_{t-j} + \sum_{j=1}^{r} \lambda_j Y_{t-j} + \sum_{j=1}^{s} \pi_j Z_{t-j} + \delta + u_{2t}, \quad (8.4)$$

$$Z_t = \sum_{j=1}^{a} \eta_j X_{t-j} + \sum_{j=1}^{b} \psi_j Y_{t-j} + \sum_{j=1}^{c} \omega_j Z_{t-j} + \zeta + u_{3t}, \quad (8.5)$$

where X, Y, and Z are stationary time series, γ, δ, and ζ are constants, and u_{1t}, u_{2t}, and u_{3t} are white noise. The above definition of causality conditional on the presence of the third variable implies that Y causes X if X_t is better predicted by including Y_{t-j}s on the right-hand side of equation (8.3) than by excluding them and that X causes Y if Y_t is better predicted by including X_{t-j}s in equation (8.4). Since the chapter's main concern is to focus on the exchange rate–price causality relationship rather than the whole structure of causal relationships among the three variables, equation (8.5) will not be analyzed.[5]

THE CHOICE OF LINEAR FILTERS

An examination of causality-feedback relationships requires stationary series of exchange rates, relative prices, and relative money supplies. In many economic time series, departures from stationarity occur because of the lack of central tendency toward mean values. If a time series is assumed to be "homogeneous nonstationary"— that is, if it moves freely without affinity for a particular location, but its behavior at different periods in time is essentially the same— then stationarity can be achieved by successive changes or differences. Therefore if we can find any linear operator $\phi(L)$, where L is the lag operator ($L^i X_t = X_{t-i}$), that transforms a given time series X_t into a stationary process $\phi(L) \cdot X_t$, then we can use the latter for our empirical examination.

In the money-income causality literature, many authors have used a linear operator, $\phi(L) = (1 - 0.75L)^2$, originally suggested by Sims (1972), without providing sufficient rationale for applying this specific form of an operator. In a second type of causality analysis, authors have tried a linear operator $\phi(L) = (1 - \phi_1 L)(1 - \phi_2 L) \cdots (1 - \phi_k L)$ by varying each of the values $\phi_1, \phi_2, \cdots, \phi_k$ between 0.1 and 0.9 for a fixed k and choosing that combination of $\phi_1, \phi_2, \cdots, \phi_k$ that yields the best prediction of the variable with serially uncorrelated residuals. Another group of authors has taken a different procedure to stationarize a variable. They run Sims' two-sided distributed lag regression equation by including a time variable as one of the explanatory variables in the right-hand side of the equation with the hope that the time variable removes the secular time trend existing in the variable and thus achieves stationarity.

This chapter attempts to endogenously obtain such a linear operator $\phi(L) = (1 - \phi_1 L - \phi_2 L^2)(1 - L)^d$, where d is the number of differences to be determined, that transforms exchange rates, relative prices, and relative money supplies into stationary time series.[6] If $(1 - \phi_1 L - \phi_2 L^2)(1 - L)^d X_t$ is serially uncorrelated (white noise), then the operator $(1 - \phi_1 L - \phi_2 L^2)(1 - L)^d$ should be considered as a good transfer function since white noise is a typical stationary process. Unlike Sims' or Pierce's procedure, however, the filtered series does not have to be white noise for our investigation.

In order to estimate ϕ_1 and ϕ_2, the following regression is run for each country.

$$(1 - L)^d \, \ell n SI_t^e = \phi_1 (1 - L)^d \, \ell n SI_{t-1}^e \qquad (8.6)$$
$$+ \phi_2 (1 - L)^d \, \ell n SI_{t-2}^e + v_{1t},$$
$$(1 - L)^d \, \ell n RWPI_t^e = \phi_1 (1 - L)^d \, \ell n RWPI_{t-1}^e$$
$$+ \phi_2 (1 - L)^d \, \ell n RWPI_{t-2}^e + v_{2t},$$
$$(1 - L)^d \, \ell n RCPI_t^e = \phi_1 (1 - L)^d \, \ell n RCPI_{t-1}^e$$
$$+ \phi_2 (1 - L)^d \, \ell n RCPI_{t-2}^e + v_{3t},$$
$$(1 - L)^d \, \ell n RMI_t^e = \phi_1 (1 - L)^d \, \ell n RMI_{t-1}^e$$
$$+ \phi_2 (1 - L)^d \, \ell n RMI_{t-2}^e + v_{4t},$$

where $\ell n SI_t^e$, $\ell n RWPI_t^e$, $\ell n RCPI_t^e$, and $\ell n RMI_t^e$ are the natural logarithms of the effective indexes of spot exchange rates, relative WPIs, relative CPIs, and relative money supplies narrowly defined, respectively,[7] and v_{1t}, v_{2t}, v_{3t}, and v_{4t} are the disturbance terms that are possibly related to one another. Note that the regression coefficients ϕ_1 and ϕ_2 are constrained to be the same for four equations so that the same filter can be obtained for each variable in the same country. The seemingly unrelated estimation technique is applied to system (8.6) for each country by varying the value of d between 0 and 4.

The estimation results, which are not reported here but are available from the author upon request, show that both $\hat{\phi}_1$ and $\hat{\phi}_2$ are highly statistically significant for all countries. The Box-Pierce Q-statistics[8] calculated from the estimated residuals indicate that the hypothesis of serial independence of the final residuals has to be rejected. The order of differences to achieve stationarity is 2 or 3, and it can be shown that no statistically significant time trend exists in $(1 - \hat{\phi}_1 L - \hat{\phi}_2 L^2)(1 - L)^d X_t$.

The seemingly unrelated regression technique transforms the variance-covariance matrix of the residuals into an identity matrix multiplied by a constant scalar, which implies that, for example, $(1 - \hat{\phi}_1 L - \hat{\phi}_2 L^2)(1 - L)^d$ ℓnSI_t^e and $(1 - \hat{\phi}_1 L - \hat{\phi}_2 L^2)(1 - L)^d$ $\ell nRWPI_t^e$ are approximately contemporaneously uncorrelated. This rationalizes our approach of concentrating on "proper" or "non-instantaneous" causality and feedback only.

SYSTEM ESTIMATION PROCEDURE

Define a set of new variables, S_t, W_t, C_t, and M_t, as the filtered variables of the natural logarithms of the effective or trade-weighted indexes for spot exchange rates (ℓnSI_t^e), relative wholesale prices ($\ell nRWPI_t^e$), relative consumer prices ($\ell nRCPI_t^e$), and relative money supplies ($\ell nRMI_t^e$), respectively. For example, $S_t \equiv (1 - \hat{\phi}_1 L - \hat{\phi}_2 L^2)(1 - L)^d \ell nSI_t^e$ where $\hat{\phi}_1$ and $\hat{\phi}_2$ are the estimated coefficients in regression (8.6) and d is the order of differences. Let P_t represent either W_t or C_t.

Our first purpose is to detect the causality between exchange rates and prices within a two variable framework. For this purpose, we have to estimate the following equations:

$$S_t = \sum_{j=1}^{m} \alpha_j S_{t-j} + \sum_{j=1}^{n} \beta_j P_{t-j} + \gamma + u_{1t}, \quad P_t = W_t \text{ or } C_t, \quad (8.7)$$

$$P_t = \sum_{j=1}^{n} \lambda_j P_{t-j} + \sum_{j=1}^{q} \theta_j S_{t-j} + \delta + u_{2t}, \quad P_t = W_t \text{ or } C_t, \quad (8.8)$$

and to test whether P_{t-j}s and S_{t-j}s should be included in equations (8.7) and (8.8), respectively. The usual ordinary least squares (OLS) estimation can be applied to each equation. An obvious difficulty of this specification is to determine the optimum numbers of lags, m, n, r, and q, in the right-hand side of the equations.

In determining optimum orders of lags, this chapter adopts the minimum final prediction error (FPE) criterion proposed by Akaike (1969; 1970) and applied in the study of money-income causality detection by Hsiao (1978a; 1978b). The FPE of a predictor is nothing but the mean squared prediction error. For example, in the case of equation (8.7),

$$FPE = E[S_t - \hat{S}_t]^2 = \frac{T + m + n + 1}{T - m - n - 1} \cdot \frac{SSR}{T},$$

where $\hat{S}_t$ is the predicted value of S_t given the estimated coefficients $\hat{\alpha}_j$, $\hat{\beta}_j$, and $\hat{\gamma}$; T is the total number of observations; and the SSR is the sum of squared residuals of OLS regression (8.7). Akaike's criterion suggests that we pick the regression equation that yields the minimum mean squared error or final prediction error. This minimum FPE criterion is obviously different from that of the minimum standard error of the regression, which is $\sqrt{SSR/(T - m - n - 1)}$ and sometimes is adopted in the literature.[9]

The minimum FPE of $\hat{S}_t$ in equation (8.7) can be obtained by varying m between 0 and N and n between 1 and N. We arbitrarily choose N to be 20. Then there would be $N(N + 1)$ combinations of m and n so that $N(N + 1)$ regressions would have to be run and $N(N + 1)$ FPEs would have to be compared in order to identify an optimum lag structure of each of the equations. Instead, we take the following two step procedure suggested by Hsiao (1978a; 1978b) for computational efficiency.

Consider equation (8.7). First, we regard S_t as a single autoregressive process; regress S_t on its own past values and a constant only; compute its $N + 1$ FPEs; and choose the optimum order, $\hat{m}$, which yields the minimum FPE. Denote this final prediction error by $FPE(S)$:

$$FPE(S) = \frac{T + \hat{m} + 1}{T - \hat{m} - 1} \cdot \frac{SSR(\hat{m}, 0)}{T},$$

where the $SSR(\hat{m},0)$ is the sum of squared residuals of regression equation (8.7) where m and β_j are constrained to be $\hat{m}$ and zero, respectively. Second, we regard S_t as a two variable autoregressive process; regress S_t on its own past values whose order of lags is fixed at $\hat{m}$, the past values of P_t and a constant; compute N FPEs by varying the order of lags of P_{t-j} between 1 and N; and choose the optimum order of P_{t-j}s, $\hat{n}$, which yields the smallest FPE among the N. Define this final prediction error as $FPE(S,P)$:

$$FPE(S,P) = \frac{T + \hat{m} + \hat{n} + 1}{T - \hat{m} - \hat{n} - 1} \; \frac{SSR(\hat{m},\hat{n})}{T},$$

where the $SSR(\hat{m},\hat{n})$ is the sum of squared residuals of equation (8.7) when the orders of lags of S_{t-j} and P_{t-j} are $\hat{m}$ and $\hat{n}$, respectively.

A simple test suggested by Hsiao (1978a; 1978b) is to see whether $FPE(S,P)$ is greater or less than $FPE(S)$. If $FPE(S) > FPE(S,P)$, then P is said to cause S. Another standard test would be to test $H_0: \beta_j = 0$ $(j = 1, 2, \ldots, \hat{n})$ for the best equation to be chosen. An F-statistic would be the relevant test statistic in this case.[10] A similar procedure would be applied to equation (8.8).

The above tests are based on the assumption that there is no other variable that causes exchange rates and/or prices. Suppose the underlying true economic structure indicates that two variables, X and Y, have no causal relationship and are independent, but that a third variable, say Z, causes both X and Y; then X (or Y) might spuriously appear to cause Y (or X) even though this is not the case (Sims 1972). Hence it is of great interest to examine how the causal structure of exchange rates and prices in a two variable system is affected by introducing a third variable.

This chapter chooses effective or trade-weighted relative money supply (narrowly defined) as the third variable to be considered. This choice is consistent with the recent approach to exchange rate determination, which focuses on the importance of relative asset supplies (in particular money supplies) as a critical determinant of exchange rates.[11]

In order to detect the causality between exchange rates and prices in a three variable framework, we have to estimate the following system of equations:

$$S_t = \sum_{j=1}^{m} \alpha_j S_{t-j} + \sum_{j=1}^{\ell} \epsilon_j M_{t-j} + \sum_{j=1}^{n} \beta_j P_{t-j}$$

$$+ \gamma + u_{1t}, \qquad P_t = W_t \text{ or } C_t, \tag{8.9}$$

$$P_t = \sum_{j=1}^{r} \lambda_j P_{t-j} + \sum_{j=1}^{s} \pi_j M_{t-j} + \sum_{j=1}^{q} \theta_j S_{t-j}$$

$$+ \delta + u_{2t}, \qquad P_t = W_t \text{ or } C_t. \tag{8.10}$$

In identifying the best specifications of equations (8.9) and (8.10) —best in the sense of Akaike's minimum final prediction error criterion—the following three step procedure is adopted. Consider regression equation (8.9). First, S is regressed on the past values of S and M separately, and six best orders of lags are chosen, according to the minimum FPE criterion, for each of the regressions by varying the lag between 0 and 20. Second, S is regressed on the past values of S and M together for thirty-six different combinations of the lag structure based on the first step, and the best equation is selected among these thirty-six specifications. Call those optimum lags for S and M $\hat{m}$ and $\hat{\ell}$, respectively, and express the minimized final prediction error as $FPE(S,M)$. Then the third step is, for given $\hat{m}$ and $\hat{\ell}$, to regress S on the past values of S, M, and P together, by varying the order of lags of P between 1 and 20, and to select the best equation. Express the final prediction error in the last step as $FPE(S,M,P)$, which is defined as:

$$FPE(S,M,P) = \frac{T + \hat{m} + \hat{\ell} + \hat{n} + 1}{T - \hat{m} - \hat{\ell} - \hat{n} - 1} \frac{SSR(\hat{m},\hat{\ell},\hat{n})}{T},$$

where the $SSR(\hat{m},\hat{\ell},\hat{n})$ is the sum of squared residuals for regression equation (8.9) with the orders of lags m, ℓ, and n constrained to be $\hat{m}$, $\hat{\ell}$, and $\hat{n}$, respectively. The $FPE(S,M)$ is defined as:

$$FPE(S,M) = \frac{T + \hat{m} + \hat{\ell} + 1}{T - \hat{m} - \hat{\ell} - 1} \frac{SSR(\hat{m},\hat{\ell}, 0)}{T},$$

where the $SSR(\hat{m},\hat{\ell}, 0)$ is obtained for OLS regressions (8.9) by constraining all the β_js to be zero and m and ℓ to be $\hat{m}$ and $\hat{\ell}$, respectively.

A simple test of causality is to compare $FPE(S,M)$ with $FPE(S,M,P)$. If $FPE(S,M) > FPE(S,M,P)$, then P is said to cause S conditionally on the presence of M. Another standard test is an F-test under the null hypothesis $H_0 : \beta_j = 0$ ($j = 1, 2, \ldots, \hat{n}$) for the best equation chosen in the last step above.

Identification of equation (8.10) and causality testing from exchange rates to prices in the presence of money follow a similar procedure.

This three step procedure would greatly contribute to computational efficiency in the sense that only 56 (= 6 × 6 + 20) regressions will have to be run as opposed to 8,400 (= 21 × 20 × 20) possible regressions. Since the object of the present chapter is not to analyze the whole structure of causal relationships, the tests of whether money causes exchange rates or prices and of whether exchange rates or prices cause money are not developed.

A final additional remark would be useful on our estimation procedure. Strictly speaking, our method of contructing effective exchange rates and relative prices implies that S_t and P_t can be each related across different countries. An unanticipated increase in one country's effective exchange rates must mean an unanticipated decline in another country's effective exchange rates, and the same should be true for effective relative prices. Hence, the correct estimation technique would require us to take account of correlations of disturbances for S_t and P_t across ten countries. However, this aspect will be neglected in our estimation, and only the ordinary least squares method will be applied, mainly because of computational efficiency and partly because of the author's belief that this consideration would not change the estimation results very much.

EMPIRICAL RESULTS

Tables 8-1 through 8-4 report the optimum orders of lags, the corresponding FPEs, and the F-statistics in a two variable framework. For example, take a look at Table 8-1. The first column represents $\hat{m}$, the optimum order of lags of S_{t-j}, when S_t is regressed on its own past values and a constant only. It is not surprising to observe that many of the optimum lags are nonzeros because of the existence of serial correlations of S_t, as has been discussed earlier. The optimum lags for France and the United States are zero, consistent with serial independence of the final residuals v_{1t} in regression (8.6). The third column is the corresponding final prediction error, $FPE(S)$. The second column is $\hat{n}$, the optimum order of lags of W_{t-j}, when S_t is regressed on the past values of S_t, whose order of lags is now fixed at $\hat{m}$, the past values of W_t, and a constant. The corresponding final prediction error, $FPE(S,W)$, is shown in the fourth column. The fifth column is the F-statistic to test the null hypothesis that all the coefficients of the W_{t-j}s are zeros. If $FPE(S) > FPE(S,W)$, then we say W "weakly" causes S. If the F-statistic is significant at least at the upper 5 percent level of significance, then we say W "strongly" causes S.[12] Tables 8-2, 8-3, and 8-4 are similarly interpreted.

Table 8-1. Causality Test from WPI to Exchange Rates in the Absence of Money.

	Optimum Order of Lags of S_t	Optimum Order of Lags of W_t	$FPE(S) \times 10^{-4}$	$FPE(S,W) \times 10^{-4}$	F-statistics
Belgium	6	1	1.177	1.227	F(1,40)0.049
Canada	9	2	1.957	1.947[a]	F(2,36)1.754[b]
France	0	1	2.132	2.036[a]	F(1,46)4.211[b]
Germany	7	16	1.874	1.917	F(16,24)1.642
Italy	4	1	3.957	4.087	F(1,42)0.416
Japan	18	8	5.376	5.024[a]	F(8,21)1.717
Netherlands	14	1	0.501	0.513	F(1,32)0.724
Switzerland	17	4	3.001	2.989[a]	F(4,26)1.488
United Kingdom	4	1	3.033	3.156	F(1,42)0.098[b]
United States	0	12	0.997	0.907[a]	F(12,35)2.446[b]

Note: The regression equation is $S_t = \Sigma\alpha_j S_{t-j} + \Sigma\beta_j W_{t-j} + \gamma + u_t$.
[a] $FPE(S,W) < FPE(S)$.
[b] F-statistics are significant at the upper 5 percent level.

Table 8-2. Causality Test from CPI to Exchange Rates in the Absence of Money.

	Optimum Order of Lags of S_t	Optimum Order of Lags of C_t	$FPE(S) \times 10^{-4}$	$FPE(S,C) \times 10^{-4}$	F-statistics
Belgium	6	15	1.177	1.075[a]	F(15,26)2.074[b]
Canada	9	; 1	1.957	2.032	F(1,37)0.220
France	0	1	2.132	2.171	F(1,46)1.097
Germany	7	4	1.874	1.874	F(4,36)1.715
Italy	4	17	3.957	3.855[a]	F(17,26)1.900
Japan	18	7	5.376	5.439	F(7,22)1.380
Netherlands	14	8	0.501	0.492[a]	F(8,25)1.608
Switzerland	17	1	3.001	3.152	F(1,29)0.002
United Kingdom	4	1	3.033	3.163	F(1,42)0.004
United States	0	1	0.997	1.036	F(1,46)0.149

Note: The regression equation is $S_t = \Sigma\alpha_j S_{t-j} + \Sigma\beta_j C_{t-j} + \gamma + u_t$.
[a] $FPE(S,C) < FPE(S)$.
[b] F-statistics are significant at the upper 5 percent level.

Table 8-3. Causality Test from Exchange Rates to WPI in the Absence of Money.

	Optimum Order of Lags of W_t	Optimum Order of Lags of S_t	$FPE(W) \times 10^{-5}$	$FPE(W,S) \times 10^{-5}$	F-statistics
Belgium	2	1	2.464	2.483	F(1,44)1.516[b]
Canada	8	9	6.575	5.585[a]	F(9,30)2.574[b]
France	3	6	5.727	5.727	F(6,38)1.846
Germany	18	10	1.094	1.059[a]	F(10,19)1.545
Italy	15	2	3.587	2.426[a]	F(2,30)9.392[c]
Japan	8	1	2.173	2.226	F(1,38)0.731
Netherlands	1	1	3.457	3.602	F(1,45)0.024[b]
Switzerland	12	17	1.992	1.445[a]	F(17,18)3.628[b]
United Kingdom	1	1	4.475	4.665	F(1,45)0.002
United States	0	2	1.532	1.524[a]	F(2,45)2.085

Note: The regression equation is $W_t = \Sigma\gamma_j W_{t-j} + \Sigma\theta_j S_{t-j} + \delta + u_t$.
[a] $FPE(W,S) < FPE(W)$.
[b] F-statistics are significant at the upper 5 percent level.
[c] F-statistics are significant at the upper 1 percent level.

Table 8-4. Causality Test from Exchange Rates to CPI in the Absence of Money.

	Optimum Order of Lags of C_t	Optimum Order of S_t	$FPE(C) \times 10^{-5}$	$FPE(C,S) \times 10^{-5}$	F-statistics
Belgium	3	10	0.834	0.776[a]	$F(10,34)2.238$[b]
Canada	14	9	1.520	1.309[a]	$F(\ 9,24)2.200$
France	9	3	0.868	0.881	$F(\ 3,35)1.454$
Germany	11	13	1.017	0.667[a]	$F(13,23)3.365$[c]
Italy	0	5	3.194	2.906[a]	$F(\ 5,42)2.985$[b]
Japan	14	1	7.408	7.661	$F(\ 1,32)0.413$
Netherlands	5	9	2.267	2.126[a]	$F(\ 9,33)2.139$
Switzerland	11	1	1.131	1.144	$F(\ 1,35)1.187$
United Kingdom	0	1	4.727	4.885	$F(\ 1,46)0.411$
United States	4	9	1.326	1.143[a]	$F(\ 9,34)2.705$[b]

Note: The regression equation is $C_t = \Sigma \lambda_j C_{t-j} + \Sigma \theta_j S_{t-j} + \delta + u_t$.
[a] $FPE(C,S) < FPE(C)$.
[b] F-statistics are significant at the upper 5 percent level.
[c] F-statistics are significant at the upper 1 percent level.

Tables 8-5 through 8-8 report the optimum orders of lags, the *FPEs*, and the *F*-statistics in a three variable framework. The analysis is essentially the same as that of Tables 8-1 through 8-4 except that money is included in the right-hand side of the regression equation. The first and second columns of Table 8-5, for example, represent a pair of optimum orders of lags, $\hat{m}$ and $\hat{\ell}$, when S_t is regressed on S_{t-j} and M_{t-j} jointly. When the second column is zero, *M* does not contribute to explaining *S*, and hence, the remaining columns are identical to Table 8-1. The fourth column is the corresponding *FPE(S,M)*. The third column is $\hat{n}$ when S_t is regressed on S_{t-j}, M_{t-j}, and W_{t-j} by constraining *m* and ℓ to be $\hat{m}$ and $\hat{\ell}$, respectively, in regression equation (8.9). The corresponding *FPE(S,M,W)* is shown in the fifth column. The last column is the *F*-statistic to test $H_0:\beta_j = 0$ ($j = 1, 2, \ldots, \hat{n}$) in equation (8.9).

Tables 8-1 through 8-8 indicate that the causal relationship between unanticipated movements in exchange rates and in relative prices do exist for most of the countries but that their patterns are different depending on whether the relative money supply is absent or present and on whether the relevant price is WPI or CPI. The tables also reveal that for more than a half of the countries, feedback relationships are observed regardless of whether money exists or not. These observations should be discussed in some detail.

First, all countries except for the United Kingdom have experienced causal relationships in some form or another. On the average, unanticipated movements in wholesale and consumer prices have strongly caused unanticipated changes in exchange rates for 20 and 15 percent of the cases, respectively, and unanticipated

Table 8-5. Causality Test from WPI to Exchange Rates in the Presence of Money.

	Optimum Orders of Lags of		Optimum Order of Lags of W_t	FPE(S,M) $\times 10^{-4}$	FPE(S,M,W) $\times 10^{-4}$	F-statistics
	S_t	M_t				
Belgium	6	0	1	1.177	1.227	F(1,40)0.049
Canada	9	0	2	1.957	1.947[a]	F(2,36)1.754
France	0	1	1	2.123	2.040[a]	F(1,45)3.834
Germany	6	15	1	1.480	1.612	F(1,25)3.257
Italy	4	1	2	3.708	3.831	F(2,40)1.076
Japan	9	2	6	4.191	3.633[a]	F(6,30)2.613[b]
Netherlands	18	3	1	0.427	0.450	F(1,25)0.008
Switzerland	13	2	7	2.485	2.226[a]	F(7,25)2.089
United Kingdom	4	2	1	2.685	2.801	F(1,40)0.019
United States	0	0	12	0.997	0.907[a]	F(12,35)2.446[b]

Note: The regression equation is $S_t = \Sigma\alpha_j S_{t-j} + \Sigma\epsilon_j M_{t-j} + \Sigma\beta_j W_{t-j} + \gamma + u_t$.
[a] $FPE(S,M,W) < FPE(S,M)$.
[b] F-statistics are significant at the upper 5 percent level.

Table 8-6. Causality Test from CPI to Exchange Rates in the Presence of Money.

	Optimum Orders of Lags of		Optimum Order of Lags of C_t	FPE(S,M) $\times 10^{-4}$	FPE(S,M,C) $\times 10^{-4}$	F-statistics
	S_t	M_t				
Belgium	6	0	15	1.177	1.075[a]	F(15,26)2.074[b]
Canada	9	0	1	1.957	2.032	F(1,37)0.220
France	0	1	1	2.123	2.194	F(1,45)0.413
Germany	6	15	1	1.480	1.807	F(1,25)0.204
Italy	4	1	18	3.708	3.351[a]	F(18,24)2.109[b]
Japan	9	2	1	4.191	4.276	F(1,35)0.875
Netherlands	18	3	3	0.427	0.402[a]	F(3,23)1.940
Switzerland	13	2	6	2.485	2.476[a]	F(6,26)1.521
United Kingdom	4	2	1	2.685	2.771	F(1,40)0.441
United States	0	0	1	0.997	1.036	F(1,46)0.149

Note: The regression equation is $S_t = \Sigma\alpha_j S_{t-j} + \Sigma\epsilon_j M_{t-j} + \Sigma\beta_j C_{t-j} + \gamma + u_t$.
[a] $FPE(S,M,C) < FPE(S,M)$.
[b] F-statistics are significant at the upper 5 percent level.

Table 8-7. Causality Test from Exchange Rates to WPI in the Presence of Money.

	Optimum Orders of Lags of		Optimum Order of Lags of S_t	FPE (W,M) $\times 10^{-5}$	FPE (W,M,S) $\times 10^{-5}$	F-statistics
	W_t	M_t				
Belgium	2	0	1	2.464	2.483	F(1,44)1.516
Canada	8	0	9	6.575	5.585[a]	F(9,30)2.574[b]
France	3	0	6	5.727	5.727	F(6,38)1.846
Germany	18	5	1	0.864	0.913	F(1,23)0.016
Italy	15	1	2	3.323	2.342[a]	F(2,29)8.173[c]
Japan	7	9	14	1.645	0.978[a]	F(14,17)3.314[c]
Netherlands	1	0	1	3.457	3.602	F(1,45)0.024
Switzerland	12	2	15	1.914	1.637[a]	F(15,18)1.986
United Kingdom	1	0	1	4.475	4.665	F(1,45)0.002
United States	0	11	12	1.218	0.831[a]	F(12,24)3.280[c]

Note: The regression equation is $W_t = \Sigma\lambda_j W_{t-j} + \Sigma\pi_j M_{t-j} + \Sigma\theta_j S_{t-j} + \delta + u_t$.
[a] $FPE(W,M,S) < FPE(W,M)$.
[b] F-statistics are significant at the upper 5 percent level.
[c] F-statistics are significant at the upper 1 percent level.

Table 8-8. Causality Test from Exchange Rates to CPI in the Presence of Money.

	Optimum Orders of Lags of C_t	Optimum Orders of Lags of M_t	Optimum Order of Lags of S_t	FPE(C,M) $\times 10^{-5}$	FPE(C,M,S) $\times 10^{-5}$	F-statistics
Belgium	3	8	12	0.670	0.653[a]	F(12,24)1.695[b]
Canada	14	2	9	1.464	1.074[a]	F(9,22)2.902[b]
France	8	19	3	0.582	0.552[a]	F(3,17)1.643
Germany	10	12	1	0.645	0.682	F(1,24)0.001[b]
Italy	4	1	5	2.979	2.706[a]	F(5,37)2.701[b]
Japan	16	12	1	6.279	6.420	F(1,18)0.823
Netherlands	5	2	9	1.779	1.695[a]	F(9.31)1.969
Switzerland	11	0	1	1.131	1.144	F(1,35)1.187
United Kingdom	0	0	1	4.727	4.885	F(1,46)0.411[b]
United States	4	0	9	1.326	1.143[a]	F(9,34)2.705[b]

Note: The regression equation is $C_t = \Sigma \lambda_j C_{t-j} + \Sigma \pi_j M_{t-j} + \theta_j S_{t-j} + \delta + u_t$.
[a] $FPE(C,M,S) < FPE(C,M)$.
[b] F-statistics are significant at the upper 5 percent level.

fluctuations in exchange rates have strongly caused unanticipated changes in wholesale and consumer prices for 30 and 40 percent of the cases, respectively. If weak causality is included within the calculation, the above percentage ratios would increase to 50, 35, 50, and 60 percent, respectively. This is not in accordance with Brillembourg's conclusion that "there does not seem to be any causal relationship between the exchange rate and PPP" (Brillembourg 1976).

Second, money matters for France, Germany, Japan, and Switzerland. On the one hand, in the presence of money, S causes C for France, S causes W (very strongly) for Japan, and C causes S for Switzerland, whereas in the absence of money these causations are not found. On the other hand, S causes W and C (very strongly for the latter) for Germany without money, whereas once money is introduced, the causality ceases to operate. The degree of causality is also influenced by the existence of money for some countries.

Third, the choice of price variables is important. A causal relationship between S and W found in a given country is not necessarily accompanied by a causal relationship between S and C for the same country. They coincide in only about 20 percent of the cases. From overall inspection of Tables 8-1 through 8-8, unanticipated changes in exchange rates tend to cause prices more frequently than vice versa regardless of money. This tendency is more strongly observed if CPI is used as a relevant price variable than if WPI is used. This observation is partly comparable to Frenkel's finding that "prices do not 'cause' exchange rates (in the Granger sense), while exchange rates do 'cause' prices" (Frenkel 1978: 183) for the early 1920s, although our conclusion is not so clear-cut as Frenkel's, particularly for wholesale prices.

Fourth, feedback relations between S and W are observed for Canada, Japan (with money only), Switzerland, and the United States, and a feedback between S and C for Belgium, Italy, and the Netherlands. It is expected that small open economies such as Belgium, the Netherlands, and Switzerland should exhibit bidirectional causality between exchange rates and relative prices, and this is supported by our empirical finding. Italy has been considered a typical example of the "vicious circle" country (Brillembourg 1976; Falchi and Michelangeli 1977), and this hypothesis is also supported. However, the United Kingdom, which is an open economy and sometimes believed to be another "vicious circle" country, does not disclose any sign of causal relationships. One might be skeptical about the observed feedback for the United States, which is viewed as a large and relatively closed economy, since fluctuations in the United State's effective exchange rates and wholesale prices might not strongly cause each other (and much less for consumer prices). One must be cautious at this point, however; the variables that we investigate are effective exchange rates and effective relative wholesale prices, relative to the rest of the world. That is, to the extent that fluctuations in exchange rates and the rest of the world's wholesale prices affect each other, one can observe a feedback relationship between S and W even for the United States. The behavior of Japan and Switzerland may be explained by the "virtuous circle" hypothesis and of Italy and the United States by the "vicious circle" hypothesis.

Since whenever a feedback is observed in a two variable model, the same feedback is found in a three-variable framework, spurious causality of the two variable case does not appear to be too serious. In this sense, the introduction of money as the third variable does not drastically alter exchange rate–price causal and feedback relationships. However, this is not to deny the importance of money in influencing exchange rates and prices; Tables 8-5 through 8-8 show that money contributes to explaining exchange rates, the WPIs, and the CPIs for seven, five, and seven countries, respectively, out of ten.

CONCLUSION

In this chapter we have detected causality directions between unanticipated movements of effective exchange rates and of effective relative prices (WPI and CPI) in both a two variable and a three variable model. Effective relative money supplies are also included as the third variable, reflecting the importance of monetary parameters in determining prices and exchange rates. Endogenous linear filters have been obtained by the seemingly unrelated regression technique in order to eliminate contemporaneous correlations of the disturbances so that we can concentrate on "proper" causality and feedback.

Using the autoregressive specification and the minimum final prediction error criterion, the following empirical results have been observed during the period of 1975-1978. First, weak and strong causalities have been observed in about 25 percent and 50 percent of the cases, on the average, respectively. Second, the introduction of money as the third variable does not appear to drastically alter the overall conclusion about exchange rate–price causality; but for such countries as France, Germany, Japan, and Switzerland, an explicit consideration of money can be very important. Spurious feedback relationships that may have appeared in a two variable model turns out to be insignificant. Third, different causal relationships can be found depending on which price variable is used, WPI or CPI. Causation from changes in exchange rates to changes in the WPIs is observed almost as many times as the opposite direction, whereas changes in exchange rates tend to cause changes in the CPIs rather than vice versa.

Fourth, the fear that exchange rate changes will eventually lead to price changes is supported for slightly more than a half of the ten industrial countries. However, it is quite difficult to draw general conclusions for those pegged countries, mainly the LDCs, that are concerned with the impacts of exchange rate devaluations upon domestic inflation. More specific analysis should be presented for these countries.

Fifth, for Belgium (CPI), Canada (WPI), Italy (CPI), Japan (WPI with money only), the Netherlands (CPI), Switzerland (WPI), and the United States (WPI), feedback relationships between exchange rates and prices are found, but not for the United Kingdom, as is often claimed by economists. Our study would lead us to the hypothesis that Switzerland and Japan experienced the process of the "virtuous" circle, and Italy and the United States the "vicious" circle, during the period of January 1975 through December 1978 on a monthly basis.

Other causality detection methods suggested by Sims (1972) and by Pierce (1977) and Pierce and Haugh (1977) have not been analyzed. If these methods were applied, twenty observations would be sacrificed due to the fact that the regression equation would have to include future values in its right-hand side. In addition, it is not clear how effective these methods are in detecting causality in a three variable framework.

APPENDIX

This appendix explains how effective or trade-weighted indexes for exchange rates, relative prices (wholesale and consumer prices), and relative money supplies are constructed in a multilateral world.

The effective exchange rate index should ideally measure a change in a country's exchange rate that has taken place since the base period relative to that of the rest of the world. In order to correctly compute the effective exchange rate, economic relationships among countries that influence exchange rate movements have to be truly reflected in the weights. However there is no ideal single variable to capture true economic relationships among countries, since commodity trade, autonomous capital transactions, banking behavior, governmental policy actions, and other factors such as expectations influence exchange rates. In constructing weights, authors have concentrated on commodity trade only by neglecting capital flows and other factors. Even when using commodity trade only, as Rhomberg (1976) summarizes, different trade weights have been proposed by different economists and organizations. In this chapter, the quantity of exports plus imports within a group of big ten countries is chosen to represent correct trade patterns. Our method is similar to that of Morgan Guaranty Trust Company (1978) except that the letter includes all the OECD countries and uses manufactures trade only. The effective or trade-weighted spot exchange rate index for country j at time t, SI_{jt}^e, is computed as

$$SI_{jt}^e = \frac{SI_{jt}}{\displaystyle\prod_{k=1}^{10} SI_{kt}^{\,w_{jk}}}, \qquad (8A.1)$$

where SI_{kt} is the spot exchange rate index at time t for country k with the year 1975 as a base period and with the United States as the standard country (hence $SI_{US,t} \equiv 1$ for all t), and

$$w_{jk} = \frac{\text{country } j\text{'s total trade volume with country } k}{\text{country } j\text{'s total trade volume with the rest of nine countries,}}$$

which implies that $\sum_{k=1}^{10} w_{jk} = 1$ and $w_{jj} = 0$. Note that these weights are fixed throughout the period. The denominator in definition (8A.1) can be thought of as the rest of the world's exchange rate index vis-à-vis the U.S. dollar and, hence SI_{jt}^e is the spot value of the jth currency vis-à-vis the rest of the world aggregate currency.

The effective relative price index, RPI_{jt}^e, and the effective relative money supply index, RMI_{jt}^e, between country j and the rest of the world, respectively, can be computed in the similar fashion:

$$RPI_{jt}^e = \frac{PI_{jt}}{\prod_{k=1}^{10} PI_{kt}^{w_{jk}}}, \tag{8A.2}$$

$$RMI_{jt}^e = \frac{MI_{jt}}{\prod_{k=1}^{10} MI_{kt}^{w_{jk}}}, \tag{8A.3}$$

where PI_{kt} and MI_{kt} are the price and money supply indexes of country k at time t. The denominators of equations (8A.2) and (8A.3) can be conceived of as the rest of the world's price and money supply indexes, respectively. Both wholesale and consumer prices are used as the price index, and $RWPI_{jt}^e$ and $RCPI_{jt}^e$ are defined according to equation (8A.2).

Monthly average data on exchange rates, wholesale price indexes, and consumer price indexes and end of month data on money supplies narrowly defined are mostly available from the IMF's *International Financial Statistics* (on tape) for Belgium, Canada, France, Germany, Italy, Japan, the Netherlands, Switzerland, the United Kingdom, and the United States. When only quarterly averages are available for prices, the same quarterly averages are used for all of the three months during that quarter. When only end of quarter data are available for money supplies, monthly data are obtained by interpolation. To obtain period average money supplies, two proximate end of month data are averaged. The sample period includes January 1975 through December 1978, and the year 1975 is taken as a base period. January 1975 is selected as a starting month, under the assumption that international disturbances caused by the OPEC's oil price increase in the fall of 1973 had mostly tapered off by then. September 1978 is the most recent year for which complete data were available at the time of the study.

Trade weights w_{jk} are computed based on the trade patterns during 1975 and 1978 obtained from the IMF's *Direction of Trade* and are available from the author upon request.

NOTES

1. See Officer (1976) and Kawai (1979b) for surveys and several important issues involved in the PPP doctrine.

2. An exception would be Frenkel (1978), who has examined the causality relationship for the early 1920s and tried different regression specifications. But he does not report the empirical result of causality. Brillembourg (1976) interprets the PPP doctrine as either a causal or an equilibrium relationship between exchange rates and prices and attempts to find out which relationship is indicated by the data.

3. Bilson (1979) clarifies some of these issues. Falchi and Michelangeli (1977) relate the "vicious circle" hypothesis to exchange rate—price causality.

4. Sims' method has been applied to many economic issues such as money-income causality (Williams, Goodhart, and Gowland 1976), wage-price linkage (Mehra 1977), and money-price causal relationships (Frenkel 1977, and Kincaid and Nakajima 1978), among others.

5. In other words, we will be interested in examining how equations (8.1) and (8.2) should be modified when the third variable is introduced to the system—that is, we would like to compare equation (8.1) with equation (8.3) or equation (8.2) with equation (8.4). However this does not mean that equation (8.5) should be neglected. To the extent that Z reacts to the past values of X and Y, equation (8.5) can become quite important.

6. For computational efficiency, only the second order polynomial form is tried.

7. The appendix shows how $\ell n SI^e_t$, $\ell n RWPI^e_t$, $\ell n RCPI^e_t$, and $\ell n RMI^e_t$ are constructed.

8. See Box and Pierce (1970) for Box-Pierce Q-tests.

9. It can be easily proven that the optimum total number of lags, $m + n$, under the standard error of the regression criterion is no smaller than that under the FPE criterion.

10. The FPE criterion is equivalent to applying an F-test with a large significance level and, hence, with large type I error (Hsiao, 1978b). The standard error of the regression criterion would be also the same as an F-test with a much greater significance level.

11. See Frenkel (1978) and Isard (1978) for good surveys of the literature on the asset market view of exchange rate determination.

12. The words "weak" and "strong" reflect differences in the significance level of F-tests (see footnote 10).

REFERENCES

Akaike, H. 1970. "Statistical Predictor Identification." *Annals of the Institute of Statistical Mathematics* 22, no. 2: 203-17.

———. 1969. "Fitting Autoregressive Models for Prediction." *Annals of the Institute of Statistical Mathematics* 21, no. 2: 243-47.

Bilson, J.F.O. 1979. "The 'Vicious Circle' Hypothesis." *IMF Staff Papers* 26, 1 (March): 1-37.

Box, G.E.P., and D.A. Pierce. 1970. "Distribution of Residual Autocorrelations in Autoregressive Integrated Moving Average Time Series Models." *Journal of the American Statistical Association* 65, no. 332 (December): 1509-26.

Brillembourg, A. 1976. "Purchasing Power Parity Tests of Causality and Equilibrium." International Monetary Fund, December. Unpublished.

Falchi, G., and M. Michelangeli. 1977. "IMF Surveillance of Exchange Rates and Problem of the Vicious Circle." Rome: Office of International Organizations, April. Unpublished.

Frenkel, J.A. 1978. "Purchasing Power Parity: Doctrinal Perspective and Evidence from the 1920's." *Journal of International Economics* 8, no. 2 (May): 169-91.

———. 1977. "The forward Exchange Rate, Expectations, and the Demand for Money: The German Hyperinflation." *American Economic Review* 67, no. 4 (September): 653-70.

Granger, C.W.J. 1969. "Investigating Causal Relations by Econometric Models and Cross-Spectral Methods." *Econometrica* 37, no. 3 (July): 424-38.

Hsiao, C. 1978a. "Autoregressive Modelling of Canadian Money and Income Data." Working Paper No. 7812. Toronto: University of Toronto, Institute for Policy Analysis, August.

———. 1978b. "Autoregressive Modelling and Money-Income Causality Detection". Technical Report No. 262. Palo Alto: Stanford University, Institute for Mathematical Studies in the Social Sciences, June.

International Monetary Fund. *Direction of Trade.* Various issues.

———. *International Financial Statistics.* In tape.

Isard, P. 1978. "Exchange-Rate Determination: A Survey of Popular Views and Recent Models." *Princeton Studies in International Finance* No. 42 (May).

Kawai, M. 1979a. "The Behavior of an Open-Economy Firm under Flexible Exchange Rates." The Johns Hopkins University, May. Unpublished.

———. 1979b. "An Empirical Examination of the Purchasing Power Parity Doctrine." The Johns Hopkins University, March. Unpublished.

Kincaid, G.R., and Z. Nakajima. 1978. "The Monetary Approach to the Balance of Payments: Tests for Causality." International Monetary Fund, May. Unpublished.

Magee, S.P. 1974. "U.S. Import Prices in the Currency-Contract Period." *Brookings Papers on Economic Activity* 1: 117-64.

———. 1973. "Currency Contracts, Pass-through, and Devaluation". *Brookings Papers on Economic Activity* 1: 303-23.

Mehra, Y.P. 1977. "Money Wages, Prices, and Causality." *Journal of Political Economy* 85, no. 6 (December): 1227-44.

Morgan Guaranty Trust Company of New York. 1978. *World Financial Markets* (May): 2-15.

Officer, L.H. 1976. "The Purchasing-Power-Parity Theory of Exchange Rates: A Review Article". *IMF Staff Papers* 23, no. 1 (March): 1-60.

Pierce, D.A. 1977. "Relationships—and the Lack Thereof—Between Economic Time Series, with Special Reference to Money and Interest Rates." *Journal of the American Statistical Association* 72, no. 357 (March): 11-22.

Pierce, D.A., and L.D. Haugh. 1977. "Causality in Temporal Systems: Characterizations and a Survey." *Journal of Econometrics* 5, no. 3 (May): 265-93.

Rhomberg, R.R. 1976. "Indices of Effective Exchange Rates." *IMF Staff Papers* 23, no. 1 (March): 88-112.

Sims, C.A. 1972. "Money, Income, and Causality." *American Economic Review* 62, no. 4 (September): 540-52.

Williams, D.; C.A.E. Goodhart; and D.H. Gowland. 1976. "Money, Income, and Causality: The U.K. Experience." *American Economic Review* 66, no. 3 (June): 417-23.

✳ *Chapter 9*

Exchange Rate Instability and Capital Controls: The Japanese Experience, 1978-1981

Ichiro Otani*
International Monetary Fund and
Program on U.S.-Japan Relations,
Harvard University

Since the adoption of the flexible exchange rate system in the early 1970s, exchange rates have fluctuated far more widely than had been expected by those who advocated the system. This fluctuation has been large relative to that of key macroeconomic variables considered to be fundamental factors determining the exchange rates. The Japanese experience bears out this observation.

The yen in terms of the U.S. dollar appreciated about 50 percent during three years ending in the third quarter of 1978; it depreciated by about 25 percent during the subsequent year and one-half ending in the first quarter of 1980. These fluctuations have continued up to the present. On the other hand the variability of Japanese prices, monetary aggregates, or output relative to those of the United States has been considerably less than variability of the exchange rate (Table 9-1). In view of these developments, officials of the Japanese government expressed the belief that the yen at times (as in mid-1978) appreciated well beyond what Japanese officials considered an appropriate level suggested by economic fundamentals, whereas at other times it has depreciated well below the level suggested by the underlying strength of the economy (as in late 1979 and early 1980).[1]

*The author is grateful for useful comments by J. Boorman, H. Houthaker, J. Sachs, T. Taya, and J. Wilson, and benefited from discussions with S. Tiwari. The views expressed in this chapter are the author's alone and do not necessarily represent those of the International Monetary Fund or the Program on U.S.-Japan Relations, Harvard University where the author was a visiting scholar for one year, 1981-1982.

Table 9-1. Variability of Selected Indicators, 1973:Q2-1981:Q2.

Variables	Trend Growth Rate per Quarter[b] (%)	Standard Deviation from Trend[c]
Exchange rate (yen/$)	-1.2	9.8
Export prices[a]	-1.3	4.8
Wholesale prices[a]	-0.9	4.8
Real GNP[a]	0.3	1.8
Narrow money[a]	1.0	6.6

[a]Ratio of Japanese to the U.S. variable.
[b]Coefficient of the time trend variable obtained by regressing the logarithm of the variable in column 1 on the time trend.
[c]Standard error of estimate.

Confronted by the apparent overshooting of the exchange rate, the Japanese government sometimes resorted to capital controls and other measures to moderate the fluctuations of the exchange rate[2]; these controls were exerted primarily on long-term portfolio investments and short-term capital flows.[3]

When the capital controls system was modified, some controls were tightened and others relaxed. It is difficult to state categorically, therefore, that the modification of the system led to a tightening or relaxing of the controls in any given period, although the general intentions of the government are fairly easy to identify. The modification of the system was carried out in three separate phases: In phase 1, the emphasis was on discouraging net inflows of capital; in phase 2, from early 1979 to late 1980, the focus was on encouraging net inflows; and in phase 3, from late 1980 to the present, the principle of free transactions has been in effect as far as transaction of short-term financial assets is concerned.

In light of these developments it would be interesting to examine whether or not the capital control measures implemented by the Japanese government in recent years had any significant impact on the level of the exchange rate and to determine whether this impact was consistent with the government's exchange rate policy objectives embodied in the implementation of the capital control measures.

In the remainder of this chapter a theoretical model is presented, with which the impact of capital controls on the exchange rate can be analyzed, and empirical results for the period, 1978-1981, are given Appendix 9A contains a more detailed description of recent developments in the capital control measures of the past several years.

ANALYTICAL FRAMEWORK

To provide an understanding of how various capital control measures are expected to influence the level of the exchange rate, a simple model is presented. The model can be used for analyzing the qualitative effects of capital controls on the exchange rates and thus lays a foundation for estimating the effects quantitatively in the subsequent section.

Model

One of the most important characteristics of the model adopted is its emphasis on asset views of exchange rate determination. The model also incorporates the "overshooting" hypothesis of exchange rate adjustment developed by Dornbusch (1976).

One aspect of the asset view of exchange rate determination can be represented by the interest rate parity theory in the presence of transaction costs.[4] Assuming that no unexploited profits exist—that is, the market is efficient[5]—the following equation holds *ex-ante*.

$$1 - \phi \leq \frac{S(1 + r_d)}{F(1 + r_f)} \leq 1 + \phi \ , \tag{9.1}$$

where

S = number of units of domestic currency per unit of foreign currency for immediate delivery (say, at time t_0).

F = number of units of domestic currency per unit of foreign currency for delivery at some time t_1 in the future ($t_0 < t_1$).

r_d = interest rate on the domestic-currency-denominated assets that is secured for the period from t_0 to t_1.

r_f = interest rate on the foreign-currency-denominated assets that is secured for the period from t_0 to t_1.

ϕ = total percentage cost of transacting financial assets and foreign and domestic currencies (i.e., cost as percentage of the total value of transactions).

Broadly speaking, unit total transaction costs can be thought of as consisting of three components: (1) brokerage fees and costs of gathering information, ϕ_b; (2) costs of bearing risks associated with given financial assets being issued by different agents, ϕ_r; and (3) opportunity costs of evading capital control measures and taxes, ϕ_c—

that is, fines or other financial costs to be borne by the potential transactors in case they violate the rules under the control measures and are discovered or added costs necessary to meet government regulations. As a result, $\phi = \phi_b + \phi_r + \phi_c$. (A further discussion on the relevance of decomposing total transaction cost will be provided in the next section.)

Ex post, the following relation holds at all times:

$$\frac{S\,(1 + r_d)}{F\,(1 + r_f)} = 1 \pm \phi \ . \tag{9.2}$$

The right-hand side of the equation is $1 + \phi$ when arbitrage funds flow *into* the home country and $1 - \phi$ when these funds flow *out of* the country (see Otani and Tiwari 1981).[6]

Taking the natural logarithm of equation (9.2) and representing the spot and forward exchange rates by lower case letters yields a familiar expression:

$$s - f = r_f - r_d \pm \phi \ . \tag{9.3}$$

The left-hand side of equation (9.3) is the spread P between the spot and the forward exchange rate, representing a premium on the home currency if it is positive and a discount if it is negative.

$$P = s - f \ . \tag{9.4}$$

The premium or discount on the home currency also represents the expected percentage change in the spot exchange rate during the period from t_0 to t_1. Following Frankel (1979), Hooper and Morton (1982), and Hooper, Haas, and Symansky (1981), the expected percentage change in the spot exchange rate of the yen is assumed to depend on the gap between the expected long-run equilibrium rate $\bar{s}\,^*$ and the present rate s, plus the expected percentage change in $\bar{s}\,^*$.

$$(\triangle s) = \theta\,(\bar{s}\,^* - s) + (\triangle \bar{s}^*) \ , \tag{9.5}$$

where $*$ denotes the expected value and $-$ denotes the long-run equilibrium rate. θ represents the speed of adjustment, taking a value between zero and unity.[7]

From the last three equations, the following equation is obtained:

$$s = \bar{s}^* + \frac{1}{\theta}\,\triangle\,\bar{s}^* + \frac{1}{\theta}\,(r_f - r_d) \pm \frac{1}{\theta}\,\phi \ . \tag{9.6}$$

Qualitative Effects of Capital Controls
on Exchange Rates

In order to analyze the effects of capital controls on the levels of the spot and forward exchange rates, a few qualifying remarks are in order. First, this analysis is concerned with the short run, so that the expected long-run equilibrium level of the exchange rate $\bar{s}^*$ is assumed not to be influenced by capital control measures. Second, the capital control measures are assumed to influence the domestic interest rate but not the foreign interest rate. This assumption reflects the notion that the stock of domestic-currency (yen)-denominated assets are small relative to foreign-currency (U.S. dollar)-denominated assets, and that changes in the flow of arbitrage funds that are induced by capital control measures can be a significant portion of the stock of financial assets in the domestic market but a small portion of the stock of financial assets in the foreign market. Third, changes in transaction costs are solely attributable to the capital control measures.[8] Fourth, in order to obtain the qualitative effects of the capital controls on the exchange rates, it is essential to distinguish between controls that are used to discourage net inflows of arbitrage funds and those that are used to encourage net outflows.

Effects of Capital Controls to Discourage
Net Inflows

There are two ways of discouraging net inflows of capital: discouraging gross inflows and encouraging gross outflows. For the present, suppose that the government introduced capital control measures to discourage gross inflows of capital by restricting foreign residents from acquiring domestic-currency-denominated assets issued by residents. The differentiation of equations (9.4)-(9.6), respectively, with respect to ϕ, will result in equations (9.7)-(9.9), respectively.[9]

$$\frac{dP}{d\phi} = (1 - \frac{\partial r_d (\phi)}{\partial \phi}) \tag{9.7}$$

$$\frac{ds}{d\phi} = \frac{1}{\theta} (1 - \frac{\partial r_d (\phi)}{\partial \phi}) = \frac{1}{\theta} \frac{dP}{d\phi} \tag{9.8}$$

$$\frac{df}{d\phi} = (\frac{1 - \theta}{\theta}) (1 - \frac{\partial r_d (\phi)}{\partial \phi}) = (\frac{1 - \theta}{\theta}) \frac{dP}{d\phi} \tag{9.9}$$

Equations (9.7)-(9.9) indicate several interesting results. Consider first the effect of capital controls on the domestic interest rate

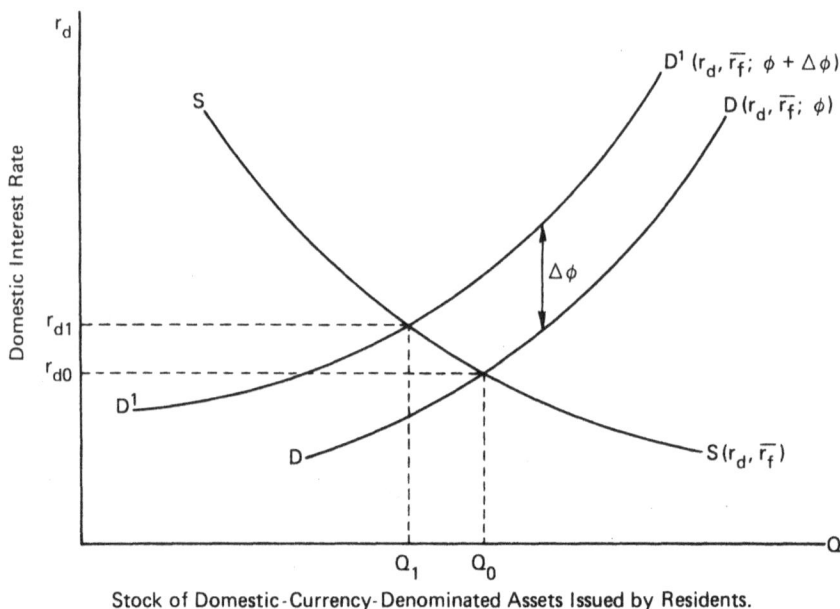

Figure 9-1. Market for Domestic-Currency-Denominated Assets Issued by Resiaents.

$(\partial r_d / \partial \phi)$. This is expected to be positive but less than unity if the interest rate elasticity of the supply schedule of the domestic currency assets is negative. This is demonstrated in Figure 9-1.

Assume that domestic residents issue domestic-currency-denominated assets and that their supply schedule for these assets is negatively related to the domestic interest rate and is depicted by SS. Nonresidents (foreigners) have a demand schedule for these assets; this schedule is positively related to the domestic interest rate and is represented by DD.[10] Suppose that capital controls are imposed, reducing foreigners' access to the domestic assets. Following the imposition of these controls, the transaction costs that must be borne by foreigners will increase by $\Delta \phi$. The demand schedule shifts upward by $\Delta \phi$, and the equilibrium domestic interest rate increases from r_{d0} to r_{d1}, while the stock of domestic-currency-denominated assets held by foreigners declines from Q_0 to Q_1. Foreigners must now liquidate a portion (amounting to $Q_0 Q_1$) of their initial holding. The proceeds from selling $Q_0 Q_1$ of the assets to the issuers or residents will be repatriated to the foreign country. The net inflow of capital in the presence of the capital controls will be lower by the distance $Q_1 Q_0$ than in the absence of the controls. It is also clear that as long as the elasticity of the supply schedule with respect to the domestic interest rate is negative, the rise in the domestic interest rate is less than the increase in the transaction costs. Therefore $(1 - \partial r_d / \partial \phi)$ is positive and less than unity, and hence the premium rises less than the increase in the transaction costs induced by the capital controls.[11]

The effect of capital controls on the current spot exchange rate is greater by $(1/\theta)$ than that of the premium; the smaller the adjustment speed, the greater the effect on the spot rate. If the speed of adjustment is instantaneous ($\theta = 1$), then the effect of the capital controls on the premium is passed on completely to the spot rate.

The effect of the capital controls on the forward rate is a product of $(1 - \theta)/\theta$ and the effect on the premium is greater than the effect on the premium if θ is less than 0.5; otherwise, it is smaller than the effect on the premium.

In short, the effect of capital controls to discourage inflows of arbitrage funds by restricting foreign demand for domestic assets will lead to (1) an increase in the domestic interest rate; (2) an increase in the forward premium on the yen; and (3) a depreciation of the yen in both the spot and the forward market.

Effects of Capital Controls to Discourage Net Outflows

The two ways of discouraging net outflows of capital are to discourage gross outflows and to encourage gross inflows. For the present analysis, suppose that the government implements measures intended to encourage gross inflows of capital by restricting foreign residents from issuing domestic-currency-denominated assets in the domestic market.[12] The effects of these capital controls on the premium, the current spot rate, and the forward rate can be obtained by differentiating equations (9.4)-(9.6), respectively. This time we must work with equation (9.6) with the minus sign attached to the expression ϕ/θ. The results are shown in equations (9.10)-(9.12).

$$\frac{dP}{d\phi} = -(1 + \frac{\partial r_d}{\partial \phi}) \ , \tag{9.10}$$

$$\frac{ds}{d\phi} = -\frac{1}{\theta}(1 + \frac{\partial r_d}{\partial \phi}) = \frac{1}{\theta}\frac{dP}{d\phi} \ , \tag{9.11}$$

$$\frac{df}{d\phi} = -(\frac{1 - \theta}{\theta})(1 + \frac{\partial r_d}{\partial \phi}) = (\frac{1 - \theta}{\theta})\frac{dP}{d\phi} \ . \tag{9.12}$$

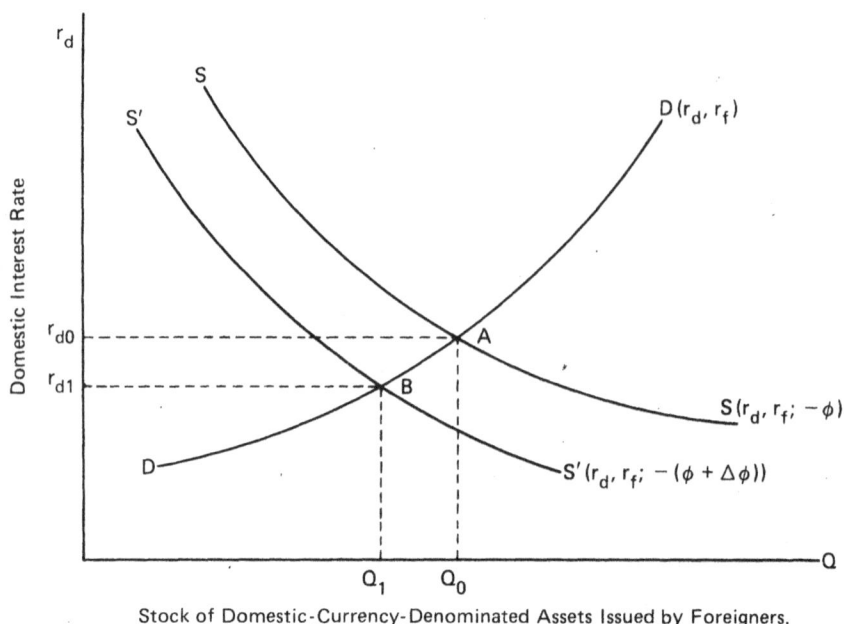

Figure 9-2. Market for Domestic-Currency-Denominated Assets Issued by Foreigners.

The effect on the domestic interest rate of capital controls to discourage outflows of arbitrage funds is expected to be negative, and the absolute value of the interest rate effect is less than the increase in the transaction costs. This is demonstrated in Figure 9-2.

The measures that restrict the supply of domestic-currency-denominated assets issued by foreigners will increase the transaction costs, representing an opportunity cost for nonresidents wishing to avoid the restrictive capital control measures or an increase cost to be borne by them to meet the government regulations embodied in these measures. As a result, the supply schedule of the domestic-currency-denominated assets shifts downward by $\Delta\phi$. Given an upward sloping demand schedule for residents, the domestic interest rate will decline by an amount less than the increase in the transaction costs; that is, $-1 < \partial r_d / \partial\phi < 0$. Therefore $(1 + \partial r_d / \partial\phi)$ is positive and less than unity. The equilibrium position shifts from the initial point at A to the new one at B, with the domestic interest rate declining from r_{d0} to r_{d1} and with the stock of the domestic-currency-denominated asset held by the residents declining from Q_0 to Q_1. This implies that domestic residents liquidate part $(Q_1 Q_0)$ of their initial holding of the yen-denominated assets (Q_0) issued by foreigners by selling it to the foreign issuers; therefore the proceeds from liquidating $Q_1 Q_0$ will be repatriated to the home country. To this extent the home country will have an inflow in the capital account, and the net outflow (inflow) will be smaller (larger) in the presence of the capital controls than in their absence.

The effect of the controls on the premium is negative, and its absolute value is less than the increase in the transaction costs. The effect on the spot exchange rate is greater than that on the premium, and the effect on the forward exchange rate is smaller than that on the spot exchange rate, since $(1 - \theta)/\theta$ is less than $1/\phi$.

In short, the effect of capital control measures to discourage net outflows or to encourage net inflows will lead to: (1) a decline in the domestic interest rate; (2) a decrease in the forward premium on the domestic currency, and; (3) an appreciation of the domestic currency (or a depreciation of the foreign currency in terms of the domestic currency) for both the spot and forward exchange rates.

EMPIRICAL RESULTS

The preceding section qualitatively analyzed how capital controls can influence exchange rates through their impact on transaction costs, the domestic interest rate, and the forward premium. This section attempts to quantify these effects. It is necessary to estimate, first, the effects of capital controls on transaction costs and, second, on the domestic interest rate and the forward premium.

Impact of Capital Controls on Transaction
Costs, Interest Rates, and Forward Premiums

The methodology to estimate the effect of the capital controls on the transaction costs can be described briefly as follows.[13] Consider two worlds, A and B. In each world, assets may be denominated in different currencies. The distinguishing characteristic of world A is that all assets are traded freely, so that there are no institutional controls or taxes on transactions by residents of any region in this world. Thus, it is expected that deviations from the interest rate parity in A reflect normal transaction costs, ϕb, and costs of bearing risks ϕr. In contrast, in world B the government of one region imposes controls on the transactions between its residents and those of other regions. Thus it is expected that in B, deviations from the interest rate parity reflect not only the normal transaction costs, ϕb, and the costs of bearing risks, ϕr, but also the costs induced by the capital control measures, ϕc.[14] If ϕb and ϕr are the same in the two worlds, we can quantify the extent of capital controls in B relative to A by comparing the deviations from the interest rate parity in A and B. Therefore it is important to note that the extent of the capital controls in B can be measured even if ϕb and ϕr vary.[15]

In order to estimate empirically the effects of the capital controls on transaction costs, we can observe two empirical counterparts to world A and world B. World A is represented by London (Eurocurrency market), where financial transactions are free of controls. We will consider one asset denominated in the Japanese yen (three-month Euroyen deposits) and another denominated in U.S. dollars (three-month Eurodollar deposits). World B is represented by the Tokyo market (including the geographical space between Tokyo and London through which capital movements can take place). The yen-denominated assets in Tokyo are represented by the three-month Gensaki bonds (bonds with repurchase agreements), and the U.S. dollar-denominated assets, by the three-month Eurodollar deposits. Therefore the yen-denominated assets in world A are different from the yen-denominated assets in world B, but the dollar-denominated assets are marketed in both worlds. The yen/dollar exchange rates for both spot and forward transactions in world A and world B are quoted in London and Tokyo, respectively.

The accuracy with which the effect of capital controls on total unit transaction costs can be estimated is crucially dependent on the validity of the assumption that ϕb and ϕr in London and Tokyo are the same. Let us now examine this assumption, therefore, before proceeding further in estimating the effect of the controls on transaction costs. Normal transaction costs ϕb, including brokerage fees and the cost of gathering information, are largely dependent on the level of technology in processing paperwork and information. Since financial institutions in both Tokyo and London use the most sophisticated electronic and communications technology, ϕb in both cities can be reasonably assumed to be the same. The cost of bearing risks, ϕr, is dependent on the credibility attached to the issuers of the financial assets. The U.S. dollar-denominated assets in Tokyo and London are identical, so the issuing agents for these assets in both markets are the same. The yen-denominated assets in Tokyo and London are issued by different agents, however, and so the risk factors associated with the issuing agents in Tokyo are different from those in London. Nevertheless, the actual cost of bearing such risks in the two cities can reasonably be assumed to be very close to each other because the issuing agencies of these yen-denominated assets are large, respectable corporations of Japanese origin.

Under these circumstances the gap between the estimated transaction costs for Tokyo and London represents the estimated effects of capital controls on transaction costs,[16] as shown in equation (9.13)

$$\phi_{\text{TKY}} - \phi_{\text{LON}} = \phi_c \quad , \tag{9.13}$$

where

ϕ_{TKY} = transaction costs in the Tokyo capital market ($\phi b + \phi r = \phi c$).

ϕ_{LON} = transaction costs in the London capital market ($\phi b + \phi r$).

ϕ_c = transaction costs associated with the capital control measures.

The estimated effects of the capital control measures on the interest rates on two types of the domestic-currency-denominated assets were based on the theoretical discussion presented in the previous section and its application to the two-market model. It has been shown that, under normal circumstances (where the demand schedule for domestic-currency-denominated assets is a positive function of the rate of return on them and the supply schedule is a negative function), capital control measures to discourage capital inflows to the home country—the Tokyo capital market—will lead to an increase in the interest rate (from r_{d0} to r_{d1} in Figure 9-1) and to an outflow of capital (amounting to $Q_0 Q_1$ in Figure 9-1). This implies that the stock of domestic-currency-denominated assets in the London market may increase somewhat as foreigners attempt to compensate for the decline in yen-denominated assets in Tokyo from Q_0 to Q_1 by acquiring additional yen-denominated assets in London, leading to a decline in the interest rate. If the supply schedule for domestic-currency-denominated assets has the same interest rate elasticity in both the Tokyo and the London market and if the decline in the stock of yen-denominated assets is offset by the increase in London, then the decline in the interest rate in London is the same as the increase in Tokyo. The converse would be true if capital control measures were introduced to encourage inflows. That is, the effect of capital controls on the interest rate on domestic-currency-denominated assets would raise the interest rate in London and lower it in Tokyo by the same amount. Therefore, the effect of the capital controls on the interest rate in Tokyo (r_c) can be estimated by equation (9.14).[17]

$$r_c = (r_{\text{TKY}} - r_{\text{LON}})/2 \tag{9.14}$$

where

r_{TKY} = interest rate on yen-denominated assets in Tokyo.

r_{LON} = interest rate on yen-denominated assets in London.

The effect of the capital controls on the interest rate in London is the same magnitude as r_c with the opposite sign (i.e., $-r_c$). Daily observations of r_{TKY} and r_{LON} are plotted in Figure 9-3.

The effect of the capital controls on the transaction costs can be distributed between the effect on the interest rate and on the forward premium according to the analyses presented in the preceding section. The results are summarized in Table 9-2.

During phase 1, when capital control measures were implemented by the government in order to ward off the speculative inflows of capital, transaction costs increased as expected; about two-thirds of this increase was transmitted as an increase in the domestic interest rate on yen-denominated assets in Tokyo, and about one-third was transmitted as an increase in the forward premium on the yen.

During phase 2, when measures were introduced to encourage capital inflows, they again led to increases in the transaction costs; these increases led to declines in the interest rate, but the estimated declines were sometimes greater than the increases in the transaction costs. The causes of these abnormal results are not entirely clear, but a possible explanation may be that it is not entirely appropriate to make the assumption that the induced capital flow into the Tokyo market depresses the interest rate on the yen-denominated assets in Tokyo just as much as the induced capital flow out of the London market raises it in London. However, the assumption that such an impact on the interest rate (in absolute terms) is less in Tokyo and greater in London than initially assumed does not change the results in any significant way (see Table 9-3). In any case the capital control measures are estimated to have had only a small impact on the forward premium.

In phase 3, the principle of free capital transactions was in effect, and the government eliminated by that time most of the capital control measures that had existed prior to the introduction of this principle. Under these circumstances the Tokyo capital market became as efficient at least, in terms of the costs of transacting financial assets, as the London market, reflecting, in part, reductions in the cost of meeting the Japanese government's regulations. As a result, the improved efficiency in transacting financial assets may have resulted in inflows of capital, as is demonstrated by a downward shift in the *DD* schedule in Figure 9-1, resulting in a decline in

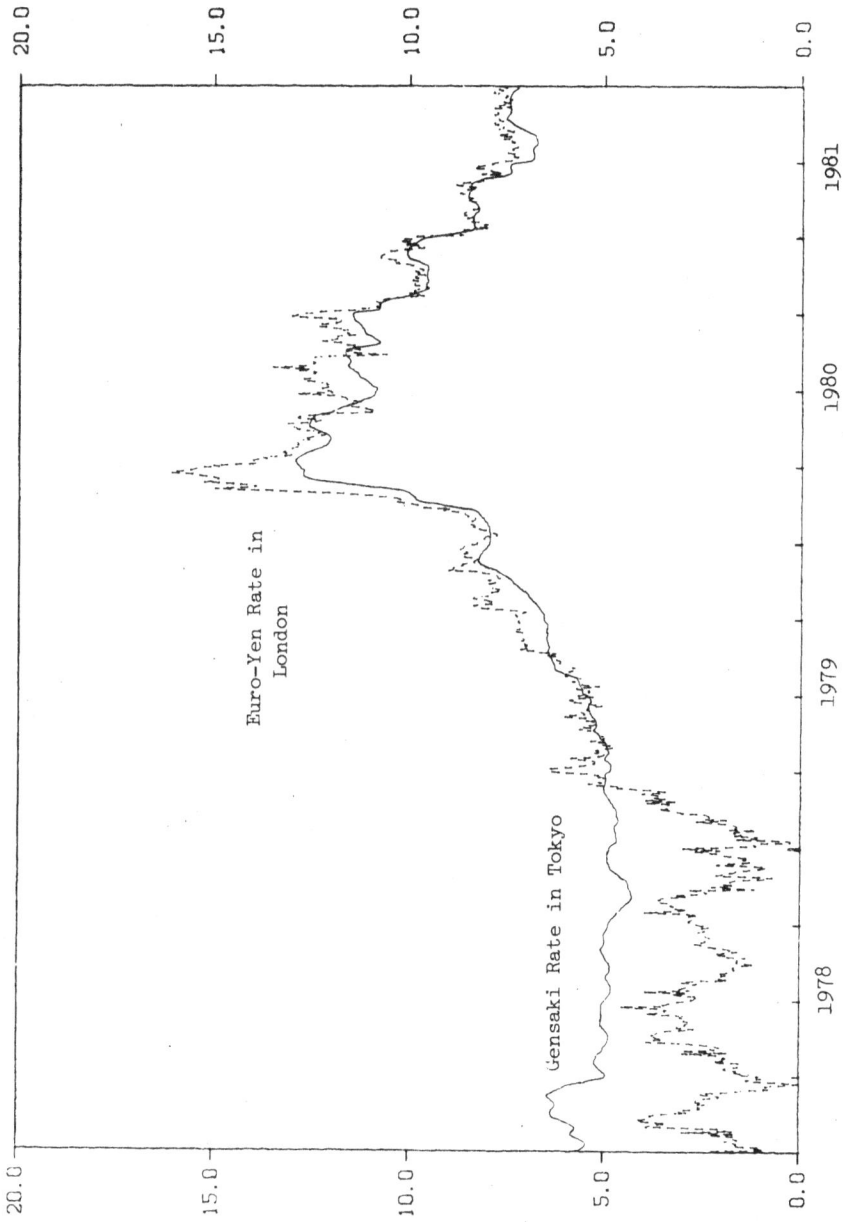

Figure 9-3. Interest Rates on Yen-Denominated Assets, 1978–1981 Daily Data (% per Annum).

Table 9-2.   Estimated Effects of Capital Controls on Transaction Costs, Interest Rates, and Forward Premiums Assuming $\alpha = 0.5$ (%).

Year	Quarter	Tokyo Market			London Market	
		Effects on Transaction Costs (ϕ_c)	Effects on Interest Rate (Gensaki)	Effects on Premium on Yen	Effects on Interest Rate (Euroyen)	Effects on Premium on Yen
		Phase 1: Period when Controls Were Introduced to Discourage Net Inflows.				
1978	1	0.676	0.466	0.210	-0.466	0.466
	2	0.460	0.293	0.167	-0.293	0.293
	3	0.477	0.324	0.153	-0.324	0.324
	4	0.444	0.305	0.139	-0.305	0.305
1979	1	0.250	0.222	0.028	-0.222	0.222
		Phase 2: Period when Controls Were Introduced to Discourage Net Outflows.				
1979	2	-0.078	-0.035	0.113	0.035	-0.035
	3	-0.021	-0.029	0.050	0.029	-0.029
	4	0.030	-0.083	0.053	0.083	-0.083
1980	1	0.169	-0.136	-0.033	0.136	-0.136
	2	0.013	-0.062	0.049	0.062	-0.062
	3	0.173	-0.107	-0.066	0.107	-0.107
		Phase 3: Period when Principle of Free Transactions Was in Effect.[a]				
1980	4	-0.030	-0.025	-0.005	0.025	-0.025
1981	1	-0.054	-0.014	-0.040	0.014	-0.014
	2	-0.052	-0.051	-0.001	0.051	-0.051

[a]In mid-1980 it became increasingly clear to the public that Japan's new Foreign Exchange and Foreign Trade Control Law was to be put into effect on December 1, 1980. As a result, the market started to adapt itself to the new law as early as the beginning of the fall in that year, and the average transaction costs in Tokyo became lower than in London from the fourth quarter of 1980. This may reflect various innovations introduced around that time to increase the efficiency of the transaction. Therefore these do not reflect the effects of the capital controls as such but indicate the effects of the improved efficiency in transacting financial assets.

Table 9-3. Estimated Effects of Capital Controls on Transaction Costs, Interest Rates, and Forward Premiums Assuming $\alpha = 0.25$ (%).

		Tokyo Market			London Market	
Year	*Quarter*	*Effects on Transaction Costs (ϕ_c)*	*Effects on Interest Rate (Gensaki)*	*Effects on Premium on Yen*	*Effects on Interest Rate (Euroyen)*	*Effects on Premium on Yen*
Phase 1: Period when Controls Were Introduced to Discourage Net Inflows.						
1978	1	0.676	0.233	0.443	-0.699	0.699
	2	0.460	0.142	0.318	-0.444	0.444
	3	0.477	0.162	0.315	-0.486	0.486
	4	0.444	0.153	0.291	-0.457	0.457
1979	1	0.250	0.111	0.139	-0.333	0.333
Phase 2: Period when Controls Were Introduced to Discourage Net Outflows.						
1979	2	-0.078	-0.018	0.096	0.052	-0.052
	3	-0.021	-0.015	0.036	0.043	-0.043
	4	0.030	-0.047	0.017	0.119	-0.119
1980	1	0.169	-0.068	-0.101	0.204	-0.204
	2	0.013	-0.031	0.018	0.093	-0.093
	3	0.173	-0.054	-0.119	0.160	-0.160
Phase 3: Period when Principle of Free Transactions Was in Effect.[a]						
1980	4	-0.030	-0.013	-0.017	0.037	-0.037
1981	1	-0.054	-0.007	-0.047	0.021	-0.021
	2	-0.052	-0.026	-0.026	0.076	-0.076

the domestic interest rate in Tokyo. The improved efficiency was estimated to have had a slightly depressing impact on the forward premium on the yen. (Of course, this result is *not* the effect of cap-ital controls as defined in this chapter.)

The effect on the London capital market of the capital control measures introduced in the Tokyo capital market can be analyzed more straightforwardly. Since the transaction costs in London can-not be affected by control measures in Tokyo, impact of these mea-sures on the London market is limited to that on the interest rate on yen-denominated assets (the Euroyen deposits) and the forward premium. As can be seen in Tables 9-2 and 9-3, during phase 1, the Euroyen deposit rate was depressed considerably by the induced flows of capital out of Tokyo into London, and the forward pre-mium on the yen is estimated to have increased by the amount of the decline in the interest rate. During phase 2, the capital control mea-sures introduced in Tokyo are estimated to have resulted in increases in the Euroyen deposit rate, and declines in the forward premium. During phase 3 the introduction of the principle of free capital trans-actions led indirectly to increases in the yen deposit rate and declines in the forward premium, as in the case of phase 2.

Reflecting the tightness of the capital control measures, their im-pact on transaction costs, interest rates, and the forward premium was much larger during phase 1 than during phase 2 and phase 3. Therefore, their impact on the spot and the forward exchange rate, as will be analyzed, is expected to be larger during phase 1 than the subsequent periods.

Impact of Capital Controls on Exchange Rates

The estimated effect on the spot and the forward exchange rate of the capital controls can be obtained by the formula represented by equations (9.8) and (9.9) for phase 1 and by equations (9.11) and (9.12) for phase 2. According to these equations the impact on the exchange rates depends crucially upon the speed of adjustment, θ. The value of θ in turn depends on the structural characteristics of the economy relevant to the market in question; and the value for the Tokyo market can be different from that for the London market.

The value of θ for the Tokyo market was taken from the estimate obtained by Hooper, Haas, and Symansky (1981), who estimated the equation for determining the spot exchange rate for the currencies of major industrial countries.[18] Their estimated value of θ was 0.488. There is no estimated value of θ for the London market. As a result, the average of 0.488 and 1 have been chosen arbitrarily, on the assumption that the lack of restrictive measures on capital controls in the London market would make the adjustment speed greater than that for the Tokyo market.[19] The estimated effects of capital controls on the spot and forward exchange rates are summarized in Table 9-4.

During phase 1 both the spot and the forward rate (yen per U.S. dollar) were higher compared to the rates that would have prevailed in the absence of capital control measures to discourage inflows of capital. To that extent these measures succeeded in depreciating the yen when the speculative inflows of capital exerted appreciatory pressure on the yen. The magnitude of the impact differed from one quarter to another; the largest impact was felt in the first quarter of 1978, and it coincided with the period when the government of Japan introduced a series of restrictive measures.[20] The estimated impact was a depreciation of about 1 yen per U.S. dollar for the spot rate and about 0.5 yen for the forward rate. During the remainder of 1978 the depreciatory impact of the capital control measures weakened somewhat as the government liberalized the capital control measures, partly because of foreign pressure to open up the capital market and its own initiative to introduce gradually the principle of freer capital transactions.[21] By the beginning of 1979 the restrictive measures had been significantly relaxed, and their depreciatory impact declined substantially, with the estimated effect on the spot and the forward rate amounting to only 0.12 yen and 0.06 yen respectively.

During phase 2 the government modified the capital control measures so as to discourage outflows and encourage inflows in response to the rapid depreciation of the yen, which started in late 1978. The results were mixed. Sometimes they had an appreciatory impact on the yen, consistent with the government's objectives, but at other times their influence was depreciatory, contrary to the government's objectives. In any case the magnitude of the impact, even if it was in the right direction, was small and insignificant. This lack of success in bringing about the desired impact on the weakening yen may reflect the limited scope in which the government had to work in introducing restrictive measures—that is, the government had to strike a balance between making the Tokyo capital market more open, on the one hand, and inducing capital inflows with the control measures, on the other. Furthermore, the failure of the controls reflects the frequently observed phenomenon concerning the effectiveness of monetary policy—namely, a tight monetary policy is effective in dampening investment demand, but an easy monetary policy is not necessarily effective in stimulating demand. Similarly, the capital

Table 9-4. Estimated Effects of Capital Controls on Spot and Forward Rate in Tokyo.

Year	Quarter	Tokyo Market[a]				London Market[b]			
		Spot Rate		Forward Rate		Spot Rate		Forward Rate	
		(%)	(Yen)	(%)	(Yen)	(%)	(Yen)	(%)	(Yen)
Phase 1:	Period when Controls Were Introduced to Discourage Net Inflows.								
1978	1	0.431	1.023	0.221	0.518	0.626	1.490	0.160	0.326
	2	0.342	0.76	0.175	0.382	0.394	0.868	0.101	0.220
	3	0.314	0.60	0.161	0.305	0.435	0.839	0.111	0.211
	4	0.285	0.543	0.146	0.272	0.410	0.780	0.105	0.195
1979	1	0.057	0.116	0.029	0.058	0.298	0.601	0.076	0.151
Phase 2:	Period when Controls Were Introduced to Discourage Net Outflows.								
1979	2	-0.088	-0.192	-0.045	-0.097	-0.047	-0.102	-0.012	-0.026
	3	0.016	0.036	0.008	0.018	-0.039	-0.085	-0.010	-0.022
	4	0.106	0.259	0.056	0.131	-0.116	-0.244	-0.029	-0.067
1980	1	-0.068	-0.165	-0.035	-0.083	-0.183	-0.446	-0.047	-0.112
	2	0.100	0.233	0.051	0.120	-0.083	-0.193	-0.021	-0.049
	3	-0.135	-0.298	-0.069	-0.153	-0.144	-0.316	-0.037	-0.081
Phase 3:	Period when Principle of Free Transactions Was in Effect.[c]								
1980	4	-0.113	-0.237	-0.058	-0.122	-0.034	-0.071	-0.009	-0.018
1981	1	-0.082	-0.169	-0.042	-0.085	-0.019	-0.039	-0.005	-0.010
	2	-0.002	-0.004	-0.001	-0.002	-0.069	-0.151	-0.018	-0.038
	3								

[a]The value of θ is estimated to be 0.488 by Hooper, Haas, and Symansky (1982).

[b]There is no estimated value for θ for the London market. It is arbitrarily assumed to be 0.744, the average between the value for the Tokyo market and unity (implying the instantaneous adjustment speed).

[c]These results are the estimated effects of the improved efficiency in transacting financial assets, not those of the capital controls as such.

controls were not always effective in inducing inflows, because sometimes they would exert little authority on international financial
transactors, especially foreigners who cannot be forced to bring funds
into the Tokyo capital market.

During phase 3, as far as the short-term financial asset market is
concerned, the Tokyo capital market became as open as the London
market and virtually free of restrictions, reflecting the implementation of Japan's new Foreign Exchange and Foreign Trade Law. As a
result, we would expect the absence of capital controls and thus no
impact on the exchange rate. The results obtained for this period also
support this expectation (Table 9-4).

The estimated effects of the control measures on the exchange
rates can be summarized as follows. These effects for the London
market are not significantly different from those for the Tokyo market for the entire sample period. During phase 1 the magnitudes of
the effects were the largest in the first quarter of 1978, diminishing
considerably in the rest of the period.[22] During phase 2 the effects
of the controls were appreciatory, but the magnitudes were very
small; and during phase 3 the implementation of the new law tended
to appreciate the yen in both the spot and the forward market, but
the magnitudes were small.

As discussed previously, the foregoing analysis of the effects of
capital controls on exchange rates was based on the arbitrary choice
of the value of θ. In order to analyze the sensitivity of the exchange
rate to the controls with different values of θ, it is useful to examine
two extreme cases: One is based on the assumption that the speed of
adjustment in the spot exchange rate in the London market is instantaneous, that is, $\theta = 1$; and the other is based on the assumption that
it is as slow as in the Tokyo market, that is, $\theta = 0.488$. Using these
values and applying to the estimated effect of the capital controls on
the premium in the first quarter of 1978 (when the controls were the
tightest), we obtain the two sets of extreme values between which

Table 9-5. Effects of Capital Controls in the London Market, 1978
First Quarter.

	$\theta = 0.488$	$\theta = 0.744^a$	$\theta = 1$
Spot rate			
Percent	0.955	0.626	0.466
Yen	2.28	1.49	1.10
Forward rate			
Percent	0.488	0.160	0.0
Yen	1.0	0.326	0.0

[a]From Table 9-4.

the estimated effects on the spot and the forward exchange rates are likely to fall. The results summarized in Table 9-5 indicate that the capital controls can be credited with depreciating the spot exchange rate by about two yen and the forward rate by one yen, but it is more likely that the true effects were probably somewhat less than indicated here.

CONCLUDING REMARKS

One of the major purposes of this chapter has been to analyze both the qualitative and the quantitative effects on the yen exchange rate of the capital control measures that have been implemented by the Japanese government in recent years and to determine whether the government has obtained the desired results from these measures.

The analysis based on the theoretical framework developed in this chapter indicates the following: (1) Qualitatively, the measures intended to discourage inflows of capital into Japan tend to depreciate the yen and those to discourage outflows from Japan tend to appreciate the yen. In this respect the nature of the capital control measures introduced and modified by the government during the period 1978–1980 were consistent with the government's exchange rate objectives. (2) Quantitatively, however, these measures were not entirely effective in influencing the exchange rates because additional transaction costs brought about by these measures were estimated to have resulted in small changes in the exchange rates. It can thus be concluded that these capital controls were ineffective instruments over this period to influence the exchange rate.

Although this empirical finding conforms to the observation made by other researchers,[23] its interpretation must be made with caution for several reasons. First, some of the assumptions made in the theoretical and empirical sections have limits in their validity. Second, within a given observation period, the government introduced measures intended to encourage (discourage) capital inflows as well as measures intended to encourage (discourage) outflows, so that it is difficult to delineate the appreciatory (depreciatory) effect of the former from the depreciatory (appreciatory) effect of the latter. Third, quantitative indicators for the exchange rate effect of these measures are based on daily averages for each three-month period; thus they cannot reveal information on the effect in the much shorter period of a week or a day.

APPENDIX 9A: RECENT DEVELOPMENTS
IN CAPITAL CONTROL MEASURES

This appendix presents a more detailed description of recent developments in the capital control measures. During the years under review the measures passed through three distinct phases. In the first phase (roughly 1977–78), the authorities intended to induce net outflows of capital by encouraging gross outflows while discouraging gross inflows. In the second phase (roughly 1979–1980), they desired to induce net inflows by discouraging gross outflows while encouraging gross inflows. In the third phase (from late 1980 to 1981), the principle of free transactions was in effect.

Phase 1

Controls on Inflows. A reserve requirement against foreign currency liabilities was established in June 1977 at a level of 25 percent. The level was raised to 50 percent in November 1977 on increases in free-yen deposits above their average level during October of that year. Reflecting sharp increases in free-yen deposits in February and March 1978, on March 15, the Bank of Japan raised the reserve requirements on free-yen deposits to 100 percent of the increase in these accounts over the daily average level in February 1978. From March 16, 1978, the Japanese authorities prohibited purchases by nonresidents of Japanese bonds and debentures with a maturity period of less than five years and one month.

Restrictions on inflows through foreign currency loans (impact loans) made by foreign banks to resident corporations were eased. From April 1978 Japanese businesses could use impact loans for operations purposes and to hedge against foreign currency assets. Previously these loans were approved only for capital investment purposes.

Controls on Outflows. As part of the process of foreign exchange control liberalization, in early January 1978 the Ministry of Finance allowed residents to hold foreign currency bank deposits up to an amount equivalent to 3 million yen in authorized foreign exchange banks in Japan. In addition, restrictions were liberalized on the sale of forward exchange contracts for the purposes of hedging exchange risks on foreign securities transactions.

The Ministry of Finance has given support to the issue of yen-denominated bonds in the Tokyo capital market. In a move to increase the interest of Japanese investors in these bonds, the ministry extended the same tax exemption on interest payments of foreign yen-denominated bonds floated by international agencies and governments to similar bonds floated by private corporations.

Phase 2

Controls on Inflows. The marginal reserve requirement of free-yen deposits, which had been 100 percent since March 1978, was reduced to 50 percent in January 1979 and eliminated in February.

In January 1979 nonresidents were again permitted to purchase securities with remaining maturities of more than one year and one month, reduced from the previous five years and one month, and in February the remaining maturity restrictions on the purchase of short-term securities were lifted. In March and again in December quotas for foreign banks' conversion of foreign currency into yen were increased and restrictions on Japanese banks' foreign currency positions were eased.

In May the Ministry of Finance introduced a seven-point program for relaxing restrictions on capital inflows. The maximum import usance period was lengthened, while the requirement for government approval for export repayments exceeding $500,000 was eliminated. The restriction on the period for conversion of yen proceeds by nonresidents borrowing by way of yen bonds or syndicated loans was lifted, while the 25 percent limit on the share of nonresidents in subscriptions to foreign yen bonds was lifted. For the first time nonresidents were given access to the Gensaki market (a short-term, three-month market dealing in repurchase agreements on securities). The process of liberalizing impact loans, begun in 1977, was carried further in the spring of 1979 when long-term impact loans could also be made to traders for long-term working capital and exchange risk hedging; the total ban on impact loans of less than one year was lifted; the Japanese banks were permitted to make short-term (though not long-term) impact loans.

Controls on Outflows. Partly reflecting the weakening of the yen as well as the balance-of-payments position, the government discouraged the issuance of the yen-denominated bonds in Tokyo by nonresidents.[24] Furthermore, the Ministry of Finance did not approve yen denominated term loans to foreign borrowers.

In March 1980 the government announced a package of "yen defense" measures. These measures included (1) removing the ceiling on the interest rate for the free-yen accounts held by nonresident official and international entities, (2) allowing Japanese banks abroad to send funds raised abroad to the head office in Japan through their interoffice accounts, and (3) allowing commercial banks to secure "impact loans" on their own account.

Phase 3

On December 1, 1980, the new Foreign Exchange and Foreign Trade Control Law came into effect, involving a change from a system of general prohibition of external transactions unless expressly permitted to one embodying a principle of free transactions unless expressly restricted. The exceptions to this principle allow the Ministry of Finance to impose restrictions under "emergency conditions" defined as "situations where a capital transaction might (1) make the maintenance of equilibrium in Japan's balance of payments difficult; (2) result in drastic fluctuations in the exchange rate; and (3) result in an international flow of funds large enough to adversely affect Japan's money or capital market (International Monetary Fund 1981: 241).

NOTES

1. Statements made by prominent officials reveal their thoughts about the overshooting of the Japanese yen. For example, Vice Minister of the Ministry of International Trade and Industry, Mr. Konno, is quoted as saying, "[The present level of the yen rate] below Y180 does not reflect the fundamental economic conditions and is clearly overvalued" (*Nihon Keizai Shimbun*, October 27, 1978); Governor of the Bank of Japan, Mr. Maekawa, expressed his thoughts on the overshooting by saying, "The present depreciation of the yen is excessive because economic conditions do not justify the depreciation by 10 or 11 yen within a one-month period" (*Nihon Keizai Shimbun*, March 3, 1980).

2. One of the measures to influence the exchange rate was the Bank of Japan's intervention in the foreign exchange market. This was analyzed by Taya (1981 and the preceding chapter in this book); he found that the effectiveness of the intervention policy was minimal, if at all, even in the short run of a day or a week, and that it was often nil.

3. Within the last several years under study, the Japanese government modified the system of capital controls regulating direct investment, long-term portfolio investments, and short-term capital flows. For the purpose of influencing the level of exchange rate, the government primarily adopted those controls that were believed to have direct bearing on flows of funds through transactions of long- and short-term financial assets. Hereafter, the capital controls refer to the controls regulating the transactions of portfolio financial assets and exclude those affecting direct investment unless otherwise expressly stated.

4. Recent literature has increasingly recognized that the notion of transaction costs be incorporated in a theoretical and an empirical study of the interest rate parity relation. For example, see Frenkel and Levich 1977, 1974, and Otani and Tiwari 1981.

5. A more detailed discussion on the validity of this assumption will be provided in the next section.

6. It is important that the plus (+) and the minus (-) signs should be assigned properly, depending on the direction in which induced movements in the arbitrage funds take place. For example, if a tax were imposed on transactions and it reduced capital inflows, a plus (+) sign would have to be attached to the term representing the transaction costs in equation (9.2). If it reduced outflows, a minus (-) sign would have to be attached. In this case the transaction costs term together with the minus sign could be interpreted as a subsidy given to transactors, who in turn reduced outflows.

7. This specification is a modified version of Dorbusch's formulation, which does not contain $\Delta \bar{s}^*$ on the right-hand side of equation (9.4). $\Delta \bar{s}^*$ can be assumed to depend on such factors as the differential between the foreign and domestic long-term equilibrium rate of inflation and other fundamental factors.

8. For the purpose of analyzing the effects of the capital controls from a theoretical point of view, it is assumed that transaction costs associated with factors other than capital controls are constant. This restrictive assumption will be relaxed in the next section.

9. In order to simplify the presentation, residents' demand for domestic-currency-denominated assets is ignored here.

10. In order to simplify the presentation, residents' demand for domestic-currency-denominated assets is ignored here.

11. In principle, the government can have domestic residents reduce the supply of domestic-currency-denominated assets available to foreigners by imposing a tax on them. Such a measure will shift the supply schedule downward by the amount of the tax. Provided that the demand schedule remains stable, $\partial r_d / \partial \phi$ will be negative, and $(1 - \partial r_d / \partial \phi)$ greater than unity, with the premium rising more than the increase in the transaction costs induced by the tax. In practice, such measures were not introduced by the government during the period covered in this study.

12. For example, the government can restrict the issuance of yen-denominated bonds in Tokyo by foreigners.

13. A more detailed and rigorous treatment of this methodology is presented in our earlier paper, Otani and Tiwari 1981.

14. It is assumed that the market is efficient in the same sense that no opportunities exist for unexploited profits. The reasonableness of such an assumption is supported by our preliminary study, which examines whether or not there are unexploited profits by the use of trading rules along the line of the study by Frenkel and Levich (1975).

15. If changes in international economic conditions have effects on risks associated with different issuing agents of financial assets, it is expected that these effects will have an equal impact in both world A and world B. Therefore changes in the deviation from the interest rate parity due to changes in the inter-

national economic environment do not affect the transaction costs associated with the capital control measures.

16. ϕ_{TKY} and ϕ_{LON} are estimated on the basis of the absolute values of the deviations from the condition for the interest rate parity. The rationale and the estimated values are provided in Otani and Tiwari 1981.

17. An infinite number of combinations can be assumed in allocating this impact as long as the following condition is satisfied:

$$r_{cTKY} = \alpha \, (r_{TKY} - r_{LON}) \ ,$$

$$r_{cLON} = - (1 - \alpha) \, (r_{TKY} - r_{LON}) \ ,$$

where r_{cTKY} and r_{cLON} are the effect of the capital controls on the interest rate on the yen-denominated assets in Tokyo and London, respectively. Since it is difficult to estimate these elasticities, we continue to use 0.5 as the value of α in this chapter, which will suffice for the present purpose; the estimated effects obtained by assuming $\alpha = 0.25$ are presented in Table 9-3, in Appendix 9A, and the substance of the chapter need not be changed as will be discussed later.

18. Their quarterly model for the exchange rate determination builds on equation (9.7) by introducing factors determining the long-run equilibrium exchange rate and other factors believed to be important in determining the exchange rate. The results obtained by them are reproduced below for the period from the second quarter of 1973 to the fourth quarter of 1979; the t-ratios are in parentheses.

$$Je = -4.70 + 0.000053 \int JBBAL \, (-1) + 2.05 \, (JRS - URS + (\Delta U\bar{p})^* - (\Delta Jp^*))$$
$$ (-3.09) \quad (2.78) \hspace{4.2cm} (2.27)$$

$$ -0.000029 \, (\Delta JNETPK) + 0.65 \, Je \, (-1) - 0.45 \, Je \, (-2) \ ,$$
$$ \quad (-1.10) \hspace{2.3cm} (2.20) \hspace{1.6cm} (-2.34)$$

$$\bar{R}^2 = .9237, \quad SER = .0409, \quad DW = 1.96 \ ,$$

where

Je	=	\$/yen exchange rate.
$\int JBBAL$	=	cumulative current account plus net direct investment inflow.
JRS	=	Japanese interest rate, three-month rate.
URS	=	U.S. interest rate, three-month rate.
$(\Delta U\bar{p})^*$	=	long-term expected rate of inflation in the United States.
$(\Delta Jp)^*$	=	long-term expected rate of inflation in Japan.
$\Delta JENTPK$	=	change in the stock of Japanese private nondirect liabilities to foreigners net of claims on foreigners (including statistical discrepancy).

The estimated coefficient, 2.05 for the third term, is equivalent to $1/\theta$ in equation (9.6) or $\theta = 0.488$.

19. Because of the arbitrary choice of the value of θ for the London market, the estimated effect of the capital controls on the exchange rates in London should be interpreted cautiously. A more detailed analysis will be provided later to examine how sensitively the estimated effects change depending on different values of the adjustment speed.

20. For example, the government implemented a 100 percent reserve requirement against increases in free-yen deposits over the daily average level of February 1978. Previously the requirement was 50 percent. It also prohibited purchases by nonresidents of Japanese bonds with a maturity of not longer than five years and one month remaining to maturity. For more details, see Appendix 9A.

21. For example, restrictions concerning the use of impact loans extended by foreign banks in Japan were eased. The new regulations allowed use of the loans for long-term operational purposes and hedging of foreign currency assets. Swap quotas for foreign banks operating in Japan were expanded. Blanket approval was given to applications for foreign loans by Japanese foreign exchange banks. For more details, see Appendix 9A.

22. Since the capital controls were tightest in the first quarter of 1978, their effects on the exchange rate in other periods were smaller than those estimated in 1978 first quarter.

23. See Komiya and Suda (1980), who reviewed developments in the Japanese government's exchange rate and capital control policies since the beginning of the generalized floating exchange rate system. They concluded that while measures intended by the government to influence short-term capital flows often appeared drastic, their impact on capital flows and the exchange rate was negligible. Their conclusion was not derived from the explicit quantification of this impact as in the present study, however.

24. The total amount of the yen bonds issued by nonresidents was Y400 billion in 1979, in comparison with Y827 billion in 1978 and Y325 billion in 1977.

REFERENCES

Dornbush, Rudiger. 1976. "Expectations and Exchange Rate Dynamics." *Journal of Political Economy* 84, 6: 1161-76.

Frankel, Jeffrey A. 1979. "On the Mark: A Theory of Floating Exchange Rates Based on Real Interest Differentials." *American Economic Review* (December): 610-22.

Frenkel, Jacob A., and Richard M. Levich. 1977. "Transaction Costs and Interest Arbitrage: Tranquil Versus Turbulent Periods." *Journal of Political Economy* 85, 6: 1207-24.

Frenkel, Jacob A., and Richard M. Levich. 1975. "Covered Interest Arbitrage: Unexploited Profits?" *Journal of Political Economy* 83, 2: 325-38.

Hooper, Peter, and John Morton. 1982. "Fluctuations in the Dollar: A Model of Nominal and Real Exchange Rate Determination." *Journal of International Money and Finance 1* (forthcoming).

Hooper, Peter, Richard Haas, and Steven Symansky. 1981. "Exchange Rate Determination in the MCM: A Proposed Revision." April. Unpublished.

International Monetary Fund. 1981. *Annual Report on Exchange Arrangements and Exchange Restrictions.* Washington, D. C.

Komiya, Ryutaro, and Miyako Suda. 1980. *Kanri Furohto Ka no Tanshiido—Sono Riron to Saikinno Keiken* (Short Term Capital Flows under Managed Floating System—Its Theory and Recent Experience). Tokyo University.

Otani, Ichiro, and Siddharth Tiwari. 1981. "Capital Controls and Interest Rate Parity: The Japanese Experience, 1978-81." *IMF Staff Papers* (December): 793-815.

Taya, Teizo. 1981. "Effectiveness of the Exchange Market Intervention in Moderating the Speed of Exchange Rate Movements: An Empirical Study of the Case of Japan." International Monetary Fund, DM/81/78, Washington, D. C.

✳ *Chapter 10*

The Causes of Export Instability: Comparing the Experiences of Two Decades*

Odin K. Knudsen
World Bank
Lloyd S. Harbert
U.S. Department of Agriculture

The causes and effects of export instability have concerned the literature on trade and development throughout the postwar era. This literature argues that developing countries experience high levels of export earnings instability due to concentration in trade on a few commodities, focus on primary products, and dependence on a few trading partners. A corollary to this argument is that the smaller the country's economic size, and hence the smaller the contribution to overall trade flows of its principal exports, the more unstable are its export earnings, because the negative correlation between price and the quantity exported is absent for these small traders. These high levels of export instability are further contended to have deterred growth by inhibiting investments, creating uncertainty in government revenues and hence in its planning, and causing domestic instability through a multiplier effect on incomes.

Empirical testing of these arguments has produced mixed results. Although Massell (1970), Knudsen and Parnes (1975),[1] and Soutar (1977) found a positive correlation between commodity concentration and instability, many other studies (Coppock 1962; Michaely 1962; Massel 1964; MacBean 1966; Lam 1980b; and Lawson and Thanassoulas 1981), have not found such a relation. In addition, MacBean and Nguyen (1980), showing that one concentration index can be consistent with a range of instabilities, challenged even the likelihood of finding such a relation.

---

*The views and interpretations in this document are those of the authors and should not be attributed to the World Bank, to its affiliated organizations, or to any individual acting in their behalf.

Empirical studies of the influence of trade in raw materials and primary products on export instability have yielded equally mixed results. MacBean (1966) found that primary product producing countries have more unstable exports than the average industrial country; Massell (1964) using 1948-1959 data obtained a positive and significant coefficient for a primary product export ratio on a regression on export instability. However, using later data, (1950-1966), Massell (1970) concluded that there is no tendency for exports of primary products to be more unstable than manufacturers. Likewise, more recent studies, Knudsen and Parnes (1975) and Lam (1980b) found no positive relation between the type of product traded and export instability.

With respect to trading partners and concentration on few markets, Massell (1970) and MacBean (1966) obtained no statistically significant relationship between geographic concentration and instability. However Knudsen and Parnes (1975) found the direction of trade to be statistically significant after accounting for the influence of other variables; and Lam (1980a), using the market share of the trading partners outside of the most important six as an index of diversification, found that countries achieving the most rapid rate of market diversification experience the lowest levels of instability *and* the slowest growth in export earnings. Lam concluded that concentrating trade to a few markets is a strategy of obtaining high growth in earnings that incidently produces high instability.

The question of the relation between economic size and export instability is related to comparing instability between developing and developed countries. Although generally studies have concluded that export instability is greater for developing countries than developed countries, once the sample is isolated to only developing countries the results are not as clear. In the 1970 article, Massell found a significant variable for gross domestic product (GDP) per capita in a regression with a dummy variable denoting developed and developing countries. However, Erb and Schiavo-Campo obtained no significant relation between both GDP per capita and a socioeconomic variable developed by Adelmen and Morris and export instability. Mathieson and McKinnon (1974) obtained a significant relation between GDP per income and instability, which becomes insignificant once the ratio of exports to GDP is included. In a sample consisting of developed and developing countries, Knudsen and Parnes (1975) found that larger countries (net of other independent variables) have *higher* instability than smaller nations.

On determining the effects of this instability on developing countries, results have been equally mixed. In fact, two studies, MacBean

(1966) and Knudsen and Parnes (1975) obtained positive, although weak, relationships between instability and investment. Likewise, Kenen and Voivadas (1972) obtain a positive and significant relationship between the growth of investment and instability. However, they found a negative and significant relation between the ratio of investment and GDP with export instability. Knudsen and Parnes found no statistically significant relation between the instability in domestic income and export instability, a result consistent with their theory of the effects of instability. Lam (1980b) obtained a positive relation between instability and the rate of expansion of exports. However, Glezakos' (1973) results indicated a negative and significant coefficient for export instability and the rate of growth of exports instability and investment.

Most of this literature and empirical work on export instability is based on data from the 1950s up to the mid-1960s.[2] Considerable changes in the economic structure of trade have taken place since this period. The economics of developing countries have diversified into manufacturing, many exchange rates have been allowed to float, and price increases of energy and price fluctuations of certain commodities have put increasing instability in trade. The structural changes in economies and in international trade justify a reexamination of the causes and effects of instability. This is particularly important as the increasing import bill of developing countries for energy has pushed countries into a more external trade orientation.

In this chapter, not only is the data base for the study extended through the 1960s into the late 1970s, but also trade is broken down into its commodity components. Along with aggregate export earnings, the trade among commodity categories are analyzed to examine how the instability of commodity flows contribute to instability. This disaggregation allows determination of whether trade in certain commodity groups is more unstable than others and whether this is systematic across the developing world. It also permits construction of an index of instability based upon the average instability of an aggregation of commodity instabilities and an index based upon the variance of commodity flows without accounting for the covariance between flows. Thus two possible effects of export instability can be differentiated.

The first is the effect of overall instability of export earning, and the second is the effect of instability of individual trade flows. Although overall earnings instability may be reduced by negative correlation between individual commodity trade flows, this lowering of aggregate instability may mask the effects on sectors of the economy dependent on earnings from particular trade flows. Therefore countries with low levels of overall earning instability might in fact be experiencing high instability in various sectors devoted to producing and exporting certain commodity groups. The measured effect of earnings instability might as a consequence be quite different if aggregate or average or variance indices of instability are used.

These propositions are examined in the following sections. First the indices of instability used are discussed, then the results on comparisons of aggregate instability, average instability, and variance instability for the 1960s and the 1970s are presented. After the causes of aggregate export earnings and instabilities are examined, whether export instability has been reflected in the instability of other important country parameters is explored. Finally, conclusions and directions for further inquiry are offered.

THE INDICES OF INSTABILITY

Export instability for the purposes of this chapter is defined as deviations from an exponential trend growth in export earnings; that is, the systematic increases in export earnings are considered as increases in expected income or, in a slightly different sense, as increases in permanent income. Deviations from this trend are unexpected or, in the second sense, transitory. This naive approach to export instability assumes that there is no adaption other than a trend adjustment of expected or permanent income to the actual experience of export earnings fluctuations. Although disregarding adaption is a definite shortcoming of this form of measuring instability, it is adopted out of expediency and the vast precedent in the literature given to this form of indexing instability.

Designating the expected or permanent component of earnings with an asterisk, we define an index of export instability for commodity flow i, for country j as the sum of squared deviations of normalized actual earnings, E from this permanent component E^*:

$$I_{ij} = \frac{1}{T} \left(\sum_{t=1}^{m} (E_{ijt}^* - E_{ijt})^2 / E_{ijt}^{*2} \right)^{1/2} , \qquad (10.1)$$

where $E_{ijt}^* = E_0 (1 + r)$, and r is the trend rate of growth of exports.

Average instability $\bar{I}_j$ for country j is defined as the weighted average of the commodity trade flows or

$$\bar{I}_j = \sum_{i=1}^{m} w_{ij} I_{ij} , \qquad (10.2)$$

where w_{ij} is the proportion of commodity flow i in total export earnings.

This average index differs from an index based on the standard deviation of aggregate earnings instability. For example, assume that there are two commodity flows; then aggregate earnings are

$$E = E_1 + E_2 \qquad (10.3)$$

and the variance is

$$\text{Var}(E) = \text{Var}(E_1) + \text{Var}(E_2) + \text{Cov}(E_1, E_2) \ . \qquad (10.4)$$

Dividing both sides by E^2 and defining w_1 and w_2 as the share of earning of each flow, we get

$$\text{Var}(E)/E^2 = w_1^2 \, \text{Var}(E_1)/E_1^2 + w_2^2 \, \text{Var}(E_2)/E_2^2$$

$$+ \text{Cov}(E_1, E_2)/E^2 \ . \qquad (10.5)$$

Defining instability as the square root of the variance divided by the square of earnings, we arrive at

$$I = (w_1^2 \, I_1^2 + w_2^2 \, I_2^2 + \text{Cov}(E_1, E_2))/E^2)^{1/2} \ , \qquad (10.6)$$

where

$$I_1^2 = \text{Var}(E_1)/E_1^2 \quad \text{and} \quad I_2^2 = \text{Var}(E_2)/E_2^2 \ .$$

Clearly, the aggregate instability index is a different measure than the average index, with the former taking into account the covariance and weighting indices by the square of their contribution to overall earnings.

A third index of instability is an aggregation of only the variances of the earnings of the individual trade flows. It is defined as

$$\hat{I}_j = \sum_i (w_{ij}^2 \, I_{ij}^2)^{1/2} \ , \qquad (10.7)$$

where I_{ij} is the instability index of country j's ith trade flow.

For the two-commodity case, it is the equivalent to the aggregate index if the covariance is zero. Thus the difference between this variance index and the aggregate index is a measure of the covariance. If the aggregate index is less than the variance index, then the covariance term is negative; if it is greater, then the covariance term is positive. As such, the difference between these indices offers a measure of how individual trade flow bundles are contributing to or reducing aggregate instability.

The aggregate index of instability, the one currently common to the literature, is of interest in examining hypotheses on the effects of export instability that operate through the overall balance-of-payments situation. It is argued that the higher the aggregate instability is the more difficult economic planning is and the less reliable the availability of foreign exchange for importing capital goods required for domestic investments. Likewise, if government revenues are dependent on the taxation of export earnings, then the more unstable aggregate export earnings are, the more unstable government revenues are and hence government expenditures for development.

The average index of instability on the other hand measures overall instability in the export sector. For example, since in general the producers and exporters of agricultural products are separate from the producers and exporters of manufactured products, each is concerned about the instability of only its own commodity flows. In the absence of government transfers, any cancellation due to one rising and the other falling is immaterial to the individual sectors. Hence the sectoral consequences of instability are better captured by the average index of instability.

The variance index of instability is similar to the average index except it offers a more theoretically attractive index as the weights are squared, thus corresponding to how variances of aggregates are constructed. It is a measure of the benefits or drawbacks of diversification since the covariance term of equation (10.6) could be either positive or negative. The former indicate that commodity trade flows tend to move in unison; the latter indicate that trade flows tend to cancel and thus to contribute to overall stability in aggregate earnings.

Although the variance index is more theoretically attractive, it weights, due to squaring, the trade flow of the major sectors disproportionately more than its contribution to the economy. Thus the average index is also included as it uses simple proportionate weighting, which is perhaps more reflective of a trade flow's importance to the economy.

INSTABILITY IN TWO DECADES

A sample consisting of thirty-seven developing countries selected according to the availability of complete data series for the 1960s and 1970s is examined.[3] Commodity trade flows are extracted from the series at the one-digit Standard International Trade Classification (SITC) level. This produces trade flows based upon the following categories:

SITC Code	Description
0	Food and live animals
1	Beverages and tobacco
2	Crude material exclusive of fuel
3	Mineral fuels, etc.
4	Animals, vegetable oil, fat
5	Chemicals
6	Basic manufactures
7	Machines, transport equipment
8	Miscellaneous manufactured goods
9	Goods not classified by kind

For each of these flows and their totals, exponential trend lines are fitted to the data for each of the two periods, and using equation (10.1) trade flow instability indices are calculated. The index based upon the total flow is the aggregate index. The index calculated by the square root of the sum of the squared weighted indices is the variance index; the index based on the simple weight average of the trade flow instabilities is the average index. The difference between the aggregate and the variance index is a measure of the covariance normalized by the flow in each year.

Then based upon the SITC classifications, commodity concentration indices are calculated:

$$C_j = (\sum_i w_{ij}^2)^{\frac{1}{2}} \ ,$$

where w_{ij} is the share of trade in SITC category i. This index has an upper limit of 1 for concentration in a single commodity group and a lower limit of $n^{-1/2}$ for equal trade flows (in the case the first digit SITC code $n = 10$).

In Table 10-1, the mean indices for the sample of countries are shown for the two periods. Each measure of instability displays a statistically significantly different mean for the two periods, with the 1970s expectedly showing significantly higher mean instability. Interestingly, the indices without the covariance effect, the variance, and the average indices show the most significant increase in instability. Although instability of aggregate earnings has increased by about

Table 10-1. Mean Instability and Commodity Concentration between the 1960s and the 1970s (Standard Deviations in Parentheses).

Index[a]	1960s	1970s
IT	8.16 (3.65)[b]	14.76 (9.94)[b]
ISQ	9.02 (4.31)[b]	19.02 (22.00)[b]
IAVG	15.03 (6.78)[b]	27.89 (24.82)[b]
CI	0.666 (0.12)	0.634 (0.12)

[a]IT   = aggregate instability;
ISQ   = aggregate instability without covariance (the variance index);
IAVG = weighted average instability;
CI   = commodity concentration.
[b]Means statistically significantly different at 0.01 level.

50 percent, the variance and average indices have increased by about 100 percent, thus pointing to much greater increases in instability of flows from sectors of the economy in the second decade than reflected in the changes in the instability of overall aggregate earnings.

By examining individual country indices, some significant differences between countries are identified (see Appendix 10A). Although for most countries export instability increased between the decades, some countries, such as Costa Rica and Upper Volta, had some decreases in aggregate instability. Also, about 40 percent of the countries in the first decade and about 47 percent in the second decade had a *lower* variance instability index than an aggregate one, indicating that diversification, at least as reflective by the first digit SITC categories, did not result in lower aggregate instability. Apparently, many countries' export earnings in commodity groups move in unison, thus creating higher aggregate instability than in the constituent flows. However, for the majority of countries a diversified export bundle resulted in lower aggregate instability.

Mean commodity concentration between the two decades remained statistically equal, at about 0.67 to 0.63. A simple correlation between the change in commodity concentration and the change in instability between the two decades showed no statistical significance.

To examine whether the instability between the trade flows of commodities differ between categories, individual commodity indices are aggregated by summing the weighted indices of categories, loosely defined as food and agricultural products (SITC codes 0, 1,

Table 10-2. Mean Instability of Agricultural Products, Raw Materials, and Manufactures: The 1960s and the 1970s.

Index[a]	1960s	1970s
AIF	15.16 (9.69)	18.70 (10.12)
AIR	15.59 (9.58)[b]	31.16 (25.03)[b]
AIM	33.88 (30.97)	28.53 (17.46)

[a]AIF = average index of instability of SITC codes 0, 1, and 4.
  AIR = average index of instability of SITC codes 2, 3, and 5.
  AIM = average index of instability of SITC codes 6, 7, and 8.
[b]Means statistically significantly different at 0.01 level.

and 4), raw materials and fuels (SITC codes 2, 3, and 5), and manufactured goods (SITC codes 6, 7, and 8). These average instability indices are a reflection of the instability in the constituent categories. Table 10-2 compares the results from the two decades.

In the 1960s, the mean instability of manufactured goods exports significantly exceeded that of raw materials and agricultural products. This is, in part, a reflection of the small flows that characterized the exports of manufactured products for many developing countries. In the 1970s, although the mean instability of agricultural products increased somewhat, manufactured goods displayed a slight fall in instability. The significant increase in the 1970s of export instability occurred in the raw material flows, which nearly doubled in instability. This increase occurred as is expected for mineral fuel exports, but it also occurred for other raw material exporters. What is unexpected is that this increase in raw material instability is not generally reflected in the other categories of exports.

THE CAUSES OF INSTABILITY

As the review of the literature reported, the primary causes of export instability have been hypothesized to be commodity concentration and the openness of the economy as often defined by the ratio of exports to GDP. In this section these hypotheses are examined and the causes of instability in individual commodity flows on aggregate instability further explored.

As shown in Table 10-3, regressions were estimated for each of the decades using commodity concentration and the ratio of exports to GDP as independent variables and the three measures of instability as dependent variables. For the 1960s sample a weak positive relation

Table 10-3. Commodity Concentration and Instability.[a]

1960s

IT = 1.43 + 9.30 CI + .03 E/GDP R^2 = 0.105
(1.81)[b]   (0.46)

IAVG = 24.82 − 16.96 CI + 0.81 E/GDP R^2 = 0.089
(−1.76)   (0.64)

ISQ = 8.95 − 0.64 CI + 0.03 E/GDP R^2 = 0.003
(−.11)   (0.34)

ICOV = −7.52 + 9.95 CI + .001 E/GDP R^2 = 0.112
(2.01)[b]   (.04)

1970s

IT = −3.11 + 13.30 CI + 0.38 E/GDP R^2 = 0.237
(1.09)   (3.06)[c]

IAVG = 1.57 + 2.97 CI + 0.98 E/GDP R^2 = 0.221
(0.10)   (3.14)[c]

ISQ = 17.35 + 18.69 CI + 1.02 E/GDP R^2 = 0.318
(0.99)   (3.67)[c]

ICOV = 16.40 − 11.60 CI − 0.53 E/GDP R^2 = 0.133
(1.02)   (−2.24)[b]

[a] IT = aggregate instability.
ISQ = aggregate instability without covariance.
IAVG = weighted average instability.
ICOV = IT − ISQ = a measure of the covariance.
CI = commodity concentration.
E/GDP = percent exports to GDP.
t-statistics in parentheses.
[b]Statistically significant at 0.05 level.
[c]Statistically significant at 0.01 level.

is found between commodity concentration and instability; for the 1970s sample no such relation is found, although the coefficient for the ratio of exports to GDP is statistically significant. Regressions on the other two indices obtained no statistically significant coefficient for commodity concentration, as is expected given that these indices do not account for the covariance term. The index of openness of the economy remains significant in the 1970s for these other regressions.

Examining the regressions on the covariance term (defined as the difference between the aggregate and variance indices) indicates that for the 1960s and the 1970s the coefficients for the concentration indices are weakly statistically significant, and positive in the first decade but insignificant in the second. Apparently by the results of these regressions commodity concentrations in the 1960s increased aggregate instability above the variance of the individual flows and in the 1970s had no effect on it.

These results indicate that diversification per se is not the solution to export instability. As the differences in instability between different commodity flows indicate, much depends on which commodities are reflected in the diversification. Increasing exports in manufactured products out of agricultural products would have resulted in higher instability in the 1960s and in the 1970s. Raw material exports although fairly stable in the 1960s were highly unstable in the 1970s, in many cases reflecting the volatility in their rapid growth.

To investigate further the effect of the type of commodity traded, the regressions reported in Table 10-4 were estimated. These regressions, besides using the conventional explanatory variables, also include variance indices for the trade categories previously defined. These indices are the square root of the sum of the square of the weighted individual flows that constitute these categories and thus reflect both the magnitude of the instability of a trade flow and its importance to overall export earnings.

These results indicate that in the 1960s the coefficient of commodity concentration is statistically significant once the instability of food exports and raw materials are accounted for. Instability in manufactured products, in part reflecting their small contribution to export earnings, is not significant. Apparently commodity concentration did matter in the 1960s, once account is taken of the relative instabilities of the individual trade flows. The results for the 1970s are dominated by the raw material instability and show no statistical significance for either commodity concentration or openness of the economy.

The third regression in Table 10-4 attempts to measure whether the changes between the two decades in concentration and the instabilities of the category trade flows are related to the changes in aggregate instability. The results indicate that countries that experienced an increase in commodity concentration also had an increase in aggregate instability. Also changes in the instability of manufactured products and raw materials are related to changes in aggregate instability. The coefficient of changes in food instability is not statistically significant.

The last regression in Table 10-4 attempts to measure whether the difference in the covariance terms between the two decades is related to the differences in the concentration indices and in the instability of trade flows. This then holds constant the cross-country differences in the level of instability and attempts to find if changes in

Table 10-4. Instability, Concentration, and Trade Flow Instability: The 1960s and 1970s.[a]

1960s

$$IT = -4.27 + 10.74\ CI + 0.59\ IF + 0.39\ IR + 0.21\ IM - .005\ E/GDP \qquad R^2 = 0.532$$
$$(2.42)[b]\ \ (3.55)[c]\ \ (3.90)[c]\ \ (1.21)\ \ \ (-0.10)$$

1970s

$$IT = -1.01 - 10.35\ CI + 0.12\ IF + 0.28\ IR + 0.71\ IM + 0.10\ E/GDP \qquad R^2 = 0.578$$
$$(1.29)\ \ \ (0.35)\ \ (3.95)[c]\ \ (2.18)[b]\ \ (0.82)$$

Differences Between Periods (1970s − 1960s)

$$dIT = 3.69 + 38.13\ dCI + 0.31\ dIF + 0.23\ dIR + 0.80\ dIM + 0.21\ dE/GDP \qquad R^2 = 0.512$$
$$(2.64)[b]\ \ (0.76)\ \ (2.87)[c]\ \ (1.94)\ \ \ (1.33)$$

$$dICOV = 3.82 + 40.04\ dCI - 0.38\ dIF - 0.75\ dIR + 0.12\ dIM + 0.16\ dE/GNP \qquad R^2 = 0.811$$
$$(2.79)[c]\ \ (-0.95)\ \ (-9.18)[c]\ \ (0.29)\ \ \ (1.06)$$

[a] IT = aggregate instability.
CI = commodity concentration.
IF = food and agricultural products instability.
IR = raw material instability.
IM = manufactured products instability.
ICOV = covariance term.
E/GDP = percent exports to GDP.
d - = difference between the two periods, 1970 minus 1960.
t-statistics are given in parentheses.
[b] Statistically significant at 0.05 level.
[c] Statistically significant at 0.01 level.

commodity concentrations and in the instabilities of trade flows results in a greater difference between the square root of the sum of the variances of trade flows and the variance of the aggregate. The regression indicates that increasing commodity concentration results in an increase in the covariance term, producing higher instability in aggregate earnings than indicated by the variances of individual trade flows. Somewhat countering this increase is the increasing importance of instability in raw material exports as indicated by the negative and statistically significant coefficient for the variable reflecting differences in raw material instability between the two decades.

EFFECTS OF EXPORT INSTABILITY

In this section, the effects of instability on other aggregate country parameters are investigated. The major question to be explored is whether instability of export proceeds is reflected in instability of gross domestic product, gross domestic investment, and government consumption expenditures. The differences in the instability of these parameters between the 1960s and 1970s will be compared to the changes in export instability. By using differences, many of the other specific country variables that would contribute to domestic instability are netted out of the regressions to a large extent. Table 10-5 reports the results.

These results indicate that disaggregation of export instability into measures that do not include the covariance term yields correlations with the level of instability in gross domestic product, private consumption, and government consumption expenditures. Further disaggregation into the instability of the constitution flows yields strong regressions with coefficients of agricultural product, raw material, and manufacture instabilities being statistically significant. The exceptions are the regressions on gross domestic investment, which are consistently insignificant. Export instability appears reflected in the instability of large aggregate parameters such as personal consumption but not in instability of domestic investment. However, in a regression estimated for the 1960s the coefficients of agricultural product instability and manufactured instability are significant:

$$IGDI = 6.9 + 1.14 \text{ IF} + 0.001 \text{ IR} + 0.08 \text{ IM} - 0.11 \text{ dE/GDP}$$
$$(2.79)^b \quad (0.005) \quad (2.06)^a \quad (-0.88)$$

$$R^2 = 0.299$$

a. Statistically significant at 0.05 level.
b. Statistically significant at 0.01 level.

Table 10-5. Export Instability and Aggregate Domestic Instability.

Gross Domestic Product

$$\text{dIGDP} = 1.74 + 0.15\ \text{dIT} - 0.08\ \text{dE/GDP} \qquad R^2 = 0.060$$
$$(1.39) \qquad (-0.72)$$

$$\text{dIGDP} = 1.94 + 0.10\ \text{dISQ} - 0.11\ \text{dE/GDP} \qquad R^2 = 0.119$$
$$(2.01)^b \qquad (-1.20)$$

$$\text{dIGDP} = 1.58 + 0.12\ \text{dIAVG} - 0.11\ \text{dE/GDP} \qquad R^2 = 0.156$$
$$(2.35)^b \qquad (-1.12)$$

$$\text{dIGDP} = 0.18 + 0.75\ \text{dIF} + 0.19\ \text{dIR} + 1.12\ \text{dIM} - 0.10\ \text{dE/GDP} \quad R^2 = 0.405$$
$$(3.23)^c \quad (3.74)^c \quad (2.68)^b \quad (-1.06)$$

Government Consumption Expenditures

$$\text{dIGCE} = 0.91 + 0.05\ \text{dIT} - 0.02\ \text{dE/GDP} \qquad R^2 = 0.006$$
$$(0.40) \qquad (-0.12)$$

$$\text{dIGCE} = 1.03 + 0.12\ \text{dISQ} - 0.12\ \text{dE/GDP} \qquad R^2 = 0.108$$
$$(1.84) \qquad (-0.86)$$

$$\text{dIGCE} = 0.65 + 0.15\ \text{dIAVG} - 0.16\ \text{dE/GDP} \qquad R^2 = 0.188$$
$$(2.55)^b \qquad (-1.17)$$

$$\text{dIGCE} = -1.48 + 0.85\ \text{dIF} + 0.24\ \text{dIR} + 1.81\ \text{dIM} - 0.09\ \text{dE/GDP} \quad R^2 = 0.473$$
$$(2.94)^c \quad (4.11)^c \quad (3.88)^c \quad (-0.78)$$

Gross Domestic Investment

$$\text{dIGDI} = 2.17 - 0.27\ \text{dIT} + 0.16\ \text{dE/GDP} \qquad R^2 = 0.053$$
$$(-1.27) \quad (0.82)$$

$$\text{dIGDI} = 1.46 - 0.10\ \text{dISQ} + 0.13\ \text{dE/GDP} \qquad R^2 = 0.028$$
$$(-0.90) \quad (0.64)$$

$$\text{dIGDI} = 1.52 - 0.05\ \text{dIAVG} + 0.09\ \text{dE/GDP} \qquad R^2 = 0.010$$
$$(-0.50) \quad (0.45)$$

$$\text{dIGDI} = 0.08 - 0.01\ \text{dIF} - 0.03\ \text{dIR} + 1.37\ \text{dIM} + 0.19\ \text{dE/GDP} \quad R^2 = .187$$
$$(-0.01) \quad (-0.25) \quad (1.45) \quad (0.92)$$

[a] dIGDP = difference in instability of gross domestic product (1970s-1960s).
dIGCE = difference in instability of government consumption expenditure (1970s-1960s).
dIGDI = difference in instability of gross domestic investment (1970s-1960s).
dIT = difference in aggregate instability.
dISQ = difference in variance instability.
dIAVG = difference in average instability.
dIF = "food and agricultural products" instability.
dIR = "raw material" instability.
dIM = "manufactured products" instability.
t-statistics are given in parentheses.
[b] Statistically significant at 0.05 level.
[c] Statistically significant at 0.01 level.

A similar regression for the 1970s found no such significant results. Perhaps the changing nature of exports instability with raw material instability becoming so much more important in the 1970s, has changed the path by which instability affects investment. Clearly more disaggregate and sophisticated country analysis is required to explore these issues with respect to investment. However, it appears clear that the effect of export instability does not operate primarily through aggregate export earnings but through the disaggregate, more sectorially related flows. Whether this domestic instability is traced to other effects in the economy is a difficult question to answer without disaggregating to the sectors affected by these flows. However, comparing differences in average savings rates with differences in trade flow instability between the 1960s and 1970s results in the following estimated equation:

$$dSAV = 2.4 - 0.38 \; dIF - 0.03 \; dIR - 0.82 \; dIM + 0.05 \; dE/GDP$$
$$(-2.21)^a \; (-0.88) \qquad (-4.79)^b \quad (0.85)$$

$$R^2 = 0.502$$

Where dSAV is the difference in the savings rate for 1960–1970 with that for 1970–1975. The other variables are defined in the tables and represent the commodity trade flow instabilities. This indicates that countries that experienced an increase in food and agricultural export instability and manufactured products export instability had a decline in average savings rate. This result runs contrary to the result found by Knudsen and Parnes (1975) using a different methodology based on the permanent income theory and a different aggregate index of instability. Other similar regressions like that reported on savings rates was estimated for difference in ICOR and GNP growth rates. These regressions were found to be statistically insignificant.

CONCLUSIONS AND DIRECTION
FOR FURTHER INQUIRY

The experience of export instability is clearly different for the 1960s and the 1970s with the recent decade displaying higher instability. However, this higher instability is not reflected equally across all commodity categories nor equally for all countries. Although raw material export instability took on primary importance in explaining export instability in the 1970s, mean instability in other categories

a. Significant at 0.05 level.
b. Significant at 0.01 level.

did not change significantly. Commodity concentration is a principal explanatory variable for intercountry differences in instability between countries once account is taken for instability in individual trade flows. Changes between decades in commodity concentration are related to the changes in the levels of aggregate instability once account is made of the instability of the commodities traded. This indicates that much of the a priori theorizing on the detrimental effects of commodity concentration to instability has justification, providing, however, that the type of commodities traded and their instabilities are taken into consideration. Besides these interdecade differences, the experience of individual countries must be accounted for, with many countries having individual trade flows that move with positive correlation, thus intensifying aggregate instability. Furthermore, the conventional aggregate instability indices in some countries overreflects sectorial instability and in others masks the instability of sector flows. In exploring the effects of instability, it is found that the differences in export earnings instability of sectoral trade flows is reflected in differences in aggregate parameters, with the exception of investment. Also, in one regression on savings rate, significant negative coefficients were found. However, with the weak results with other parameters, the effects question remains open. Perhaps, in these, differences in aggregate and sectoral instabilities is the key to discovering the effects of instability. And it is not improbable that, given the differences in the type and level of instability recorded for the 1960s and 1970s, the effects of instability are equally quite different for the two decades when further disaggregations are made.

NOTES

1. Measured for individual trade flows between countries so the result does not necessarily apply to overall trade flows.

2. The exceptions are Lam's work, which uses data up to 1974, and Lawson and Thanassoulas's study on effects of concentration, which uses 1971-1977 data.

3. The "1960s" is generally represented by data from 1962 to 1970; the "1970s" generally by data from 1971 to 1977 and in a few cases 1978 and 1979.

APPENDIX 10A: EXPORT EARNINGS
INSTABILITY AND ITS COVARIANCE[a]

		1960s			*1970s*		
		IT	VI	ICOV	IT	VI	ICOV
1.	Afghanistan	6.10	7.03	-0.93	8.60	10.27	-1.67
2.	Argentina	6.25	7.34	-1.09	16.00	10.70	5.30
3.	Bolivia	7.20	11.25	-4.05	—	—	—
4.	Brazil	6.70	4.84	1.76	13.40	8.14	5.26
5.	Burma	10.30	8.58	1.72	10.40	15.36	-4.96
6.	Cameroon	11.20	7.56	3.64	12.20	9.30	2.90
7.	Chad	12.90	14.40	-1.50	6.55	45.05	-38.50
8.	Chile	4.70	5.14	-0.44	26.30	21.81	4.49
9.	Colombia	7.50	7.38	0.12	7.20	6.57	0.63
10.	Congo	13.70	14.73	-1.03	42.10	119.71	-77.61
11.	Costa Rica	3.20	2.53	0.67	4.30	4.67	-0.37
12.	Egypt	6.30	5.12	1.18	11.50	13.31	-1.81
13.	El Salvador	4.32	5.14	-0.82	16.60	16.74	-0.14
14.	Ghana	13.20	13.45	-0.25	7.70	9.01	-1.31
15.	Honduras	11.10	9.25	1.85	7.80	13.61	-5.81
16.	India	5.85	3.41	2.44	3.90	3.94	-0.04
17.	Indonesia	—	—	—	31.20	31.75	-0.55
18.	Ivory Coast	8.60	7.45	1.15	10.60	8.65	1.95
19.	Kenya	—	—	—	13.86	13.58	0.28
20.	Korea	5.12	14.32	-9.20	16.14	9.33	6.81
21.	Madagascar	8.18	9.42	-1.24	5.82	5.46	0.36
22.	Mexico	3.50	4.86	-1.36	11.10	9.46	1.64
23.	Nicaragua	2.90	4.76	-1.86	6.50	9.09	-2.59
24.	Niger	18.67	16.89	1.79	15.01	13.23	1.78
25.	Nigeria	9.88	10.08	-0.20	29.67	31.13	-1.46
26.	Pakistan	5.70	7.05	-1.35	10.80	10.84	-0.04
27.	Panama	7.10	7.83	-0.73	16.20	17.08	-0.88
28.	Paraguay	12.30	9.64	2.66	13.10	10.58	2.52
29.	Peru	4.60	4.42	0.18	10.96	10.59	0.37
30.	Phillipines	7.85	6.33	1.52	17.65	23.99	-6.34
31.	Senegal	8.24	9.23	-0.99	14.71	14.18	0.53
32.	Sri Lanka	5.10	4.35	0.75	6.90	7.61	-0.71
33.	Thailand	7.75	8.70	-0.95	13.92	11.25	2.67
34.	Togo	_2.44	15.39	-2.95	40.85	46.68	-5.83
35.	Tunisia	4.14	20.95	-16.81	29.10	17.39	11.71
36.	Upper Volta	14.40	15.60	-1.20	3.09	3.63	-0.54
37.	Venezuela	8.28	11.11	-2.83	32.08	32.17	0.63

[a] IT = aggregate instability index.
VI = variance instability index.
ICOV = covariance instability index.

REFERENCES

Coppack, J. 1962. *International Economic Instability.* New York: Mac-Graw-Hill.

Erb, G.F., and S. Schiavo-Campo. 1969. "Export Instability, Level of Development and Economic Size of Less Developed Countries." *Bulletin of Oxford University Institute of Economics and Statistics* 31, 4 (November): 263-83.

Glezakos, C. 1973. "Export Instability and Economic Growth: A Statistical Verification." *Economic Development and Cultural Change* 21, 4 (July): 670-78.

Kenen, P.B., and Voivodas, C.S. 1972. "Export Instability and Economic Growth." *Kyklos* 25, 4 (December): 791-804.

Knudsen, O., and Parnes, A. 1975. *Trade Instability and Economic Development.* Lexington, Mass.: D.C. Heath.

Lam, W.V. 1980a. "Export Instability, Expansion and Market Concentration: A Methodological Interpretation." *Journal of Development Economics* 7, 1 (March): 99-115.

_____. 1980b. "Export Instability, Growth and Primary Commodity Concentration: A Methodological Interpretation." *Economia Internazionale* 33, 1 (February): 40-57.

Lawson, C.W., and Thanassoulas, C. 1981. "Commodity Concentration and Export Instability: A Missing Link or Hunting a Shark?" *Bulletin of the Oxford University Institute of Economics and Statistics* 43, 2 (May): 201-6.

MacBean, A.I. 1966. *Export Instability and Economic Development.* Cambridge, Mass.: Harvard University Press.

MacBean, A.I., and Nguyen, D.T. 1980. "Commodity Concentration and Export Earnings Instability: A Mathematical Analysis." *Bulletin of Oxford University Institute of Economics and Statistics* 90 (June): 354-62.

Maizels, A. 1968. *Exports and Economic Growth of Developing Countries.* Cambridge, England: Cambridge University Press.

Massell, B.F. 1970. "Export Instability and Economic Structure." *American Economic Review* 60, 4 (September): 618-30.

_____. 1964. "Export Concentration and Fluctuations in Export Earnings: A Cross-Section Analysis." *American Economic Review* 54, 2 (March): 47-63.

Mathieson, D.J., and McKinnon, R.J. 1974. "Instability in Underdeveloped Countries: The Impact of the International Economy." In *Nations and Households in Economic Growth* ed. M.W. Reder. New York: Academic Press.

Michaely, M. 1962. *Concentration in International Trade.* Amsterdam: North-Holland.

Soutar, G.N. 1977. "Export Instability and Concentration in Less Developed Countries." *Journal of Development Economics* 4, 3 (September): 279-97.

※ *Chapter 11*

Exchange Rates and the Adjustment Process*

J. de Larosière
Managing Director of the International Monetary Fund

The subject I treat in this chapter is a very broad one—exchange rates and the adjustment process—and I intend to treat it broadly, offering a series of practical reflections emerging from the experience of the last half dozen years. If one is going to discuss it in terms of broad generalizations, it is useful to have an image in mind of the system being described and how it works. What is the right image of the exchange rate system we have had for the last six years? On the one hand, more than three quarters of the members of the Fund have rates that are wholly or partially pegged to another currency or to a basket of currencies. On the other hand, about three quarters of all trade, including all or a major part of the trade of every industrial country, is carried out across floating rates. While many of those rates have been heavily managed in recent years, there has been no lack of movement. Thus, we have had a system which can justly be categorized as predominantly a flexible rate system.

How then was a flexible rate system supposed to work? There clearly was no general agreement on this subject or much of the controversy over the choice of an exchange rate regime would not have taken place. Nevertheless, a widely held view on the floating system saw flexible rates as providing countries with the freedom to pursue domestic objectives without the constraint imposed by balance of payments considerations, or more broadly without the need to be

---

*Adapted from a speech delivered at a luncheon organized in Paris on October 29, 1979 by the International Herald Tribune and Forex Research Limited.

directly and closely concerned with the behavior and policies of other countries. Indeed, many of the opponents of flexible rates shared this view and feared that exchange rate flexibility would diminish the external discipline on domestic management and lead to a fragmenting of the world economy.

I shall develop three themes: (1) that flexible rates do not insulate economies in an open world; (2) that they do not lessen the need for basic policy adjustments; and (3) that they do not diminish the need for cooperation and active international surveillance.

FLEXIBLE RATES DO NOT INSULATE
ECONOMIES IN AN OPEN WORLD

It is a matter of observation that, in today's world, a high degree of economic interdependence continues in spite of widespread floating. To some extent this is becaue the floating is not "clean": central bank intervention results in the transmission of monetary flows from one economy to another. This is an important and growing practice which I shall consider shortly in its own right. But even in the absence of intervention there are three fundamental reasons why flexible rates cannot fully insulate a domestic economy from external influences.

The first reason is that real activity in an economy will react to exchange rate changes only to the extent that relative costs adjust, and after the time lag that it takes for demand to respond to changes in these relative costs. It has long been recognized, of course, that exchange rate changes can only be effective if they lead to shifts in the costs of producing goods in one country as compared with others. To the extent, however, that devaluations set off movements in wages and prices that lead to offsetting increases in costs, while appreciations act in the direction of reducing costs, the effects of exchange rate changes can be limited in both time and amount. In a large number of cases changes in nominal rates have been offset by inflation differentials, and thus real exchange movements have often been small. The risk of such feedback is increased by the fact that, for many goods and services, trade volume only responds to relative cost changes over a fairly extended period. This varies from one country to another, from one time to another, and from one type of product to another. Nevertheless, for most devaluing or appreciating currencies it is generally a year or more before a noticeable change occurs in the country's real balance of trade, and a substantial additional period may be required to realize something approaching the full result of the change in the exchange rate. If during this period the relative cost improvement in devaluing countries is eroded by domestic inflation, while the relative cost deterioration in appreciating countries is dampened by reduced rates of inflation, then the full effects of the exchange rate changes will not come through and the need for adjustment will remain. Adoption of a realistic exchange rate is thus a necessary but not a sufficient condition for adjustment of a country's external accounts.

The second reason why flexible exchange rates cannot entirely insulate economies lies in the high level of external trade in relation to domestic production in many countries. Exchange rate changes cannot, especially given the lags I have mentioned, prevent the level of economic activity in one country from being affected directly by the demand for its products in its principal trading partners. In this important respect, therefore, the flexible rate system has a good deal of similarity to a pegged rate system, and those responsible for economic policy need to continue to take a close interest in economic developments in other countries.

The third aspect of interdependence which is important concerns those countries whose currencies are widely used for international trade and held by other countries in their international reserves. The domestic monetary policies of these major countries are naturally reflected in the external value of their currencies, and if these policies result in sharp fluctuations or in widespread shifts in confidence then the functioning of the world's markets and the economies of other countries are invariably and directly affected.

These, then, are three reasons for the continuing interdependence of national economies even under a regime of freely floating rates. Let me now turn to examine the type of exchange rate fluctuations we have seen in practice over the last few years, the factors that have led to the widespread adoption of "managed" floating, and the reasons why these developments in my view do not diminish the need for prompt adjustment of general economic policies compared with the position under the previous par value system.

FLEXIBLE EXCHANGE RATES DO NOT LESSEN THE NEED FOR BASIC POLICY ADJUSTMENTS

During the later years of the par value system, when balance of payments crises were receiving a good deal of attention, there were those who held that the introduction of flexible rates would banish stories about international payments and exchange rates to the back pages of the newspapers. Unfortunately, this has not turned out to be the case, and in recent years developments in exchange markets have often provided the lead stories for the media throughout the world.

Looked at retrospectively, three kinds of exchange rate changes can be identified in the recent experience: first, very short-term fluctuations of the day-to-day, month-to-month variety; second, intermediate-term fluctuations in which a change in one direction of six months to a year is subsequently reversed; and third, long-term structural changes in the pattern of rates.

It has long been held that the authorities should do what they can to smooth out very short-term fluctuations, although on occasion they may have to vary their intervention tactics to avoid being made a target by the market. There is similarly wide agreement that little can be usefully done by intervention alone to resist long-term structural rate changes.

It is, however, in the area of intermediate-term fluctuations that the test of principles becomes clearest, and here there have recently been substantial developments. Following the events of last year all countries are prepared to take a view on whether a movement in the value of their currencies is appropriate, and are prepared to use intervention and other policies to resist a potential intermediate-term change which they regard as undesirable. This is an important change in attitude, and when the commitment to the management of exchange rates reaches this level the distinction between a flexible rate system and an adjustable peg system has narrowed substantially.

The chief reasons for this adoption of "managed" floating are perhaps as follows. First, it has been accepted that exchange rates alone could not take the full strain of the severe external shocks to which economies have been subjected during the last few years. Second, governments have come to recognize that, because of the factors I described earlier, exchange rate movements cannot by themselves, or in the very short term, bring about adjustment between economies. This in itself implies that, while the management of exchange rates can make a contribution to stability, adjustment policies must go beyond intervention in exchange markets and also embrace general economic policies to tackle inflationary disorders directly. It is in the underlying economic conditions and policies that the key to exchange stability is to be found.

The recognition that changes in nominal exchange rates are an important, but not by themselves sufficient, policy tool has encouraged a search for alternatives to a system of flexible rates which would aim to coordinate intervention policies and also general policies of economic adjustment. The decision to establish the European Monetary System is an indication of a willingness to place more emphasis on the adjustment of other policies as well as exchange market intervention. It is clearly of vital importance that these other policies are in fact adjusted. Past experience with the par value system indicates that, if rates of inflation differ substantially among member countries, there is a need both to adjust exchange rates promptly and to make changes to general economic policies which prevent excessively frequent one-way movements. Similarly, exchange rate zones can make a contribution to the stability of markets, but their success depends on the timely adjustment of rates and on a readiness to adopt appropriately coordinated internal policies.

THE USE OF FLEXIBLE RATES DOES NOT DIMINISH THE NEED FOR COOPERATION AND ACTIVE INTERNATIONAL SURVEILLANCE

While the question of exchange rate arrangements is one that will continue to be followed closely in the Fund, this is an issue that the amended Articles of the Fund leave explicitly in the hands of individual members. It is clear, however, that while members are free to choose an exchange rate arrangement, the level of their exchange rates is a matter of mutual concern. Indeed, if an exchange rate is so high that it prevents "effective balance of payments adjustment" or so low that it enables the member "to gain an unfair competitive advantage over other members," the member is not fulfilling its obligations. The Fund is then required to act under its responsibility to "exercise firm surveillance over the exchange rate policies of members."

The Articles use the term surveillance to apply particularly to the exchange rate policies of members. It is clear from what has been said earlier, however, that the mere fact that a Fund member allows its exchange rate to adjust does not mean that other members can afford to be indifferent to the domestic policies it follows, or that it has no interest in the policies of other countries. Indeed, if a country cannot insulate its economy from that of others, it cannot fail to take a close interest in what happens in other countries. An increasing recognition of the fact that a high degree of interdependence remains under flexible rates has led to developments in the application of surveillance that encompass both surveillance over exchange rate policies and oversight over related economic policies which can affect the exchange rate.

The communiqué of the Interim Committee of March 1979 already reflected this wider view: "The Committee emphasized the importance of international economic cooperation, and, with this objective in mind, stressed the necessity of active surveillance by the Fund over the exchange rate and related policies of all members as a means of strengthening the adjustment process." Further encouragement for an active surveillance role for the Fund came at the recent Interim Committee Meeting in Belgrade, and the Committee's communiqué again called for an active exercise of the Fund's surveillance authority. In his address to the Annual Meetings Secretary Miller of the United States stated: "Without active surveillance, there is no system. The Fund has moved cautiously and prudently in applying its surveillance procedures. Bolder action is now required." It is widely accepted that, while regional exchange blocs have their virtues, international surveillance can make an important contribution to ensuring a degree of coherence in exchange rate and related policies throughout the system as a whole.

It is easy these days to be pessimistic about the long-run outlook. In recent years we have had a high degree of flexibility of rates combined with massive intervention in foreign exchange markets. This is a paradoxical situation, but in my view it does not arise from defects in the rules or legal arrangements of the system. Rather, we have to look to the same underlying economic policy errors that made the old par value system unsustainable. That system could tolerate modest differences in inflation rates with periodic adjustments in exchange rates but could not withstand divergence in economic policies on the scale experienced in the late 1960s and early 1970s. Now, as then, the difficulties encountered by the United States in containing its rate of inflation are central to the problems we are encountering. The United States is to be commended for the recent monetary policy changes that indicate the seriousness with which inflation is being regarded.

CONCLUSION

For my concluding remarks I will present a few general observations that arise from these reflections on exchange rates and the adjustment process. The first is that there has been less difference between the operation of the adjustment process under the par value system and under flexible rates than many had expected. This extends right through to the Fund's stabilization programs. Some may have thought that the nature of these stabilization programs, particularly the restraints on domestic credit expansion, would be different under flexible rates. Recent research at the Fund, however, has shown that under a flexible rate system such as the present one, in which countries exercise a degree of management over exchange rates, such a distinction does not apply.

A second observation is that, among a considerable number of swings in exchange rates, there have been over the period some significant real exchange rate changes. A substantial movement in real exchange rates occurred in the latter part of 1977 and in 1978 between the U.S. dollar and a number of other major currencies. The position stabilized in the first half of 1979 with further changes occurring recently. Balance of payments positions, in particular a much needed shift in the current account positions of the three largest industrial countries, show that these real exchange rate changes have played a role in adjustment.

A third observation is that while we are still very early in the process of applying surveillance, it can make a significant contribution to the adjustment process if used with a combination of firmness and discretion. In this connection I was very heartened in Belgrade to see that there is growing understanding in countries of the deep-seated nature of the inflationary problem confronting us. This is of particular importance in the case of the United States given the key position it occupies in the system as a whole. If the governments of the world's major trading countries persevere in the firm resolve which they have now expressed, and in a framework of active international cooperation, then the outlook must be for a smoother functioning of the exchange markets in the international adjustment process.

✳ *Chapter 12*

The Exchange Rate as an Instrument of Policy*

Otmar Emminger
President of the Deutsche Bundesbank

THE PRESENT FRAMEWORK OF EXCHANGE RATES

Since 1973 exchange rate policy has largely centered on the use of flexible exchange rates or "floating." It should not be forgotten, however, that only a minority of countries in the Western world have floating currencies. In the middle of 1978, of the one hundred and thirty-three member countries of the IMF only thirty-eight countries were "floaters" (of which six maintained common margins in the "snake" arrangement and five adjusted exchange rates according to a set of indicators), in addition to Switzerland as a nonmember of the IMF, and ninety-five members pegged their currencies either to a single other currency—predominantly the U.S. dollar—or to a basket of currencies, like the special drawing right (SDR). But currencies that are pegged are in reality also floating—namely, against all the currencies that float against their own key currency. In fact, less than one-fifth of all international trade moves across pegged exchange rates.

Pegging inside a regional bloc that floats jointly against all other currencies, as in the European Monetary System (EMS), raises particular problems. The close regional and institutional interconnections of the member countries provide an incentive for maintaining mutual exchange rates as stable as possible. On the other hand, fixed parities in relation to the dollar and other "external" cur-

---

*Revised and abridged version of a Special Lecture at the London School of Economics on December 7, 1978.

rencies are practically impossible. Thus, such a regional currency bloc is beset with the problems of fixed but adjustable rates in its internal relations and with those of floating in its external relations.

WHY DID THE SYSTEM OF FIXED PARITIES BREAK DOWN?

The transition to widespread "floating" among the major currencies in early 1973 was a reaction to the rigidities of the Bretton Woods system of fixed parities. Under this system the fixed but adjustable exchange rate has essentially been viewed as a means of providing a stable basis for external economic and monetary relations. In circumstances of "fundamental disequilibrium" alterations of the exchange rate could—and should—be used as an instrument for balance of payments adjustment. In its first twenty years or so the Bretton Woods system had worked reasonably well. But over time it turned out that countries were not sufficiently prepared to adjust their domestic demand and price level to their exchange rate, nor were they, as a rule, willing to adjust their exchange rate speedily enough to their domestic situation or to their fundamental payments position. Thus it was rightly called a system of "reluctant adjustment" by the late Professor Harry Johnson (Johnson 1968: 121). In its final stage of degeneration this system had contributed to a distorted pattern of over- and undervalued exchange rates, to a consequent dislocation of productive resources, to an inflation of currency reserves and of the money supply in Europe due to excessive obligatory dollar purchases, and—last but not least—to a never-ending succession of exchange rate crises.

Up to this day the experts have been unable to agree on the causes of the breakdown of the Bretton Woods system. Nor have they been able to agree on the role to be attributed to "floating" or even on its actual performance up to the present.

It would be superficial to ascribe the breakdown to one event —namely, the suspension of the dollar's convertibility into gold in August 1971. A more fundamental cause behind this event was the growing overvaluation of the dollar—which European critics ascribed mainly to America's policy of "benign neglect" of its payments deficit, while American critics occasionally blamed countries with strong currencies for not appreciating them speedily enough. Other observers, following the lead of Professor Triffin, held that the reserve role of the dollar would inexorably lead to a breakdown of the system; they believed that the growing need for reserves of other countries would "force payments deficits on the United

States" until its external overindebtedness in relation to its own (gold) reserves would become untenable (at least under continuing gold convertibility of the dollar). However, from 1970 to 1973 the creation of new dollar reserves was excessive by all standards and was certainly not forced upon the United States by a legitimate need for new reserves. Moreover, European countries did not go over to floating against the dollar because the dollar had become inconvertible into gold. On the contrary, since the suspension of the dollar's convertibility into gold in August 1971, they have multiplied their dollar holdings to an amazing extent. The absence of gold convertibility has not diminished the reserve role of the dollar.

In my view, the reasons for the breakdown of the fixed rate system were complex. The growing external weakness of the dollar—in part due to the Vietnam inflation in the United States, in part to other causes—certainly played an important role. But there were additional reasons: since the beginning of the 1970s, high and widely divergent inflation rates among a number of major countries made a fixed rate system increasingly vulnerable; they would have necessitated a continuing series of exchange rate adjustments that would have kept the whole system constantly embroiled in speculative expectations and turmoil. Furthermore, confidence-induced money flows from one country to another often assumed enormous proportions with the growing internationalization of banking and of money markets, in particular the Eurodollar market. "The adjustable peg opened the floodgate for disruptive speculation," as Professor Haberler put it (Haberler 1977: 245).

To this was added a fundamental monetary asymmetry of the system: in the surplus countries the central banks were obliged to intervene to support the fixed dollar rate and thus had (often involuntarily) to expand their monetary base ("imported inflation"), whereas in the deficit countries, owing to their accommodating monetary policy, foreign exchange outflows usually did not lead to a slowing down of monetary expansion. This produced a ratchet effect, an international escalation of inflation, whenever even temporary imbalances or crises of confidence occurred, with consequent large foreign exchange flows. It is no accident that in the final years of the par value system, the inflation of the money supply in Europe reached record levels: in the three and a quarter years from the beginning of 1970 to March 1973 the European money stock (in the wider definition) increased by no less than 54 percent, while in the main deficit country, the United States, the money supply, far from slowing down, also experienced a record expansion. Thus, the system of fixed par values had become a "perfect inflation machine," as it was called in 1971 by Karl Blessing, a former governor of the Bundesbank.

As one who participated in (and was partly responsible for) the decision of West Germany to go over to floating in March 1973, I can testify that the main reason for this decision was the effort to shield the German monetary system against further inflationary foreign exchange inflows, after the Bundesbank had to absorb a dollar inflow worth more than DM 20 billion within five weeks, creating money equivalent to more than double the amount of new central bank money required for a whole year. There was a very similar motivation for the Swiss decision to go over to floating a few weeks earlier (end of January 1973).

If I had to name the single most important cause of the breakdown of the Bretton Woods system of fixed parities, I would put my finger on the huge dollar flows which—as a consequence of the American payments deficits, enlarged by confidence movements and by the Eurodollar market—swamped the world monetary system at the beginning of the 1970s and which in February–March 1973 became intolerably destabilizing for a number of countries.

LESSONS FROM THE BREAKDOWN OF
THE FIXED PARITIES SYSTEM

From these historical experiences a number of lessons for exchange rate policy can be drawn:

First, a combination of a weak dollar and enormous volatile dollar holdings in the world would wreck, sooner or later, any attempt at a fixed parity or even a mere target zone for the dollar. For the foreseeable future we can, therefore, rule out any such arrangements in relation to the dollar.

Second, as long as there are wide divergences of cost and price movements in different countries, fixed parities between them are clearly not maintainable. "It is virtually impossible to operate a system of fixed parities in a world of chronic inflation" (Bernstein 1973:167). And this, in particular, because in an inflationary world, wide divergences in inflation rates are unavoidable. The sensitivity to inflation differs widely from country to country.

Third, the transition to widespread floating in 1973 was not a deliberate act in search of a better international monetary system; rather, it was forced on the major countries by events.

Fourth, the primary reason for going over to floating in 1973 was emphatically not to facilitate the adjustment of relative exchange rate levels, but to put up a defense against confidence-induced destabilizing flows of funds. It would therefore be wrong to judge the system of floating primarily according to its performance in the adjustment process.

That there was no free choice between fixed and flexible exchange rates has been demonstrated by subsequent developments. Indeed, had the major countries not gone over to floating in the spring of 1973, they would quite certainly have been compelled to do so when at the end of 1973 the oil price explosion subjected the payments pattern of the world to enormous strains. As Mr. Witteveen, the then Managing Director of the IMF, said in an address in London in January 1974, immediately after the oil shock, "In the present situation, a large measure of floating is unavoidable and indeed desirable," (Witteveen 1974: 20).

That the transition to floating was primarily a defense against destabilizing money flows,[1] and not necessarily a means of payments adjustment, is well illustrated by the German and American experiences in the initial years of floating. In Germany, the inflationary inflow of foreign exchange ceased entirely from the middle of 1973 to the end of 1975;[2] in 1976 there was again an inflow, but this was entirely due to Germany's obligation to intervene in the regional fixed rate system of the European common float (the "snake"), while there was no net inflow from outside the "snake" system. It was only from the autumn of 1977 onward—that is, with the increasing weakness of the U.S. balance of payments—that floating against the dollar no longer provided a sufficient shield against destabilizing foreign exchange inflows.

THE USE OF FLOATING FOR PAYMENTS ADJUSTMENT

As concerns payments adjustment through flexible exchange rates, this can only be expected to a significant extent in so far as "floating" leads to a change in the "real" exchange rate—that is, a change in the average ("effective") exchange rate that exceeds a mere offsetting of cost and price differentials between various countries.

Now both for the dollar and the DM there was little net change in the "real" rate of exchange in the four years from March 1973 to March 1977. There were relatively wide fluctuations up and down. But the net outcome over this period was for the dollar a "real" (i.e., price-adjusted) depreciation of only about 4 percent and for the Deutsche mark a "real" appreciation of 2 percent (measured by using trade-weighted variations in the respective exchange rates and adjusting them by relative consumer prices).[3]

In fact, the historical process correcting the long-standing over-valuation of the dollar had already been largely brought about un-der the previous fixed rate system; the "real" (price adjusted) de-valuation of the dollar between 1969 and March 1973—approximately 17 percent—was several times larger than anything achieved under the floating rate system between March 1973 and the middle of 1977. The same is true of the "real" appreciation of the DM, which was also several times larger from 1969 to 1973 than in the subse-quent years of floating.

More generally, it can be said that at least in the initial period after 1973 floating did not lead to large shifts in the "real" levels of major currencies. As the IMF summed up this experience in its an-nual report for 1976: "Trends of most countries' exchange rates over the floating period as a whole have been broadly commensurate with major differences in rates of domestic inflation" (IMF 1976: 3) And a year later, in its 1977 annual report it wrote: "Exchange rate changes do not seem, however, to have played much of a role in recent years in reducing existing external imbalances among indus-trial countries" (IMF 1977:30).

This was due in large measure to the fact that in many countries the exchange rate was deliberately exempted from the task of help-ing the adjustment process after the oil price explosion and during the worldwide recession, when financing, and not correcting, the imbalances was the order of the day. In early 1974 an international consensus came about among the IMF member countries that at least for a certain period of time, payments imbalances due to the oil price explosion should not be absorbed by the exchange rate but should be "accepted"—that is, financed out of reserves or foreign borrowing. This led not only to heavy foreign borrowing by many countries (the total amount of current account deficits that had to be financed out of reserves or net borrowing abroad jumped from $22 billion in 1973 to $77 billion in 1974!) but implied a deliberate "strong management of floating."

A few years later, in 1976, both the IMF (through its Managing Director) and the OECD appealed to member countries that now the time had come to shift from mere financing toward correcting pay-ments disequilibria. Actually, 1976 was the year when—although for quite different reasons—several major currencies, in particular those of Italy, Britain, and France, were under strong downward pres-sure, leading to an adjustment of their external value to their internal value and even below it. In these cases it was the foreign exchange market, and in particular confidence-induced capital movements, that forced this "real" depreciation on the currencies concerned.

Thus, the exchange rate was used only grudgingly as a means of payments adjustment, often only when capital movements forced "overshooting," and thus "real" adjustment of the exchange rate, on both deficit and surplus countries—Italy, Britain, France, the United States on the one side, Japan, Switzerland, Germany, et alia on the other side. This often-criticized "overshooting" has in several cases played a useful role.

THE DOLLAR AS A SPECIAL BURDEN ON THE FLOATING RATE SYSTEM

From the autumn of 1977 to the end of 1978 the pressures on the dollar were so strong that a number of countries were forced by circumstances to intervene heavily in support of the dollar in order to prevent wildly exaggerated ("erratic") swings in the exchange rate structure of the world. During this period the bilateral exchange rate relationships between the dollar and some "stronger" currencies no longer reflected either relative price movements or interest rate differentials or relative money supply movements.

It is often believed in high quarters, especially in the United States and in Britain, that this pressure on the dollar rate has mainly arisen from the huge amount of so-called "footloose" or "stateless" dollars created and held by the international banking system. In my view, however, by far the most important influence has been the sudden turnaround in the American balance on current account, to which neither the American capital balance nor the official financing measures of the American authorities were adjusted in time ("benign neglect"!). This turnaround in the current account balance amounted to no less than $32 billion within two years—from a surplus of $18 billion in 1975 to a deficit of $14 billion in 1977. This dramatic shift was due to a number of factors: structural reasons, such as the growing dependence on foreign oil or the inroads of Japan and a group of advanced developing countries into the American market; cyclical factors—namely, the faster growth of demand in the United States compared with the rest of the industrial world; and finally, an increasing inflation differential to the disadvantage of the United States. The deficit was increased by large net capital exports of the United States. The floating rate system has been severely put to the test by this abrupt change. No other exchange rate system would have been able to cope with such a sudden shift in the external fortunes of the major economic power of the world. But in the absence of proper financing by the United States themselves, this huge basic deficit—amounting to more than $30 billion in each of the years 1977 and 1978—also forced the central banks of the world to finance it by intervening in the dollar market (with the Bundesbank's share of about $10.5 billion in the two years, out of a total of nearly $70 billion, being relatively modest).

A GENERAL ASSESSMENT OF FLOATING

More recently, and particularly since the end of 1977, there has emerged a growing disenchantment and discontent with the results of the floating rate regime. This has led on the one hand to a move toward a wider area of stable exchange rates in Western Europe (EMS) and on the other hand to a greater degree of control and management of floating, including the management of the dollar rate.

As the floating rate system seems to have entered a critical phase, it is appropriate to review briefly recent experiences with floating. This is a field where prejudice and preconceived ideas abound. There can be no doubt that many high-flown expectations—entertained by uncritical believers in floating—have been disappointed. But many fears and objections of opponents to floating have not materialized either.

Let me first look at the disappointments. Some advocates had expected that in such a system, the balance of payments would look after itself, giving the national authorities more freedom to pursue domestic goals. To quote Edward M. Bernstein, the well-known economic advisor to the IMF in the 1950s: "The reasons for preferring a system of fluctuating exchange rates in a period of inflation and unsettled economic conditions is that it will facilitate adjustment to an appropriate balance of payments on both current and capital account" (EMB 1975:13). And looking at the large current account surplus that the United States had achieved in 1975 he wrote: "There can be no doubt that it [the depreciation of the dollar from 1970 to 1975] has been effective in improving the U.S. trade balance. In this respect, the system of fluctuating exchange rates has worked well—perhaps too well in a world that has massive oil deficits (sic!)" (EMB 1975: 1). The factual basis for this last judgment proved to be short-lived, however, since a few years later a combination of cyclical and structural factors, as well as a poor relative price performance, had converted the 1975 surplus into the largest American payments deficit every recorded.

Samuel Brittan, one of the early advocates of floating, had expected "that a floating exchange rate . . . , in contrast to all alternatives, is almost too good at keeping overseas payments in balance" (Brittan 1970: 66). But he is expressly warned that "it is no magic wand and will only work satisfactorily if backed by sensible internal policies" (Brittan 1970: 65).

Even with such support, trade flows often respond only slowly to changes in exchange rates, for a number of reasons that I need not enumerate in detail here. And when the volume of exports and imports has begun to change in the right direction, this is usually accompanied by a relative change in import and export prices (i.e., the terms of trade), which can produce a perverse result in value terms for a considerable time (the J-curve effect). Thus, in Japan as well as in Germany, imports increased in 1978 much more than exports in volume terms; but in dollar terms their respective surpluses on current account even increased for a while, before they definitely turned down, and shifted into deficit in 1979.

Although changes in exchange rates by themselves are no panacea, they do work

1. provided that they have led to "real" changes in exchange rates, and
2. provided that they are supported by appropriate domestic policies.

Econometric studies at the Federal Reserve Board in Washington, for instance, have shown that the American trade deficit will narrow by between $750 million and $1 billion over a period of two years with every percentage point of "real" dollar depreciation, after allowing for inflation. As the IMF stated in its 1978 annual report:

> There is considerable empirical evidence that relative price changes have a strong influence on the volume of imports and exports. Time is needed, however, . . . so that only some fraction, say one fourth to one half, of the ultimate volume effects will be observed over a period as short as a year. . . . In contrast to these volume effects, exchange rate changes can affect a country's terms of trade rather rapidly. As a result of this asymmetry of timing, the trade balance generally degenerates before it begins to move steadily in the expected direction. (IMF 1978: 41)

And this perverse initial effect may, of course, sometimes lead to misdirected speculative movements (e.g., in leads and lags of payments).

To mention a few well-known cases where "real" changes in exchange rates have produced equilibrating results: the improvement of the current account of the United States in the years 1974–1976 as a consequence of the "real" depreciation of the dollar from 1969 to 1973; the surprising reversal of the external balance of Italy, Britain, and France from very large current account deficits in 1974 to equilibrium or surplus in 1978; and finally, the considerable volume effect on the Japanese trade balance in 1978, followed by a corresponding value effect in early 1979.

Because floating has turned out not to be a fast-acting panacea by itself for payments imbalances, it has not liberated domestic economic policy from all external constraints. It has given monetary policy more freedom to pursue national monetary targets, as both Germany and Switzerland have demonstrated after their transition to floating in early 1973. But very often the dilemma between external and internal monetary considerations has cropped up again. Seemingly this was also the case when the Federal Reserve saw itself obliged to repeatedly increase interest rates in support of the external value of the dollar since January 1978; but in retrospect it has turned out that this would have been at least as necessary in order to fight domestic inflation.

Floating seems to have made some "strong" currencies stronger by a virtuous circle of appreciation leading to more domestic stability and some "weak" currencies weaker by a vicious circle of depreciation, increased inflation, and more depreciation. But here again, the considered judgment of the IMF may be quoted: "A needed exchange rate adjustment will become associated with a vicious circle only if demand management policy is sufficiently expansionary to permit it" (IMF 1977: 35).

Finally, flexible rates have sometimes moved in an abrupt and erratic manner, difficult to relate to variations in underlying economic conditions. The expected equilibrating market effect of foreign exchange speculation as well as of sort-term money flows induced by interest rate differentials has often been lacking.

Turning now to some fears of the critics and opponents which proved exaggerated: First, world trade has not been crippled. On the contrary, in the past six years of widespread floating, from the beginning of 1973 to 1978, the volume of foreign trade has continued to expand faster than total production (according to OECD estimates, the volume of international trade of the industrial countries rose from 1972 to 1978 by 37 percent, while real GNP increased by 20 percent).

Contrary to fears that flexible rates would throttle international capital movements, such movements have in recent years risen to enormous—some might even say, excessive—levels. Even more important, the floating rate system has demonstrated a high degree of shock absorption capacity. It has weathered several severe shocks and disturbances to the world economy—the oil price increases, the sudden and deep recession in the United States, inflationary crises in some countries, and the phasing out of sterling as a reserve currency —in a tolerable way.

The floating system, although it has often been criticized as fueling inflation, has in fact not prevented the world economy from gradually overcoming the worst features of the inflation of the years 1972 to 1974. In my view it has even greatly helped this movement, on the one hand by supporting monetary stabilization policies in low inflation countries through shielding them against imported inflation, and on the other hand by depreciating exchange rates, thus putting strong pressure on high inflation countries to set up domestic stabilization programs. In this connection, an overreaction of the exchange markets (or "overshooting") may occasionally have a quite positive function. On the other hand, floating by itself—if not supported by appropriate domestic policies—seems powerless against the new wave of inflation beginning near the end of 1978.

The fear that floating rates would be widely abused for competitive depreciation and would end in economic warfare has turned out to be groundless. On the contrary, when after the sudden appearance of a huge oil deficit in 1974 it was agreed that for an interim period this supposedly "irrepressible" deficit should be "accepted" —that is, bridged over by borrowing—there developed a tendency toward higher rather than lower exchange rates in order to ward off the inflationary impact of high world prices.

Finally, contrary to the fears of the opponents of floating, it has not led to a breakdown in international cooperation in the financial field. Thus, while the advocates of floating have had to digest a certain amount of disillusionment, its opponents have had to swallow a spoonful of realism.

Looking back over the last six years, and taking a broad general view, I would say that floating worked reasonably well at least up to 1977—considering the prevailing circumstances and considering also the available alternatives. Floating has, in particular, spared the world a series of exchange rate crises that would have been inevitable under a fixed rate system. This view is supported by the evaluation of the International Monetary Fund in its 1975 annual report, which in its sedate language reads: "On the whole, exchange rate flexibility appears to have enabled the world economy to surmount a succession of disturbing events, and to accommodate divergent trends in costs and prices in national economies with less disruption of trade and payments than a system of par values would have been able to do" (IMF 1975: 33).

This was like a sigh of relief after the worst of the oil crisis and the American recession had been overcome without a breakdown of the international system. In subsequent years, however, skepticism and frustration with pure floating have increased. This appears, for instance, in the more skeptical views about floating in the reports of the BIS (Bank for International Settlements), the central bankers' bank, and particularly of the chairman of the Council of Administration of the BIS, the Dutch central bank governor, Mr. Zijlstra. He wrote in an annual report of his central bank a few years ago: "For the time being there is no alternative to floating rates for the principal currencies. On the other hand it is still far too early to make a lasting virtue of that necessity" (Zijlstra 1976: 15). This skeptical view could also be expressed by adapting Churchill's famous dictum on democracy: floating may have been the worst system, except for all the other available ones.

NEW TRENDS IN EXCHANGE RATE POLICIES

The vulnerable position of the dollar in the exchange markets since the autumn of 1977 has had a considerable influence on the American attitude toward floating. In November 1978, after the dramatic fall of the dollar and the equally dramatic introduction of a massive dollar support program, a high American government official explained: "We have moved into a very activist definition of countering disorderly markets, and in fact, under present conditions, the phrase disorderly markets may be inappropriate because we are determined to have *stability* in exchange markets." But sooner or later the minds of those responsible for the dollar may again be torn between wanting the dollar rate high and stable and at the same time wanting it sufficiently "competitive."

This interest of the U.S. authorities in more exchange rate stability and in the correction of "wrong" exchange rate levels should certainly not be interpreted as a move to a target rate for the dollar. But it is a significant shift toward a firmer management of the dollar exchange rate, and above all it shows, together with other parts of the new dollar support program, that the era of "benign neglect" of the external value of the dollar is over.

A number of countries have had the sobering experience that if there is a major external imbalance, the adjustment cannot be left to the floating exchange rate alone. "Adjustment" always means a shift in real resources from the domestic to the external sector (or vice versa) and a change in relative real wages. It cannot, therefore, be "painless." The change in "real" exchange rates is a necessary, but not sufficient, condition. Demand management is often more important. The staff of the IMF (1978) have tried to estimate what the relative contributions to external adjustment of a change in real demand versus a change in the exchange rate were for various countries. In reality, a fundamental disequilibrium can be adjusted only by a combination of both demand and relative price (i.e., exchange rate) measures. This realization has had some influence on the application of exchange rate changes. If domestic measures could not be dispensed with, why not put the emphasis mainly on the domestic stabilization program and give the exchange rate only a minor supporting role?

It has been recognized that the exchange rate is a two-edged instrument. The effect of exchange rate variations on the balance of trade and on current account is often disappointingly slow and during a transitional period often perverse (the J-curve effect). On the other hand, the impact on domestic prices has often been felt very quickly. Recently, a European central bank claimed that a depreciation of its currency would rapidly raise domestic costs and prices not only to the same degree but possibly by even more than would correspond to the devaluation; thus the country would, after a short transitional period, be no better, but may be even worse off as concerns price competitiveness than before the depreciation. Such reasoning has given rise to the theory of the vicious circle. In reality, this theory is an oversimplification. Everything depends on the combination of exchange rate policy with domestic policy. It has been shown, both in theory and in practice, that the vicious circle of depreciation, leading to more inflation and again to more depreciation, can be broken by an appropriate policy mix.

As the inflation rates of the mid-1970s gave the fight against inflation a high priority, the emphasis in using the exchange rate shifted in a number of countries toward its stabilizing possibilities. Formerly, the main emphasis was on the role that exchange rates could play in improving external competitiveness and thereby adjusting payments imbalances. I would call this the period of "competitive" exchange rate policy. Those were the times when international organizations like the IMF and the OECD feared "competitive devaluations" on the model of the 1930s (although this is one of many myths in this field, as in the 1930s there were few competitive devaluations and many more cases of obstinate overvaluation of currencies).

Today, some countries give precedence to the direct effect of their exchange rate on domestic costs and prices. As they look at exchange rates as potential "price stabilizers," they are more interested in relatively higher rather than lower exchange rates.

A good illustration of the change in emphasis from a competitive to a stabilizing exchange rate is the recent development in Britain. When the pound went over to floating in June 1972, the first reaction in Britain "was one of almost jubilation" (*Euromoney* 1972: 3). The predominant view was that Britain now had a chance to get rid of the "pseudoproblems artificially created by the attempt to freeze exchange rates" (Brittan 1970). The balance of payments and the external value of the pound could—so it appeared—be safely left to the flexible exchange rate. This would at last provide more freedom of action in domestic demand management. Now compare this to the "Conclusions" in the British Government's recent Green Paper, of November 24, 1978, on the European Monetary System where we read: "The Government for its part has made it clear that it does not regard exchange rate depreciation as a solution to the economic problems still facing the U.K. . . . Only an improvement in our industrial performance and victory in the battle against inflation can provide a lasting basis for stability of the exchange rate" (Great Britain. Chancellor of the Exchequer 1978: 12).

We can also discern a new trend concerning exchange rate policy in one or two surplus countries. Surplus countries have benefited from the virtuous circle—the balance of payments surplus leading to appreciation of the currency and thus to greater domestic price stability with the consequence of further appreciation.

The Swiss case is a first class example of the extremes to which a one-sided virtuous circle may lead. A few years ago, the president of the Swiss National Bank explained his country's position: "We had to give up fixed rates because the volume of dollar purchases by the Swiss National Bank was just too big. Inflation was almost 12 per cent in 1973. . . . With the float we regained control of our domestic money supply" (*International Herald Tribune* 1976). In October 1978, after the Swiss franc had been pushed up in the markets way above anything that could be justified by relative price trends or any other underlying factors, the Swiss National Bank announced a sort of ceiling rate for the Swiss franc, by defining the maximum appreciation of the Swiss franc vis-à-vis the Deutsche mark that it would henceforth tolerate. It also announced that in order to hold the Swiss franc below the ceiling, it would, if necessary, intervene on a massive scale in the foreign exchange markets, irrespective of the ensuing expansion of domestic liquidity. This was followed up in January 1979 by the official suspension of a quantitative monetary target. For the time being—as long as inflationary pressures do not reemerge more visibly—control of the money supply has been sacrificed for the sake of better control of the exchange rate. The Swiss National Bank has made it clear, however, that adequate control of the money supply will be reintroduced as soon as there are signs that the offsetting effect of the high exchange rate on prices is no longer assured.

In Germany we have also had a touch of a virtuous circle and a similar trade-off between money supply policy and exchange rate policy, but to a lesser degree than in Switzerland. For the year 1978 the target was an average increase in the stock of "central bank money" of 8 percent, but the actual expansion was 11.5 percent. The main justification for this overshooting was that the appreciation of the Deutsche mark had been acting as an offsetting counterinflationary force—so much so, indeed, that the rate of price increase in 1978 (consumer prices rose 2.6 percent) was slightly below our own official forecast.

German exchange rate policy has continued to adhere to the principle that the exchange rate of the Deutsche mark—as far as it is not a fixed rate in relation to other EEC currencies—should follow the underlying market trends and that we intervene in the dollar market only to counter disorderly conditions (in a broad sense) and to try to smooth abrupt and excessive swings. Nevertheless, the appreciation of the mark, which from 1977 to the end of 1978 somewhat exceeded the average inflation differentials vis-à-vis major countries, gave us a welcome trade-off aginast the inflationary potential of an excessively expanding money supply, the excessive expansion being mainly due to interventions of the Deutsche Bundesbank both against the dollar and inside the European fixed-rate system. The goal of German monetary policy in this period had been to keep the inflationary effect of foreign exchange intervention and the deflationary effect of mark in balance.

The recent Swiss experience, which our experience in Germany parallels (although not in such extreme terms), demonstrates that floating rates can exert strong pressures just as much on surplus as on deficit countries. In this sense it is a more symmetrical system.

FINAL REMARKS

It has sometimes been said that with a fixed exchange rate, a country no longer has any power over its inflation rate because it is forced to follow the level of international inflation. On the other hand, it is alleged that with a floating rate it no longer has any power over its level of employment, as the appreciation or depreciation of its exchange rate determines the rate of capacity utilization and profits.

The first thesis is partly borne out by our own experience in Germany. During the last stage of fixed rates from 1970 to 1973, Germany was unable to dissociate itself from the average rate of price inflation in the major countries (the United States, Britain, France, and Italy). In the 1950s and 1960s, however, it had significantly more price stability than its European neighbours—with the consequence of an undervalued currency with a structural misallocation of resources and occasional currency crises followed by belated up-valuations. At the same time, however, it had some disinflationary influence on its trading partners: it exported stability and imported inflation.

The second thesis, concerning the effect of floating on growth, cannot so easily be proven by actual experience. Growth and employment are determined not only by the level of the exchange rate. They are affected even more by domestic policies and developments, which by themselves also greatly influence the exchange rate. It is the combination of domestic policies and exchange rate developments that counts for the result.

This seems to me to be the most important general lesson to be learned from the experience of the last six to ten years. Whether the exchange rate is used as a competitive tool for balance of payments adjustment or as a stabilizing influence on domestic costs and prices, the result will always depend on the support that exchange rate policy is given by other economic and financial polices.

NOTES

1. In the case of Germany and Switzerland against destabilizing inflows, in the case of Britain (1972) and Italy (January 1973) against destabilizing outflows.

2. Germany's dollar holdings even declined by about $3.7 billion during these two and a half years.

3. Measured by a comparison of relative unit labor costs, both the average "real" depreciation of the dollar and the average "real" appreciation of the DM were larger.

REFERENCES

Bernstein, E.M. 1973. "New Devaluation of the Dollar", A prepared statement of Edward M. Bernstein. *In Hearings before the Subcommittee on International Finance of the Committee of Banking and Currency, House of Repre-*

sentatives, Ninety-third Congress, First Session on H.R. 4546, a Bill to Amend the Par Value Modification Act. Washington, D.C.: U.S. Government Printing Office: 164-8.

Brittan, S. 1970. *The Price of Economic Freedom: A Guide to Flexible Rates.* London: Macmillan.

EMB (Ltd.) Research Economists. 1975. *Economic Aspect of Floating Dollar,* Report No. 75/15 (August). Washington, D.C.: EMB (Ltd.)

Euromoney. 1972. "The Real Worries about Sterling". In *Euromoney,* London: Euromoney Publications Ltd. (July): 3-5.

Great Britain. Chancellor of the Exchequer. 1978. *The European Monetary System.* London: HMSO.

Haberler, G. 1977. "The International Monetary System After Jamaica and Manila." In *AEI Studies on Contemporary Economic Problems, 1977,* ed. W.J. Fellner. Washington: American Enterprise Institute for Public Policy Research: 239-288.

International Herald Tribune. 1976. "Policy of Floating the Franc, Fights Inflation While Aiding Recovery." (May 10).

International Monetary Fund. 1975. *Annual Report 1975.* Washington, D.C.: International Monetary Fund.

———. 1976. *Annual Report 1976.* Washington, D.C.: International Monetary Fund.

———. 1977. *Annual Report 1977.* Washington, D.C.: International Monetary Fund.

———. 1978. *Annual Report 1978.* Washington, D.C.: International Monetary Fund.

Johnson, H. 1968. "Problems of Balance of Payments Adjustment in the Modern World". *In Essays in Money and Banking in Honour of R.S. Sayers,* London: Oxford: 113-29.

Witteveen, H.J. 1974. "The Role of the International Monetary Fund", Address delivered to the World Banking Conference in London on January 15, 1974. Printed in *IMF Survey* (January 21): 17, 20-22.

Zijlstra, J. 1976. "The President's Report". In *De Nederlandsche Bank n.v. Report for the Year 1975.* Amsterdam: the Nederlands Bank (April): 11-20.

✳ *Chapter 13*

On the Efficacy of the Generalized Floating System

Hideo Suzuki
Advisor to the President, the Nomura Securities Co.,
Ltd. and former Special Advisor to the Minister of
Finance in Japan.

FLOATING EXCHANGE RATE

Over the past few years, we have seen disturbances on the foreign exchange markets and wide fluctuations of exchange rates. This instability is attributable to two reasons. One is the balance of payments disequilibrium between major countries. The other is the declining role of the U.S. dollar as a reserve currency and the disorganized shift from the dollar to other reserve currencies.

The conceptually structured floating system presumes (1) that the exchange rate is determined through the demand and supply mechanism and (2) that balance of payments disequilibrium rectifies itself through changes in the exchange rate. Although the flexibility of the exchange rate has been abundantly proved in the recent past, the effectiveness of the floating system in restoring balance of payments equilibrium has come to be questioned. The reasons are that (1) the price elasticities of exports and imports were too low to correct trade account imbalances effectively and (2) the interest rate was not flexible enough to adjust adequately the capital account of the balance of payments.

As is often pointed out, under the floating system, changes in the exchange rate take place only gradually, so that the price elasticities at the initial stage are likely to be small. People can easily get accustomed to a newly set exchange rate, while the terms of trade do not always reflect changes in the exchange rate. Furthermore, even after substantial changes in the terms of trade take place, the resultant changes in trade volume tend to be limited.

In 1978, Japan witnessed what might be described as the "reverse" J-curve—a process where the rate of decrease in export volume is exceeded by the rate of increase in export price. Consequently, the dollar value of Japan's exports continued to increase sharply. Furthermore, a massive inflow of foreign capital into Japan occurred in anticipation of further appreciation of the yen. From January to July 1978 in particular, Japan's current account registered a surplus of $10.5 billion, and the Bank of Japan supported the value of the U.S. dollar by purchasing approximately $10 billion on the exchange market. Nevertheless, the market value of the U.S. dollar vis-à-vis the yen declined by 26 percent during this period. The massive inflow of foreign capital was the major cause of the yen's overshooting.

In order to halt such foreign capital inflow, one may simply take the low interest rate policy. However, taking into account other domestic considerations such as inflation, the monetary authorities are often slow in taking timely measures. The experience in Japan in 1977–1978 as well as in West Germany in 1973–1974 suggests that balance of payments disequilibrium is quite often amplified by the concurrence of trade surplus (or deficit) and capital surplus (or deficit). This would inevitably cause overshooting (or undershooting) of the exchange rate. Counterspeculation, that was expected to serve as a stabilizer, was often void. Rather, by the time overshooting became obvious in everyone's eyes, changes in exchange rates had become ineffective in correcting trade account imbalances, and an offsetting flow of capital had not taken place.

GUIDELINE FOR FLOATING

Even if the floating system is effective in absorbing sudden shocks from outside such as the quadrupling of oil prices in 1973, incessant changes in exchange rates are not sustainable from the view point of a private enterprise, as far as investment decisions in particular are concerned. Hence, joint efforts of market intervention by the monetary authorities of the countries concerned are needed. Actually such efforts have been made from time to time to smooth out excessive fluctuations of exchange rates.

However, past intervention has been unsatisfactory in combating speculative capital flows, and there is every reason for the need to reexamine the role of intervention in the floating system. In the author's view, an aggressive intervention policy sufficient to bring exchange rates back to the levels justified by economic fundamentals is more necessary than simply smoothing out wide fluctuations of exchange rates. Also, in order for the intervention policy to be successful, it is important to introduce an element of predictability into the floating system, thereby reducing uncertainties regarding future exchange rates.

Then, what indicator can be used to objectively measure the potential strengths and weaknesses of the currency in question? The Committee of Twenty, which was set up in the autumn of 1972, explored, under the U.S. initiative, the possibility of adopting a reverse indicator, whereby the countries whose foreign exchange reserves reached certain limits should automatically take corrective actions, including revaluation or devaluation of their currencies. However, this approach was discarded in the subsequent years, and instead, inflation differentials began to be used to measure the desirable changes in exchange rates.

A question still remains, however, as to whether the exchange rate change geared to inflation differentials or the rate based upon the purchasing power parity is sufficient to bring about an adequate correction of external disequilibrium, especially when it stems from the divergence in economic growth rates. As was the case with Japan in 1977–1978, rather belated economic expansion gave rise to huge payments imbalances that could not be removed even by an obvious overvaluation of the yen. In this respect, a point can justifiably be made to define the role of the exchange rate in the adjustment process. Specifically, the role placed on the exchange rate should be lessened to a certain extent, and a greater emphasis should be placed on domestic economic policy to restore the external equilibrium. This may partly be achieved by strengthening multilateral surveillance by international organizations of the economic policies of member countries. Also, a subcommittee with the authoritative power to implement its decisions could be established under the auspices of the summitteers (group of seven countries) to design a guideline for floating. This is particularly advisable considering that the construction of the exchange rate regime has been more a matter of advanced countries, and a small committee may be better fitted to work out practical solutions. In order to facilitate adjustment of payments imbalances and to avoid unnecessary disturbances on the exchange markets, it is of the utmost importance to initiate domestic economic policies in the first stage and thus reduce heavy reliance on the exchange rate. If this approach is followed, only a relatively small real revaluation (or devaluation as the case may be) may well ensure a balance of payments equilibrium.

CURRENCY DIVERSIFICATION OF
INTERNATIONAL LIQUIDITY

Recently, another problem has arisen that has an important bearing upon the exchange rate policy of major countries. It is the problem of diversification of international currencies in general, or diversification of portfolio holdings away from the U.S. dollar to other internationally used currencies such as the Deutsche mark and the Japanese yen in particular.

In order to augment international monetary stability, it is ideal to forge a system of a single currency standard. After World War II, the international monetary system was long dominated by the U.S. dollar, and a certain degree of stability was maintained at least until the late 1960s. But the U.S. primacy in the field of international trade and finance has gradually been surpassed by other countries, and the shift from the dollar to other currencies, especially as reserve assets, is likely to be a long-term trend. Since there will be no candidate that is able to take over the role of the U.S. dollar, a kind of multicurrency system should be contrived where several major currencies are to be used as reserve assets. A question arises as to how we can alleviate the dampening effects upon the dollar that would be brought about in the process of shifting out of the dollar into other currencies. In this respect, it is worth a further attempt to establish a substitution account outside the exchange markets to absorb the funds that will flee from the dollar.

Another question is whether the system contrived generates an intermittent source of instability. Under the multicurrency system, many financial centers would be formed, each with its own key currency. Capital flows between different currency centers will be so huge and volatile as to easily give rise to disturbances on the foreign exchange markets. Thus, international arrangements for coordinated action, especially in the field of monetary policy between the countries of major financial centers, are needed to attain orderly capital movements. At the same time, the idea of a basket currency unit, similar to the IMF's SDR but stronger and less complicated than the SDR, could be developed to diversify the risks involved in the multicurrency system. The basket currency unit could be a weighted average of five or six leading currencies—which could be used as reserve currencies—and might well be used in private transactions. For each component currency, a movable band linked to and denominated in the currency unit could be worked out to delineate the upper and lower limits of the fluctuations of individual currencies, and either a semiannual or quarterly review of the system may be done to monitor and revise the movable bands. In setting and revising the movable bands, some form of purchasing power parity would be taken into consideration.

To sum up, a more stable and structured international monetary system could be constructed by maintaining orderly capital movements between different currency areas. Orderly capital movements could be secured primarily by domestic economic policies aimed at equilibrating the current account of the balance of payments, while reducing the role of the exchange rate in the adjustment process. Also, some form of the crawling movable band system that reflects inflation differentials might be worked out to introduce an element of predictability into the exchange market.

※ *Chapter 14*

Floating Exchange Rates: A Practical Lesson on the Automaticity of Adjustment Mechanisms

Guido Carli
Confederazione Generale dell'Industria Italiana
and former Governor of the Bank of Italy

Faced with the turbulence of present conditions in international monetary relations, it is tempting to believe in the existence of automatic adjustment mechanisms to avoid such problems. Many economic commentators, nostalgic for the supposed stability of the past, consider the gold standard to have been such an automatic system, while more modern experts look to freely flexible rates of exchange as the prerequisite to stability. Yet, the supposed automatic adjustment provided by the gold standard was not without cost. In language that foreshadowed the terminology and the preoccupations of present-day economists, Keynes noted that "sensitive reciprocal action, of the kind which the pre-war gold standard was supposed to provide, involved every country in a subordination of internal equilibrium to every external change however trifling or transitory" (Keynes 1930: 320). Under such a system, "even when a change in bank rate is only required as a temporary corrective . . . to preserve external equilibrium, it cannot be prevented from reacting . . . on the volume of output and employment" (Keynes 1930: 314).

The cost of this international adjustment mechanism could be clearly identified in terms of the lost output and reduced employment due to internal disequilibrium. One way this cost could be reduced was by holding sufficient reserves of internationally liquid assets. The failure of the growth of world gold supplies to satisfy this need led to the conditions that produced the gold exchange standard as a means of augmenting available international liquidity.

But

> insofar as national systems develop devices and maintain large liquid re-
> serves with the express object of having the power to maintain internal
> equilibrium . . . without too sensitive a regard for external events, recip-
> rocal action will necessarily become less dependable—except in the event
> of major movements. (Keynes 1930: 320)

In such a system, positive action for adjustment becomes not
only less reciprocal, but asymmetric, for "major movements" that
require the outflow of reserves cannot be permanently sustained
and internal deflationary action must be initiated eventually to defend finite reserves. At the same time the concommitant increases
in reserves in the rest of the world may not be of "major" proportion and thus easily absorbed without requiring an internal adjustment via expansion, while the decrease in world exports due to the
deflationary actions could lead to income deflation on a worldwide
scale.

It was the risk of the asymmetry of adjustment via deflation in
deficit countries spreading to create a worldwide deficiency of aggregate demand that the founders of the Bretton Woods Agreement
attempted to eliminate. As the preparatory documents for the
Agreement indicate very clearly, there was a divergence of opinion
on the way that this could best be achieved. This divergence represented, to a large extent, the different national histories of the two
major protagonists of postwar reconstruction, the United States
and the United Kingdom. The United Kingdom had encountered
great difficulties in attempting to reestablish the pre-1914 sterling
parity. As the issuer of the key currency of the sterling area, the U.K.
negotiators were also well aware that the autonomous growth of gold
supplies would not be adequate to the needs of the hoped for postwar expansion in world trade. Thus, the draft of the Keynes plan
first put forward for official discussion (Horsefield 1969: III, 3,) calls
for an "international bank money . . . fixed (but not unalterably)
in terms of gold"—that is, the British were mainly concerned to establish a nonnational reserve asset that could provide liquidity in the
proportions required for the expected postwar expansion of trade.
Alternatively, the first purpose of the White plan was to create a
fund "to stabilize foreign exchange rates" (Horsefield 1969: III,
41), so as to resume exchange convertibility and thus multilateral
trade as soon as possible without recourse to the bilateral agreements
and trade restrictions that had characterized the interwar period
especially after the 1933 devaluation of the dollar—that is, elimina-

tion of discrimination against U.S. exports was the main economic priority. (It should be remembered that, beside problems of postwar reconstruction and trade, the position of London as the dominant international financial center was under challenge from New York, a fact that strongly influenced the acceptance of the various proposals in both countries.)

The more direct purpose of the Keynes plan was to seek to reintroduce directly the "reciprocal" actions of both debtor and creditor nations. The final agreement, based primarily on the White plan, did, nonetheless, allow for borrowed exchange reserves that would allow debtor countries to eliminate deficits in a manner more consistent with the maintenance of internal equilibrium. What it did not do, however, was to create a reserve asset to supplement gold in the reserves of those countries who wished to seek additional independence in internal policy at the expense of increased reserves, nor did it create a mechanism that would relate the expansion of such reserves to the expansion of world trade. The need for such expansion was amply demonstrated, for in the absence of an official international reserve asset, the dollar filled this role de facto up until the late 1950s. The force of events turned the gold exchange standard into the dollar exchange standard. In the event, the drawing rights of members of the Fund proved inadequate to the expanding liquidity needs of trade and payments, and the U.S. deficit on capital account provided the liquidity required to finance the postwar deficits of war-damaged Europe. This latter action, of course, had a more political than economic motivation.

The process of postwar reconstruction and development of the various European countries went on at varying rates; patterns of national productivity, wages, national incomes, and trade patterns also changed. The exchange rates of particular European countries soon bore little relation to their new economic realities. Likewise, the trading relations between the United States and the rest of the world changed. Exchange rates established in the postwar period soon became outmoded, and some, under the provisions of the articles of the Fund, were adjusted. Yet, the Fund itself and a majority of central banks attached great value to preserving the initial rates, and in some countries once again the costs in terms of internal equilibrium of external equilibrium became noticeable.

Already in the 1950s economists were discussing the idea that the costs of adjustment implicit in the gold exchange standard and explicit in a rigid exchange rate system such as Bretton Woods had become could be eliminated by means of a diametrically opposed adjustment mechanism—flexible exchange rates. If exchange rates were free to equilibrate the external position, then internal policy would be independent to preserve internal equilibrium. (It is of interest to note that this argument has an obverse—namely, as a defense against inflation imported from the rest of the world—but this only became important somewhat later). The mechanism of floating exchanges thus automatically frees a country to pursue policies to avoid both inflation and deflation.

Although the question of flexible versus fixed rates was hotly debated in academic circles for some time in the 1950s and early 1960s, the conclusion of policymakers was that insofar as the problem of the conflict of internal and external balance was concerned, it could be satisfactorily dealt with via measures to ensure adequate liquidity and proper identification of objectives and instruments.[1]

As academic interest in such questions began to fade, the implications of decisions taken at Bretton Woods concerning the form of the IMF were becoming explicit in the ever more frequent adjustments in exchange rates as the role of the dollar as a provider of liquidity and as a reserve asset with fixed relation to gold came into conflict. The first signs of this process, which became visible in 1960 when the price of gold in the London market rose above the official dollar rate, leading to the creation of the Gold Pool, eventually culminated in President Nixon's dramatic announcement in August 1971 of dollar inconvertibility. These and other well-known events (see Carli 1978) testify to the fact that floating rates emerged as a solution to a dilemma concerning the mechanism of international trade and payments that had its origin in the Bretton Woods Agreements. It is perhaps ironical, from an academic perspective, that floating rates emerged not because fixed rates proved to be so great a constraint on the ability of national governments to determine independent internal policy, but as a result of the lack of an internationally controlled reserve asset capable of supporting the needs of the international economy, in which trade was expanding at a more rapid rate than the ever more unequal national growth rates.

It is also interesting to note that floating does not provide an objective solution to the reserve problem within the Bretton Woods framework, for it completely eliminates the possibility of any national currency bearing a fixed value to gold or any other currency at the same time as it eliminates (theoretically) the need for reserve currencies. It is thus not surprising that the first actions taken after 1971 were the reimposition of fixed rates in the Smithsonian Agreements and the creation of the "special drawing rights" by the IMF. Whether the Smithsonian parities were more directly influenced by economic or political conditions soon became irrelevant as the outbreak of the Yom Kippur war led to a quadrupling of petroleum prices and havoc in both national economic policies and international trade. The old Bretton Woods problem of an imbalance of purchasing power in the hands of a group of countries who were unable to spend in the same amounts, and unwilling to spend in the same pattern, made the need for liquidity by the non-OPEC countries acute. Again the dollar, this time in the nature of the off-shore currency markets, filled the vacuum. The role that the U.S. capital account deficit had played in postwar reconstruction was taken by the Eurodollar market financing. But due to the absence of any mechanism for the control of the creation of liquidity in these markets, the reserve currency role of the dollar was permanently weakened, thus destroying the credibility of the Smithsonian Agreements. In the absence of an internationally controlled reserve asset, the problem of recycling the petrodollars fell to the Eurobanking system and to the U.S. banks (see Carli 1976: 177). The instability that resulted (both in national banking systems and in international trade) eliminated the possibility of a system of stable rates, for there was no alternative reserve asset.

Of course, the floating exchange rate regime established after 1973 could only eliminate the need for a reserve asset and for liquidity if it succeeded in eliminating persistent surpluses and deficits. This did not happen, and indeed could not, since without coordinated control of internal policy, adjustment could not take place. While it may be true that floating rates give the freedom to follow policies of internal stability, they also give the freedom not to follow such policies. In the modern world, forces leading to just such actions as would prevent the process of internal adjustment have become increasingly strong. The freedom from conflict between internal and external objectives that floating rates were to have brought does not make the resolution of internal conflicts over real wages, growth, and income distribution any easier. The freedom to act on the external balance is then complete only when there is agreement on policy for internal stability. When this is not the case, floating rates produce a situation in which internal and external objectives conflict in the presence of conflict over internal objectives.

The petroleum price revolution of 1973 required a massive transfer of purchasing power from petroleum purchases to producers. Real incomes had to be reduced. Naturally, in many countries specific groups attempted to avoid the inevitable reduction in their own real incomes by increasing their nominal earnings. The result was an increasing divergence in national rates of productivity growth, prices, output, and employment. The failure of internal adjustment was simply passed on to the foreign exchange market, increasing the already volatile conditions of such markets due to the uncontrolled growth of international liquidity due to the expansion of the Eurodollar markets. Many national governments lost control not only of internal price movements and employment levels but also their external deficit, despite large adjustments in exchange rates.

The response to these conditions was a generalized policy of deflation in almost all countries. Since such deflationary policies seem to be the only policy adequate to resolve the conflicts that produce internal disequilibrium and since this seems to be true irrespective of external positions of deficit or surplus, the international monetary system in the period after 1973 has had an even more pronounced tendency toward deflation than that which was feared at Bretton Woods. In the present system, the "beggar my neighbor" policies of competitive devaluation have been replaced by a system of competitive deflation in order to try to keep unit wage costs and prices in line with the country with the lowest rates of increase in wages and prices. As the experience of the United States has demonstrated, any attempt to expand at a more rapid rate that results in a rise in wages and prices above the world average produces a sustained decline in the exchange rate. The result is much similar to that which Keynes attributed to the gold standard regime except that now the asymmetry in favor of deflation is increased, for even surplus countries are induced to follow deflationary policies in order to keep their competitive position and to avoid the risk of internal disequilibrium that loss of control of their exchange rates seems to imply.

There are a number of reasons that may encourage deflationary policies in surplus countries. First, the lack of any ready substitute for the dollar as a reserve currency has meant that the uncontrolled mass of liquidity created by the Eurodollar markets has to be continually shifted between the strongest currencies if losses are to be avoided, creating revaluations of some currencies far in excess of that justified by trade and autonomous capital flow conditions. Surplus countries thus find their currencies overvalued in terms of relative purchasing power and vice versa for the currencies in the rest of the world. Allowing exchange rates to rise reduces export profit margins and foreign competitiveness of these countries while attempting to hold exchange rates at levels that preserve export competitivity often means loss of control of money supply creation and internal instability. Thus there is pressure to dampen the rate of increase in costs by means of internal expansion at a lower rate than would be justified at a lower exchange rate. The result is the contradictory position in which strong currency countries urge deflation on the rest of the world as the answer to their overvalued exchange rates. At the same time, in the face of generally rising raw material and petroleum prices, an increasing number of countries view a strong exchange rate as a certain counterinflationary weapon and adopt tight monetary policies to this effect. This line of reasoning, which is compatible with "international monetarist" doctrine, suffers from a fallacy of composition, for relative adjustment is impossible if both surplus and deficit countries raise interest rates to strengthen their currency. The effects of such a generalized increase in the level of interest rates on output and employment is not neutral. The weak currency countries seem all too ready to respond with deflationary policies.

From this point of view, the experience with floating rates since 1973 has not been an academic exercise, nor has it resembled the academic description—nor was it introduced for the reasons often debated in the academic literature. The system of floating rates emerged because the decisions taken at Bretton Woods and subsequently left little choice. From a pragmatic point of view, to the extent that the system has survived, floating rates have functioned satisfactorily. But this is not the relevant question. It is more pertinent to enquire into the implications that they have had on the system. Indeed, rather than provide the freedom for each country to proceed to price stability and full employment, they have in the presence of uncontrolled international liquidity produced a tendency toward deflation. From this point of view we might conclude that they are not preferable to fixed rates, which imposed this discipline only on deficit countries.

History does not repeat itself, and it is no doubt true that the age of Bretton Woods has ended. Yet the same problems that exercised the founders of the modern international monetary system remain current. It is perhaps not without significance that Europe has chosen to form, by means of the EMS, an area of exchange stability in an attempt to eliminate this tendency to deflation that has been associated with the recent experience of floating rates. Given the inability of floating rates to eliminate the deflationary tendencies that were thought to have been associated only with fixed rates, this is a choice that I can only approve. Yet this initiative cannot succeed unless it benefits from the lessons of past experience. The attempt at European stability can only succeed if it provides a way of resolving two interrelated problems—the OPEC surplus and the dollar overhang. The creation of an international asset that would attempt to deal with the needs of the Arab countries for an asset to preserve the real value of their petroleum reserves and the needs of the industrialized countries to avoid continued inflation and unemployment due to the deflationary aspects of the large continuing unspent OPEC reserves has been proposed as a solution to the former. The recent increases in petroleum prices and the stated hesitancy of some producers to continue to supply oil to satisfy the uncontrolled expansion of demand in the industrialized countries makes such a guarantee of the value of the Arab countries' petroleum reserves an even more pressing necessity.[2]

The second part of the problem may be faced, within the auspices of the European Monetary System, by allowing the ECU to become a reserve asset that could replace unwanted dollars in national (and private) reserves. The alternative to the creation of such reserve instruments would be the risk of a major deflation in the United States and thus in the rest of the industrialized world. The move to create an area of stability must be clearly seen as a move to avoid the disastrous consequences of such a policy on world trade and on Europe's economic survival.

NOTES

1. See the now abundant literature linked to the contributions of Tinbergen, Theil, and subsequently, Mundell.

2. For descriptive purposes I have called this asset an "advance payment purchase bond" or APPB. The novel aspect of the approach is that any OPEC country could be able to purchase these bonds from any country willing to issue them, on the expectation of eventually spending the proceeds in the issuing country. They would be nonmarketable, although provision for redemption on demand at a small penalty during the first ten years and for redemption in any amount, at any time, after this period to final maturity of, say, twenty-five years with interest accrued to the date of actual redemption could be arranged. The interest on the bonds might best be credited and compounded annually and paid only on redemption or maturity.

The rate of interest could be variable and could be determined, retroactively, for each year on the basis of three criteria: (1) the average real growth of the issuing country for the year, plus (2) the average overall price increase for the year in the country of issue, less (3) the average increase (if any) in the delivered price of OPEC oil to the country over the same year. The rate of interest should not, in any event, fall below the market rate for government securities of comparable maturity for the year of issue in the issuing country (see Carli 1979).

REFERENCES

Carli, G. 1979. "Finance and Trade in the 1980's: What Action if Required to Promote the Economic Regeneration of Europe." Paper delivered at *Financial Times* World Business Conference, Frankfurt, February 15.

———. 1978. "Perspectives on the Evolution of the International Monetary System." *Journal of Monetary Economics* 4: 405-14.

———. 1976, "Address." *The New Inflation and Monetary Policy*, ed. M. Monti, pp. 173-81. London: Macmillan.

Horsefield, J.K., ed. 1969. *The International Monetary Fund 1945-1965.* 3 vols. Washington, D.C.: International Monetary Fund.

Keynes, J.M. 1930. *Treatise on Money.* vol. 1. London: Macmillan.

Name Index

Abel, A., 27
Akaike, H., 192, 197, 199
Alexander, S.S., 68
Aliber, R.E., 105, 106
Archibald, G.C., 162
Arrango, S., 102
Artus, J.R., 86

Balassa, B., 81, 84
Barro, R.J., 149, 184
Basevi, G., 28
Bell, G., 47
Bernstein, E.M., 274
Bigman, David, xviii, 102
Bilson, J.F.O., 67, 91, 92-93, 94,
    155, 175, 184, 209
Black, S., 4, 155, 156
Blanchard, Oliver, xviii
Blessing, K., 270
Bolin, W.H., xxv
Box, G.E.P., 196, 209
Boyer, R., 28, 184
Branson, W., xviii, 28, 142, 155, 156
Brillembourg, A., 204, 205, 209
Brittain, B., 102
Brittan, S., 275, 280
Britton, A.J.C., 103
Bruno, M., 156
Buiter, Willem, xx, 156

Calvo, G., 74, 157
Cassel, G., 77, 80
Christ, C., 156, 157

Claasen, E.M., 162
Clark, P.B., 162, 175, 182
Clements, K., 27
Clower, R., 162
Cohen, B.J., 162
Coombs, C.A., 48
Cootner, P.H., 49
Coppack, J., 241
Cornell, W.B., 67
Courchene, T.J., 182-183
Cuddington, J., 123

De Grauwe, P., 28
Del Canto, J., xxv
De Macedo, J., 155, 156
Dietrich, J.K., 67
Dooley, M., 45, 46, 53, 56, 57, 58, 59,
    60, 66, 68
Dornbusch, Rudiger, xix, 28, 81-82,
    94, 135, 142, 143, 155, 156, 157,
    184, 215
Driskill, R., 103

Erb, G.F., 242

Falchi, G., 205, 209
Fama, E.F., 16, 67, 156
Farber, A., 156
Fischer, S., 28, 94, 157, 170, 173, 184
Fisher, F.M., 167
Flanders, M., 162
Fleming, J.M., 10-13, 27, 143, 156
Flood, R., 28, 155

301

Subject Index

Fisher parity equations, 144–145
Fixed exchange rates, xix–xx, 38;
  breakdown, 268–271, 293–294;
  and money supply, 34, 269–270
Foreign assets. *See* External assets
Foreign exchange dealers, 101, 104,
  112–118
Forward market, 51–53, 97; and
  capital controls, 217, 219–220, 221,
  228–232; and covered interest
  arbitrageurs, 105–107, 118;
  efficiency, 28–29, 89; and
  martingale, 49–51; and purchasing
  power parity, 87–91
France, 64, 272–273, 276; prices,
  189, 200, 204, 206, 208
French franc, 60

Gensaki bonds, 222, 234
Germany, 122, 273, 276; current
  account, 275; and filter rule, 64;
  growth, 25; inflation, 129, 270,
  281–282; monetary policy, 24, 151,
  281; prices, 189, 204, 206, 208
Gold Pool, 294
Gold standard, 268–269, 291–295,
  296
Goods market, 39
"Greater fool" hypothesis, 47

Hard currency countries, 19–20
Heckscher-Ohlin model, 180
Helicopter rain, 152–153
Herstatt failure, 66
Hicksian fix-price goods, 104, 107,
  108, 109

Imports, 22–23; propensity to,
  162–163, 176–181
Indexation, 20
Indexes: exchange rate, 207–208;
  money supply, 208; price, 39,
  80–81, 86, 91–92, 208
Inflation, 34, 129, 147–148, 277,
  281–282; and balance of payments,
  38; and commodity arbitrage,
  90–91; and depreciation, 4, 20, 35,
  279; and exports, 4; and fixed rate
  breakdown, 269–271; and interest
  rates, xix, 92; and less developed
  countries, xxi, xxii, xxiii; and policy
  decisions, 129, 264, 269, 273, 275
Information, 21–22, 45, 49, 66
Interest rates, 92–93, 97, 135–141,
  285; and bond market, 119–122;
  and capital controls, 217–219, 220,
  222, 223–228; and capital flow,

9–10, 12, 13, 19, 286; and commodity arbitrage, 90–91; and
  current account, 151, 152–153;
  differentials, 16–17, 35–36, 46, 53,
  54, 55, 67, 77, 92, 93–94, 105;
  and Eurocurrency, 53, 54, 55, 67;
  and expectations, 21; and imports,
  22–23; and inflation, xix, 92; and
  interdependence, xix; and less
  developed countries, xx, xxii, xxiii,
  xxiv; and money supply, 11–12;
  and output, 10
Interest rate parity theorem, 106, 215
International Financial Statistics
  (IMF), 208
International Monetary Fund, xx, xxi,
  34, 275, 276, 277–278; and adjustment, 279; Article IV, 38;
  Article VIII, 122; exchange rate
  data, 208; and fixed rate, 293; and
  less developed countries, xxi,
  xxii–xxiii, xxv; and payment adjustment, 272–273; surveillance,
  263–264, 265
International reserves, demand for,
  161–184; determinants, 162–168
Intervention, 40, 122–123, 286–287;
  "aggressive," 38; and bonds, 138;
  and central banks, 41, 48, 52–53,
  65, 73, 129, 138, 260, 274, 281;
  and purchasing power parity, 28–29,
  83–84
Invoicing, 101, 103, 104–105,
  107–108, 118–119
Italy, 58, 59, 60, 272; current
  account, 276; prices, 189, 205, 206,
  208; reserves, 60

Japan, 273, 287; capital controls, 122,
  214–238; current account, 275,
  286; and filter rate, 64; Foreign
  Exchange and Foreign Trade Law,
  231, 235; growth, 25; prices, 189,
  204, 205, 206, 208; reserve requirements, 238
J-curve effect, 37, 96, 275, 279; and
  capital flows, 121–122, 123–214;
  and speculators, 101, 103, 104,
  107–109, 111, 119

Konno, 235

Less developed countries: balance of
  payments, 246; competitiveness, 25;
  current account, xxi, 37; domestic
  investment, xx, xxi, 243, 253;
  exports, xxi, xxii, 241–256; foreign

Epilogue

Exchange Rate Regimes:

The Lessons of the Past Two Decades

David Bigman
Wageningen University

Teizo Taya
Bank of Japan

INTRODUCTION

The breakdown of the Bretton Woods system of fixed, although adjustable, exchange rates in 1973 ushered in a new era in the international financial system in which the major currencies were floated, capital mobility increased very substantially, and a growing number of countries opened up their domestic financial market while keeping the autonomy of their monetary policy. The convertibility of the U.S. dollar into gold had ended two years earlier yet the dollar remained at the center of the system, although in future years the emergence of the Euro is likely to introduce a new factor. The increasing integration of the global capital market, especially during the 1990s, was the strongest and most obvious signal of the growing integration of the world economy; it also became a major factor that attracted the developing countries into the global market. These countries were encouraged to liberalize their trade and capital account by means of comprehensive structural adjustment programs under the stewardship of the IMF and the World Bank and under the pressures to meet the conditions to join the WTO; at the same time, the gravitational pull of the global capital market gave these countries incentives to further liberalize their current account transactions in order to benefit from the large flows of private capital.

Globalization has increased openness to international trade, internationalized the balance sheets of many companies and has given strong incentives to diversify production and trade. It also exposed, however, countries and enterprises to higher foreign exchange risks while the scope for risk diversification has diminished owing to the growing integration and greater correlation of the financial markets. Moreover, as more countries have integrated into the global financial market, available policy options diminish, and the relatively free movements of capital in and out of the country make government intervention less effective. In particular, capital controls aimed at introducing a wedge between the domestic and the foreign capital markets and give the monetary authorities greater independence and reduce the spillovers of external shocks, have become more complex and costly and less effective. The evolving global markets make it therefore necessary to increase current account convertibility and liberalize the capital account by gradually removing the existing restrictions. At the same time, though, financial liberalization and the internationalization of the capital markets have become associated with speculative attacks, financial crises and instability, despite the stabilizing effect of the international institutions like the IMF, as a crisis in one country spills over to others.

Under the Bretton Woods system, a wide range of controls had been established to insulate the 'real' economy and the commodity markets from unstable short-term capital flows; indeed, the raison d'être of that system was the establishment of a web of international agreements and institutions aimed at preventing the race of competitive depreciations to "beggar thy neighbor" that undermined the global trading system under the gold standard. After the breakdown of that system, most developed and developing countries adjusted their exchange rate system, some making it more flexible while others pegging it more firmly. The choice of the most effective exchange rate system differed among countries depending on the level of development of their economic system and institutions and the level of their integration with the global market. These countries faced a wide choice of possible exchange rate regimes, and no single regime could be prescribed by the IMF or the World Bank as best for all countries, or even for a given country at all times. The objective of this brief survey is to review the development of exchange rate regimes in developed and developing countries during the past three decades.

Exchange rate regimes of the major currencies

The currencies of the three largest industrial countries, the U.S. dollar, the Japanese yen, and the deutsche mark, have floated against each other since 1973, and the variability of the bilateral exchange rates has increased very sharply (see Table 15.1). These currencies exhibited not only substantial short-run volatility but also large medium-term swings in nominal as well as real terms that were much higher than under the Bretton Woods system. The mounting instability of the major currencies' exchange rates entailed considerable external costs for third countries; although the direct effect of exchange rate volatility on net trade volumes is generally assumed to be fairly small, large exchange rate swings between close trading partners are likely to create substantial sectoral adjustment costs. The positive externality of reducing that volatility motivated the European Union countries to make efforts to reduce the variability of exchange rates among member countries, initially through the creation of the exchange rate mechanism of the European monetary system and ultimately through the creation of the Euro. However, despite expectations that the emergence of the Euro would lead to a bi- or tri-polar system, the U.S. dollar remained by far the major international currency for trade in both goods and assets.

Table 15.1.
Variability of Bilateral Exchange Rates.

		1970s	1980s	1990s	1970s	1980s	1990s
			¥/$			DM/$	
Daily	SD	0.59	0.68	0.74	0.62	0.72	0.67
	MAD	0. 30	0.49	0.53	0.38	0.53	0.49
Monthly	SD	2.47	3.10	3.07	2.70	3.05	2.53
	MAD	1.78	2.42	2.32	1.91	2.48	2.03
Annual	SD	12.91	15.18	10.40	11.82	16.04	9.62
	MAD	9.86	10.81	9.13	8.31	11.27	7.05

Note: *SD* and *MAD* are the standard deviation and the mean absolute deviation, respectively.

Under the Bretton Woods system, temporary official financing of payments imbalances, mainly through the IMF, were considered adequate to smooth the adjustment process of the exchange rates and avoid undue disturbances to the current account, trade flows, output, and employment. In the system that emerged since then, exchange rates among the major currencies fluctuated primarily in response to market forces in both the commodity and the capital markets. In the 1980s, the medium-term swings have increased very significantly with the sharp appreciation of the dollar in the first half of the decade followed by its equally sharp depreciation in the mid-1980s.[1] The range between the maximum and minimum values of the bilateral nominal index for the deutsche mark against the US dollar shot up to 130 percent in some years—well above the range that reflects fluctuations in the economic fundamentals. These wide swings in the medium-term exchange rates of the major currencies have often been identified with "misalignments," and they have driven the efforts to secure a greater alignment of policies on the one hand, and introduce financial innovations aimed at reducing the risks associated with the short-term volatility on the other hand. Nevertheless, these wide swings indicate that there has been a relatively small decline in the extent of the volatility of the main bilateral exchange rates also during the 1990s despite these measures and despite periods of relative stability in some years.

International private capital flows have increased several-fold and have become the primary factor in financing current account imbalances in many countries. According to the BIS survey, turnover in foreign exchange markets has nearly tripled from $590 billion in 1989 to $1,490 billion in 1998, although it then decreased to $1,200 billion in 2001 in the aftermath of the Asian crisis and its Latin American ramifications. Fluctuations in the flows of private capital have become a significant cause in macroeconomic disturbances, and the easy capital mobility across financial markets has transmitted these fluctuations to the entire international system. These large flows have also motivated the industrial countries to abandon the efforts to control their exchange rates since it has become clear that by preventing an appreciation or depreciation of the exchange rate they primarily provide hefty subsidies to investors that drive these capital inflows or outflows.

Capital mobility has reached unprecedented levels[2] owing to the steep reduction in the obstacles on cross-country trade in real and financial as-

---

1   This can be attributed, in part, to the sharp appreciation of the yen and the deutsche mark against the U.S. dollar in the mid-1980s following the Plaza agreement.

2   In relative terms, these flows even match the large flows under the gold standard.

sets, to the dramatic improvements in information and communication technologies that enabled a sharp reduction in transaction costs in the financial markets, to the wave of financial innovations that facilitated capital movements across national boarders and markets by reducing the short-term risks,[3] and to the increasing integration of the world's financial markets in the balance sheets of multinational companies. These changes have prompted large capital movements even in response to relatively small yield differentials between real or financial assets in different countries, or even in response to shifts in the perception of relative risks. As a result, the waves in the aftermath of a shock in any one of the more significant capital markets tend to spread across many other markets around the world.

In Japan, a prolonged monetary easing fostered overly bullish expectations, leading to large investments in real estate and stocks within the country that created an asset price bubble, and huge investments in external securities (mainly bonds), by Japanese institutional investors that were facilitated by the easing of the regulations on investments abroad. Even after the asset price bubble burst at the end of the 1980s, the Japanese current account surplus remained large, and the yen continued to strengthen.

In the U.S., the highly secure local financial markets, the safety of local financial investments and the nearly intoxicating rise in the price of local stocks through most of the decade attracted massive inflows of foreign capital from all over the world. Despite the large and growing U.S. current account deficit, these capital inflows led to a real appreciation of the dollar during the latter part of the 1990s, after its substantial depreciation from the mid-1980s to the mid-1990s. Most U.S. industries, particularly the high-tech industries, agro-industries and many multinational corporations, had no real difficulties in remaining competitive, whereas many others, like the steel industry, had to seek refuge in the bosom of the big government.

Theoretical models of exchange rate determination conduct the analysis at three separate time dimensions: the short, medium, and long run. In the long run, the exchange rates are still widely considered to be determined according to the purchasing power parity. In the medium run, they are generally assumed to be function of the inflation rate differential, the

---

3   The development of derivatives that reduce short-term exchange rate fluctuation has reduced also the risks on medium-term investments; these instruments cannot, however, deal with medium-term, cyclical swings.

real interest rate differential, and variables expressing the risk on foreign currency–denominated assets. In the short run, exchange rate movements are generally perceived to be a random walk. These theoretical models have seen little progress since the 1970s, despite several new empirical studies that emphasize the role and potential impact of current account imbalances. In these models, the medium- and long-term exchange rates are assumed to reflect the "fundamentals" that restore the long-term equilibrium level of the *current account* (e.g., the level that maintains the saving-investment balance); discrepancies between the current and the medium-term equilibrium exchange rates are taken as an indication of exchange rate "misalignment" and a valuable input in determining future policies.

In quite a few cases, however, these discrepancies need not indicate a misalignment. This, for example, would be the case if the discrepancies were due to a stable flow of remittances to local citizens from abroad or to transfers of private capital by local residents to foreign banks or by foreign residents to local banks in response to the conditions in the global financial markets that are likely to persist in the medium term. In all these cases, the discrepancies are due to certain fundamental factors (e.g., higher safety of the country's banking system; a large community of the country's natives that reside abroad, etc), and they reflect conditions that make a stable flow of transfers highly likely to persist in the future. Most of these factors are relevant, however, to the country's capital account only, and they are not captured therefore by the fundamentals that underlie the country's trade and current accounts. These factors represent very significant features in the balance of payments of many developed and developing countries, but they are rarely taken into account in the estimation of misalignments in the country's exchange rate in models that guide macro-economic policies.[4]

EXCHANGE RATE REGIMES IN DEVELOPING COUNTRIES

Despite the pressures to liberalize the trade and the capital accounts since the collapse of the Bretton Woods system, most developing countries left the restrictions on the capital account in place until the mid-1980s. Only

---

4   This is also the approach employed by the IMF's Coordinating Group on Exchange Rate Issues in its evaluation of exchange rates misalignment.

since then, in part in the aftermath of the debt crisis and with the advent of structural adjustment programs and in part as an effect of the internationalization of the global capital market and the banking industry, an increasing number of developing countries liberalized their capital account more rapidly and permitted foreign financial institutions to operate within their borders.

During the past decade, the net capital flows to developing countries increased sharply owing to the rise in the flows of private capital, mostly foreign direct investments, that became the main source capital for many of them. Net private capital flows to developing countries have risen from less than 0.5 percent of their GDP in the early 1980s to over 3 percent in the mid-1990s – although the Asian crisis reversed these capital flows in the late-1990s. The flows of private capital are distributed, however, very unevenly between the developing countries: The lion's share goes to only twelve developing countries, while most other developing countries have benefited only marginally from the steep rise in these flows, and nearly all their capital imports consist of official capital and trade-related lending.

For the majority of the developing and transition countries, the choice of an exchange rate regime has become the key policy decision and its importance has increased with the rise in the countries' involvement in the global economy. Several exchange rate regimes have been suggested for the developing countries, especially for the ~30 more advanced ones (often referred to as *emerging economies*), and a number of models have been developed to evaluate these regimes and identify the "most effective" one. The effectiveness of a regime depends, however, on the specific conditions in the country, which include not only the level of reserves and the composition of its debts but also its past experience with alternative exchange rate regimes, the stability of the country's financial system, the past experience with inflation, and the strength of its political system and public institutions.[5] Empirical cross-country studies also have concluded that no single regime can be suitable for most countries and, in most cases, the effectiveness of the regime and its suitability depend on

---

5   The experience in the past decade shows, however, that sound macroeconomic and financial fundamentals are necessary but not sufficient to reduce the risk of a crisis, since that may also come as a result of the contagion effect of a foreign crisis—as illustrated in the East Asia financial crisis of 1997/1998 that spread to Eastern Europe and Latin America.

the (economic and political) conditions in the country, and even the effectiveness of the interest rate in stabilizing the exchange rate varies widely among countries.

Figure 1: Exchange Rate Regimes in Developed and Emerging Markets Countries: 1991 and 1999 (number of countries[1] and percent of total)

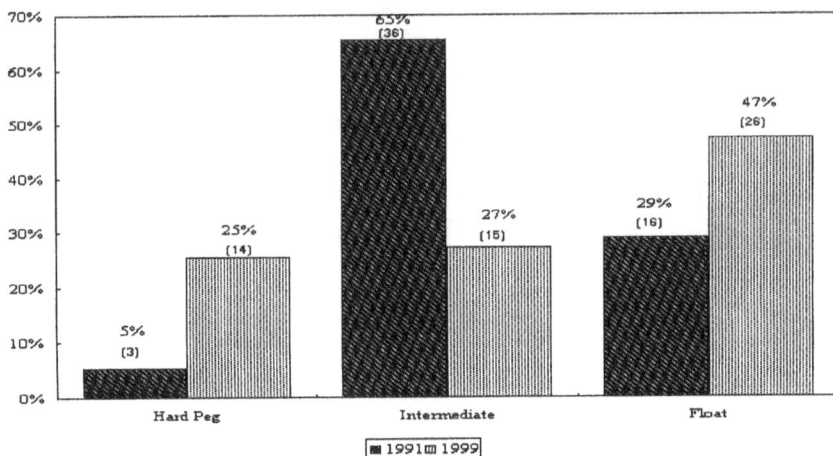

In the 1990s, an increasing number of countries gravitated to corner solutions of either "hard peg" — by means of a currency board or "dollarization"— or free floating (Figure 15.1). The flexible exchange rate regime was adopted to provide greater monetary independence and allow the country to respond to shocks by adjusting its exchange and/or interest rates. In a country that is well integrated into the global economy, fixed exchange rate robs the central banks of the autonomy of monetary policy since the country's interest rate is then effectively pegged to the rate in the international financial markets, and the economy may be affected by any movement in the relative value of the currency to which the country's exchange rate is pegged.

The majority of the developing countries, however, are not yet sufficiently integrated into the global financial markets, and their domestic financial institutions are far less developed. In particular, their exchange market is thin, lacking adequate financial sector regulations and supervision, and is often dominated by a relatively small number of agents. The

---

1   Number of countries in parenthesis. Source: IMF

embryonic state of their foreign exchange market and the lack of proper institutions to regulate its activities make hedging against exchange rate risk more difficult and costly and raise the economic costs of exchange rate volatility. In these countries, a more credible and stable anchor for trade and for the financial market may be necessary to prevent excessive volatility; a stable anchor may also be necessary to guide the country's monetary policy and provide a simple and effective method for determining the value of the local "money" in terms of alternative assets with a stable value. Pegging offers a simple, transparent, and credible anchor; the rigors of maintaining a pegged exchange rate regime are less demanding, and it offers the most rapid and credible route to stop the inflation cycle and stabilize expectations. Indeed, many of the countries that officially maintain a "managed float" in practice maintain some sort of exchange rate peg.

Hard peg has also been a viable alternative in the early days of the ex-centrally planned economies when the central bank was still at the base of the learning curve and the other financial institutions were hardly functioning. Simplicity in operation and transparency in execution are the main virtues of a hard peg for these countries. Hard peg reduces also the risk of self-fulfilling inflationary expectations, but it may not eliminate it altogether; a certain risk premium, albeit smaller, might still be required, thus making even the hard peg costly. Formal pegging and stringent management of the exchange rate were therefore viable alternatives, but they required a strong and clear commitment (formal or informal), combined with tightly managed monetary policy to support that peg. To stabilize their exchange rate, these countries had to give up a great deal of their monetary independence since market arbitrage linked also their interest rate to that in the anchor currency.

Fixed exchange rates proved to be a particularly effective anchor for expectations and an efficient tool to bring the country's inflation rate under control. During the Asian crisis, countries that maintained fixed exchange rates with capital control (China, Malaysia) were affected less than countries that allowed unrestricted capital transactions and rapid depreciation (Indonesia). China's official policy is managed float, but effectively, the yuan has been tightly linked to the U.S. dollar since mid-1995; the peg is maintained with tight controls over short-term capital flows, large foreign exchange reserves, and a large current account surplus. To combat inflation and prevent speculative attacks on the currency, some countries "hardened" their peg by establishing a currency board or by abandoning the local currency altogether in favor of "dollarization." In the Western Hemisphere in particular, the adoption of a hard peg by several key countries was an important factor that contributed to sharply reduce the rate of inflation in the hemisphere from an annual average of 420 percent in 1988-1991 to 9.5 percent in 1996-1998. In countries with a history of high inflation the public often has an endemic fear of floating, and their authorities are particularly reluctant to let their exchange rate float; they continue to interfere heavily in the foreign exchange markets even if they officially have made the transition from fixed rates to floating.

"Hard peg" in particular, is a draconian measure but in certain critical cases also an effective tool to put both the fiscal and the monetary policies under tight control and thus make them more credible. By allowing devaluation only in extreme conditions and by exacting very high political costs of unsustainable fiscal or monetary policies that might lead to the system's collapse, they further increase their credibility. In many countries that went through a high inflation spiral, these hard conditions were essential to convince a very suspicious public that has often been traumatized by past hyperinflation that the government will neither devalue the exchange rate nor manipulate the economic variables to justify devaluation. The added credibility that a hard peg gives to the country's economic policy and the discipline it imposes on the fiscal and monetary authorities due to the high political costs of reneging on their exchange rate commitment were the main advantages of this option for a number of key countries. The prolonged period of stability and rapid growth in Argentina during most of the 1990s and the collapse of its currency board in the early 2000s highlight both the advantages and the pitfalls of hard peg.[6] Outright dollarization represents an even more complete renouncement of sovereignty but, provided it can be sustained, offers the most rapid route to halt an inflation cycle and stabilize expectations. to the more stable financial centers and force the country to either use its foreign exchange resources or raise its interest rate to defend the exchange rate, thus triggering inflation and real depreciation.

---

6   Lack of fiscal discipline under fixed rates may, however, widen the balance-of-payments deficit and accelerate the loss of foreign exchange reserves, thus raising doubts about the government's capacity to defend the peg—as the experience in Argentina has demonstrated.

The fixed exchange rate regime, particularly the hard peg, has a number of notable disadvantages, however:

- Doubts about the government commitment or capacity to defend the peg may prompt the public to take measures ahead of time to protect its assets, primarily by converting its financial assets to harder currencies. The attacks on the exchange rate may be, and often are, pure speculations that reflect mostly the public fancy about the stability of the currency rather than facts about the country's fundamentals. Nonetheless, expectations for depreciation can trigger an outflow of capital to the more stable financial centers and force the country to either use its foreign exchange resources or raise its interest rate to defend the exchange rate, thus triggering inflation and real depreciation.

- For the monetary authorities to maintain a credible currency board, they must hold foreign exchange reserves that exceed their monetary liabilities. Only then can they protect the entire stock of liquid monetary assets against speculative attacks of domestic and foreign agents in the event that they try to convert their domestic financial assets (and the banks' liabilities) to foreign currency.

- The commitment for a fixed peg may create a moral hazard—as was the case in Indonesia when banks entered into large dollar-denominated debts.

- With a currency board or full dollarization the monetary authorities are not free to extend credit, and the central bank cannot therefore operate as "lender of last resort" and provide credit to banks in difficulty or even to the government.

- With a fixed peg, the monetary policy is entirely subordinate to the exchange rate regime; changes in the base money-and therefore also in the interest rate are determined by the foreign exchange. No room is left for adjustments in the real exchange rate through changes in the nominal exchange rate, and these adjustments require other means—including changes in domestic prices and costs. Hard peg therefore requires greater flexibility in the labor market and in prices in order to allow the necessary adjustments in relative prices.

- With a hard peg, the country may lose its competitiveness against its trading partners that have flexible rates and can therefore react to external shocks by devaluing their currencies. Indeed, during the Asian crisis, some countries that had floating or *de facto* flexible exchange rate gained a competitive advantage against countries like Argentina that continued to adhere to a hard peg. The loss in competitiveness was a major reason for the sharp recession in Argentina in 1998–1999 after the Asian crisis and the devaluation in Brazil.

For these and other reasons, hard peg may not be sustainable over a longer time period, and a strategy for a timely and orderly "exit" from the peg may be necessary. Indeed, these effects of external shocks have led many countries to abandon the peg and effectively float: In the mid-1970s, over 85 percent of the developing countries pegged their exchange rate; by mid-1980s, that percentage had declined to 55 percent, and by the mid-1990s, only around one-third of the developing countries had fixed exchange rates (although quite a few countries *managed* their float).

The Asian crisis of the late-1990s also highlights potential pitfalls and difficulties in defending a fixed exchange rate: First, with fixed exchange rates, these countries found it increasingly difficult to make the adjustments to the changes in relative prices in the world markets that were necessary to maintain their competitive position. Second, countries that sought to stabilize their exchange rate, either by means of formal pegging or with effective controls on their foreign exchange market, were often unable to impose the necessary constraints on their monetary policy and their financial system. Third, the globalization of financial markets and the growing activities of multinational banks and other financial enterprises in these developing countries made it considerably more difficult for their central banks to conduct an independent monetary policy, and, in particular, to buffer speculative attacks on their currency. Fourth, despite the rapid development of their banking system that was precipitated by their interactions with the multinational financial corporations, the public institutions that supervise the banks' operations failed to evolve in that rapid pace, and the financial system in many of these countries was marred by bankruptcies, scandals, and corruption that rocked the confidence in the currency.

During the past decade, an increasing number of countries made a successful transition to more flexible exchange rates, primarily because this regime gives the central bank more flexibility in the conduct of monetary policy. With flexible exchange rates, the economy is losing, however, its most visible nominal anchor and must replace it with an alternative anchor that is also highly visible and credible. In several countries, inflation targeting has been selected as an alternative anchor; this, however, is not a common indicator in developing countries–due in part to their limited awareness of and in part to their limited confidence in inflation figures. The main problem with this anchor—as well as with other indicators that are based on official statistics—is that they do not have the same clear meaning and do not represent the same formal and clear-cut restriction on the discretionary powers of the monetary authorities as does the exchange rate. This is also the reason why even those developing countries that maintain a relatively flexible exchange rate regime tend to use much more extensively both monetary policy measures and official intervention in the exchange market to influence the exchange rate and to maintain it as a significant guide even when it is no longer the formal anchor.

Concluding remarks

The experience of the past decade offers a number of useful lessons on the choice of an exchange regime:

- The high short- as well as medium-term volatility of the exchange rates of major currencies remains a significant problem that will have to find a proper solution in the coming years even though its direct effect on net trade volumes may be limited and these fluctuations need not be the result of significant misalignments. At the same time, large exchange rate swings are likely to create substantial sectoral adjustment costs both in the leading industrial countries themselves and in their trading partners.

- A considerable number of developing countries experimented during the 1990s with floating exchange rates even though they did not have the necessary institutional infrastructure. The most obvious examples are some of the ex-centrally planned economies that issued, at the beginning of the decade, their independent currencies. These courtiers floated their currencies although they had neither the expertise nor the institutions to maintain an efficient exchange market. In subsequent years, practically all these countries moved to formally stabilize their currencies.

- Some developing countries that experimented with floating exchange rates found out that this regime requires thorough preparation and necessary institutions to succeed.

- The most important and difficult aspect of monetary policy is to convince a skeptical public to accept money as a "store of value" even though its future value is uncertain. With a fixed exchange rate and, even more so, with a hard peg, the future value seems more certain, and in some countries this may have been the only way to convince the public that the future of the currency holds a better promise than its bitter past.

- Governments that attempted to extract an inflation tax from the public by monetizing an excessive fiscal budget often found out that they have lost even the seignorage.

- For the more advanced developing countries, floating exchange rates offer considerable advantages, particularly given the need to adjust to the relatively sharp and rapid changes in relative prices in the world markets as an effect of technical changes.[7] To be able to gain from these advantages, the monetary and fiscal authorities in these countries must be fully and consistently aware of the need to keep the public confidence in the currency.

- The present day's conditions in the global financial markets and the rapid flow of funds across countries and continents make this task far more difficult, however, than at any time in the past. Prudent fiscal and monetary policies are no longer sufficient conditions to ensure the stability of the exchange rate, nor are they even the most important conditions. Equally important are the efficiency, competitiveness, and transparency of the foreign exchange markets and of the financial institutions that trade in this market.

- The global operations of multinational corporations in general and of the multinational banks in particular considerably complicate the supervision over financial institutions and over their foreign exchange operations. Several outstanding episodes of the recent years in the United States highlight these difficulties. In a developing country, effective supervision is essential, however, to maintain the confidence in the currency and the economic costs of similar episodes can therefore be much higher.

These general lessons cannot and should not, however, be used to construct a general formula for the structure of an exchange rate system, as has been done so often in the past. Instead, the policymakers in each country and their advisors must go through the elaborate process of analyzing the

---

7   This is the advantage of the floating exchange regime that has been highlighted in the Mudell-Flemming model.

www.ingramcontent.com/pod-product-compliance
Lightning Source LLC
Chambersburg PA
CBHW020334270326
41926CB00007B/177

specific conditions in the country and designing an exchange rate regime, as part of the entire financial system, that can take advantage of the country's strengths and overcome most effectively the country's weaknesses. Equally important, the key to the success of this strategy is a timely exit from an exchange rate peg once it has completed its job and a transition to a more flexible system, combined with a credible commitment to defend the exchange rate (possibly within a band) if speculative attacks risk the system's stability.

REFERENCES

Calvo, G., and C. Reinhart. (2000). "Fear of Floating," Paper presented to the Conference on Currency Unions, Hoover Institutions, Stanford University.

Frankel, J., S. Schmuckler, and L. Serven. 2000. "Global Transmission of Interest Rates: Monetary Independence and Currency Regime." The World Bank. Unpublished.

Mussa, M., P. Masson, A. Swoboda, E. Jadresic, P. Mauro, and A. Berg. 2000. "Exchange Rate Regimes in an Increasingly Integrated World Economy." Occasional Paper 193. International Monetary Fund.